BIOGRAPHICAL DICTIONARY OF GEOGRAPHY

BIOGRAPHICAL DICTIONARY
OF
GEOGRAPHY

ROBERT P. LARKIN
AND
GARY L. PETERS

GREENWOOD PRESS
Westport, Connecticut • London

Library of Congress Cataloging-in-Publication Data

Larkin, Robert P.
  Biographical dictionary of geography / Robert P. Larkin and Gary
L. Peters.
     p.   cm.
  Includes index.
  ISBN 0–313–27622–6 (alk. paper)
  1. Geographers—Biography—Dictionaries. I. Peters, Gary L.
II. Title.
G67.L37   1993
910.922—dc20   92–18364

British Library Cataloguing in Publication Data is available.

Library of Congress Catalog Card Number: 92–18364
ISBN: 0–313–27622–6

First published in 1993

Greenwood Press, 88 Post Road West, Westport, CT 06881
An imprint of Greenwood Publishing Group, Inc.

Printed in the United States of America

∞™

The paper used in this book complies with the
Permanent Paper Standard issued by the National
Information Standards Organization (Z39.48–1984).

10 9 8 7 6 5 4 3 2 1

To John Willmer and David Lantis,
two extraordinary human beings and professors of geography.

Contents

Contents

Preface

The evolution of the modern discipline of geography is a history of interesting people who have been instrumental in its development. This book outlines the lives and contributions of a selected group of those people. Because it would have been impossible to determine a definitive list of the most important geographers in the history of the field, we decided to include people who have made significant contributions and represent a cross section of geographers from a variety of subfields within the discipline, from ancient to modern. Most of the geographers selected are deceased, although a dozen have made significant contributions to the field and are currently alive.

Each entry is divided into four sections. The first section is an essay that highlights the life of the person and discusses his or her contributions to the evolution of geography. The second section is a selected bibliography that lists some of the major works published by the geographer. The third section is a chronology that outlines the highlights of the person's life. Where appropriate, the final section gives biographical reference sources for further reading. Throughout the dictionary, a cross-reference to another geographer is indicated by an asterisk on first mention in an entry. Three appendices have also been included: an alphabetical list of the geographers (Appendix 1), a chronological list by date of birth (Appendix 2), and a list by a country of birth (Appendix 3).

The descriptions of the life and contributions of the geographers in this work would not have been possible without assistance from the *Geographers Biobibliographical Studies*, an excellent journal published on behalf of the Working Group on the History of Geographical Thought of the International Geographical Union and the International Union of the History and Philosophy of Science. The journal's former editor, T. W. Freeman, and its current editor, G. J. Martin, have performed an invaluable service to geographers by providing detailed discussions of the lives and contributions of many geographers.

This book would also not have been possible without the help of several students and colleagues. We would like to thank Carol Donaldson, Scott Roscoe, Elaine Schantz, and Sandra Salisbury for their help in the preparation of this manuscript. Of course, we alone remain responsible for whatever errors and shortcomings the book may have.

THE DICTIONARY

Roald Amundsen

Roald Amundsen was born in the little Norwegian village of Borge on July 16, 1872. Soon afterward his family moved a few miles south to Oslo, where Roald was reared and educated. When Roald was only fourteen, his father died. Subsequently, his brothers moved out on their own and left him with his mother (Finley, 1929), who urged him to attend medical school; however, Amundsen approached a medical career without enthusiasm and ultimately set it aside in favor of a life of exploration. Reflecting on his life many years later, Amundsen wrote, "When I was fifteen years old, the works of Sir John Franklin, the great British explorer, fell into my hands. I read them with fervid fascination, which has shaped the whole course of my life" (1927:2).

He recognized early that both physical and mental preparation would be required for his chosen work. His preferred physical conditioning came from skiing, which he pursued with considerable enthusiasm. At the university where he had started in pursuit of his medical education, however, he was less interested and left at the age of twenty-one. Joining the Norwegian military, he completed his obligation before going on to train as a ship's skipper.

Beginning in the summer of 1894, and working for two successive summers after that, Amundsen became a sailor on a sailing vessel, where he gradually worked his way up to a mate's position. In 1897 he was chosen as first mate aboard the *Belgica*, which was heading to study the south magnetic pole as part of the Belgian Antarctic Expedition. Though this mission never reached the South Pole, it served to provide Amundsen with considerable sailing experience as the *Belgica* became the first ship ever to spend a winter in the Antarctic region.

Upon returning to Norway, Amundsen purchased the *Gjöa*, a 45-foot sailing vessel with which he navigated the Northwest Passage. Following that achievement, he planned a drifting expedition across the North Pole in *Fridtjof Nansen's ship, the *Fram*. As Amundsen's plans were being made, news arrived that Peary had successfully reached the North Pole in September 1909.

It was then that he set his sites on the South Pole, which locked him into a race with Robert Scott. Amundsen chose to stage his assault on the South Pole from The Bay of Whales, a stable portion of the Great Barrier ice field, which he reached without difficulty in the *Fram*. This put him about 60 miles closer to the South Pole than was Scott, who worked from his old camp at McMurdo Sound, near the eastern edge of the Ross Ice Shelf.

In October 1911, Amundsen and four companions, along with four sleds and fifty-two Siberian huskies, headed toward their southernmost supply station, which they reached on November 3, 1911. By the middle of November, Amundsen and his party had advanced to within about 270 miles of the pole, and plenty of time remained to reach his goal. That final push was not without a struggle, however, as they had to find an acceptable route to the upper plateau that stretched out to the South Pole, finally climbing up a tongue of ice that Amundsen named the Axel Heiberg Glacier. Deep snow slowed the dogs considerably, however, and it was necessary to change routes when ice blocks barred progress toward the upper plateau.

On December 7, 1911, Amundsen and his group reached the southernmost extent to which *Ernest Schackleton had gotten in his failed attempt in 1909, and in another week, on December 14, 1911, they stood at the bottom of the world. On January 17, 1912, a very disappointed Robert Scott reached the South Pole as well, only to find Amundsen's tent and a letter addressed to him from Amundsen.

For Amundsen it was the triumph of a lifetime, one for which he had prepared as thoroughly as possible by studying the works of earlier explorers of the high latitudes, by learning all that he could about inhabitants of those high latitudes and the ways in which they coped with the harsh environment, and by apprenticing himself as a sailor.

Having accumulated some funds from his Antarctic expedition, Amundsen established a thriving shipping business, though his adventuresome spirit remained. After failing to reach the North Pole by sea, he sought to get there by air in 1925, though he was to come within only about 170 miles of it. In 1926, with Lincoln Ellsworth and Umberto Nobile, he was able to pass over the North Pole in a dirigible on a flight from Spitsbergen, Norway, to Alaska.

Today Amundsen Gulf, the southeastern extension of the Beaufort Sea, remains as a tribute to Amundsen, who, perhaps fittingly, died at sea while trying to rescue Nobile from a dirigible crash near Spitsbergen, not far from the shores of his native Norway.

Selected Bibliography

1908   *The North West Passage*. New York: Dutton.

1912   *The South Pole*. London: John Murray.

1927   With Lincoln Ellsworth. *First Crossing of the Polar Sea*.

            My Life as an Explorer. New York: Doubleday, Page.

Chronology

1872	Born July 16 in Borge, near Oslo, Norway.
1897	First mate on a Belgian expedition that was the first to winter in the Antarctic.
1903	Sailed the Northwest Passage, east to west in the *Gjöa* (voyage lasted until 1906).
1910	Set sail in June for South Pole.
1911	Began trip by sledge and fifty-two dogs to South Pole on October 19. Reached the pole on December 14.
1918	Failed arctic voyage.
1925	Tried to reach the North Pole by air; flew within 170 miles of it.
1926	Flew over the North Pole in a dirigible, crossing from Spitsbergen to Alaska.
1928	Died June 18, trying to rescue Umberto Nobile from a dirigible crash near Spitsbergen.

Reference

Finley, John H. 1929. "Amundsen: Supreme Adventurer." *Geographical Review* 19:145–46.

Aristotle

Aristotle was born in 384 B.C. in the small town of Stagira, near Macedonia. His father was a physician in the court of the King of Macedonia.

At the age of seventeen he joined Plato's Academy, where he remained until Plato's death almost twenty years later. He was sometimes viewed as a troublesome student and often and openly disagreed with Plato. In 335 B.C., at the age of forty-nine, Aristotle returned to Athens after travelling widely around Greece and the lands adjacent to the Aegean and established his own school, the Lyceum, in Athens. According to *Preston James and Geoffrey Martin (1981:26), "By this time he was convinced that the best way to build theory was to observe facts, and the best way to test a theory was to confront it with observations." Aristotle's methodology was quite different from what Plato had taught, and between them they had developed what we now recognize as deduction (Plato) and induction (Aristotle). As Adler (1978:xiii) noted, "Aristotle's thinking *began* with common sense, but it did not *end* there. It went much further. It added to and surrounded common sense with insights and understandings that are not common at all. His understanding of things goes deeper than ours and sometimes soars higher."

Though he has long been recognized as one of the greatest systematic thinkers of ancient Greece, Aristotle's contributions to geographic thought are less well known. His views on the earth and the universe were serious early contributions to geography, even though some are obviously now unacceptable, and his systematic approach to reasoning about natural and human processes has provided a guide for geographic inquiry.

About a century before Aristotle, Empedocles (490–430 B.C.) had argued that the world was composed entirely of four basic elements: air, fire, water, and earth. To this list, Aristotle added a fifth element, ether, which comprised the heavenly bodies. Modifying the work of Empedocles, Aristotle, according to James and Martin (1981:27), "developed the theory of natural places. Everything had its natural place in the universe, and, if removed from this place, it would seek to return.''

Aristotle accepted Plato's argument that the earth was a sphere and sought observations to test the hypothesis. He noted that during an eclipse of the moon the shadow has a circular edge, for example, and also recognized the changing position of the stars overhead as one travelled from south to north.

Aristotle also noted the relationship between latitude and climate, though the model with which he worked seems simplistic today. His observations, of course, were limited to the inhabited region around the Mediterranean Sea, and from those observations, coupled with his acceptance of the spherical earth, he concluded that three latitudinal zones could be recognized and related to human habitability. He knew that south of the Mediterranean, in what is now Libya, temperatures were much hotter than they were in Greece; thus he concluded that temperatures must be even hotter yet near the equator, and his low latitude zone was recognized as the torrid zone, which he thought was totally uninhabitable. At the other end of the spectrum, Aristotle reasoned that the polar latitudes must be permanently frozen, a frigid zone, and thus uninhabitable as well. In between the frigid zone and the torrid zone, however, he found the temperate zone, which formed the *ekumene*, or inhabited portion of the earth's surface. As James and Martin (1981:28) noted, ''This notion of habitability as a function of latitude has had a long history and, in fact, is still widely accepted, especially by nongeographers.''

Aside from these major views of the earth, Aristotle speculated on the nature and causes of volcanic activity and earthquakes, and was probably the first person in the world to suggest a relationship between earthquakes and weather, arguing specifically that the majority of earthquakes occur when the weather is calm. He also believed that most major earthquakes would occur in regions where the earth is hollow and the seas full of currents, and that they were likely to occur in association with lunar eclipses as well. Earthquakes, Aristotle believed, were caused by the wind, or ''exhalation.''

Not only did Aristotle make contributions to an understanding of the natural world in his day, but he was also interested in what we would now label environmental and urban issues as well, and was even concerned with such modern problems as the conflict between the rich and the poor. He wrote about the best locations for cities, for example, considering what we would recognize as both site and situational characteristics (Kish, 1978). Clean air and water were essential for the sake of human health, Aristotle thought, especially as people gathered in cities.

Selected Bibliography

Athenai: on politeia

De anima

De generatione animalium

De motu animalium

De plantis

Meteorologica

On the Heavens

On the Cosmos

Organum

Poetics

Politics

Chronology

384 B.C.	Born in Stagira.
367 B.C.	Joined Plato's Academy near Athens. Remained there until Plato's death in 348.
348 B.C.	Began travels around Greece and the Aegean.
335 B.C.	Returned to Athens and founded his own school, the Lyceum.
322 B.C.	Died.

References

Adler, Mortimer J. 1978. *Aristotle for Everybody: Difficult Thought Made Easy.* New York: Macmillan.

James, Preston E., and Geoffrey J. Martin. 1981. *All Possible Worlds: A History of Geographical Ideas.* 2d ed. New York: Wiley.

Kish, George, ed. 1978. *A Source Book in Geography.* Cambridge, Mass.: Harvard University Press.

Wallace Walter Atwood

Wallace Walter Atwood was born on October 1, 1872, in Chicago, where his father owned a planing mill. The family traced its lineage back to early Massachusetts settlers. Wallace graduated from West Division High School in 1892 and enrolled at the University of Chicago, where he studied geology.

Before receiving his S.B. degree in geology in 1897, Wallace Atwood experienced a field trip with *Rollin D. Salisbury in the Devil's Lake area of Wisconsin, near Baraboo. That experience transformed Atwood's thinking, and afterward he committed himself to studying and interpreting landforms and landscapes. In 1903 he went on to receive his Ph.D. in geology from the University of Chicago, where he had been an instructor during his last two years of graduate school, then taught there in the Department of Geology from 1903 to 1913. During his graduate years at the University of Chicago, he had been exposed to John Dewey and his ideas about education, which stimulated Atwood's interest in teaching and learning.

Wallace Atwood's first professional publication was coauthored with Rollin Salisbury and focused on the geography and geology of the Devil's Lake region, where they had done fieldwork together. Atwood subsequently worked on several projects with Salisbury, including state geological surveys in New Jersey and Wisconsin.

In 1913 Wallace Atwood accepted an appointment at Harvard as a professor of physiography following the retirement of *William Morris Davis. Atwood's teaching and field experience drew a number of students to him, and he expanded the physical geography curriculum to include new advanced courses and a field course in the western United States, where he had already done considerable fieldwork.

In 1920 Atwood accepted the presidency of Clark University, and in 1921 he became the director of Clark's Graduate School of Geography. Clark's was only the second geography department in the United States to have a fully staffed and independent Ph.D. program in geography, and under Atwood the program excelled. Though fieldwork and physiography were essential to the program, geographical education and land-use studies became important also. In addition, in 1925 Atwood established the journal *Economic Geography*, which is still housed at Clark. Both domestic and foreign students were attracted to Clark's geography program under Atwood.

Since receiving his Ph.D., Atwood had concentrated on field studies in physiography, culminating with the publication of his monography on the San Juan Mountains in 1932, a work coauthored with K. F. Mather and completed several years before its actual publication date.

Atwood's primary scientific interest focused on the understanding and sequential reconstruction of landscapes, with an emphasis on the importance of field observation and testing of hypotheses. Gradually his work became more discernible as environmental determinism, arguing that human geography was influenced strongly by the characteristics of landform regions. Many of his ideas were institutionalized in the curriculum of Clark University in the 1920s and 1930s under his leadership. As Koelsch (1979:14) puts it:

Geography, as Atwood saw it, was a science of relationships linking man to the natural environment, expressed in terms of the "great human dramas" of men responding or adapting to natural advantages, and partially transcending natural disadvantages through the development of interdependent networks of communication and trade between distinct "natural regions."

His major publications, from the earliest with Rollin Salisbury, dealt primarily with glaciation, first in Wisconsin then in such western mountains as the San Juans, the Wasatch, and the Uintas. Broader physiographic concerns showed up occasionally as well in his written work, including his work on topographic map interpretation with Salisbury, his work with Mather on the San Juan Mountains, and, perhaps his best-known work today, *The Physiographic Provinces of North America*. His last book, published in 1945, was *The Rocky Mountains*, which appeared as one of a series of books on American mountains.

Atwood's interest in education found another outlet as well in a series of school geography works and educational aids. He was also president of the Association of American Geographers in 1934 and retired in 1946. It is easy to agree with Koelsch (1979:15) when he says of Atwood:

His record of innovation in the advancement of popular geographical knowledge through untraditional teaching aids such as films, visits to museums and study tours; his enormous impact on school geography; his conservation efforts and his organizing talents earned him an honoured place in the history of American geography.

Selected Bibliography

1897   With R. D. Salisbury. "Drift Phenomena in the Vicinity of Devil's Lake
                and Baraboo, Wisconsin." *Journal of Geology* 5:131–47.

1900   With R. D. Salisbury. "The Geography of the Region about Devil's Lake and the Dells of Wisconsin." *Wisconsin Geology and Natural History Survey Bulletin No. 5.* State of Wisconsin, Madison.

1903   Glaciation of the Uinta Mountains, Ph.D. dissertation, Department of Geology, University of Chicago.

1908   With R. D. Salisbury. "The Interpretation of Topographic Maps."*U.S. Geological Survey Professional Paper No. 60.* Washington, D.C.: Government Printing Office.

1909   "Glaciation of the Uinta Mountains." *U.S. Geological Survey Professional Paper No. 61.*

1911   "A Geographic Study of the Mesa Verde." *Annals of the Association of American Geographers* 1:95–100.

1912   With K. F. Mather. "The Evidence of Three Distinct Glacial Epochs in the Pleistocene History of the San Juan Mountains, Colorado." *Journal of Geology* 20:385–409.

1919   "Geography in America." *Geographical Review* 7:36–43.

1920   *New Geography: Book Two.* Boston: Frye-Atwood Geographical Series.

1921   With H. G. Thomas. *Teaching the New Geography: A Manual for Use with the Fry-Atwood Geographical Series.* Boston.

        "The New Meaning of Geography in American Education." Inaugural Address. Clark University Library, 6:25–37. See also *School and Society* 13:211–18.

1925   With Harriet T. B. Atwood. *The Problem Method in Comparative Map Studies.* Boston.

1928   With H. G. Thomas. *Home Life in Faraway Lands.* Boston.

        Series of ten regional-political wall maps of the continents and the world. Chicago.

1929   With H. G. Thomas. *The Americas.* Boston.

1930   With H. G. Thomas. *Nations Beyond the Seas.* Boston.

1931   *The World at Work.* Boston.

1932   With K. F. Mather. "Physiography and Quaternary Geology of the San Juan Mountains, Colorado." *U.S. Geological Survey Professional Paper No. 166.*

1933   "The Correlation of Ancient Erosion Surfaces." *Comptes-Rendus, Congres Internationale de Geographie.* Paris, 1931, 588–91.

1936   With H. G. Thomas. *The Growth of Nations.* Boston.

1938   With W. W. Atwood, Jr. "Working Hypothesis for the Physiographic History of the Rocky Mountain Region." *Geological Society of America Bulletin* 49:967–80.

1940   *The Physiographic Provinces of North America.* Boston: Ginn.

1943   With H. G. Thomas. *The American Nations.* Boston.

1945   *The Rocky Mountains.* American Mountain Series. New York: Vanguard.

1946   With H. G. Thomas. *Nations Overseas*. Boston.

1948   With Ruth Pitt. *Our Economic World*. Boston: Ginn.

Chronology

1872   Born in Chicago, Illinois, on October 1.

1892   Graduated from West Division High School in Chicago.

1897   Earned S.B. degree at the University of Chicago. Published his first paper,
            written jointly with Rollin D. Salisbury, "Drift Phenomena in the Vicinity
            of Devil's Lake."

1901   Appointed Instructor in Geology at the University of Chicago. Appointment
            to U.S. Geological Survey.

1903   Ph.D. degree.

1908   Secretary, Chicago Academy of Sciences.

1913   Appointed Professor of Physiography, Harvard University.

1920   Appointed President of Clark University.

1921   Appointed Director, Graduate School of Geography, Clark University.
            President, National Council of Geography Teachers.

1929   President, National Parks Association.

1932   President, Pan American Institute of Geography and History.

1944   Sc.D. Worchester Polytechnic Institute.

1946   Appointed President Emeritus on his retirement from Clark University.

1949   Died July 24 at Annisquam, Massachusetts.

Reference

Koelsch, William A. 1979. "Wallace Walter Atwood." *Geographers Biobibliographical
      Studies* 3:13–18.

Henri Baulig

Henri Baulig was born in Paris on June 17, 1877. He was the only son of a farm worker from Brie who had moved to Paris to work as a *concierge* in a factory. Although Henri came from these modest circumstances, from early on he was regarded by his teachers as exceptionally bright. He was awarded a scholarship that made it possible for him to attend the lycée of Louis-le-Grand, the most respected and important "high school" in Paris, and then to continue his studies at the Sorbonne, where he concentrated on history and geography. While at the Sorbonne, he was attracted by the teaching of the famous French geographer *Paul Vidal de la Blache. Baulig was for some time Vidal's assistant and planned on writing a thesis about Paris. All these plans changed, however, when he gave up this post at the age of twenty-seven and left for the United States in 1905.

On the advice of Vidal de la Blache, Baulig went to Harvard University to work with the American geomorphologist *William Morris Davis, who had a profound influence on his future career. Baulig stayed in America for seven years attending Davis's major courses and working under his direction.

Upon his return to Paris in 1913, Baulig arranged to write a thesis on the Central Plateau of France under the direction of Vidal de la Blache and carried out the fieldwork for the next three years. Baulig, according to *Jean Gottmann (1963:612), "brought to France the teaching of Davis and the ideas of *Grove Karl Gilbert" and became "one of the two main leaders of French physical geography." In order to support himself during this time, Baulig taught at the Sorbonne and later at Rennes.

After his return from World War I, Baulig was appointed to the chair of geography at the University of Strasbourg in 1919. He spent his early years at Strasbourg developing the Institute of Geography and continuing his research. He was over fifty years of age when, in 1928, he defended his doctoral thesis on Central France. Using a Davisian framework, he sought to determine the

varied processes involved in the emergence of the landscape of the Massif Central
region of France. Although Baulig's ideas were challenged, his contemporaries
recognized in him a remarkable gift for observing and interpreting physical
landforms. He was invited to London in 1935 to give a series of lectures that
were later published as *The Changing Sea Level* by the Institute of British
Geographers.

Baulig's interests, however, were not solely confined to topics of physical
geography. He wrote two large volumes that dealt with the economic and regional
geography of the United States and Canada. These volumes were regarded by
many scholars of the time as the best available regional description of this part
of the world. The American Geographical Society awarded him the Charles P.
Daly medal for ''the best regional geography of North America in any language.''

During World War II, the activities of the University of Strasbourg were
moved to Clermont-Ferrand, and Baulig was concerned with the treatment of
Alsatian and Jewish students who were refugees. Baulig's concern for these
students, along with his openly expressed anti-Nazi views, brought about his
arrest and imprisonment for two months in 1944.

The war took its toll on Baulig, and he was physically worn out by its end.
His intellectual vitality, however, was still strong, and after the liberation, he
reestablished the Institute of Geography at Strasbourg. He continued to live in
Strasbourg after his retirement in 1947 and wrote a number of papers on a variety
of geographical ideas. He died on August 8, 1962, at Igwiller and left an
endowment at Strasbourg University to establish the Baulig Foundation.

Selected Bibliography

1909   ''Les Ressources Naturelles du Nord et du Nord-Ouest Canadien.'' *Annales
            de Géographie* 18:451–62.

1913   ''Les Plateaux de Lave du Washington Central et la Grand Coulée.''
            Annales de Géographie 22:149–69.

1921   ''La Population de l'Alsace et de la Lorraine en 1921.'' *Annales de Géo-
            graphie* 32:12–25.

1925   ''La Notion de Profil d'Équilibre: Histoire et Critique.'' *Congrès Inter-
            national de Géographie* (Cairo) 3:51–63.

1926   ''Sur une Méthode Altimetrique d'Analyse Morphologique Appliquée à la
            Bretagne Peninsulaire.'' *Bulletin de l'Association des Géographes Fran-
            cais* 10:7–9.

1928   *Le Plateau Central de la France et sa Bordure Méditerranéenne.* Doctoral
            Dissertation, Sorbonne, 591.

1933   ''À Propos du Relief Armoricain de l'Origine du Loess Breton.'' *Bulletin
            de l'Association des Géographes Francais* 67:51–55.

1935   ''The Changing Sea Level.'' Four lectures given at the University of
            London. *Institute of British Geographers* 3:46pp.

Amérique Septentrionale. Tome 13 of Géographie Universelle. 2 vols.,
640 pp.

1939   "Sur les Gradins de Piedmont." *Journal of Geomorphology* 2: 281–304.

1940   "Reconstruction of Stream Profiles." *Journal of Geomorphology* 3:3–12.

1948   "Problèmes des Terrasses." *International Geographical Union Commission for the Study of Terraces* 109(6):16pp.

            "Le Problème des Méandres." *Bulletin de la Societé Belge d'Etudes Géographiques* 17:103–43.

            "Les Chaînons du Grand Bassin." *Annales de Géographie* 57:258–63.

            "La Géographie est-elle une Science?" *Annales de Géographie* 57:1–11.

1949   "La Vallée et le Delta du Mississippi." *Annales de Géographie* 58:220–32.

1950   "W. M. Davis: Master of Method." *Annals, Association of American Geographers* 40:188–95.

1951   "Isaiah Bowman (1878–1950)," *Annales de Géographie* 60:48–50.

1952   "Surfaces d'Aplannissement." *Annales de Géographie* 61:161–83, 234–62.

Chronology

1877   Born in Paris, June 17.

1905   At Harvard University (to 1910) doing research with W. M. Davis; travelled extensively in U.S.A.

1908   Published first article in *Annales de Géographie*: "Sur la Distribution des Moyens de Transport et de Circulation chez les Indegenes de l'Amérique du Nord."

1913   Director, Geographical Laboratory, Rennes University.

1928   Promoted to Professor at Strasbourg and became Head of the Centre d'études germainiques. Completed doctoral thesis on the central plateau of France.

1933   Gave lectures at London University, published in 1935 by the Institute of British Geographers as a monograph, *The Changing Sea Level.*

1938   Published *Amérique Septentrionale* (regional text of North America), Tome 13 of Géographie Universelle, 2 vols.

1939   Published "Sur les Gradins de Piedmont" in the *Journal of Geomorphology.*

1948   Received the Charles P. Daly gold medal from the American Geographical Society and was Chairman of the International Geographical Union (I.G.U.) Commission on the study of terraces, 1948–52.

1962   Died at Igwiller, August 8.

Reference

Gottmann, Jean. 1963. "Henri Baulig," *Geographical Review* 53: 611–12.

Brian J. L. Berry

According to the Social Science Citation Index, Brian Berry has been the world's most frequently cited geographer since the early 1960s. He has authored more than three hundred books, articles, and other professional publications while teaching at some of America's most prestigious institutions.

Berry was born on February 16, 1934, in Sedgley, in the English Midlands. He attended primary school in Nottinghamsire and Lincolnshire and the Queen Elizabeth's Grammar School in Gainsborough, Lincolnshire. After leaving school at the age of sixteen, he took Britain's civil service entrance examinations and intended to go to work. He was persuaded, however, to return for further education (sixth form) in order to better prepare himself for a governmental career.

Berry attended the Acton County Secondary School where the headmaster, G. T. Giles, encouraged him to study history and geography, as well as mathematics. The geography teacher at Acton School, H. Urch, was a stickler for performance and encouraged Berry to pursue a university degree. In 1952 he won a state scholarship that enabled him to attend university, and he was accepted into the program at University College, London, where he was to pursue a degree in economics. He was the first member of his family to attend university and was awarded a Bachelor's degree with First Class Honors in 1955.

Since many geographers at University College were encouraged to attend graduate schools in the United States, Berry applied to several American graduate programs. The first acceptance, with an assistantship included, came from the University of Washington. He obtained a Fulbright travel award and was off to the United States in the fall of 1955. He worked closely with William Garrison and coauthored his first paper with him, part of a study on a civil defense plan for the State of Washington. In 1956 Berry was awarded an M.A. degree in Geography with a thesis entitled *Geographic Aspects of the Size and Arrangement of Urban Centers*. After completing his M.A., he prepared several papers for publication but several were rejected because they were either "not geography" or "too mathematical." He spent two more years at Washington and was awarded the Ph.D. in 1958.

Berry was invited to the University of Chicago in 1957 to give a lecture and to interview for a position as Assistant Professor of Geography. The following year he started his first full-time teaching position at Chicago. He rose through the professorial ranks and was appointed Associate Professor in 1962, Full Professor in 1972, and Irving B. Harris Professor of Urban Geography and Department Chairman in 1972. During his eighteen years at Chicago, Berry's research branched out into a variety of areas including city-systems, systems of cities, and central-place theory, as well as associated work in spatial analysis and statistical geography. He was one of the geographers that sparked the so-called "quantitative revolution" that took place in geography during the 1960s. While at Chicago, he also started his work in developing countries, and his experiences in Calcutta were instrumental in sparking his interest in regional development.

Berry left Chicago in 1976 to take a position as Williams Professor of City and Regional Planning and Director of the Laboratory for Computer Graphics and Spatial Analysis at Harvard University. Five years later in 1981, he became Dean of the School of Urban and Public Affairs and University Professor of Urban Studies and Public Policy at Carnegie-Mellon University. Berry's current position, which he has held since 1986, is the Lloyd Viel Berkner University Professor of Political Economy and the Director of the Bruton Center for Development Studies at The University of Texas at Dallas. His recent research has focused on long-wave rhythms that pattern economic development and political behavior.

Berry has served on the editorial board or as editor-in-chief for many scholarly journals including *Urban Geography, Growth and Change, Journal of Regional Science, Journal of Urban Economics, Regional Studies, Urban Studies, Demography, Annals of the Association of American Geographers, Geographical Analysis, Geographical Review*, and the *Journal of the American Institute of Planners*. He has also held a variety of positions in scholarly societies such as Vice President (1977–78) and President (1978–79) of the Association of American Geographers, a Fellow of the Urban Land Institute, a Fellow of the American Academy of Arts and Sciences, a Fellow of the American Association for the Advancement of Science, and a Corresponding Fellow of the British Academy.

Berry's scholarly contributions have been recognized with the Meritorious Contributions Award in 1968 from the Association of American Geographers, the James R. Anderson Medal of Honor in 1987 from the Association of American Geographers, and the Victoria Medal from the Royal Geographical Society in 1988.

Selected Bibiography

1956   With J. D. Nystuen. "Food Supply." Chapter 3 in *Washington State Survival Plan Studies*, 7.45–7.178. Seattle: University of Washington.

1957   With W. Garrison. "A Source of Theory for Highway Impact Studies."
        Economic Impact of Highway Improvement. Special Report No. 28. High-
        way Research Board, 79–83.

1958   With W. Garrison "The Functional Bases of the Central Place Hierarchy."
        Economic Geography 34:145–54.

        With W. Garrison. "Recent Developments of Central Place Theory."
        Papers and Proceedings of the Regional Science Association 4:107–20.

        "A Note Concerning Methods of Classification." *Annals of the Association
        of American Geographers* 48:300–303.

1959   "Recent Studies Concerning the Role of Transportation in the Space Econ-
        omy." *Annals of the Association of American Geographers* 49:329–42.

1961   "City Size Distributions and Economic Development." *Economic Devel-
        opment and Cultural Change* 9:573–88.

1963   With J. Simmons and R. Tennant. "Urban Population Densities: Structure
        and Change." *Geographical Review* 53:389–405.

1967   *Geography of Market Centers and Retail Distribution*. Englewood Cliffs,
        N.J.: Prentice-Hall.

1968   With D. Marble. *Spatial Analysis: A Reader in Statistical Geography*.
        Englewood Cliffs, N.J.: Prentice-Hall.

        With C. Harris. "Walter Christaller. An Appreciation." *Geographical
        Review* 60:116–19.

1969   *Growth Centers and Their Potentials in the Upper Great Lakes Region*.
        Washington, D.C.: Upper Great Lakes Regional Commission.

        With P. Rees. "The Factorial Ecology of Calcutta." *American Journal of
        Sociology* 74:445–91.

        With P. Schwind. "Information and Entropy in Migrant Flows." *Geo-
        graphical Analysis* 1:5–14.

1970   With F. Horton. *Geographic Perspectives on Urban Systems*. Englewood
        Cliffs, N.J.: Prentice-Hall.

        "The Changing Internal Structure of the Daily Urban Systems." In *The
        Great Lake Megalopolis: A Comparative Study of Growth Trends*. Athens:
        Doxiadis Associates, 171–230.

1971   "The Logic and Limitations of Factorial Ecology." *Comparative Factorial
        Ecology*, 209–19.

1972   "Social Change as a Spatial Process." *International Social Development
        Review* 4:11–20.

1973   *The Human Consequences of Urbanization: Divergent Paths in the Urban
        Experience of the Twentieth Century*. New York: St. Martins.

1974   With F. Horton. *Urban Environmental Management: Planning for Pol-
        lution Control*. Englewood Cliffs, N.J.: Prentice-Hall.

        A National Resource Inventory and Evaluation Program for Indonesia.
        Washington, D.C.: The World Bank.

1976   With E. Conkling and M. Ray. *The Geography of Economic Systems.*
        Englewood Cliffs, N.J.: Prentice-Hall.

1979   "Inner City Futures: An American Dilemma Revisited." *Transactions of
        the Institute of British Geographers.* New Series 5:1–28.

1980   "Creating Future Geographies." Presidential Address to the Association
        of American Geographers, published in the *Annals of the Association of
        American Geographers* 70:449–58.

1987   With E. Conkling and D. Ray. *Economic Geography: Resource Use,
        Locational Choices, and Regional Specialization in the Global Economy.*
        Englewood Cliffs, N.J.: Prentice-Hall.

1988   With J. Parr. *Market Centers and Retail Location. Theory and Applica-
        tions.* Englewood Cliffs, N.J.: Prentice-Hall.

1989   "Migration Reversals in Perspective: The Long-Wave Evidence." *Inter-
        national Regional Science Review* 11:245–51.

Chronology

1934   Born in Sedgley, England.

1952–55 Attended University College, London.

1955   Awarded Bachelor's degree with first class Honors and enrolled at the
        University of Washington.

1956   Awarded M.A. degree in geography from the University of Washington
        with a thesis entitled *Geographic Aspects of the Size and Arrangement of
        Urban Centers.*

1958   Completed Ph.D. in geography at the University of Washington and took
        position as Assistant Professor of Geography at the University of Chicago.

1962   Appointed Associate Professor of Geography, University of Chicago.

1967   Published first book, *Geography of Market Centers and Retail Distribution.*

1968   Published *Spatial Analysis: A Reader in Statistical Geography.*

1970   Published *Geographic Perspectives on Urban Systems.*

1972   Appointed Irving B. Harris Professor of Urban Geography and Department
        Chairman, University of Chicago.

1974   Published *Urban Environmental Management: Planning for Pollution
        Control.*

1976   Took position as Williams Professor of City and Regional Planning and
        Director of the Laboratory for Computer Graphics and Spatial Analysis at
        Harvard University.

1980   President of the Association of American Geographers.

1981   Appointed Dean of the School of Urban and Public Affairs and University
        Professor of Urban Studies and Public Policy, Carnegie-Mellon University.

1986   Appointed University Professor of Political Economy and Director of the
        Bruton Center for Development Studies, The University of Texas at Dallas.

John R. Borchert

An American geographer whose work has been extensively used in public-policy decisions, John R. Borchert was born in Chicago, Illinois, on October 24, 1918. He grew up in a small town forty miles from downtown Chicago, and his frequent visits as a youngster to both the inner city and affluent suburbs raised a variety of questions about geographic processes. His father was a railway mail clerk and that job "raised endless questions about what lay beyond the horizon" (Personal correspondence, March 27, 1991).

Borchert's undergraduate education was at DePauw University, where he majored in geology with minors in math and chemistry. There was no geography program at DePauw, but according to Borchert, "Geology served two needs. One was a lifelong curiosity about land and its use. . . . A second need was to be sure my college years would lead to a job. For it was during the Great Depression." It was also at this time that Borchert developed a strong interest in college teaching. Upon graduation from DePauw in 1941, with an A.B. degree, he shifted to graduate work, first in geology and then in meteorology at the Massachusetts Institute of Technology.

Borchert's graduate work was interrupted by the outbreak of World War II, when he became a member of the central operational forecasting team for the 8th Air Force over Europe. At the end of the war, he learned for the first time that there was an academic field of geography and that the geographic method, though underdevoloped, was a very powerful and useful discipline. He quickly became committed to geography and started graduate work at the University of Wisconsin. As a graduate student, he was strongly influenced by Finch, Trewartha, Hartshorne, *Arthur H. Robinson, and Kollmorgen. Borchert completed his M.A. in 1946 and his Ph.D. in 1949, both from the University of Wisconsin.

In 1949 Borchert took a teaching position as an Assistant Professor at the University of Minnesota. He rose through the professorial ranks at Minnesota to Associate Professor in 1951 and full Professor in 1956, and in 1981 he was appointed Regent's Professor. He also held a variety of administrative positions during this time.

Most of Borchert's research dealt with geography in relation to public policies in land use and resource management. He has been an active member on a variety of policy-making committees and commissions. Much of his work has focused on the United States, particularly the Upper Midwest region. As Director of the Center for Urban and Regional Affairs at the University of Minnesota from 1968 to 1977, he authored or coauthored many studies on urban problems and development issues.

Borchert has served on numerous committees of the Association of American Geographers and was Vice President (1967–68) and President (1968–69) of that organization. He has been Chairman of the Earth Sciences Division of the National Research Council (1967–69), Chairman of the National Academy of Sciences–National Research Council Committee on Geography (1970–72), and Director-at-Large, Social Science Research Council (1965–67); he was elected as a member of both the National Academy of Sciences and the American Academy of Arts and Sciences in 1976.

As a result of his contributions to urban geography, Borchert was awarded the Eugene Van Cleef Gold Medal from the American Geographical Society in 1971. The National Council for Geographic Education gave him its Master Teacher Award in 1984, and he received the John Brinckerhoff Jackson Award from the Association of American Geographers in 1988.

Selected Bibiography

1947   "A New Map of Climates of China." *Annals of the Association of American Geographers* 37:169–76.

1948   "The Agriculture of England and Wales: 1939–45." *Agricultural History* 22:56–62.

1950   "The Climate of the Central North American Grasslands." *Annals of the Association of American Geographers* 40:1–49.

1953   "Regional Differences in the World Atmospheric Circulation." *Annals of the Association of American Geographers* 43:14–26.

1954   "The Surface Water Supply of American Municipalities."*Annals of the Association of American Geographers* 44:15–32.

1955   *A Reconnaissance Atlas of Minnesota Agriculture*. Minneapolis: University of Minnesota, Department of Geography and Minnesota Council for Geographic Education.

1959   *The Twin Cities*. New York: Doubleday.

            Minnesota's Changing Geography. Minneapolis: University of Minnesota Press.

1960   *Belt Line Commercial Industrial Development: A Case Study in Minneapolis–St. Paul Metropolitan Area*. Minneapolis: University of Minnesota Highway Research Project.

"Industrial Water Use in the United States." *Polish Geographical Review* 32:63–83.

1961   "The Twin Cities Urbanized Area: Past, Present, Future." *Geographical Review* 51:47–70.

Geography of the New World. Chicago: Rand McNally.

Geography of the Old World. Chicago: Rand McNally.

1963   *The Urbanization of the Upper Midwest: 1930–1960*. Minneapolis: Upper Midwest Economic Study.

With R. Adams. *Trade Centers and Trade Areas of the Upper Midwest*. Minneapolis: Upper Midwest Economic Study.

1964   With T. Anding and M. Gildemeister. *Urban Dispersal in the Upper Midwest*. Minneapolis: Upper Midwest Economic Study.

1965   "The Dimensions of Geography in the School Curriculum." *Journal of Geography* 44:244–49.

With W. Anderson and R. Olson. *Minnesota Land Ownership*. St. Paul: Minnesota Outdoor Recreation Resources Commission.

1967   "American Metropolitan Evolution." *Geographical Review* 57:301–32.

"Geography and Systems Theory." Chapter 18 in Saul Cohen, ed., *Problems and Trends in American Geography*. New York: Basic Books, 264–73.

1968   "Remote Sensors and Geographical Science." *Professional Geographer* 20:6:371–75.

1969   With D. Yaeger. *Atlas of Minnesota Resources and Settlement*. St. Paul: Minnesota State Planning Agency.

1971   "The Dust Bowl in the 1970s." *Annals of the Association of American Geographers* 61:1–22.

1972   "America's Changing Metropolitan Regions." *Annals of the Association of American Geographers* 62:352–73.

1973   With T. Mortenson and A. Alanen. *Public College Enrollment in Minnesota's Changing Population Pattern 1970–1985*. Minneapolis: University of Minnesota, Center for Urban and Regional Affairs.

1978   "Major Control Points in American Economic Geography." *Annals of the Association of American Geographers* 68:214–32.

1980   With N. Gustafson. *Atlas of Minnesota Resources and Settlement*. Minneapolis: University of Minnesota, Center for Urban and Regional Affairs and St. Paul: Minnesota State Planning Agency.

"Geography and Environmental Controls in the United States: The Case of Surface Mining." *Proceedings of the Third Scientific Symposium of the IGU Commission on Environmental Problems*. Moscow: Academy of Science of the U.S.S.R., 188–97.

1983   "Instability in American Metropolitan Growth." *Geographical Review* 73:124–46.

1984	With D. Gebhard, D. Lanegran, and J. Martin. *Legacy of Minneapolis: Preservation Amid Change*. Minneapolis: Voyageur.
1986	"Persistent Places and Paths on the Midwestern Plain." *Journal of Geography* 87:218–23.
1987	*America's Northern Heartland*. Minneapolis: University of Minnesota Press.
1990	"GIS: Science, Application, Coherence." *GIS/LIS Conference Proceedings*, Washington D.C.: American Society for Photogrametry and Remote Sensing.

Chronology

1918	Born in Chicago on October 24.
1941	Graduated from DePauw University, A.B. in geology.
1942	Member of the central operational forecasting team for the 8th Air Force in Europe.
1946	Graduated from the University of Wisconsin, M.A. in geography.
1947	Published first article in the *Annals of the Association of American Geographers*.
1949	Graduated from the University of Wisconsin, Ph.D. in geography. Took first teaching position as an Assistant Professor of Geography at the University of Minnesota.
1951	Appointed Associate Professor of Geography, University of Minnesota.
1956	Appointed Professor of Geography, University of Minnesota and Chairman of the Department of Geography.
1959	Published *Minnesota's Changing Geography*.
1965	Appointed Associate Dean, Graduate School, University of Minnesota.
1968	Appointed Director, Center for Urban and Regional Affairs, University of Minnesota. Elected President of the Association of American Geographers.
1971	Awarded the Eugene Van Cleef Gold Medal from the American Geographical Society.
1976	Elected Member, National Academy of Sciences.
1981	Named Regents' Professor, University of Minnesota.
1984	Master Teacher Award, National Council for Geographic Education.
1988	John Brinckerhoff Jackson Award, Association of American Geographers.

Isaiah Bowman

Isaiah Bowman was one of the monumental figures in the development of modern geography. According to George Carter (1950:335), "Possibly no geographer since [Alexander] *Von Humboldt has contributed so much to so many aspects of the broad field of geography." Bowman had a penetrating intellect and was a valued advisor to students, colleagues, statesmen, and presidents.

Isaiah Bowman was born on December 26, 1878, in Berlin (now Kitchener), Ontario, the third child and first son of Samuel and Emily Bowman. When he was eight weeks old, his family moved to a log cabin in Brown City, Michigan, where he developed an early interest in reading, natural history, and geography. Work on the family farm, combined with a rigorous country schooling, prepared Bowman for attendance at the Ferris Institute in Big Rapids, Michigan in 1900. At the Ferris Institute, he studied under Harlan H. Barrows, but after only a year he decided to transfer to Michigan State Normal School in Ypsilanti in order to study with Charles T. McFarlane.

When Bowman arrived in Ypsilanti in 1901, he found out that McFarlane had been replaced by *Mark Jefferson. Bowman became one of the first students, and probably the most notable, who studied under Jefferson. It was Jefferson who arranged for Bowman to study at Harvard University under the tutelege of *William Morris Davis, Nathan Shaler, and R. T. Jackson. It was Davis, however, who had the most influence on the young Bowman. They had frequent meetings and corresponded regularly until the death of Davis in 1934. Unlike Davis, Bowman departed from the concentration on physiography to look at the integration of the human and physical environments.

Upon completion of his B.S. degree from Harvard in 1905, Bowman accepted a faculty position in the Department of Geology and Geography at Yale University, where Bowman developed an ontographic geography in a regional setting. He was among the first American geographers to develop regional courses, and he was especially interested in the study of the influences of the geographic environment. While at Yale, he established geography as a respected discipline and went on three expeditions to South America in 1907, 1911, and 1913. *Desert Trails of the Atacama* and *The Andes of Southern Peru* were the two books that were written about these field experiences in South America. *Desert Trails of the Atacama* was one of the first regional geography books written in the United States and is still considered an important work on the Pleistocene history of Bolivia. *The Andes of Southern Peru* involved a 200-mile transect along the coastal desert of Peru and included the first regional diagrams ever published. There were also a variety of notes, articles, and reviews that were the result of these field excursions.

In the summer of 1915, Bowman left Yale to become director of the American Geographical Society. He directed the society in a variety of scholarly pursuits, including a strengthening and upgrading of the monographic series and a revision of the format of the *Geographical Review*. He also made important changes to the map collection and library of the society.

During the twenties, Bowman developed his own research interests in pioneer belts and settlement patterns, the results of which were published in the *Geographical Review* as well as other scholarly journals. In his book *The Pioneer Fringe*, he attempted to outline his ideas on a science of settlement.

While at the American Geographical Society, Bowman also initiated a Latin American mapping project. His goal was to map Latin America on the millionth scale (1:1,000,000). The project ran for twenty-five years and was recognized as a major geographic contribution. Several of the more than one hundred maps produced were later used to adjudicate boundary disputes.

Bowman became involved in preparing materials for the peace conference after World War I, since he was chief officer of the inquiry and territorial advisor to the American Commission to Negotiate Peace 1918–19. He played an important role in preparing numerous maps for United States and Allied use. As a result of his interest in political issues, Bowman wrote the first political geography book, *The New World*, to be published in the United States.

Although Bowman had been involved in a variety of specific research projects, he also was interested in the broad scope of geography. In 1934 he published *Geography in Relation to the Social Sciences*, his attempt to look at geographic concepts and methodologies. At that time it was probably the most comprehensive statement of its kind, and it exerted an important influence on educators, professional geographers, and administrators.

In 1935, during the depths of the depression, Bowman left the American Geographical Society and took the presidency of Johns Hopkins University in Baltimore. He found a university in considerable financial difficulty, but through his energetic leadership, he was able to overcome these difficulties and make a positive impact on Johns Hopkins. His ideas about the place of the university and the educated man (Bowman's term) in our society were published in a book entitled *A Design for Scholarship*.

During his thirteen-year presidency of Johns Hopkins, Bowman continued to write and to publish a considerable amount of geographical works. He created departments of geography and oceanography at Johns Hopkins and gave special attention to the development of graduate programs. He felt that the production of geography scholars was very important and that this could only be done with a strong graduate program. His ideas about the development of geography programs were sought by more than one hundred colleges and universities. His experience with the development of graduate programs inspired him to write *The Graduate School in American Democracy* for the Office of Education in Washington, D.C.

During the course of World War II, Bowman was involved with a variety of important governmental positions. Three days a week he spent at the U.S. State Department as a special advisor to Secretary Cordell Hull. He was a member of numerous missions, delegations, and conferences and also was an advisor to President Franklin D. Roosevelt.

In January 1948, Bowman retired from the presidency of Johns Hopkins. The following year he devoted a considerable amount of time to the Economic Cooperation Administration and concurrently assembled materials for a series of studies. Shortly thereafter, on January 6, 1950, he died.

Isaiah Bowman left a legacy of immense importance to the development of geography in the United States. He wrote more than 180 scholarly articles, 12 books, and numerous book reviews and notes. He was awarded thirteen honorary degrees, six medals, and nine honorary fellowships. He was president of the Association of American Geographers, the International Geographical Union, and the American Association for the Advancement of Science. His record of achievement in publication, scholarship, and public affairs was monumental.

Selected Bibliography

1904   "Deflection of the Mississippi." *Science* 20:273–77.

            "A Typical Case of Stream-Capture in Michigan." *Journal of Geology* 12:326–34.

1905   "A Classification of Rivers Based on Water Supply." *Journal of Geography* 4:212–20.

1906   "Northward Extension of the Atlantic Preglacial Deposits." *American Journal of Science* 22:313–25.

1907   Assisted by Chester A. Reeds. *Water Resources of the East St. Louis District*. Illinois State Geological Survey Bulletin.

1909   "The Physiography of the Central Andes." Vol.1: "The Maritime Andes." Vol.2: "The Eastern Andes."*American Journal of Science* 28: 197–217, 373–402.

            "The Distribution of Population in Bolivia." *Bulletin of the Geographical Society of Philadephia* 7:74–93.

            "The Highland Dweller of Bolivia: An Anthropogeographic Interpretation." *Bulletin of the Geographical Society of Philadelphia* 7:159–84.

1911   *Forest Physiography: Physiography of the United States and Principles of Soils in Relation to Forestry.* New York.

         Well Drilling Methods. U.S. Geological Survey Water Supply Paper no. 257. Washington, D.C.

1912   "The Valley People of Eastern Bolivia." *Journal of Geography* 11:114–19.

1912–13   "Asymmetrical Crest Lines and Abnormal Valley Profiles in the Central Andes." *Zeitschrift fur Gletscherkunde* 7:119–27.

1915   *South America: A Geography Reader.* New York.

1916   *The Andes of Southern Peru: Geographical Reconnaissance along the Seventy-Third Meridian.* Published for the American Geographical Society by Henry Holt.

1917   "The Frontier Region of Mexico: Notes to Accompany a Map of the Frontier." *Geographical Review* 3:16–27.

1919   "The American Geographical Society's Contribution to the Peace Conference." *Geographical Review* 7:1–10.

1921   *The New World: Problems in Political Geography.* New York.

1922   "A Note on the Political Map of Turkey." *Foreign Affairs* 1:158–61.

1923   "An American Boundary Dispute: Decision of the Supreme Court of the United States with Respect to the Texas-Oklahoma Boundary." *Geographical Review* 13:161–89.

         "The Boundaries of Turkey According to the Treaty of Lausanne." *Geographical Review* 13:627–29.

         "Geographical Elements in the Turkish Situation: A Note on the Political Map." *Geographical Review* 13:122–29.

1924   *Desert Trails of the Atacama.* American Geographical Society Special Publication No. 5. New York.

1926   "The Analysis of Landforms: Walther Penck on the Topographic Cycle." *Geographical Review* 16:122–32.

         "The Scientific Study of Settlement." *Geographical Review* 16:647–53.

1927   "The Pioneer Fringe." *Foreign Affairs* 6:49–66.

1930   *International Relations.* American Library Association. Chicago.

         "The Political Geography of the Mohammedan World." *Moslem World* 20:1–4.

         "Antarctica." *Scientific Monthly* 30:341–51.

1931   "Jordon Country." *Geographical Review* 21:22–55.

         The Pioneer Fringe. American Geographical Society Special Publication No. 13. New York.

1932   "Planning in Pioneer Settlement." *Annals of the Association of American Geographers* 22:93–107.

1933   "Correlation of Sedimentary and Climatic Records." *Proceedings of the National Academy of Science* 19:376–86.

1934	*Geography in Relation to the Social Sciences*. New York.
	"William Morris Davis." *Geographical Review* 24:177–81.
1935	"The Land of Your Possession." *Science* 82:285–93.
1936	*A Design for Scholarship*. Baltimore.
1937	*Limits of Land Settlement: A Report on Present-Day Possibilities*. Council on Foreign Relations, New York.
1939	*The Graduate School in American Democracy*. U.S. Office of Education Bulletin No. 10. Washington, D.C.
1940	"John Houston Finley, 1863–1940." *Geographical Review* 30:355–57.
	"Science and Social Effects: Three Failures." *Scientific Monthly* 50:289–98.
1941	"Peace and Power Politics 1941." *Baltimore Bulletin of Education* 18:171–80.
	"The Ecuador-Peru Boundary Dispute." *Foreign Affairs* 20:757–61.
1942	"Geography and Geopolitics." *Geographical Review* 32:646–58.
1943	"A Department of Geography." *Science* 98:564–66.
1946	"The Millionth Map of Hispanic America." *Science* 103:319–23.
1951	"Pioneer Settlement." In Griffith Taylor, *Geography in the Twentieth Century*. New York.

Chronology

1878	Born at Berlin, Ontario, Canada, December 26.
1905	Awarded the B.S. Degree from Harvard University, then joined the faculty at Yale University.
1907	Went on first expedition to South America.
1909	Awarded a Ph.D.
1911	Went on second field trip to South America.
1915	Appointed Director, American Geographic Society, and published *South America: A Geography Reader*.
1918	Chief of territorial experts for U.S. delegates at Paris Peace Conference.
1921	Became a member of the Board of Directors of the Council on Foreign Relations and a member of the Editorial Advisory Board of *Foreign Affairs*.
1931	President of the Association of American Geographers and publication of *The Pioneer Fringe*.
1934	Publication of *Geography in Relation to the Social Sciences*.
1935	President, Johns Hopkins University.
1936	Publication of *A Design for Scholarship*.
1937	Publication of *Limits of Land Settlement*.
1943	President, American Association for the Advancement of Science.

1946	Declined an appointment to the Atomic Energy Commission.
1948	Retired from the Presidency of Johns Hopkins University.
1950	Died January 6.

Reference

Carter, George F. 1950. "Isaiah Bowman, 1878–1950." *Annals of the Association of American Geographers* 40:335–38.

Albert Perry Brigham

Albert Perry Brigham was one of the forty-eight original members of the Association of American Geographers, and during the first decade of its existence he played an important role in shaping its professional affairs. The half-century of Brigham's professional life was divided between a decade as a minister and four decades as a professional geographer.

Brigham was born on a farm in Perry, a small upstate New York town, on June 12, 1855, the son of Horace A. and Julia (Perry) Brigham. Although his mother died when he was fifteen, her influence remained throughout his life. She made the world both interesting and exciting to her son although she never travelled more than 40 miles from her home. She gave him a geography book by S. Augustus Mitchell, *A System of Modern Geography* (1849), that contained 197 pictures. He was fascinated by both pictures and maps, which he studied for hours.

Young Brigham entered Madison University (now Colgate) in 1875 at the age of twenty and graduated in 1879. He took the standard liberal arts curriculum and was conspicuously brilliant, especially in speaking and writing. During his junior year, he took a Natural History course from Professor Walter T. Brooks, in which Brooks presented the earth's history as changing and developing. Although this idea intrigued Brigham, in accordance with his father's wishes, he entered the Theological Seminary at Hamilton, New York and was ordained to the ministry in 1882.

For the next decade, Brigham devoted his life to the ministry, first as a pastor in Stillwater, New York, then from 1885 to 1891 as minister of a church in Utica, New York. During this time, however, he still continued to have an interest in natural history and spent much of his spare time studying the rocks and geography of the local area. Working on his own, he completed a survey of the rocks and landforms around Utica that was published in 1888.

During the summer of 1889, Brigham attended two field courses offered by Nathan Shaler and *William Morris Davis of Harvard University. After these courses Brigham decided that he would be of greater service as a teacher of geography than as a minister. He concluded that nature was all about him, and its meaning should be learned and given to the world.

In 1891 he resigned from the ministry to attend Harvard University and study with Shaler and Davis. In 1892 he completed his Master of Arts degree and returned to Colgate University as an instructor in geology.

Brigham's scholarly work focused on the border area between geology and geography. He had a broad view of geography, and in 1924 in an article in the *Annals of the Association of American Geographers* (14:110) he said that "essential content of geography is so large that the successful cultivation of the whole demands the energies of many experts."

Brigham's geographic contributions to the literature ranged from glacial geology and physiography to the relationship between geography and history. He also wrote books for elementary and high school students as well as students in normal schools and universities (Martin, 1932:500).

Brigham's early research and writing, after starting his career at Colgate, showed the strong influences of his mentors at Harvard. His paper of 1892 on "Rivers and the Evolution of Geographic Forms" was centered around William Morris Davis's landform sequence model. Brigham used examples from his field research in New York to illustrate Davis's ideas. The multiple hypotheses method expounded by *Grove Karl Gilbert and Davis can clearly be seen in Brigham's 1893 paper on "The Finger Lakes of New York." He was also concerned with teaching physiography, and in his 1895 paper on "The Composite Origin of Topographic Forms," he wrote, "The teacher of physiography has no greater reward than is his when a student assures him that henceforth his native state will be to him a new country, or that he shall see the hills and valleys of his old home with new eyes."

In 1901 Brigham published his *Textbook of Geology* followed one year later by his *Introduction to Physical Geography*, coauthored with Gilbert. In his physical geography book, Brigham stressed the interaction between people and the physical environment. In 1903 he published another book entitled *Geographic Influences in American History*, an interesting topic for one who had been primarily trained in physical geography.

In the early 1900s, Brigham continued to publish papers in the area of historical geography, including several works dealing with routes across the Appalachians. These studies included detailed map studies and field observations. A summary of these studies appeared in his 1907 book *From Trail to Railway Through the Appalachians*. Brigham arranged special round-table discussions at the annual meetings of the Association of American Geographers in 1907 and 1909 to look more closely at "geographic influences" and invited historians and anthropologists to participate in these meetings. In 1914, as President of the Association of American Geographers, he centered his presidential address on the problems of geographic influence. He felt it was the geographer's task to be cautious when asserting the influence of the physical environment on human behavior. He was especially concerned about the works of *Ellsworth Huntington and *Ellen Churchill Semple and their emphasis on climatic influences.

After a visit to Cape Cod during the summer of 1915, Brigham spent several years looking at the human landscape impact of that region. The result was a book published in 1920 entitled *Cape Cod and the Old Colony*. *Preston E. James believed this was Brigham's greatest work because Cape Cod was a perfect place to illustrate his ideas concerning geographic interpretation and study.

After World War I, and before his retirement in 1925, Brigham's sphere of instruction grew; he taught summer courses at Cornell, Harvard, Wisconsin, Oxford, the Royal Geographical Society in London, and other centers of learning. He also received a variety of scholastic honors, including an Sc.D. from Syracuse University in 1918; a Litt. D. from Franklin College in 1920; and an LL.D. from Colgate in 1925 at the time of his retirement.

Brigham continued to lead an active professional life after retirement from Colgate. In 1930 he was appointed "Consultant in Science" at the Library of Congress in Washington. In the same year, he was elected Vice Chairman of the Division of Geology and Geography in the National Research Council and was selected as one of the official delegates of the American Geographical Society to the centenary of the Royal Geographical Society. On the seventy-fifth anniversary of his birth in 1930, the June issue of the *Annals of the Association of American Geographers* (Keith, 1933:207) was devoted entirely to tributes, dedicated to him by his colleagues. Brigham's many years as Secretary of the Association of American Geographers (1904–13) and as President in 1914 were greatly appreciated. He died in Washington, D.C., on March 31, 1932.

Selected Bibliography

1888   "The Geology of Oneida County." *Transactions of the Oneida Historical Society 1887–1889*, 102–18.

1892   "Rivers and the Evolution of Geographic Forms." *Bulletin of the American Geographical Society* 24:23–43.

1893   "The Finger Lakes of New York." *Bulletin of the American Geographical Society* 25:203–23.

1895   "Drift Boulders Between the Mohawk and Susquehanna Rivers." *American Journal of Science*. 3d series, 49:213–28.

            "The Composite Origin of Topographic Forms." *Bulletin of the American Geological Society* 27:161–73.

1897   "Glacial Flood Deposits in Chenango Valley." *Bulletin of the Geological Society of America* 8:17–30.

1898   "Topography and Glacial Deposits of Mohawk Valley." *Bulletin of the Geological Society of America* 9:183–210.

1901   *Textbook of Geology*. New York.

1902   With G. K. Gilbert. *Introduction to Physical Geography*. New York.

1903   *Geographic Influences in American History*. Boston.

1904   "The Geography of the Louisiana Purchase." *Journal of Geography* 3:243–50.

            "Good Roads in the United States." *Bulletin of the American Geographical Society* 36:721–35.

            "Geography and History in the United States." In *Report of the 8th International Geographical Congress*, 958–65.

1905   "Great Roads Across the Appalachians." *Bulletin of the American Geographical Society* 37:321–39.

1906   "The Fiords of Norway." *Bulletin of the American Geographical Society* 38:337–48.

1907   *From Trail to Railway Through the Appalachians*. Boston.

1911   *Commercial Geography*. Boston.

1916   With C. T. McFarlane. *Essentials of Geography*. New York.

1920   *Cape Cod and the Old Colony*. New York.

            With C. T. McFarlane. *Results of the World War*. New York.

            "Geography and the War." Presidential Address, National Council of Geography Teachers. *Journal of Geography* 19:89–103.

1921   "The Teaching of Geography." *Journal of the New York State Teachers Association* (February): 16–18.

            "Geographic Education in America." *Annual Report, Smithsonian Institution*, 487–96.

1924   "The Appalachian Valley." *Scottish Geographical Magazine* 40:218–30.

1927   *The United States of America—Studies in Physical, Regional, Industrial, and Human Geography*. London.

1929   *The Glacial Geology and Geographic Conditions of the Lower Mohawk Valley*. New York State Museum Bulletin, Albany.

Chronology

1855   Born at Perry, New York, June 12.

1879   Graduated from Madison (Colgate) University.

1888   First publication, "The Geology of Oneida County."

1891   Resigned from ministry; entered Harvard.

1892   M.A. degree; appointed to teach geology at Colgate University.

1901   Publication of *Textbook of Geology*.

1902   Chief interest shifted to human geography. Publication of *Introduction to Physical Geography*, with Grove K. Gilbert.

1903   Published *Geographic Influences in American History*.

1904   Secretary-Treasurer, Association of American Geographers (secretary until 1913, treasurer until 1907).

1907	Publication of *From Trail to Railway Through the Appalachians*.
1914	President of the Association of American Geographers.
1927	Science adviser, Library of Congress; Publication of *The United States of America*.
1929	Vice Chairman, Division of Geology and Geography, National Research Council; Publication of "The Glacial Geology and Geographical Conditions of the Lower Mohawk Valley."
1930	American Geographical Society delegate to Royal Geographical Society centenary; lectured in Havana, Cuba.
1932	Died in Washington, D.C., March 31.

References

Keith, Arthur. 1933. "Memorial of Albert Perry Brigham." *Bulletin of the Geologic Society of America* 44:307–11.
Martin, Lawrence. 1932. "Albert Perry Brigham." *Geographical Review* 22:499–500.

Anton Friedrich Büsching

One of the most influential geographers of the later half of the eighteenth century was Anton Büsching. Many geographical publications of the nineteenth century were based upon his work and several scholars at that time considered Büsching to be the* "Strabo" of contemporary geography. *Immanuel Kant, the German philosopher who made important geographical contributions, based many of his lectures on geography after passages in the works of Büsching.

Büsching was born in Stadhagen on September 27, 1724. He was from a wealthy and established Westphalian family and the only survivor of a family of nine children. He attended the municipal school from the age of six, and at the age of seventeen he left the basic Latin school. After Latin school, he was tutored by Eberhard Hauber, who taught him several languages as well as gave him an understanding of the interrelationship between sciences, especially geography. In his *Autobiography*, Büsching says that Hauber "when lecturing on history, familiarized us with geography, and with history, when lecturing on geography" (1789:41). In 1743, Büsching left Stadhagen and attended the Latin school at Halle for a year, in order to prepare for the university. In April 1744, he enrolled at the University of Halle as a theology student. He acquired a master's degree from Halle in 1747 and the following year became a private tutor for the son of Friederich Rochus, The Count of Lynar. In 1749, the Count was transferred to St. Petersburg and Büsching went along.

This first journey, according to Buttner and Jakel, "had some influence on Büsching's later work, for he was stimulated to work out decisively his description of the earth and to begin the collection of geographical data" (1982:9). Büsching explains in his *Autobiography* how this journey pointed out the inadequacy of the geographic works he had read. From this time on, he began to concentrate on his geographic writings, and in 1752 he left for Copenhagen to use the library of his former tutor, Eberhard Hauber. While working at Hauber's home, he completed works on the Nordic lands as well as Southern and Western Europe.

In 1754, Büsching was offered an appointment as a professor in the philosophical faculty at the University of Göttingen. He continued his geographic research and published part of his major geographical work, *New Earth Description*. A year after going to Göttingen, he married Polxene Auguste.

His *New Earth Description* would eventually encompass eleven volumes in numerous editions. Büsching preceded his description of various countries with his general views on geography. He believed geography had three areas of emphasis: mathematical geography, physical geography, and cultural—or human—geography. He thought the purpose of geography was

to give a complete account of the nature and political state of the known territory of the earth. The known territory of the earth must be studied with regard to its physical and also its political shape. Its physical shape includes mathematical studies on its characteristics as a celestial body . . . and related studies; on the other hand it included the knowledge of everything that is above and below the surface of the earth. (Vol. 1, 1785: 19–20)

In 1754 Büsching received his Doctor of Theology degree, but eventually his theological ideas caused a rift with his colleagues at Göttingen, and he left the university in 1761. In that year, he accepted the position of pastor of the Lutheran congregation at St. Peters in St. Petersburg. He resigned that position in 1765, and the following year became senior consistorial counsel and director of the two senior high schools in Berlin. Management of the schools was very time-consuming and greatly curtailed his geographic work.

Büsching did however publish two journals between 1767 and 1788. One journal, *Weekly Information on New Maps and Geographical Statistical and Historical Books and Data*, was published between 1773 and 1787. Most of the contributions of this journal were written by Büsching himself, and he selected materials he thought would be of interest to geographers. The journal also included bibliographic and geographical literature. The second journal, *Magazine of the New History and Geography*, was published between 1767 and 1788. It contained a variety of scientific papers written by Büsching's fellow scientists. Büsching also wrote reports of minor trips he took, as well as textbooks for his high school classes. In total, Büsching's publications numbered more than one hundred.

Büsching was a major force in the development of geography in the later half of the eighteenth century. According to Buttner and Jakel, "Until well into the nineteenth century, most geographical publications were based, to some degree, on Büsching's writings, sometimes even taking whole passages, as often as not referring to Büsching by name" (1982:12). Büsching's works were also the basis for the geographical education of the famous German geographer *Carl Ritter. Ritter praised Büsching's work, referring to Büsching's *Europa* as a masterpiece of its era. Aside from his emphasis on exact delimitation of areas, Büsching was also responsible for introducing statistical methods and the study of census data to the science of geography. Büsching's greatest achievement, according to Oscar Peschel, was to "have understood . . . that the study of population density should be one of the tasks of geography" (1878:16). Many of Büsching's ideas are still of interest and relevant to current geographical studies. Büsching died on May 25, 1793, in Berlin.

Selected Bibliography

1754   *New Earth Description* (Neue Erdbeschreibung). London.

1766   *Description of the Dead Sea in Palestine* (Beschreibung des todten Meers in Palästina). Hamburg.

1775   *Complete Topography of the Province of Brandenburg* (Vollstandige Topographie der Mark Brandenburg). Berlin.

            Teaching Natural Science (Unterricht in der Naturgeschichte). Berlin.

            Description of a Journey from Berlin through Potsdam to Rekahn in the Brandenburg Hinterland (Beschreibung seiner Reise von Berlin über Potsdam nach Rekahn unweit Brandenburg). Leipzig.

1780   *Description of a Journey from Berlin to Kyritz in the Prignitz Region* (Beschreibung seiner Reise von Berlin nach Kyritz in der Prignitz). Leipzig.

1782   *History of the Weather in Brandenburg Province* (Ältere Wettergeschichte der Mark Brandenburg). Berlin.

Chronology

1724   Born at Stadhagen, ca. September 27.

1747   Graduated with a master's degree.

1754   After a short stay in Halle, went to Göttingen University as a professor; published part of his *Neue Erdbeschreibung* (New Earth Description), of which the remainder appeared in 1757, 1759, 1761, and 1768.

1757   Became a Doctor of Theology.

1766   In October went to Berlin and became head of a grammar school; published his description of the Dead Sea in Palestine.

1767   First publication of the *Magazim für die neue Histoire und Geographic* (Magazine for the New History and Geography).

1771   Asked Emperor Joseph II to appoint him as "Imperial Geographer," but this was not possible.

1773   Began the publication of a weekly news sheet on new maps.

1775   Further publication on the topography of Brandenburg, the teaching of natural science, and his journey to Rekahn.

1782   Published *History of the Weather in Brandenburg Province.*

1793   Died in Berlin on May 25.

Reference

Büttner, Manfred, and Hoheisel Jakel. 1982. "Anton Friedrich Büsching." *Geographers Biobibliographical Studies* 6:7–15.

Walter Christaller

Walter Christaller was born in Berneck, a small village in Germany's *Schwarz-wald* (Black Forest region), on April 21, 1893. His mother, Helene, was a well-known novelist, and on her side of the family there had been considerable interest in geography. His father, Erdmann, was a clergyman who retired early and authored a number of critical essays.

Despite the family's apparent success, resources were scarce and travel was uncommon, though it appealed very much to young Walter. According to *Brian Berry and *Chauncy D. Harris (1970:116):

Maps provided solace; he would pore over them by the hour, taking imaginary journeys. A nagging question emerged. Why was it that towns were so regularly spaced along the routes: Why did large towns follow small ones, and small towns follow large ones, in apparently regular progressions?

These early ruminations were to interest Christaller throughout his professional life, and answers to those questions culminated in his major work, *Die zentralen Orte in Süddeutschland*.

Christaller's early university studies were in philosophy and economics, but World War I intervened before he graduated. He served in the military, returned for a semester to the university, then worked at a variety of jobs, including journalism and construction. He was influenced considerably by left-wing causes during the 1920s and ultimately ran into problems because some of his work was used as the basis for Nazi settlement planning in Eastern Europe.

In 1928, after a variety of different work and intellectual experiences, he again matriculated at the University of Erlangen, where he came under the influence of Robert Gradmann, who was at that time engaged in laying the foundation for a location theory of cities. Christaller had found his intellectual home, where he pursued answers to those early childhood questions that had remained with him. Fundamentally, he searched for laws or generalizations that would explain the size, number, and spatial arrangement of cities. He received his doctorate in 1932, with his dissertation on central places in southern Germany, cited already, and his *habilitation* degree in 1938, with a dissertation, *Rural Settlement Patterns in the German Reich and Their Relationship to the Organization of Local Government.*

Though Christaller personally viewed his work as a contribution in economics, it was within geography—first from Robert Gradmann, then from others—that he became well-known. At least partly as a result of his paradoxical position, Christaller was not to experience a successful academic career—he did not fit into economics departments, yet he refused to make any commitment to the broader field of geography beyond location theory. Additionally, he seemed unaware of the political abuse of the application of his theory to Eastern Europe during and after World War II. After the war, according to Hottes, Hottes, and Schöller (1983:12), "Christaller returned, as he had done so often in periods of crisis, to his parents' home, the 'Blue House' in Jugendheim. His income was scanty and irregular. In part he directed lower-level statistical works, or was out of work."

Given the difficulties of employment, Christaller's creative work probably suffered considerably, thus his dissertation at Erlangen, published as *Die zentralen Orte in Süddeutschland* in 1933, remains his major contribution. It was in that work that he developed what is now widely accepted by geographers and others as *central place theory.* As Hottes, Hottes, and Schöller (1983:12) phrased it, "He brought site and distribution, size and the range of services offered in the different locations all into a logical system of organization, which helped to open new horizons." The hexagonal arrangement of settlement patterns that he developed rested on what in retrospect seems—as is often the case once new ideas are introduced and understood—quite simple.

In Christaller's case, one initial principle was that central places provide goods to their populations and to people in surrounding areas. The range of goods offered by a particular central place, then, was conditioned by demand—the smaller the central place, the smaller would be the range of goods offered, leading to the idea that there is some regular hierarchical arrangement of central places as well as a hexagonal, spatial arrangement of the system. Once such basic principles were understood, Christaller began looking at possible variations in systems of central places, such as those introduced by topographic variations or administrative divisions. As he saw it, he wanted to do for the geography of settlement patterns what *Johann Heinrich von Thünen had done for agricultural location and Weber had done for industrial location. According to Berry and Harris (1970:118), Christaller "judged, prophetically, that the work would be of enduring value for human geography in general and for settlement geography in particular by suggesting ways in which human geography could rise above the simple Linnaean state."

Early reviews of Christaller's work by geographers failed to comprehend its value. However, August Lösch, a well-known German location theorist, valued Christaller's work highly and introduced it to *Edward Ullman, who was in turn the first geographer to present Christaller's work to American geographers.

Honors accorded Christaller included the *venia legendi* for geography at the university in Freiburg in 1938 and the Outstanding Achievement Award from the Association of American Geographers in 1964. Christaller died of cancer on March 9, 1969, in Germany.

Selected Bibliography

1934   *Die zentralen Orte in Süddeutschland. Eine ökonomischgeographische Untersuchung über die Gesetzmässigkeit der Verbreitung und Entwicklung der Siedlungen mit städtischen Funktionen* (Central Places in Southern Germany: An Economic-Geographical Investigation into the Regularities of the Distribution and Development of Settlements with Urban Functions). Jena: University of Erlangen.

1937   *Die ländliche Siedlungsweise im Deutschen Reich und ihre Beziehungen zur Gemeindeorganisation* (Rural Settlement Patterns in the German Reich and Their Relationship to the Organization of Local Government). Stuttgart-Berlin.

1938   "Rapports fonctionnels entre les agglomerations urbaines et les campagnes." *Comptes Rendus Congres Internationale de Géographie Leiden Géographie Humaine.* 2:123–38.

1941   "Die zentralen Orte in den Ostgebieten and ihre Kultur- und Marketbereiche" (Central Places in the Eastern [occupied] Regions and Their Market and Cultural Realms). *Struktur und Gestaltung des deutschen Ostens.* Leipzig.

        "Raumtheorie und Raumordnung" (Spatial Theory and Spatial Organization). *Archiv für Wirtschaftsplanung* 1:122–26, 131–33.

1950   *Das Grundgerüst der räumlichen Ordnung in Europa* (The Basic Framework of Spatial Organization in Europe). Monograph. In W. Hartke, ed., *Frankfurter Geographie Hefte* 24 (1) .

1955   "Beiträge zu einer Geographie des Fremdenverkehrs" (A Contribution to the Geography of Tourism). *Erdkunde* 9:1–19.

1957   "Der Berufsverkehr in der industriellen Grosstadt" (Occupational Transportation in Large Industrial Cities) and "Formen und Gründe des Pendelns" (The Form and Basis of Commuting). Two essays in *Standort und Wohnort* (Location and Dwelling Place). Köln-Oplanden.

1960   "Die Hierarchie der Städte" (The Hierarchy of Cities). *Proceedings of IGU Symposium of Urban Geographers*, Lund, 1960 (pub. 1962), 95–105.

1961   *Das Gesicht Unserer Erde: Räume, Völker, Kontinente, Ein Kompendium der Geographie unserer Tage* (The Face of our Earth: Regions, Peoples, Continents. A Compendium of Modern Geography). Text by Christaller; general editor, H. R. Fischer. Munich.

1963	"Wandlungen des Fremdenverkehrs und der Bergstrasse, im Odenwald und im Neckarthal" (Changes in Tourist Traffic and Mountain Tracks in Odenwald and the Neckar Valley). *Geographische Rundschau* 15:216–22.
1964	"Some Considerations of Tourism Location in Europe—the Peripheral Regions, Underdeveloped Countries, Recreation Areas." *Papers of the Regional Science Assocciation, European Congress*, Lund, 95–105.

Chronology

1893	Born on April 21 at Berneck, Germany.
1913–14	Student at the universities of Heidelberg and Munich.
1914–18	Served in the German Army and received a commission.
1921–24	Employed by German civil service in Berlin; worked on rural problems.
1925–28	Employed by a building firm in Berlin.
1930	Master's degree.
1932	Doctoral degree—his thesis was the basis for his work on central places in Southern Germany.
1939–45	Worked in Berlin, continuing research.
1945–69	Worked as a journalist and author.
1969	Died on March 9 at Königstein, Taunus.

References

Berry, Brian, and Chauncy D. Harris. 1970. "Walter Christaller." *Geographical Review* 60:116–19.

Hottes, Karlheinz, Ruth Hottes, and Peter Schöller. 1983. "Walter Christaller." *Geographers Biobibliographical Studies* 7:11–16.

Captain James Cook

Captain James Cook was born in the small village of Marton-in-Cleveland, England, on October 27, 1728. He joined the Britannic Majesty's Naval Service on June 17, 1755, and set out on a career in exploration that was to leave an imprint on the world's geography (Beaglehole, 1974).

Three major voyages remain his legacy. The first of those, taken between August 26, 1768, and July 13, 1771, on the *Endeavour*, took Captain Cook to the South Pacific, where he carried out a series of observations on the transit of Venus across the sun, then on to Tahiti. Though those observations proved to be of little use, Cook sailed southward from Tahiti to about 40 degrees south in search of Terra Australis, then, finding no land, turned westward toward New Zealand. After demonstrating that New Zealand was not a part of any major southern land body, thus rejecting a concept suggested earlier by *Ptolemy, he went on to Australia, where he worked on a careful mapping of the eastern coast, then passed through the Torres Strait, which separates Australia and New Guinea.

Captain Cook's second voyage was far more successful in its accomplishments and was among the first exploratory voyages to go beyond simply gathering information about coastal configurations and nautical information. Because of his outstanding record, he was given command of two ships, the *Resolution* and the *Adventure*. This voyage, which took place between 1772 and 1775, carried him even farther south than the previous one, reaching to approximately 71 degrees south, and it confirmed what he had concluded earlier about Ptolemy's southland—though Cook believed that still further south there might have been a landmass that he never reached. Cook returned to England in 1775 with considerable information to report, especially about the vastness of the southern hemisphere oceans and his explorations in the South Pacific. During the voyage, he added much to the world's knowledge of the outline of the Pacific Ocean, to which he was to return on his final voyage.

Cook's third voyage left England on July 11, 1776, again with two ships, the

Resolution and the *Discovery*, and carried him into the North Pacific in that same year and finally to the Hawaiian Islands on January 18, 1778. He landed at Waimea, Kauai, on January 20, 1778, and named the islands Sandwich Islands in honor of the Earl of Sandwich. After that, he followed along the coast of North America to the Aleutian Islands, reaching a latitude of about 70 degrees north before being turned back by ice. Cook returned to Hawaii for the winter, then journeyed off again early in 1779. That journey was cut short because of the need to repair one of his ship's masts. He returned to Hawaii to do the repairs and was killed there in a fight with some of the native Hawaiians on February 14, 1779. His ship sailed on without him and returned to England in 1780. By that time, with the information that he had gathered in his voyages, the world for the first time had a reasonably clear map.

Selected Bibliography

1893   Journal during his first voyage around the world made in *H. M. Bark Endeavor*, 1768–71. London: Elliot Stock.

            Journals and logs from his trips aboard the *Eagle, Solebays, Pembroke, Northumberland*, and *Grenville*.

Chronology

1728   Born at Marton-in-Cleveland, England, on October 27.

1755   Entered his Britannic Majesty's Naval Service.

1759   Held Master's warrant when he sailed for Canada.

1763   Received a letter of recommendation and a bounty from Admiral Lord Calville, for his landing in Quebec and his ability at naval survey.

1768   Command of the bark *Endeavour*. Sailed from Plymouth for the South Seas to observe the transit of Venus.

1770   Anchored in Australian waters on April 29.

1771   Arrived back in England, July 13.

1772   Command of the ships *Resolution* and *Adventure*. Sailed for the South Seas in July. Promoted to Post-Captain.

1776   Led an expedition to discover the Northwest Passage. Departed from England on July 11.

1778   Enroute, discovers the islands of Oahu and Kauai in January. Named the group of Sandwich Islands, in honor of the Earl of Sandwich, who was First Lord of the Admiralty and Cook's patron.

1779   Killed in Hawaii during an altercation on February 14.

Reference

Beaglehole, J. C. 1974. *The Life of Captain James Cook*. Stanford: Stanford University Press.

Nicolaus Copernicus

With the advent of the Age of Exploration in the last fifteenth century, the geographic horizons were about to be pushed back. According to *Preston James and Geoffrey Martin (1981:91), "There were a few brilliant flashes of genius . . . that illuminated the road ahead." A major question at the time was whether the earth was the fixed center of the universe with the sun and stars revolving around it, or whether the sun was the center of the universe with the earth in orbit about it. Up until the fifteenth century, the geocentric, or earth-centered, universe of Ptolemy was the most commonly held idea. The idea of a heliocentric, or sun-centered, universe was not new, but by the latter part of the fifteenth century, it was increasingly challenged.

The scholar most noted for his advocacy and research of the heliocentric universe was Nicolaus Copernicus. Copernicus was born at Torun, Poland, on February 19, 1473. He was the son of Barbara Watzenrode and Nicolaus Copernicus, a city assessor and shopkeeper. Nicolaus's father died in 1483 when he was only a little more than ten years old. Along with his sisters, Barbara and Catherine, and his older brother, Andrew, he was reared by his maternal uncle Lucas Watzenrode, a bishop at Varmia.

Copernicus went to the University of Cracow from 1491 to 1495, where he studied natural philosophy, cosmography, and astronomy. Through the influence of his uncle, Copernicus was elected a canon of the cathedral chapter of Frombork. The income from this position supported him for the rest of his life. The chapter gave him permission to continue his studies in Italy, where he attended Bologna University from 1496 to 1501, studying Roman and Canon Law, as well as classical philology and astronomy. As a result of his contacts with eminent Italian Renaissance scholars and his interest in classical works, he began to question the validity of the geocentric theory.

In 1501 Copernicus's chapter granted him permission to return to Italy to study for two more years. This time he went to Padua University to study medicine. His chapter wanted him to be a "helpful physician" to both the bishop and other chapter members. He continued his interest, however, in classical works and started developing a model of a heliocentric universe. He returned to Varmia in 1503 after receiving a doctoral degree in canon law from the University of Ferrara. The remaining forty years of his life were spent at Varmia in the service of his chapter.

Copernicus built a tower in 1513 to house his astronomical instruments and took a series of observations. He wrote the first draft of his new astronomical system, *Commentariolus*, in 1514 and discreetly circulated it to friends for comments. In this work, he challenged the astronomical system that had dominated Western thought since the days of *Aristotle and *Ptolemy. He proclaimed that the center of the earth was not the center of the universe and that the earth revolved around the sun along with the rest of the planets. Copernicus continued his work on the heliocentric theory and in 1542 published his major work *De Revolutionibus Orbium Collestium* (Revolutions of the Heavenly Spheres).

Book 1 of *De Revolutionibus* contains a number of concepts related to geography and geology, although geography was taught as a part of geometry in the time of Copernicus, whose heliocentric ideas made it necessary for him to define more precisely some of the earth's features. According to Babicz, Buttner, and Nobis (1982:25), "Having proved the sphericity of the cosmos, Copernicus proves the spherical shape of the earth by astronomical arguments."

Copernicus was also interested in the structure of the earth. The reports of travellers at the time and the discovery of new continents were dealt with in a variety of scientific works and led Copernicus to abandon Aristotle's conviction that the mass of waters was ten times greater than that of the lands (Babicz, Buttner, and Nobis, 1982:25). Copernicus's ideas about the structure of the earth, its gravity and gas and water covers led him to discard ancient beliefs that the earth's motion was impossible. According to Babicz, Buttner, and Nobis (1982:25), "The concept of the earth and the cosmos, as part of the heliocentric theory, made Copernicus a discoverer not only of a new heaven but also of the new earth."

Although Copernicus is primarily known for his astronomical observations, he was also a pioneer in the field of mapmaking and cartography. He used his astronomical knowledge and instruments for measuring latitudinal position, a basic concept of cartography. He also drew political maps of the Polish kingdom that were used to settle a variety of boundary disputes. The impact of Copernicus's work on future generations was monumental; it laid the groundwork for further confirmation by such notable scientists as Bruno, Galilei, Kepler, and Newton. Copernicus died at Frombork on May 24, 1543.

Selected Bibliography

1507			*Commentariolus*. Varmia.

1509			"Eyne Gemeelte." Map in *Regesta Copernicana*. Wroclaw.

1519	"Topographicam Eius Loci Descriptionen, Quam Doctor Nicolaus Depinxit." In *Regesta Copernicana*. Wroclaw.
1523	*De Revolutionibus*. Frombork.
1542	*De lateribus et angulis triangulorum*. Frombork.

Chronology

1473	Born February 19 at Torun.
1491–95	Studied at Cracow University, including natural philosophy, astronomy, and cosmography.
1496–1501	At Bologna, where he studied law, classical philology, and astronomy.
1501–3	Undertook medical studies at Padua University with wide reading on scientists of antiquity.
1503	Awarded doctorate of Canon Law at Ferrara University.
1506–10	Still in the service of his uncle, as physician and adviser, he began to design political maps to illustrate the territories contested between Poland and the Teutonic Order.
1515	Began to study the works of the Cracow astronomers.
1519–21	Still concerned largely with ecclesiastical estates and also with cartography.
1521–37	General administrator of the Varmia dioceses; at this time he was publishing his major works.
1535	At Frombork, produced his work on the astronomical calendar for 1536.
1540–41	Joachim Rheticus stayed in Varmia for some time and Copernicus agreed to the publication of *De Revolutionibus*.
1543	Died at Frombork on May 24.

References

Babicz, Josef, Manfred Buttner, and Heribert M. Nobis. 1982. "Nicolaus Copernicus." *Geographers Biobibliographical Studies* 6:23–29.

James, Preston E., and Geoffrey J. Martin. 1981. *All Possible Worlds: A History of Geographical Ideas*. 2d ed. New York: Wiley.

Charles Andrew Cotton

Charles Andrew Cotton was born in Dunedin, New Zealand, in 1885. He had a lifelong interest in geomorphology and landforms, probably the result of his boyhood travels with his father along the New Zealand coasts. After attending Christchurch Boys High School, he entered the School of Mines at Otago University in Dunedin, where he received the Sir George Grey Scholarship. In 1907 he graduated from Otago with a B.Sc., with first class honors in geology.

After spending a year as director of the Coromandel School of Mines, he accepted a position as a lecturer in the Geology Department at Victorial College, the University of New Zealand, in Wellington. Later, in 1915, he received a D.Sc. from the University of New Zealand [now Victoria University] at Wellington.

Cotton was an admirer of *William Morris Davis, and his early work was strongly influenced by Davis. Cotton did field work on both sides of Cook Strait and gathered evidence on the sequential phases in the evolution of both inland and coastal features. Although this early work was Davisian in nature, Cotton did not accept a rigid concept of successive cycles and denudation chronology as applied to the New Zealand landscape. These early works were well written and clearly illustrated with block diagrams and well-chosen photographs.

Cotton's greatest contribution to geomorphology can probably be found in his textbooks, which were clearly written in a logical manner with particular attention given to the cyclical approach. The illustrations were excellent and considerable care was given to the use of precise definitions. For example, in his *Geomorphology: An Introduction to the Study of Landforms* (1942), Cotton makes a distinction between a *cirque* and a *corrie*, the first term referring to a valley head feature, and the second to a feature hanging along valley sides.

Many of Cotton's later papers, mostly reviews of works of other writers, clearly show his ability to analyze geomorphic problems. According to Soons and Gage (1978:28), "Such papers were not only the outcome of the very wide reading which characterized the whole of Cotton's career, but also models of cool, incisive and unprejudiced comparison of evidence and interpretation. Moreover they say much for Cotton's ability to envisage the landscape of areas which were personally unknown to him.''

The developments in geomorphology associated with statistical analysis and quantitative measurements were not fully accepted by Cotton in his later years. He did, however, recognize mistakes he had made in his earlier works, and he had no hesitation in referring to these previous works and publicly correcting inaccurate or misconceived ideas.

In all, Cotton wrote more than 160 scientific papers and books. He retired as the Chair of Geology at Victoria University in 1953. The following year he received an honorary LL.D from the University of New Zealand. Other honors received by Cotton were the Hutton Medal from the Royal Society of New Zealand in 1947, the Victorial Medal in 1951 from the Royal Geographical Society in London, and the Dumont Medal in 1954 from the Geological Society of Belgium. He died in Wellington in 1970.

Selected Bibliography

1922   *Geomorphology of New Zealand*. Part 1: *Systematic: An Introduction to the Study of Landforms*. New Zealand Board of Science and Art, Manual No. 3, Dominion Museum, Wellington.

1941   *Landscape as Developed by the Processes of Normal Erosion*. London. 2d ed., 1948.

1942   *Geomorphology: An Introduction to the Study of Landforms*. Christchurch. Presented as 3d ed. of *Geomorphology of New Zealand*. 4th ed., 1945; 5th ed., 1949; 6th ed., 1952; 7th ed., 1958.

        Climatic Accidents in Landscape Making. Christchurch. 2d printing, 1947.

1944   *Volcanoes as Landscape Forms*. Christchurch.

1945   *Earth Beneath: An Introduction to Geology for Readers in New Zealand*. Christchurch.

        Living on a Planet. Christchurch.

1955   *New Zealand Geomorphology: Reprints of Selected Papers 1912–1925*. Wellington: New Zealand University Press.

1974   *Bold Coasts*. Edited by B. W. Collins. Wellington.

Chronology

1885   Born in Dunedin, New Zealand.

1907   Graduated with B.Sc. from Otago University.

1908   Graduated with M.Sc. with first class honors in geology.

1909   Lecturer in charge of the first department of geology at Victoria College, University of New Zealand, Wellington.

1915   Awarded D.Sc., University of New Zealand.

1916–19   Editor, New Zealand Institute.

1922   Publication of *Geomorphology of New Zealand*. Part 1: *Systematic: An Introduction to the Study of Landforms*.

1941   Publication of *Landscape as Developed by the Processes of Normal Erosion*.

1942   Publication of *Climatic Accidents in Landscape Making and Geomorphology: An Introduction to the Study of Landforms*.

1944   Publication of *Volcanoes as Landscape Forms*.

1945   Publication of *Living on a Planet*.

1947   Awarded the Hutton Medal, Royal Society, New Zealand.

1951   Awarded the Victoria Medal, Royal Geographic Society, London.

1954   Received an honorary LL.D. from the University of New Zealand and the Dumont Medal from the Geologic Society, Belgium.

1970   Died at Wellington.

1974   Publication of *Bold Coasts*. Edited by B. W. Collins.

Reference

Soons, Jane M., and Maxwell Gage. 1978. "Charles Andrew Cotton: 1885–1970." *Geographers Biobibliographical Studies* 2:27–32.

George Babcock Cressey

George B. Cressey was born on December 15, 1896, in Tiffin, Ohio. His father, Dr. Frank G. Cressey, was a Baptist minister and his mother, Minnie Babcock, was the first woman graduate of the University of Chicago and a teacher of Latin at Denison University in Ohio. George enrolled as an undergraduate at Denison University in 1915 and graduated in 1919 with a B.S. in geology. He continued graduate study at the University of Chicago and received an M.S. degree in geology in 1921. He went on with his doctoral studies at Chicago under the direction of *Rollin D. Salisbury and completed his Ph.D. in geology in 1923 with a dissertation entitled, "A Study of Indiana Sand Dunes."

Cressey had planned to do fieldwork in North Africa, but instead he was appointed to the faculty at Shanghai College, an American Baptist college in China. As was customary at the time, he spent a year in the College of Chinese Studies in Peking before going to Shanghai College. It was while at Peking that he met another young American, Marion H. Chatfield, whom he married two years later in 1925.

Cressey taught both geology and geography at Shanghai College until 1929 which afforded him the opportunity to observe China firsthand. Between 1923 and 1929 (James 1964:254), "He travelled some thirty thousand miles, visiting at least parts of the twenty-eight provinces and all fifteen of the geographic regions. Copious field notes and photographs recorded the results of his travels." At one time, in 1926, Cressey was even accosted by bandits and beaten and robbed. The materials he gathered on these field excursions eventually were the basis for his first book on Chinese geography.

In 1929, Cressey returned to the United States and entered the Clark University Graduate School of Geography. His thesis supervisor was *Wallace W. Atwood, and he completed his second Ph.D. in 1931 with a dissertation on the Ordos Desert of Inner Mongolia. After completing his graduate work at Clark, he was appointed Chairman of the Department of Geology and Geography at Syracuse University in 1931 at the age of thirty-five.

Shortly after being appointed at Syracuse, Cressey found out that all his text materials, along with the photos and maps for his forthcoming book on China, had been destroyed in a fire in Shanghai. He then rewrote the book from notes and other materials he had, and it was published in 1934. This book, *China's Geographic Foundations*, was instantly welcomed as an excellent piece of scholarship about an area of the world that was little understood in both the United States and Europe. According to Herman (1965:361), "The main theme was the adjustment of man to the physical environment. . . . The physical environment was presented systematically, supported by original maps, many statistics, and excellent photographs."

Cressey continued his research in Asia in the 1930s and became interested in the Soviet Union. In 1937, he attended the International Geological Congress in Moscow and then travelled in Siberia and the Arctic for three months.

As a result of his specialized knowledge of Asia, Cressey was brought to Washington as a consultant during World War II. He worked for the Board of Economic Welfare, the Department of State, and Army Intelligence. He was also busy at Syracuse, teaching in the accelerated army training program. During this time he also wrote he second book, *Asia's Lands and Peoples*, which brought information about the geography of the Soviet Union to American students.

In 1945, geology and geography were separated at Syracuse University, and Cressey was appointed as the new chairman of geography, which was included in the Maxwell Graduate School. After twenty years of service to Syracuse University, he retired as chairman in 1951 and became the first recipient of the distinguished Maxwell Professorship. He continued his travels and field study with a particular focus on Southwest Asia. In 1955–56, he was a Fulbright Research Scholar in Iraq and in 1957–58 a Smith-Mundt Professor in Lebanon. The result of this work appeared in his book published in 1960 titled *Crossroads: Land and Life in Southwest Asia*. He continued his research studies up until the time of his death in 1963, when he was studying the resources of the world's oceans.

Cressey's works made a major contribution to geographic knowledge. According to *Preston James and Andrew Perejda (1981:22), "His books were widely used and read not only as textbooks in the colleges and universities, but also by people employed in government work dealing with, particularly, the various realms of Asia." Cressey was a meticulous researcher who believed that field work was an essential element for anyone interested in writing books about geography. He also believed that the myriad problems associated with poverty in developing countries could only be solved with the assistance of the industrialized nations.

In addition to his teaching and scholarly work, Cressey was very active in a variety of professional organizations. He was president of the International Geographical Union from 1949 to 1952 and also served several times as vice president of that organization. From 1949 to 1956, he represented the union on the Executive Board of the International Council of Scientific Unions. He was a member of the Council of the Association of American Geographers from 1947 to 1949 and was honorary president of the association in 1957. He was a member of the American Geographical Society from 1952 until the time of his death, and he served as President of the Association for Asian Studies from 1959 to 1960.

Cressey also received many honors and awards. He was a member of Sigma Xi and Phi Betta Kappa and was appointed National Visiting Scholar of Phi Beta Kappa in 1961–62. In 1945 he was awarded the Doctor of Humane Letters degree from Denison University, and the American Geographical Society awarded him its George Davidson Medal in 1952. In 1957 he received the Distinguished Service Award from the National Council for Geographic Education.

In writing Cressey's obituary for the *Geographic Review*, Preston James (1964:257) highlighted Cressey's career and stated in conclusion that Cressey's "devotion to geographical studies was expressed fundamentally by his service as a teacher. It was not enough to see and understand the interconnections of man and the land throughout the world—he had to communicate his understanding. He did this with a rare vitality and enthusiasm, which sent his students away with a new excitement about learning."

Selected Bibliography

1928   "The Geology of Shanghai." *China Journal* 8:334–45; 9:89–96.

The Indiana Sand Dunes and Shore Lines of the Lake Michigan Basin. Chicago.

"The Meaning of Geology." *Voice Quarterly* 18:24–39.

1930   "The New Map of China." *Geographical Review* 20:652–56.

"The Geographic Regions of China." *Annals of the Association of Political and Social Science* 152:1–9.

1932   "Chinese Colonization in Mongolia: A General Survey." In I. Bowman, ed., *Pioneer Settlement*. American Geographical Society, New York, 273–89.

1934   *China's Geographic Foundations.* New York.

"Agricultural Regions of Asia." Part 4: "China." *Economic Geography* 10:109–42.

1935   "The Major Geographic Regions of Eurasia." *Journal of Geography* 34:197–301.

1936   "The Fengsien Landscape: A Fragment of the Yangtze Delta." *Geographical Review* 26:396–413.

1938   "The Landforms of Chekiang." *Annals of the Association of American Geographers* 38:259–76.

"News from Siberia." *Harper's Magazine* 177:148–57.

1939   "Frozen Ground in Siberia." *Journal of Geology* 47:472–88.

With A. D. Perejda and V. Washburn. Translation of Vol. 1 of 1938 edition of *Great Soviet World Atlas*.

1940   "The Place of Geography in Far Eastern Studies." *Notes on Far Eastern Studies in America* 6:1–2.

1942   "A Russian View of the Economic Geography of Asia." *Far Eastern Quarterly* 1:180–84.

"Siberia's Role in Soviet Strategy." *Journal of Geography* 41:81–88.

1944   *Asia's Land and Peoples*. New York.

1945   "Geographical Education in China and India." *Geographical Review* 35:486–88.

1946   "The Place of Geography in General Education." In *The Clark Graduate School of Geography: Our First Twenty-five Years*. Worcester, Mass. 27–33.

1948   "To Understand and Deal with the Physical Aspects of Geography." In C. F. Kohn, ed., *Geographic Approaches to Social Education*. Washington, D.C., 53–62.

1949   "Wallace W. Atwood, 1872–1949." *Annals of the Association of American Geographers* 39:296–306.

"U.S.S.R.: Geographic Bases for Agricultural Planning." *Land Economics* 25:334–6.

"China's Prospects." In H. Weigert, V. Stefansson, and R. E. Harrison, eds., *New Compass in the World*. New York, 249–61.

1950   "Asia Looks at Latin America." *Journal of Geography* 49:305–12.

1952   "The Land of the Five Seas." *Journal of Geography* 51:221–30.

1953   "China." In H. R. Anderson, ed., *Approaches to an Understanding of World Affairs*. 25th yearbook of the National Council for the Social Studies, Washington D.C., 171–80.

"Changing the Map of the Soviet Union." *Economic Geography* 29:198–207.

1954   *How Strong Is Russia?* Syracuse, N.Y.

"Advice to Speakers." *Professional Geographer* 6(6):12–13.

1955   "Changing the Map of China." *Economic Geography* 31:1–16.

Land of the 500 Million: A Geography of China. New York.

1957   "Swasia." *Professional Geographer* 9(5):11–12.

"Land for 2.4 Billion Neighbors." *Economic Geography* 29:1–9.

1960   "The Deserts of Asia." *Journal of Asian Studies* 19:389–402.

1962   *Soviet Potentials: A Geographical Appraisal*. Syracuse, N.Y.

1963   "How Rich Is the Earth, with Illustrations from the Mustard Seed Garden Manual of Chinese Painting, 1679–1701." Address at annual chancellor's dinner for faculty at Syracuse University for those with twenty-five years service or who were retiring.

Chronology

1896	Born in Tiffon, Ohio, December 15.
1919	Awarded B.S. degree from Denison University.
1923	Awarded Ph.D in geology at the University of Chicago and entered the College of Chinese Studies in Peking. Travelled in China until 1929.
1931	Awarded Ph.D. in geography, Clark University, and became Chairman of the Geology and Geography Department, Syracuse University.
1934	Publication of *China's Geographic Foundations*.
1937	Consultant on the *Great Soviet World Atlas*, Vol. 1
1947–49	Served on the Council of the Association of American Geographers.
1949–52	President of the International Geographical Union.
1952	Awarded the George Davidson Medal, American Geographic Society.
1954	Publication of *How Strong Is Russia?*
1955	Publication of *Land of the 500 Million: A Geography of China*.
1955–56	Fulbright Research Scholar in Iraq.
1957	Distinguished Service Award, National Council for Geographic Education.
1959–60	President, Association for Asian Studies.
1963	Died at Syracuse, New York, October 21.

References

Herman, Theodore. 1965. "George Babcock Cressey: 1896–1963," *Annals of the Association of American Geographers* 55(2):360–64.

James, Preston E. 1964. "George Babcock Cressey: 1896–1963." *The Geographical Review* 54(2):254–57.

James, Preston E. and Andrew D. Perejda. 1981. "George Babcock Cressey." *Geographers Biobibliographical Studies* 5:21–25.

Raymond E. Crist

One of America's foremost regional geographers who has had an important influence on geographic field investigations, particularly in Latin America, is Raymond E. Crist. Crist was born on a farm in southwestern Ohio, near the village of Seven Mile, on October 11, 1904. He was the third child in a family of six children. His rural roots, according to Allen Bushong (1989:121), "gave him a firm, practical understanding of the land and empathy for those who work it."

Crist's early education was in a one-room schoolhouse in Seven Mile, a town with a population of 340 in 1910. He went to high school in the town of Hamilton, where he focused on languages, especially Latin, French, and German. When Crist entered the University of Cincinnati in 1921, he intended to major in the classics, but switched to geology after taking a course from Walter W. Bucher. Another professor he had at Cincinnati was Nevin M. Fenneman, a charter member of the Association of American Geographers and its president in 1918. Crist graduated from the University of Cincinnati with a Bachelor of Arts degree on June 13, 1925, with a double major in German and Geology. At graduation, he was given the McKibben medal, "awarded to that young man of the senior class who in the judgment of the Faculty best exemplified the ideas of young manhood" (McGrane, 1963:206).

For the 1925–26 academic year, Crist was appointed to his first teaching position as an instructor in physiography at the Howe School in Howe, Indiana. In 1926, he took a one-year position to do surveying in Mexico with the El Aguila Oil Company, the start of his lifelong interest in Latin America. Crist decided to spend the 1927–28 academic year doing post-graduate, nondegree study in geology at Cornell University. He returned to Latin America in 1928 for a three-year position as an assistant geologist doing topographic mapping and geological survey work for the Sinclair and Atlantic Refining Company.

This work was carried out in Venezuela and thus began his association with the country that has been the subject of much of his geographical research.

In 1931 Crist decided to leave the oil company and pursue further study in geology at the University of Zurich, where he took several geography field courses and was introduced to the field of cultural geography. In 1932 he went to the University of Bonn to study with Leo Waibel. While in Germany, he was notified that he had received an American Field Service Fellowship for study at the University of Grenoble under Raoul Blanchard, an important turning point in Crist's career. According to Crist, "I had crossed the Rubicon, as it were, and realized that my interest was no longer concentrated in geology, but in cultural geography" (Personal correspondence from Raymond Crist, January 18, 1990).

Crist returned to the United States in 1936 and took a teaching position at the University of Illinois in Urbana. During his first year there, he completed work on his doctorate, which was awarded in the spring of 1937. In 1940 he was awarded his first John Simon Guggenheim Memorial Fellowship, which gave him fifteen months to do field work in Andean South America, another important milestone in his career. According to David Clawson (1989:3), "The insights and recognition that Ray gained through the experiences provided by the fellowship propelled him into the leading ranks of Latin Americanist geographers and established him as perhaps the most field-oriented scholar in the discipline."

In 1942 Crist left the University of Illinois for a position at the University of Puerto Rico at Rio Piedras. At this time, during the war, he was a field technician for the Rubber Development Corporation; he traveled extensively in parts of Latin America with which he was previously unfamiliar. He returned to the United States in 1943, however, to marry Hilda Buttenwieser, a professor of classics at the University of Cincinnati. According to Bushong (1989:126), Hilda "shared in much of Ray's travels during their forty-five years of marriage, and his writings benefited from her literary sensibilities and critical editorial eye."

After spending three years at the University of Puerto Rico's Institute of Tropical Agriculture, Crist accepted a position at the University of Maryland at College Park in 1947. Four years later he accepted a position with the University of Florida as a Research Professor, where he finished his career and retired in 1975.

Since his first publication with Raoul Blanchard in 1935, Crist has published more than 250 books, articles, book reviews, research notes and commentaries. Most of his writings have dealt with Latin America, focusing on field investigations that were concerned with frontier colonization and the pioneer settlement processes. Many of these publications appeared in either the *Geographical Review* or the *American Journal of Economics and Sociology*. His 80 book reviews all share a common feature: "It is his philosophy of book reviewing that a bad book does not deserve even the publicity of a negative review, and he has declined to submit reviews of books assigned to him that he has been unable to speak about favorably. His reviews thus promote works which he can truly speak well of'' (Bushong, 1989:128).

Aside from his prodigious research output, Crist has been a mentor to many geographers interested in Latin America. At the time of his retirement in 1975, he had chaired more dissertations on a Latin American area than anyone else in American academic geography—a record that still stands. His greatness as a mentor, according to his last doctoral student, David Clawson (1989:5), "was grounded in his conviction that our development was his highest professional responsibility."

In recognition of his excellent research and teaching, Crist has received numerous awards. In 1969 the University of Cincinnati at its sesquicentennial awarded him an honorary Doctor of Science degree in recognition of his "intensive field studies of cultural geography in the West Indies, in Andean South America, and in the Mediterranean Basin." The National Council for Geographic Education awarded him the Master Teacher Award at its 1979 annual meeting, and in 1985 the Association of American Geographers conferred on him one of its Honors Awards. In recognition of his lifelong contributions to the development of Latin American geography, the Conference of Latin Americanist Geographers gave him its Eminent Latin Americanist Geographer Career Award for 1987.

Selected Bibliography

1932   "Along the Llanos-Andes Border in Zamora, Venezuela." *Geographical Review* 22:411–22.

1935   With Raoul Blanchard. *A Geography of Europe*. New York: Henry Holt.

1939   "The Pulque Industry." *Economic Geography* 15:189–94.

1940   "The Peasant Problem in Yugoslavia." *Scientific Monthly* 50:385–402.

1941   "The Bases of Social Instability in Venezuela." *American Journal of Economics and Sociology* 1:37–44.

            "Land Tenure in Tunisia: Inter- and Intra-national Implications." *Scientific Monthly* 52:403–15.

1944   "Cultural Crosscurrents in the Valley of the Rio Sao Francisco." *Geographical Review* 34:587–612.

1945   "Bolivia and Chile in the Concert of the La Plata Nations." *American Journal of Economics and Sociology* 5:130–34

1950   "The Personality of Popayan." *Rural Sociology* 15:130–40.

1952   "The Canning of Guava Fruits: An Item in the Industrialization of Cuba." *Journal of Geography* 51:338–41.

            The Cauca Valley, Colombia: Land Tenure and Land Use. Baltimore: Waverly Press.

            "Cultural Dichotomy in the Island of Hispaniola." *Economic Geography* 28:105–21.

1953   "Fixed Physical Boundaries and Dynamic Cultural Frontiers: A Contrast." *American Journal of Economics and Sociology* 12:221–30.

1954   "Changing Cultural Landscapes in Antigua, B.W.I." *American Journal of Economics and Sociology* 13:225–32.

1956   "Along the Llanos-Andes Border in Venezuela: Then and Now." *Geographical Review* 46:187–208.

           "Some Notes on Recent Trends in Rice Production in Cuba." *Economic Geography* 32:126–31.

1960   "Some Recent Trends in French Geographic Research and Thought." *Professional Geographer* 12:26–28.

1963   "Why Move a Capital? Brasilia's Origins." *Americas* 15:13–17.

1964   "The Indian in Andean America." Vol. 1: "From Encomienda to Hacienda." *American Journal of Economics and Sociology* 23:131–43.

1966   "Politics and Geography: Some Aspects of Centrifugal and Centripetal Forces Operative in Andean America." *American Journal of Economics and Sociology* 25:349–58.

1968   "The Latin American Way of Life." Vol. 1: "A Culturally Diverse Continent—Balkanized." *American Journal of Economics and Sociology* 27:63–76.

1969   "Geography." *Professional Geographer* 21:305–07.

           With E. P. Leahy. *Venezuela: Search for a Middle Ground.* New York: Van Nostrand Reinhold.

1971   "Migration and Population Change in the Irish Republic." *American Journal of Economics and Sociology* 30:253–58.

1973   With Charles M. Nissly. *East from the Andes: Pioneer Settlements in the South American Heartland.* Gainesville: University of Florida Press.

1980   With Louis A. Paganini. "Pyramids, Derricks and Mule Teams in the Yucatan Peninsula: A Second Effort in 2,500 Years to Develop a Jungle and Forest Area." *American Journal of Economics and Sociology* 39:217–26.

1981   "Jungle Geopolitics in Guyana: How a Communist Utopia That Ended in Massacre Came to Be Sited." *American Journal of Economics and Sociology* 40:107–14.

1983   "Land for the People—A Vital Need Everywhere: In Latin America and the Caribbean It's Now 'a Prey to Hastening Ills' and Decay." *American Journal of Economics and Sociology* 42:275–90.

1984   "Development and Agrarian Land Reform in Venezuela's Pioneer Zone." *American Journal of Economics and Sociology* 43:149–58.

Chronology

1904   Born in Seven Mile, Ohio.

1925   Graduated with a B.A. from the University of Cincinnati majoring in

	German and Geology and took first teaching position at Howe School in Indiana.
1926	Took a position to do surveying work with the El Aguila Oil Company in Mexico.
1927–28	Post-graduate work at Cornell University.
1928	Returned to Latin America working for the Sinclair and Atlantic Refining Company in Venezuela.
1931	Entered the University of Zurich.
1932	Awarded American Field Service Fellowship for study at the University of Grenoble.
1936	Took teaching position at the University of Illinois in Urbana.
1937	Awarded Ph.D. degree.
1943	Married Hilda Buttenwieser, a professor of classics at the University of Cincinnati.
1947	Took position at University of Maryland at College Park.
1951	Took position at University of Florida.
1969	Awarded honorary Doctor of Science degree from the University of Cincinnati.
1979	Awarded the Master Teacher Award from the National Council for Geographic Education.
1987	Received the Eminent Latin Americanist Geographer Career Award from the Conference on Latin Americanist Geographers.

References

Bushong, Allen D. 1989. "Raymond E. Crist: A Biographical Essay." *Journal of Cultural Geography* 9:121–33.

Clawson, David L. 1989. "Folks in the Road: Raymond E. Crist and Geographical Field Work in Latin America." *Journal of Cultural Geography* 9:1–13.

McGrane, Reginald C. 1963. *The University of Cincinnati: A Success Story in Urban Higher Education*. New York: Harper and Row.

Charles Darwin

Charles Darwin was one of the most important figures in the historical development of science, and although he did not consider himself a geographer and never held an academic position as a geographer, he had a significant influence on the development of geography as a science. Although he described himself as a ''naturalist,'' he published significant works in the fields of paleontology, geology, psychology, zoology, botany, and geography.

He was born in Shrewsbury, England on February 12, 1809, the son of Dr. Robert Darwin, an eminent physician and a person who played an important role in shaping his son's career. Charles's grandfather, Erasmus Darwin, was a surgeon, poet, naturalist, and philosopher who had written the work *Zoomania*.

Charles was sent to a day-school run by a Unitarian minister in 1817 and the following year entered Shrewsbury School, where he received a classical education, including some history and geography. In 1825, at the age of sixteen, he left Shrewsbury School and enrolled at Edinburgh University to study medicine; however, he disliked medical studies and left after two years.

In 1828, Darwin entered Christ's College, Cambridge, with the intention of studying to be a clergyman. He was not especially successful at Cambridge and was even rebuked by his father, who thought at that time that he would be a disgrace to the family. While at Cambridge, however, Darwin developed an interest in natural history, first stimulated by the geologist Adam Sedgwick and encouraged by John Henslow, professor of botany. Another scientist who had a great influence on Darwin at Cambridge was the geographer *Alexander Von Humboldt. Although Darwin did not meet Humboldt at Cambridge, he did get a copy of Humboldt's book *Personal Narrative of Travels to the Equinoctial Regions of a New Continent* and was enthralled by Humboldt's account of a journey in South America between 1799 and 1804. This book gave Darwin a burning desire to travel, and he considered Humboldt the greatest scientific traveller who had ever lived.

In 1831, Darwin received his B.A. from Cambridge and a few months later was offered the position of Ship's Naturalist aboard the *H.M.S. Beagle*. [The naturalist's position had originally been offered to Professor Henslow but when he was unable to go, he suggested Darwin.] The ship was to go on a charting expedition to South America, then continue across the Pacific and Indian Oceans, eventually circumnavigating the globe. Darwin left England aboard ship on December 27, 1821, with two books in his possession, Humboldt's *Personal Narrative* and Charles Lyell's *Principles of Geology*.

The voyage lasted from 1831 to 1836 and Darwin was "able to experience the biological richness of the rain forests of South America, to see volcanic islets and coral reefs, to climb the spectacular Andes and find marine fossils thousands of meters above sea level, and to note the distinctiveness of the animals and plants on several islands and archipelagoes" (Armstrong, 1985:38).

On returning to England, Darwin published, in 1839, an account of his voyage in *A Naturalist's Voyage on the Beagle*. Within a few years he published two books, *Structure and Distribution of Coral Reefs* (1842) and *Geological Observations on Volcanic Islands* (1844), that had a strong focus on geology and geography. These early works received critical acclaim from both Humboldt and Lyell. For the next twenty years, Darwin amassed evidence in support of his theory of evolution by natural selection, which became published as *On the Origin of Species by Means of Natural Selection* (1859) and *The Descent of Man* (1871).

Darwin's impact on the life sciences was monumental, but his influence spread even further. According to D. R. Stoddart (1966:683), "Darwin's work so changed the nineteenth century world view that the development of geography as a science itself became possible." Darwin had always been concerned with geographic distributions, and it was "largely facts of geographical distribution in a spatial setting which provided Darwin with the germ of his theory" (Stoddart, 1966:683).

One area of geography on which Darwin had a direct impact was geomorphology. When he developed his ideas about the transformation of fringing reefs into barrier reefs and the cyclical processes involved, he set the stage for the "cyclical" ideas later developed by *William Morris Davis in the study of landforms. According to Stoddart (1966:686), "Davisian geomorphology was deductive, time-oriented, and imbued with mechanistic notions of causation. . . . Its theme of change through time at least partly derived from a simplified view of evolution."

Similar views were also proposed in the field of plant geography and ecology. In his pioneer work on plant succession, F. E. Clements (1916:3) emphasized succession as the "universal process of formation development . . . the life-history of the climax formation."

The idea of change through time has been an important theme in human geography. The Berkeley School, under the influence of *Carl Sauer, analyzed the American southwest and other areas with a focus on changes in the landscape over time. Derwent Whittlesey's model for cultural landscape change, which he called "sequent occupance," also looks at this theme.

Another major idea of Charles Darwin that eventually made its way into the geographic literature was the concept of interrelationships and connections between all living things and their environment. Ernst Haeckel introduced the term *ecology* only a decade after Darwin published *The Origin*. The American geographer Harlan H. Barrows used the term *human ecology* and in an important paper in 1923 (1923:1) stated that "the centre of geography is the study of human ecology of specific areas."

Darwin's powerful ideas of struggle and selection also made their way into geographic writings. In political geography, *Friedrich Ratzel developed his seven laws of the growth of states. He noted that "just as the struggle for existence in the plant and animal world always centres about a matter of space, so the conflicts of nations are in great part only struggles for territory" (1896:351). This view of Ratzel, in conjunction with ideas from Rudolph Kjellen, also served as a basis for the development of *Geopolitik* under *Karl Haushofer.

Stoddart believes that modern geography would be "inconceivable" without the advances made by Darwin. Perhaps Darwin said it best in a letter to Joseph Hooker: "When we are dead and gone, what a noble subject will be Geographical Distribution" (Armstrong, 1985:43).

Selected Bibliography

1837   "On Certain Areas of Elevation and Subsidence in the Pacific and Indian Oceans as Deduced from the Study of Coral Formations." *Proceedings of the Geological Society of London* 2:552–54.

1839   *Journal of Researches*. Vol. 3 of *Narrative of the Surveying Voyages of His Majesty's Ships Adventure and Beagle*, later published as *A Naturalist's Voyage* and now known as the *Voyage of the Beagle*. London: Henry Colheum.

          "Observation on the Parallel Roads of Glen Roy." *Philosophical Transactions of the Royal Society of London*, 39–81.

1842   *The Geology of the Voyage of the Beagle*. Vol. 1: *The Structure and Distribution of Coral Reefs*. London: Smith Elder.

          The Geology of the Voyage of the Beagle. Vol. 2: *Geological Observations on the Volcanic Islands Visited on the Voyage*. London: Smith Elder.

1846   *The Geology of the Voyage of the Beagle*. Vol. 3: *Geological Observations on South America*. London: Smith Elder.

1851   *The Monograph of the Sub-Class Cirripedia with Figures of All the Species; the Lepadidae; or Pedunculated Cirripedes*. London: Ray Society.

          A Monograph of the Fossil Lepadidae; or Pedunculated Cirripedes of Great Britain. London: Palaeontographical Society.

1854   *The Balanidae (or Sessile Cirripedes), the Verrucidae etc*. London: Ray Society.

1859   *On the Origin of Species by Means of Natural Selection, or the Preservation of Favoured Races in the Struggle for Life.* London: John Murray.

1862   *The Various Contrivances by Which Orchids Are Fertilised by Insects.* London: John Murray.

1865   "The Movements and Habitats of Climbing Plants." *Journal of the Linnean Society.*

1868   *The Variation of Animals and Plants Under Domestication.* London: John Murray.

1871   *The Descent of Man, and Selection in Relation to Sex.* London: John Murray.

1872   *The Expression of Emotions in Man and Animals.* London: John Murray.

1875   *Insectivorous Plants.* London: John Murray.

1876   *The Effects of Cross- and Self-Fertilisation in the Vegetable Kingdom.* London.

1877   *The Different Forms and Flowers on Plants of the Same Species.* London: John Murray.

1880   *The Power of Movement in Plants.* London: John Murray.

1881   *The Formation of Vegetable Mould Through the Action of Worms, with Observation on Their Habits.* London: John Murray.

Chronology

1809   Born at the Mount, Shrewsbury, February 12.

1831   Graduated from Cambridge University (Bachelor of Arts degree); geological excursion into North Wales with Professor Adam Sedgwick. Departed December 27 on voyage of *H.M.S. Beagle.*

1836   Visited Australia and completed circumnavigation of the world aboard the *Beagle*, returning to England on October 2.

1837   "Conversion" to evolutionary outlook. Opened species notebook.

1839   Publication of *Journal of Researches* into the geology and natural history of the various countries visited during the voyage of *H.M.S. Beagle* around the world, later known as *The Voyage of the Beagle.*

1853   Awarded Royal Medal of the Royal Society.

1858   Received Alfred Russel Wallace's paper and presentation of joint Darwin-Wallace papers to the Linnean Society of London, July 1.

1859   Publication of *The Origin of Species by Means of Natural Selection, or the Preservation of Favoured Races in the Struggle for Life.*

1860   The Huxley-Wiberforce Debate at the British Association for the Advancement of Science meeting at Oxford.

1864   Awarded the Copley Medal of the Royal Society.

1882   Died at Down House, April 19; buried in Westminster Abbey, April 26.

References

Armstrong, Patrick. 1985. "Charles Darwin." *Geographers Biobibliographical Studies* 9:37–45.

Barrows, H. H. 1923. "Geography as Human Ecology." *Annals of the Association of American Geographers* 13:1–14.

Clements, F. E. 1916. *Plant Succession: An Analysis of the Development of Vegetation.* Washington, D.C.: Carnegie Institution.

Ratzel, F. 1896. "The Territorial Growth of States." *Scottish Geographical Magazine* 12:351–61.

Stoddart, D. R. 1966. "Darwin's Impact on Geography." *Annals of the Association of American Geographers* 56:683–98.

William Morris Davis

William Morris Davis is considered by many scholars to be one of the major figures in the development of geography in America. He came from a prominent Philadelphia Quaker family and was born in that city on February 12, 1850. His father, Edward, had a wide variety of business interests, and his half-brother eventually became a member of Congress. William was educated partly at home, but after the age of sixteen he enrolled at Harvard University.

Davis's formative years at Harvard were primarily spent under the tutelage of Nathanial Southgate Shaler. Although Shaler was a trained geologist, he was deeply concerned with the human impact on the resource base and natural systems. According to *Preston James and Geoffrey Martin (1981:281–82), Davis learned from Shaler three distinct habits of thought. First, he developed the ability to carefully observe field activities; second, he gained an appreciation for the role of man as part of the landscape; and third, he acquired an appreciation of the processes of change in explaining various earth features. He graduated from Harvard in 1869 and the following year received a Master of Engineering degree.

After completing his studies at Harvard, Davis took a position as an assistant at the Argentine Meteorological Observatory in Cordoba, Argentina, from 1870 to 1873. In early 1873, he left Argentina and crossed the Andes on a long-distance expedition by foot, horse, train, and boat. He eventually ended up in Philadelphia working as a bookkeeper for the Barclay Coal Company, of which his father was president.

Davis worked for Shaler, teaching a field geology course during the summer of 1875, and the following year accepted Shaler's offer of an assistantship at Harvard. In 1878, he was promoted to Instructor in Physical Geography.

Davis's early years as a teacher, however, did not appear to be very successful. As a result when he was reappointed as an instructor in 1882, he received an interesting letter from President Charles W. Eliot that said the following:

The Corporation offers you a reappointment . . . quite aware that this position is not suitable for you as a permanency. . . . In considering whether it is in your interest to accept this offer temporarily, I hope that you will look in the face of the fact that the chances of advancement for you are by no means good, although the Corporation have every reason to be satisfied with your work as a teacher. (Chorley, Beckinsale, and Dun, 1964:623)

After receiving this letter from President Eliot, Davis began to write a great deal and to look for new and exciting ideas. Three years later, in 1885, he was appointed Assistant Professor, and five years after that was granted a full professorship.

Davis is perhaps most well known for his contributions to the field of geomorphology. The basis for his study of landforms was a result of his geological fieldwork and his friendship with *John Wesley Powell, T. C. Chamberlain, and *Grove K. Gilbert. Davis's work in the 1880s focused on the "cycle of erosion" and was strongly aided by the use of official topographic maps of medium and large scales. According to Davis (Beckinsale and Chorley, 1981:28), the cycle

is initiated by crustal uplift and proceeds through a sequence of erosional downweaving to an ultimate plain of imperceptible relief. The sequential forms are dependent on the amount of erosion and are capable of systematic description in terms of the stage of cycle they have reached. All landforms are dependent on structure, process and stage, the last being a function of time.

Davis not only provided names for the stages of his cycle, but he also precisely defined technical terms for the various landforms. Many of these terms, such as *river piracy*, *peneplain*, and *monadnock*, still survive today.

In conjunction with his geomorphological research, Davis produced geographical illustrations that were of exceptional quality. He used an abundance of visual illustrations in his work, and their complexity was awe-inspiring to the less gifted illustrator. A major criticism of Davis, however, was the lack of quantitative measurements in his work. Although in 1919 he discussed the importance of qualitative statements being supported by quantitative measurements, he rarely used statistics in his own works. This lack of precision in measurement, particularly in slope processes, has led since the 1950s to a decline in those who advocated a Davisian approach to geomorphology.

Aside from his scientific endeavors, Davis was very concerned with the teaching of geography. He believed the teaching of geography was focused too much on the teaching of factual knowledge and not enough on an understanding of the organizational concepts by which these facts could be understood. In an article on geographic education in 1932, Davis outlined some of his concerns. "Unhappily, geographers are often so impressed with the innumerable facts of their subject that much of their attention is given to individual occurrences in specified localities rather than to principles which the occurrences exemplify; and this is regrettable'' (1932:215).

Davis was also concerned with the advancement of what he thought of as geography. He proposed that geography should have a professional society similar to that of the Geological Society of America. In 1904 the Association of American Geographers was formed and Davis became the first president; he was reelected in 1905 and served a third term as president in 1909.

Another major accomplishment of Davis that furthered geography was the Transcontinental Excursion of the American Geographical Society in 1912. Some forty-three European geographers, accompanied by over one hundred American geographers, took a coast-to-coast train ride that traversed over 12,000 miles. The results of the excursion were the writing and publication of a variety of professional papers. Also, many close personal friendships developed among geographic leaders from both Europe and America.

Davis's contributions to geography were also involved with his responsibilities as associate editor of a variety of scholarly journals. At one time or another, he was associate editor of *Science, American Naturalist, Journal of Geography, American Journal of Science*, and *American Meteorological Journal*.

Davis received numerous medals and awards. Although he never received a Ph.D., he was given several honorary doctorates. After his retirement from Harvard, he held temporary appointments at a variety of universities including Arizona, Stanford, Oregon, California, and the California Institute of Technology. His influence on the development of geography was succinctly stated by Beckinsale and Chorley in their biographical essay (1981:30):

Because of his large literary output, his activity in editing and founding journals, his initiation of the Association of American Geographers, his own lecturing and tutoring at home and abroad, and his great efforts to establish geography as an independent specialized study, Davis had more direct global influence on geography as a discipline than any other scholar before or since.

William Morris Davis died in Pasadena, California, on February 5, 1934.

Selected Bibliography

1882   "Glacial Erosion." *Proceedings of the Society of Natural History* 22:19–
            58.

1888   "The Triassic Formation of Connecticut Valley." *7th Annual Report of
            the U.S. Geological Survey, 1885–86*, 455–90.

1889   "The Rivers and Valleys of Pennsylvania." *National Geographic* 1:183–
            258.

1892   "Theories of Artificial and Natural Rainfall." *American Meteorological
            Journal* 8:493–502.

1893 "Winter Thunderstorms." *American Meteorological Journal* 9:164–70, 238–39.

1894 *Elementary Meteorology*. Ginn.

1898 "The Triassic Formation of Connecticut." *18th Annual Report of the U.S. Geological Survey, 1896–97*. Part 2, 1–192.

 With W. H. Snyder. *Physical Geography*. Ginn.

1899 "The Drainage of Cuestas." *Proceedings of the Geological Association of London* 16:75–93.

 "The Circulation of the Atmosphere." *Quarterly Journal of the Royal Meteorological Society* 25:160–69.

 "North America: The United States." In H. R. Mill, ed., *International Geography*. London: Newnes, 664–78, 710–73.

1900 "Continental Deposits of the Rocky Mountain Region." *Bulletin of the Geological Society of America* 11:569–601.

1902 "The Terraces of the Westfield River, Mass." *American Journal of Science* (4th series) 14:77–94.

 "River Terraces in New England." In *Geographical Essays*, 514–86.

 "Base Level, Grade and Peneplain." *Journal of Geology* 10:77–111.

 Elementary Physical Geography. Ginn.

1903 "A Scheme of Geography." *Geographical Journal* 22:413–23.

1905 "The Geographical Cycle in an Arid Climate." *Journal of Geology* 13:381–407.

1909 *Geographical Essays*. (Dover edition, 1954.)

 "The Systematic Description of Landforms." *Geographical Journal* 34:300–318.

 "Glacial Erosion in North Wales." *Quarterly Journal of the Geological Society* 65:281–350.

1913 "Nomenclature of the Surface Forms on Faulted Structures." *Bulletin of the Geological Society of America* 24:163–216.

1915 "The Principles of Geography in the United States." *Annals of the Association of American Geographers* 14:159–215.

1918 *Handbook of Northern France*. Cambridge, Mass.: Harvard University.

1920 "Features of Glacial Origin in Montana and Idaho." *Annals of the Association of American Geographers* 10:75–147.

1924 "The Progress of Geography in the United States." *Annals of the Association of American Geographers* 14:159–215.

1926 *The Lesser Antilles*. New York: American Geographical Society.

1928 *The Coral Reef Problems*. New York: American Geographical Society.

1930 "Origin of Limestone Caverns." *Bulletin of the Geological Society of America* 41:475–628.

"Physiographic Contrasts, East and West." *Science Monthly* 30:394–415, 501–19.

1931   "Elevated Shore Lines of the Santa Monica Mountains, California." *Bulletin of the Geological Society of America* 42:309–10.

1932   "A Retrospect of Geography." *Annals of the Association of American Geography* 22:211–30.

1933   "Glacial Epochs of the Santa Monica Mountains." *Bulletin of the Geological Society of America* 44:1041–1133.

1934   "The Faith of Reverent Science." *Science Monthly* 38:395–421.

1938   "Sheetfloods and Stream Floods." *Bulletin of the Geological Society of America* 49:1337–1416.

Chronology

1850   Born in Philadelphia, February 12.

1866   Entered Lawrence Scientific School, Harvard University.

1870   Master of Mining Engineering, summa cum laude.

1878   Instructor in Geology at Harvard responsible for Physical Geography and Meteorology.

1890   Appointed full Professor of Physical Geography at Harvard University.

1904   Founding member and first president of Association of American Geographers (president in 1904 and 1905).

1906   President of the Geological Society of America.

1908–9 Visiting Professor at the University of Berlin.

1909   President of the Association of American Geographers.

1911   President of the Geological Society of America. October 1911–April 1912, Professor at the Sorbonne, Paris.

1912   Organized American Transcontinental International Expedition.

1928   Publication of *The Coral Reef Problems*.

1934   Died in Pasadena, California, February 5.

References

Beckinsale, Robert P., and Richard J. Chorley. 1981. "William Morris Davis." *Geographers Biobibliographical Studies* 5:27–33.

Chorley, R. J., R. P. Beckinsale, and A. J. Dun. 1964. *History of the Study of Landforms.* Vol. 1. London: Methuen, 621–41.

James, Preston E., and Geoffrey J. Martin. 1981. *All Possible Worlds: A History of Geographical Ideas.* 2d ed. New York: Wiley.

Sten de Geer

Sten de Geer was born in Stockholm, Sweden, in 1886. His father, Gerard de Geer, was a distinguished Swedish geographer noted for his work in glaciology and geochronology; he was the first scientist to establish a date for the last glacial retreat by counting varves in glacial lakes.

Sten de Geer received his doctorate from the University of Uppsala in 1911, taught at the University of Stockholm from 1911 to 1928, then went on to teach at the University of Göteborg from 1928 until his untimely death in 1933. De Geer's interests in geography were more practical than theoretical, and his work on population mapping was long a standard. Though he emphasized the practical side of geography, he certainly was also an early adherent of quantitative methods. While regional studies at many scales, from local to national, interested him, he rejected the works of environmental determinism. Probably his most influential work was his atlas of population in Sweden, which is considered a classic example of the combining of careful observation and systematic mapping.

De Geer's earliest published works were written when he was in his early twenties. Two papers on rivers in Sweden, one on the Dal and another on the Klar, were among his first works. These detailed local or regional studies allowed him to develop an approach that was to remain with him. In 1908 de Geer wrote an article on Gotland that included a population map that was the predecessor of his famous 1917 population atlas. A 1912 study of three lakes near Orebro continued his regional research, and in 1913 he produced a short study of glaciation in Spitzbergen.

Most of his major writings were condensed into the period 1912–28, and he wrote on a variety of topics, from rivers, lakes, and glaciers to population distributions, cities, and political geography, as is apparent in the bibliography below. In his work on distribution mapping, de Geer differentiated between absolute and relative distributions, aiming toward determining patterns of regionalization. As Freeman (1967:126) noted:

The idea not only of the simple, or absolute, distribution occurs here, but also that of the interaction of phenomena, or relative distributions. And this introduces the concept of synthesis, for one distribution can only be understood in relation to another, and the character of the relationship distinguishes one area from another.

Expressed in his own work, de Geer (1923:10) suggested that "geographical provinces and regions form a synthesis of characteristic complexes of important distribution phenomena within limited parts of the earth's surface."

De Geer was well before his time in his consideration of quantification and cartographic design. He was concerned that earlier descriptive geographies should be replaced with more reliable quantification and the development of "genetic geography." In map design, he experimented with various ways of producing thematic maps, concerned always about methods of representation and interpretation. He was the first cartographer to use dot maps for showing population distributions in Sweden, though as Freeman (1967:152) noted:

Sten de Geer was not the initiator of the distribution map, but he made it effective without being over-dramatic in its demonstration of the wide disparities in the land-use pattern of Sweden; his inclusion of forest limits and other landscape features introduced a measure of correlation that contributed to the regional study of the country.

From the localized nature of his earlier writings, de Geer's interests gradually evolved toward bigger pictures, often with broad generalizations that have subsequently reduced their usefulness. Such broader interests included European historical geography, the Nordic lands, and the United States. His early study of the American manufacturing belt is one of the better examples of his later studies, and again the work was based strongly on distributional maps.

Certain traits marked all of de Geer's work. He was soundly based in his time, looked for data with which to support arguments, and believed that careful observation and measurement were essential to improving geographic studies. De Geer focused on mapping distributions and interpreting those distributions with respect to both their absolute and relative characteristics, seeking out relationships and interactions that would help to explain the mapped distributions. As Freeman (1967:1973) commented, "If *Ellsworth Huntington stands out as a man possessing great assurance with a mind sweeping across the world and through human history like a whirlwind, Sten de Geer stands out as a man of caution, patience, and practical good sense."

Selected Bibliography

1906   "Dalälfen och dess utskärnigar nedom Alfkarlebyfallen." *Ymer*. 26:83–92.

        "Om Klarälfen och des dalgång." *Ymer*. 26:383–414.

1908   "Befolkningens fördelning på Gottland." *Ymer*. 28:240–53. (A population study)

1912	"Niplandskap vid Dalälven." *Sveriges Geologiska Undersökning, Årsbok.* 9.
	"Storstäderna vid Ostersjön." *Ymer.* 32:41–87. This article deals with harbors and appeared in a shorter form as "Die Grosstädte an der Ostsee." *Zeitschrift der Gesellschaft für Erdkunde zu Berlin*, 754–66.
	"Geografisk undersökning, av sjöarna Toften, Testen och Tysslingen i Närke." *Sveriges Geologiska Undersökning, Årsbok* 4. (An article on lake analysis)
1913	A study of a glacier in Spitzbergen is found in *Ymer*. 33:148–57.
1917	*Karta over Befolkningens Fördelning i Sverige den 1 Januari, 1917*. Stockholm. (Atlas of twelve maps showing the population of Sweden)
1918	Political regions of Scandinavia. *Ymer*. 24–38.
1919	Reprint of atlas with a text volume in Swedish.
1920	"Europas statsgränser och statsområden efter varldskriget." *Ymer*. 40:553–62. (An article on political geography)
1922	*Storstaden Stockholm ur geografisk synpunkt*. Stockholm.
	Det Nya Europa. Stockholm. (A book on political geography)
1923	A shorter version of the work on Stockholm, in English, is found in *Geographical Review* 13:497–506.
	"On the Definition, Method and Classification of Geography." *Geografiska Annaler* 5:1–37.
1925	"Om Sveriges geografiska regioner." *Ymer*. 45:392–415. (Major human regions of Scandinavia)
1926	"Norra Sveriges Landsformsregioner." *Geografiska Annaler* 8:125–36.
	"The Kernel Area of the Nordic Race." *The Racial Characters of the Swedish Nation*. Uppsala.
	"The American manufacturing belt." *Geografiska Annaler* 9:233–359.
1928	"Das geologische und das geographische Baltoskandia." *Geografisker Annaler* 10:120–39. (An article on the delimitation of Fennoscandia, in German)
	"The Subtropical Belt of Old Empires." *Geografiska Annaler* 10:205–44.
1929	"A Map of the Distribution of Population in Sweden: Method of Preparation and General Results." *Geographical Review* 12:72–83.

Chronology

1886	Born in Stockholm.
1908	Began experimenting with new method of showing population, using dots. Travelled to Spitzbergen.
1910	Travelled to Bohemia and Silesia and later to France and Italy.
1911	Received Doctorate, University of Uppsala. Taught Geography at Högskola in Stockholm (University of Stockholm).

1922	Travelled in the United States for one year.
1928	Appointed chair of geography department at the University of Göteborg.
1933	Died June 2 in Göteborg, Sweden.

Reference

Freeman, T. W. 1967. *The Geographer's Craft*. New York: Manchester University Press.

Vasily Vasilyevich Dokuchaev

Vasily Dokuchaev was born in March 1846 in the village of Milyukovo in the Smolensk district. His early education was at an ecclesiastical school in the town of Vyazama. He continued his education at the Smolensk Seminary, from which he graduated in 1867 with an honors diploma. He then studied for a year at the Ecclesiastical Academy of St. Petersburg, but decided that he did not want a career as a minister and left the academy to enter the physics and mathematics department at St. Petersburg University.

In 1871, he graduated, and the following year he was appointed curator of the university's Geological Laboratory. He completed work for a master's degree in mineralogy and geology in 1878 and was appointed an assistant professor in 1879. One of the courses he taught in his early career dealt with quaternary deposits and is believed to be the first course of this type taught at a university (Esakov, 1980:33).

In 1883, Dokuchaev was appointed head of the Department of Mineralogy and Crystallography, and four years later he ran a course on soil science. According to *Preston James and Geoffrey Martin (1981:228), "Dokuchaev deserves a major place among the world's geographers because of his innovative studies of soil. . . . He was the first scientist to realize that soil is not just disintegrated and decomposed rock." His primary interest was the study of quaternary rock deposits with a particular emphasis on the Chernozem soils of European Russia. His large-scale study of the Chernozem soil region titled *Russkii Chernozem* (Russian Chernozem) was published in 1883 and earned him a doctorate in mineralogy and geology.

Dokuchaev believed that the development of soil was the result of a complex interaction of slope, plants, animals, climate, and parent material. He also recognized the crucial role humans played as a major change agent. The development of soil science as a new branch of science was due to the pioneering work of Dokuchaev. He pointed out that "very few scientists treated soils as natural, historical bodies, and nobody investigated all the main properties of all these interrelated bodies" (Esakov, 1980:35).

Dokuchaev's influence was far-reaching. His ideas about natural landscape zones laid the foundation for the development of physical geography in Russia. His studies of swamps and forests contributed greatly to the geography of plants. The American soil scientist C. P. Marbut believed Dokuchaev's work in the area of soil science was similar to that of Charles Lyell in the history of geology or C. Linneaus in the history of botany (James and Jones, 1954:383).

In 1897, primarily due to a nervous disease and extreme fatigue, Dokuchaev resigned from St. Petersburg after twenty-five years of service. After his health improved, he resumed work, and in 1898 he even went on an expedition in Bessarabia to analyze soil development processes. He also made trips to the Caucasus, Transcaucasus territory, and Transcospian district. He delivered a number of lectures in 1900 in Tbilisi. These lectures dealt with his three-year study of the soils in the Caucasus. Shortly thereafter he returned to St. Petersburg where he suffered from severe mental depression for the last three years of his life. He died on November 8, 1903, at the age of fifty-seven.

Selected Bibliography

1872   "The Drift Formations Found Along the Kachna River in the Sychev Region of Smolensk Province." *Trudy St. Petersburg: Obshchestva Yestestvoispytateley* 3:xxix–xxxiii.

1875   "On the Draining of Swamps in General and of Polesyia in Particular." *Trudy St. Petersburg: Obshchestva Yestestvoispytateley* 6:131–85.

1877   "Results of Work on the Russian Chernozem." *Trudy Volnogo Ekonomicheskogo Obshchestva* 1:415–32.

1878   *Types of Valley Formation in European Russia.* St. Petersburg.

            Cartography of Russian Soils. St. Petersburg.

1883   *Russkii Chernozem.* St. Petersburg.

1892   *Our Steppes Past and Present.* St. Petersburg.

1893   *The Russian Steppes.* St. Petersburg: Ministry of Crown Domains.

1898   *Place and Role of Modern Soil Science.* Warsaw.

1899   *On the Theory of Natural Zones, Horizontal and Vertical Soil Zones.* St. Petersburg.

Chronology

1846   Born in village of Milyukovo in the Smolensk district, March.

1867   Graduated from the Smolensk seminary and student at St. Petersburg University (to 1871).

1871   Conducted geological and soil explorations in European Russia to 1878.

1878	Defended his thesis for master's degree on mineralogy and geology. Publication of *River Valley Formation in European Russia* and *Cartography of Russian Soils*.
1883	Defended doctoral thesis (geology) and appointed head of the Department of Mineralogy and Crystallography at St. Petersburg University (to 1897). Publication of *Russkii Chernozem*.
1885	Secretary of the St. Petersburg Naturalists Society (to 1891).
1892	Headed the Special Expedition of Forestry Department. Publication of *Our Steppes Past and Present*.
1898	Explored the soils in Bessarabia and Caucasus. Publication of *Place and the Role of Modern Soil Science*.
1899	Made two trips to the Caucasus (to 1900) and publication of *On The Theory of Natural Zones*.
1900	Displayed soil map of European Russia, and so forth, in Paris.
1903	Died in St. Petersburg, November 8.

References

Esakov, Vasily Alexeyevich. 1980. "Vasily Vasilyevich Dokuchaev." *Geographers Biobibliographical Studies* 4:33–42.

James, Preston E., and C. Jones. 1954. *American Geography, Inventory and Prospect*. Syracuse: Syracuse University Press.

James, Preston E., and Geoffrey J. Martin. 1981. *All Possible Worlds: A History of Geographical Ideas*. 2d ed. New York: Wiley.

Eratosthenes

The first writer to use the term *geography* for one of his works was the Greek scholar Eratosthenes, who has been referred to by many scholars as ''the father of geography.'' He was born in the Greek colony of Cyrene in Libya during the 126th Olympiad, around 275 B.C. Although accounts of his early upbringing are sketchy, he apparently came from a somewhat wealthy family and had an excellent education. The town of Cyrene was a prosperous meeting place for travellers from both the Mediterranean basin and the interior of Africa. It is believed Eratosthenes studied under Lysanias the grammarian, a disciple of Homer and an erudite scholar, and Callimachus, a native of Cyrene. He received his early mathematical training from some of the disciples of Euclid.

Eratosthenes left Cyrene while still a youth and continued his education in Athens. He probably attended both the New Academy and the Lyceum. He was impressed with the intellectual activity in Athens at that time and was exposed to a variety of philosophical doctrines. As a student of the New Academy, he came under the influence of Arcesilaus and thus acquired the best geometric and astronomical teaching of the time.

In about 244 B.C., the king of Egypt invited Eratosthenes to be the royal tutor, and, at the same time, he was named as ''alpha fellow'' at the museum in Alexandria. Ten years later when the chief librarian of the museum died, Eratosthenes was named head of the library at Alexandria, one of the most coveted and prestigious posts in the Greek scholarly world. It afforded him the opportunity to live with, or come in contact with, some of the finest scholars in both literature and science, and he held the library post until his death at over age eighty in 195 B.C. It was during his tenure as head librarian that he did most of his geographic work.

The diversity of interests possessed by Eratosthenes seemed to astonish other scholars at the time. The range of his works point out a broad interest. According to Aujac (1978:40), he was ''capable of vigorous logic, he loved discussion and especially paradox; a well-informed philologist, he was always dubious about the subtleties of literary commentators and laughed at those who looked for scientific teaching in poetry; interested in philosophical doctrines, he committed himself to none of them.''

Eratosthenes' intuition also played an important role in his contributions to the development of geography. *Strabo wrote (Jones, 1953:41), ''Frequently Eratosthenes digresses into discussions too scientific for the subject he is dealing with, but the declarations he makes after his digressions are not rigorously accurate, but only vague, since, so to speak, he is a mathematician among geographers and yet a geographer among mathematicians.''

The major contributions of Eratosthenes were related to mathematical geography. His most famous work had to do with his elegant measurement of the circumference of the earth. Although Eratosthenes was not the first to measure the circumference of the earth—both *Aristotle and Archimedes tried—he was the most accurate. His geometric assessment of the earth's circumference was both simple and elegant. His method, involving the geometry of a sphere, consisted of measuring the distance between two places on the same meridian. If one could calculate the differences in latitude between these two places, it would then be possible to deduce easily the length of 1 degree or of the whole meridian. Eratosthenes believed Syene was directly on the Tropic of Cancer, and he calculated the distance from Syene to Alexandria. His calculations, however, involved two minor errors. ''One of these arose from the belief that the earth was a perfect sphere, instead of being flattened at the poles—a mistake which was unavoidable according to the knowledge of that time. The other error was caused by Syene being regarded as lying directly under the tropic, whereas in reality it was 37 miles to the northward of it'' (Kish, 1978:76). Despite these minor errors, the measurements of Eratosthenes were astonishingly accurate.

Another major contribution of Eratosthenes was in the field of cartography. He prepared a ''world map'' in which he mapped parallels to the north and south of Rhodes and meridians to the east and west, which was a major improvement over previous maps. ''Henceforth a map was no longer an empirical sketch, or a mere guide book for sailors but an accurate diagram, showing the position of any place in terms of latitude and longitude'' (Aujac, 1978:41). This new map marked a major advance in cartography since it involved the selection of an orthogonal map projection that was easy to read, simple to draw, and involved little distortion in narrow latitudinal stretches.

Eratosthenes also produced an accurate analysis of tidal currents in straits. He was the first scholar to show there was a connection between oceanic tides and currents in straits. Strabo (Book 1, Chapter 3, p. 11) describes Eratosthenes' theory: ''And Eratosthenes says that this is the reason why the narrow straits have strong currents, and in particular the strait of Sicily which, he declares, behaves in a manner similar to the flow and ebb of the ocean; for the current changes twice within the course of every day and night and, like the ocean, it floods twice a day and falls twice a day.''

Eratosthenes also wrote a book describing the *ekumene*, or inhabited area of the earth. He described the five zones: a torrid zone, two temperate zones and two frigid zones. According to *Preston James and Geoffrey Martin (1981:33):

He improved on Aristotle by giving the mathematical boundaries of these zones. The torrid zone he thought was forty-eight degrees of the whole circumference (twenty-four degrees north and south was calculated as the location of the tropics). The frigid zone extended twenty-four degrees from each pole. The temperate zone was between the tropic and the polar circles.

Eratosthenes believed that geography was a science and that certain general laws control the functioning of the world. He became quite famous during his lifetime and remained well known for many centuries thereafter. His geographic works were widely circulated for over three centuries and led to the conviction by Christopher Columbus that he could reach India by sailing across the Atlantic Ocean. Eratosthenes died in 195 B.C. from voluntary starvation, induced by despair at his blindness.

Selected Bibliography

Some of Eratosthenes' works can be found in:

1789	Siedel, G. *Eratosthenes Geographicorum Fragmenta*. Gottingen.
1822	Bernhardy, G. *Eratosthenica*. Berlin.
1872	Hiller, E. *Eratosthenis carminum reliquiae*. Leipzig.
1880	Berger, H. *Die Geographischen Fragmente des Eratosthenes*. Leipzig.
1883	Mass, P. *Analecta Eratosthenica*. Berlin.
1948	Bentham, R. M. "The Fragments of Eratosthenes." Unpublished thesis, University of London.

Chronology

ca. 275 B.C.	Born in the Greek colony of Cyrene.
ca. 244 B.C.	Invited by the King of Egypt to be a royal tutor and named as "alpha fellow" at the museum at Alexandria.
234 B.C.	Named head of the library at Alexandria.
195 B.C.	Died from voluntary starvation induced by despair of his blindness.

References

Aujac, Germaine. 1978. "Eratosthenes c.275–c.195 B.C.," *Geographers Biobibliographical Studies* 2:39–43.

James, Preston E., and Geoffrey J. Martin. 1981. *All Possible Worlds: A History of Geographical Ideas*. 2d ed. New York: Wiley.

Jones, H. L. ed. 1954. *Strabo-Geography*. London.
Kish, George, ed. 1978. *A Source Book in Geography*. Cambridge, Mass.: Harvard
    University Press.

James Geikie

James Geikie was born on August 23, 1839, in Edinburgh, Scotland. He was the third child in a family of eight children and the younger brother of Archibald Geikie, another distinguished scientist. He came from a well-to-do family; his uncle Walter was a well-known Scottish painter, and his maternal grandfather, a sea captain, enthralled the Geikie children with his tales of voyages to the outside world.

Geikie's early education was at a private school, but in 1850 he entered Edinburgh High School, where he did well as a classical scholar. Along with his older brother and friends, he rambled through his Edinburgh neighborhood in search of fossils. In 1854 he was apprenticed to an Edinburgh printer, but found the work unacceptable and detrimental to his health. He left the apprenticeship in 1858 and attended lectures in geology and natural history at the University of Edinburgh, while holding a variety of temporary jobs. In 1861, a vacancy occurred at the Scottish Geological Survey, and he was hired to survey glacial drift deposits.

As a result of his early work in glacial drift deposits, Geikie developed an interest in glacial processes. Field exercises to Norway in 1865 and to the Rhineland and Switzerland in 1868 stimulated his interest in glaciation and helped him visualize the nature of glacial processes. One of the results of this early work on glaciers was the publication in 1874 of his major work *The Great Ice Age and Its Relation to the Antiquity of Man*. The following year, Geikie married and was elected a Fellow of the Royal Society.

This book on glacial activity was probably Geikie's greatest scientific contribution. According to Marsden (1979:55), "*The Great Ice Age* established Geikie as the leading protagonist of the land ice theory." The book also introduced the idea that climatic changes had taken place during glacial periods, and many glacial deposits were of an interglacial nature. Geikie advocated the position that there were several interglacial periods and they played an important role in understanding the nature of glacial deposits.

When Geikie's older brother Archibald left the Chair of Geology at Edinburgh to take the position of Director General of the Geological Survey of Great Britain in 1882, James was offered the position as Professor of Geology. These first years at Edinburgh were trying in that he found it difficult to prepare lectures, and he missed the camaraderie with his friends at the Geological Survey.

During Geikie's first decade at Edinburgh, however, he made a number of significant contributions. He established the Scottish Geographical Society and became Honorary Editor of its publication, the *Scottish Geographical Magazine*. He contributed regularly to the magazine and helped establish its reputation.

Geikie emphasized the interrelationship between geology and geography. He felt geography was a prerequisite for geological investigations. Similar, geography needed the underpinning of geology. According to Geikie in an article written for the *Scottish Geographical Magazine* (1887:401), the physical geographer ''can describe the actual existing condition; without the aid of geology, he can tell us nothing of their origin and cause.''

In the early 1890s, Geikie spent much time preparing a new edition of *The Great Ice Age*. He expanded the text from 600 to 850 pages and included much new material. In 1894, he was promoted to the position of Dean of the Faculty of Science at Edinburgh. He continued writing and, in 1898, published his major contribution to the science of geomorphology, *Earth Sculpture, or The Origin of Landforms*.

After age sixty, at the turn of the century, Geikie continued lecturing and writing both articles and books. His last three books were *Structural and Field Geology for Students, Mountains: Their Origin, Growth and Decay*, and *The Antiquity of Man in Europe*. From all accounts, his pedagogical skills were considerable. Although he had been in middle age when he became a professor, he apparently had an easygoing, colloquial style of lecturing. According to Newbigin and Flett (1917:185), ''He spoke fast, and covered a very large part of his subject in the course of the one hundred lectures which constituted the winter class.'' He also emphasized field excursions as an essential part of his courses.

Geikie was also a strong supporter of those who wanted to establish geography as a university subject. One of the objectives of the Scottish Geographical Society was to press for the full recognition of geography as a legitimate branch of scientific knowledge. Geikie ardently supported efforts to improve geographical education, and in his first article for the *Scottish Geographical Magazine* (1885:28) ''The Physical Features of Scotland,'' he discussed the importance of Ordinance Survey maps as pedagogical tools:

With such admirable cartographical work before them, how long will intelligent teachers continue to tolerate those antiquated monstrosities which so often do duty as wall-maps in their school-rooms? . . . With a well-drawn and faithful orographical map before him, the school-boy would not only have his labours lightened, but geography would become one of the most interesting of studies.

Geikie made many contributions to the development of both geology and geography. His influence abroad was almost as great as that at home. The distinguished German scientist *Albrecht Penck saw himself as a disciple of Geikie's, and on his death Penck sent a tribute to Geikie's wife. "James Geikie belongs to those who have influenced most my scientific evolution. His clear way of seeing things and his reasoning made a convincing impression on me, and though I never listened to one of his lectures, I felt always to be one of his students. He was my master" (Newbigin and Flett, 1917:137). In America, *William Morris Davis referred to *The Great Ice Age* as the "standard work on the subject." Geikie had developed an international reputation for both his teaching and writing.

In 1900, to honor Geikie, the United States Geological Survey named a peak in Wyoming after him. He was made an honorary member of the New York Academy of Science in 1901, and in 1913 was elected President of the Royal Society at Edinburgh. After giving his last lecture at age seventy-six in June 1914, Geikie retired from the university, and less than a year later, on March 1, 1915, he died suddenly from a heart attack.

Selected Bibliography

1867   "On the Buried Forests and Peat Mosses of Scotland, and the Changes of Climate They Indicate." *Transactions of the Royal Society of Edinburgh* 24:363–84.

1868   "On Denudation in Scotland Since Glacial Times." *Transactions of the Royal Geological Society of Glasgow* 3:54–74.

1871   "On Changes of Climate During the Glacial Epoch." *Geological Magazine* 8:545–53; 9:23–31, 61–69, 105–11, 164–70, 215–22, 254–65.

1872   "On the Glacial Phenomena of the Long Island or Outer Hebrides." *Quarterly Journal of the Geological Society* 29:532–45.

1874   *The Great Ice Age and Its Relation to the Antiquity of Man.* London, 2d ed., 1894.

1875   *Geology.* London.

1880   "On the Glacial Phenomena of the Long Island or Outer Hebrides." *Quarterly Journal of the Geological Society* 34:819–67.

            Pre-Historic Europe: A Geological Sketch. London.

1882   "The Aims and Methods of Geological Inquiry." Inaugural Lecture. *Nature* 27:44–46, 64–67.

1885   "The Physical Features of Scotland." *Scottish Geographical Magazine* 1:26–41.

1886   *Outlines of Geology.* London. 2d ed., 1888; 3d ed., 1896; 4th ed., 1903.

"Mountains: Their Origin, Growth and Decay." *Scottish Geographical Magazine* 2:145–762.

"The Geographical Evolution of Europe." *Scottish Geographical Magazine* 2:193–207.

1887   "Geography and Geology." *Scottish Geographical Magazine* 3:398–407.

1890   "The Evolution of Climate." *Scottish Geographical Magazine* 6:59–78.

"Glacial Geology." Presidential Address to British Association, Section C. *Geological Magazine* 6:461–77.

1892   "On the Glacial Succession in Europe." *Transactions of the Royal Society of Edinburgh* 37:127–49.

"Geographical Development of Coastlines." *Scottish Geographical Magazine* 8:457–79.

1983   *Fragments of Earth Lore: Sketches and Addresses, Geological and Geographical.* Edinburgh.

1895   "The Morphology of the Earth's Surface." *Scottish Geographical Magazine* 11:56–67.

"Classification of European Glacial Deposits." *Journal of Geology* 3:241–69.

1897   "The Last Great Baltic Glacier." *Journal of Geology* 5:325–39.

1898   *Earth Sculpture, or the Origin of Landforms.* London. New ed., 1902; 2d ed., 1909.

1901   "Mountains." *Scottish Geographical Magazine* 17:449–60; 18 (1902):76–84.

1905   *Structural and Field Geology for Students.* Edinburgh. 2d ed., 1908; 6th ed., 1953.

1906   "From the Ice Age to the Present." *Scottish Geographical Magazine* 22:449–63.

1909   "Calabrian Earthquakes." *Scottish Geographical Magazine* 25:113–26.

1911   "The Architecture and Origin of the Alps." *Scottish Geographical Magazine* 27:393–417.

1913   *Mountains: Their Origin, Growth and Decay.* Edinburgh.

1914   *The Antiquity of Man in Europe.* Edinburgh.

Chronology

1839   Born August 23 in Edinburgh.

1854–58   Apprenticed to printer; later attended natural history classes at Edinburgh University.

1861   Joined the Geological Survey. Early work mapping drift deposits.

1866–67   First publication on glacial processes, "On the Buried Forests and Peat Mosses of Scotland."

1874   Publication of *The Great Ice Age and Its Relation to the Antiquity of Man.*

1875	Publication of *Geology* (Elementary science manual).
1880	Publication of *Pre-historic Europe: A Geologic Sketch.*
1882	Succeeded Archibald Geikie as Professor of Geology at the University of Edinburgh. Publication of "The Aims and Method of Geological Inquiry (Inaugural Lecture)."
1889	Awarded the Macdougall-Brisbane Medal of the Royal Society at Edinburgh; Murchison Medal of the Geological Society of London.
1892	President of the Geographical Section of the British Association (Edinburgh).
1898	Publication of *Earth Sculpture, or the Origin of Landforms.*
1904–10	President of Royal Scottish Geographical Society.
1905	Publication of *Structural and Field Geology for Students.*
1913	President of the Royal Society of Edinburgh. Publication of *Mountains: Their Origin, Growth and Decay.*
1914	Retirement from the Chair of Geology at Edinburgh University. Publication of *The Antiquity of Man in Europe.*
1915	Died March 1 at age 76, in Edinburgh.

References

Marsden, W. E. 1979. "James Geikie." *Geographers Biobibliographical Studies* 3:39–52.

Newbigin, M. I., and J. S. Flett. *James Geikie: The Man and the Geologist.* Edinburgh.

Grove Karl Gilbert

Grove Karl Gilbert was one of the early pioneers in the development of modern scientific geomorphology. He was born in 1843 in Rochester, New York, the fifth child in a large family of seven children (although only three of his siblings survived to maturity). He attended Rochester High School and graduated in 1862 at the age of nineteen from the University of Rochester. After graduation, in order to pay off his college debts, Gilbert took a job as a school teacher in Jackson, Michigan. Unfortunately, he had great difficulty in controlling the students, and before the end of the school year he resigned and returned to Rochester.

Fortunately for Gilbert, at this time he met Professor Henry A. Ward, who offered him a job to help in the preparation of geological and zoological materials that Ward was selling to museums and colleges. Gilbert found the work rewarding, and he remained with Ward for five years, primarily preparing specimens for display in museums or laboratories. He was also sent to a variety of places in the eastern United States to install the exhibits.

While working at the New York State Museum in Albany, he developed an interest in the gorge of the Mohawk River near Cohoes. He traced the old glacial drainageway by examining some 350 potholes and dating the dwarf cedar trees growing on the steep sides of the gorge. According to *Preston James, "This experience was the turning point in Gilbert's life. He now knew that he wanted to devote his life to the study of the earth's surface features and to the search for general principles that would account for their origin" (1977:26).

In 1869, he took a job at the Geological Survey of Ohio working with the geologist J. S. Newberry, mapping the landforms of the Maumee Valley of northwestern Ohio. Gilbert did this for three years, then accepted an appointment as a geologist on the United States Geological Survey (U.S.G.S.) West of the One Hundredth Meridian, under the direction of Lt. George M. Wheeler. He spent three seasons in the field (1871–73), then returned to Washington to write reports about the areas in Arizona and Utah that were surveyed. It was also in 1874 that he married Fannie Porter, who was the sister-in-law of one of his friends.

In 1874, he joined the United States Geographical Survey of the Rocky Mountain Region, under the direction of his friend *John Wesley Powell, and it afforded him the opportunity to study intensely the landforms and geology of the western territories. In 1875–76, he did a detailed study of the Henry Mountains that was published by the survey the following year. This was Gilbert's first major work and probably his most famous. In it he carefully outlined the landforms and geologic structure of the region, but he did not stop at this "mere description." In the latter half of this report, he developed a model of landform development by running water. He finished the report with a short economic assessment of the resources found in the Henry Mountains.

This report broke new ground in a number of ways. According to James (1977:27), "Gilbert's model of landform development was the most complete statement of the laws of river erosion that had been presented up to that time, and it was done without reference to earlier European attempts to formulate such laws." Gilbert's analyses led him to recognize the interdependence of all parts of a drainage system:

Every slope is a member of a series, receiving the water and the waste of the slope above it, and discharging its own water and waste upon the slope below. If one member of the series is eroded with exceptional rapidity, two things immediately result: first, the member above has its level of discharge lowered, and its rate of erosion is thereby increased; and second, the member below, being clogged by an exceptional load of detritus, has its rate of erosion diminished. (Report on the geology of the Henry Mountains, 1877:118)

These ideas associated with the relationship between slope, water volume, and stream load, which he called grade, has become an important concept and an essential foundation of modern geomorphology.

Upon finishing his work on the Henry Mountains in Utah, Gilbert initiated a study of Lake Bonneville, the extinct glacial lake near the Salt Lake City region in Utah. This study was published by the United States Geological Survey in 1890, and it also broke new ground and demonstrated his ability as a creative thinker. Without knowledge of previous work done by Charles Lyell, Gilbert's view of Lake Bonneville provided some new insights into marine processes. He clearly delineated the different erosional processes associated with waves, currents, and rivers.

In 1881, when John Wesley Powell became the second director of the United States Geological Survey, Gilbert moved to Washington. In 1888 he made his first and only trip to Europe, where he gave a speech to the British Association for the Advancement of Science and met many prominent French geomorphologists in Paris. He was promoted to Chief Geologist at the survey in 1889, and for three years worked closely with Powell, primarily on administrative details.

In 1892, political conflicts arose concerning the work of the survey and its budget was cut in half. This caused the resignation of Powell and the elimination of the Chief Geologist position. Gilbert remained at the survey; however, he was given the title of Geologist. He had been tempted to accept a professorship at Cornell University but had decided to stay on at the survey.

In 1892, Gilbert was assigned the task of mapping the geology of the eastern plains of Colorado near the town of Pueblo. He did an excellent job. "His ability to present descriptions of rock structure and surface features in a language understandable to laymen was no more clearly demonstrated" (James, 1977:27).

Gilbert had a longstanding interest in landforms associated with displacement along faults and fatefully, he was in San Francisco almost exactly on the San Andreas fault in 1906. At the time of the earthquake, he was in the field measuring and photographing the movement of objects along the fault line.

In 1909, Gilbert was slowed down somewhat due to a stroke. Within a year, however, he was back to studying the transportation of detrital material by streams. In 1914, the results of this work were published by the Geological Survey as *The Transportation of Debris by Running Water*. This monograph focused on the debris carried by the Sacramento River in California, and Gilbert had worked out the precise relationships between the velocity of the stream and its load.

Gilbert was involved with a variety of professional societies throughout his career. He was one of the original members of the Geological Society of America and served as its fourth president in 1892. In the same year, he also served as president of the Philosophical Society of Washington. At the turn of the century, he was president of the American Association for the Advancement of Science and gave a presidential address on "Rhythms and Geologic Time." He was one of the original forty-eight members of the Association of American Geographers and became its fourth president in 1908. His presidential address focused on his recent work on the San Andreas fault and was entitled "Earthquake Forecasts." The range of Gilbert's influence, according to James, "cannot be measured only by the variety of his published works. He also had a remarkable personal influence on those with whom he came in contact" (1977:30). Gilbert died at Jackson, Michigan, on May 1, 1918.

Selected Bibliography

1867   "The American Mastodon."*Moore's Rural New Yorker*.

1873   "Reports on the Surface Geology of the Maumee Valley, and on the Geology of Williams, Fulton and Lucas Counties, and West Sister Island." *Geological Survey of Ohio* 1:535–90.

1875   "Report on the Geology of Portions of Nevada, Utah, California, and Arizona Examined in the Years 1871–1872." *Report of the United States Geographical and Geological Survey West of the 100th Meridian* 3:17–187.

1876 "The Colorado Plateau Province as a Field for Geological Study." *American Journal of Science* 12:16–24, 85–103.

1877 "Report on the Geology of the Henry Mountains." *United States Geographical and Geological Survey of the Rocky Mountain Region.*

1880 "The Outlet of Lake Bonneville." *American Journal of Science* 19:341–49.

1884 "The Sufficiency of Terrestrial Rotation for the Deflection of Streams." *American Journal of Science* 27:427–32.

1885 "The Topographic Features of Lake Shores." *Geological Survey, Fifth Annual Report.* Washington, D.C.

1890 *Lake Bonneville.* Washington, D.C.: United States Geological Survey Monograph.

1893 "The Moon's Face: A Study of the Origin of Its Features." *Philosophical Society of Washington Bulletin* 12:241–92.

1895 "Niagara Falls and Their History." *National Geographic Monograph* 1:203–36.

"New Light on Isostasy." *Journal of Geology* 3:331–34.

1896 "The Origin of Hypotheses." *Science* 3:1–13.

1898 "Origin of the Physical Features of the United States." *National Geographic Magazine* 9:308–17.

"Recent Earth Movement in the Great Lakes Region." *United States Survey Eighteenth Annual Report* 2:601–47.

1900 "Rhythms and Geologic Time." *Proceedings of the American Association for the Advancement of Science* 49:1–19.

1904 "Glaciers and Glaciation, Alaska." *Harriman Alaska Expedition.* Vol. 3.

1909 "The Convexity of Hilltops." *Journal of Geology* 17:344–50.

"The California Earthquake of 1906." *American Journal of Science* 27:48–52.

"Earthquake Forecasts." *Science* 29:121–38.

1914 "The Transportation of Debris by Running Water." *United States Geological Survey Professional Paper No. 86.*

"The Interpretation of Anomalies of Gravity." *United States Geological Survey Professional Paper No. 85.*

Chronology

1843 Born in Rochester, New York.

1862 Graduated from the University of Rochester.

1867 First publication, "The American Mastodon."

1876 Publication of *The Colorado Plateau.*

1879 Assigned to U.S. Geological Society; Great Basin—Lake Bonneville studies.

1889	Appointed Chief Geologist U.S.G.S. (until 1892).
1892	President, Geological Society of America; President, Philosophical Society of Washington; work on plains in eastern Colorado.
1895	President, Geological Society. Publication of "Niagara Falls and Their History."
1896	Publication of "The Origin of Hypothesis"
1898	Publication of "Recent Earth Movements in the Great Lakes Region."
1904	Moved to Berkeley, California, for work on the Sacramento River region and earthquake studies. Publication of "Glaciers and Glaciation."
1908	President of the Association of American Geographers.
1909	Suffered a stroke. Publication of "The Convexity of Hilltops" and "Earthquake Forecasts."
1914	Publication of "Transportation of Debris by Running Water."
1918	Died at Jackson, Michigan on May 1.

Reference

James, Preston E. 1977. "Grove Karl Gilbert." *Geographers Biobibliographical Studies* 1:25–33.

John Paul Goode

Born on a farm on the pioneer fringe near Stewartville, Minnesota, on November 21, 1862, John Paul Goode was the product of a demanding pioneer life in a land of cold, long winters. His father, Abraham John Goode, came from eastern Pennsylvania and his mother, Huldah Jane Van Valkenburgh, came from a well-known family from New York. Although John Paul enjoyed some advantages not common to those from this area of Minnesota, he was always fond of the fact that he had to struggle and work to obtain his education. He worked his way through preparatory school and the University of Minnesota, partially from the funds he obtained from singing in choirs and quartets.

Goode graduated from the University of Minnesota in 1889 with a Bachelor of Science degree. After graduation he accepted a position to teach natural science in the newly opened Minnesota State Normal at Moorhead. While teaching at Moorhead, Goode also attended graduate school at Harvard and the University of Chicago during summer breaks. He stayed at Moorhead until 1898 when he left for a position as Professor of Physical Science and Geography at Eastern Illinois State Normal School. The lure of graduate school, however, drove him to enter the University of Pennsylvania and he received his Ph.D. in 1901. Although his doctoral work dealt with a variety of geographic topics, the degree was awarded in the faculty of economics.

When the University of Chicago established a Department of Geography in 1903 under *Rollin D. Salisbury, Goode was invited to be included. Goode's primary function was to develop courses in economic geography: at that time Chicago had the largest concentration of such courses in the United States (Pattison, 1978:3–8). He developed a reputation as an expert in Economic Geography and as such was sent by the Chicago Harbor Commission in 1908 to study the leading European ports. The following year he received an appointment by President Taft to assist in conducting a distinguished group of Japanese financiers, the Honorary Commercial Commissioners, on a tour of fifty-five American cities.

Goode also held a number of significant offices during this early period of his career. He served as coeditor of the *Journal of Geography* from 1901 to 1904 and was President of the Geographic Society of Chicago from 1904 to 1906. He was also one of the founding members of the Association of American Geographers in 1904 and went on to be councillor in 1907, second vice president in 1916,and president in 1926. During 1907–8 he was also General Secretary of the American Association for the Advancement of Science.

In 1907 Goode presented his first paper on the program of the Association of American Geographers at the annual meeting in Chicago. His paper, entitled "A College Course in Ontography," focused on the interaction between life and the physical environment. He used the term *human ecology* to describe the study of the geographic conditions of human culture. This idea of human ecology was further advanced in sociology by Park, Burgess, and McKenzie, and in 1922 H. H. Barrows used it as a theme for his presidential address to the Association of American Geographers.

Goode's major interest, and the area where he probably had the most influence, was in cartography. In 1908 he taught a course entitled "Cartography and Graphics," the first course of this type taught in the United States. He shared this enthusiasm for cartography with colleagues in a series of papers presented at the annual meetings of the Association of American Geographers. According to Haas and Ward (1933:244), "He spoke before the Association eleven times after the Baltimore meeting and at each of his appearances, with one exception, he recorded advancement in map making." The culmination of this work was when he gave the Presidential Address (at the 1928 meeting in Philadelphia) entitled, "The Map as a Record of Progress in Geography."

Dissatisfied with what he called the "evil Mercator," Goode made several significant advances in map projections. In 1916 he designed the interrupted homolographic projection and several years later combined his ideas about the sinusoidal and homolographic projections into what he called the homolosine projection.

Significant advances were made by Goode in cartography and map projections, but his chief ambition was to produce a school atlas, and it was this atlas that was to perpetuate his name. It was a great source of personal satisfaction to him when his preliminary atlas was published in 1923, and a revised and enlarged edition was completed shortly before he died. The atlas was to continue for over sixty years with many editions after its initial appearance. The name was changed to *Goode's World Atlas*, and it is now used extensively throughout the United States.

Aside from his publications and inspirations to students, Goode was an enormously successful public speaker. He was asked to speak before a variety of business groups, teachers' associations, community assemblies, and many other types of organizations. During 1926 alone, he had at least seventy engagements, speaking to geographical and scientific societies, associations of commerce, teachers' associations, and university groups. According to Haas and Ward

(1933: 244), "With characteristic energy and thoroughness, he developed the art of lecturing before the public to a degree that won him acclaim from all. . . . He brought vividness to all parts of the United States and to every large city." His melodious voice, in conjunction with lantern slides showing maps and graphs, were very popular on the lecture circuit. According to C. C. Colby (1932: 348), Goode was responsible for bringing geography to the attention of a large number of people in all walks of life. His lectures were so successful that he had to engage a professional lecture company to manage his affairs. He even financed his own leave from the university with funds he obtained from the lecture circuit. Some of the titles of his more popular lectures were "The Significance of the Forest," "When Coal Is Gone, What Then?" and "Chicago, a City of Destiny."

Many economic geographers and cartographers are indebted to Professor Goode and his pioneering work. He was also an eloquent spokesperson who brought geography to many outside the academic community. He died in 1932, happy and satisfied, after receiving many congratulatory messages on the publication of his *School Atlas*.

Selected Bibliography

1899   "Foucault's Pendulum." *Journal of School Geography* 3:298–303.

1903   "Geographical Societies of America." *Journal of Geography* 2:343–50.

1904   "Function of Map-Drawing in the Teaching of Geography." *School Review* 12:67–69.

              "The Human Response to the Physical Environment." *Journal of Geography* 3:333–43.

1905   "A New Method of Representing the Earth's Surface." *Journal of Geography* 4:369–73.

              "A Model Series of Base Maps." *Journal of Geography* 4:373–77.

1906   "Laboratory Work with the Sun." *Journal of Geography* 5:97–108.

              Lantern Slide Illustration for the Teaching of Meteorology. Edited by J. Paul Goode and Henry J. Cox. Geographic Society of Chicago.

1908   *The Development of Commercial Ports*. Report to the Chicago Harbor Commission, Chicago.

1909   "Story of the Manchester Ship Canal." *World Today* (June 16):617–25.

1910   "Fundamental Principles of Japanese Education." *School Review* (November):634–36.

1912   "The Forests of the Philippines." *Bulletin of the American Geographical Society* 44:81–89.

1913–17   *Physical and Political Wall Map Series*. Chicago: Rand McNally. (Eighteen maps, for nine areas, political and physical)

1918   "A Course in Economic Geography." *School and Society* 7 (February 23):216–22.

1919	"Studies in Projections: Adapting the Homolographic Projection to the Portrayal of the Earth's Surface Entire." *Bulletin of the Geographical Society of Philadelphia* 17:103–13.
1923	*Goode's School Atlas, Physical, Political and Economic, for American Schools and Colleges.* Chicago: Rand McNally.
1925	"The Homolosline Projection: A New Device for Portraying the Earth's Surface Entire." *Annals of the Association of American Geographers* 15:119–25.
1926	*The Geographic Background of Chicago.* Chicago: University of Chicago Press.
1927	"The Map as a Record of Progress in Geography." *Annals of the Association of American Geographers* 17:1–14.
	"The Polar Equal Area: A New Projection for the World Map." *Annals of the Association of American Geographers* 19:167–71.

Chronology

1862	Born November 21, Stewartville, Minnesota.
1901	Awarded a doctorate at the University of Pennsylvania for "The Influence of Physiographic Factors upon the Occupations and Economic Development in the United States."
1901–4	Coeditor of the *Journal of Geography*.
1904–6	President of the Geographic Society of Chicago.
1907	Presented his first paper at the annual meeting of the Association of American Geographers.
1908	Published *What the Ports of Europe Are Doing*. Offered the first course in the United States on "Cartography and Graphics."
1913–17	Produced the series of eighteen wall maps.
1923	Designed the homosline projection and the first publication of *Goode's School Atlas*. Awarded the Culver Gold Medal by the Geographic Society of Chicago.
1926	President of the Association of American Geographers.
1932	Died August 5, Little Point Sable, Michigan.

References

Colby, C. C. 1932. "John Paul Goode." *Journal of Geography* 31:347–48.

Haas, W. H., and H. B. Ward. 1933. "J. Paul Goode." *Annals of the Association of American Geographers* 23:241–46.

Pattison, W. D., 1978. "Goode's Proposal of 1902: An Interpretation." *Professional Geographer* 30:3–8.

Jean Gottmann

Jean Gottmann is a geographic scholar of international renown. He has had a variety of academic appointments in France, the United States, and England, as well as political and administrative appointments. He was born in 1915 in Kharkov [Ukraine], of prosperous parents, but two years later both parents were killed and he was taken by his uncle to Paris. "His uncle became the art critic of a Russian newspaper . . . and drew around him a number of expatriate intellectuals. . . . Cosmopolitan, travelled and talkative was the household in which Gottmann spent his formative years; the influence of his childhood surroundings on his intellectual development must have been profound" (Patten, 1983:xii).

Gottmann studied at the Lycée Montaigne and the Lycée St. Louis and then went to the Sorbonne to study law. Influenced by several distinguished geographers there, he decided to forego the study of law. Of particular interest to him was the geographic and historic development of the world's great cities. He received his Diplôme d'Études Supérieures in 1934 and his Licencie es Lettres in 1937, both were in geography and history.

When the Nazi's occupied France, Gottmann fled Paris to Montpellier and then, via the Iberian Peninsula, he reached the United States. He was especially fascinated by New York City and its surrounding urban region. His first job in American was at the Institute for Advanced Study in Princeton. He also did some teaching at Johns Hopkins University and served as a consultant to several agencies, including the United States Board of Economic Warfare.

After World War II, Gottmann returned to Paris and served on the staff of the minister of the national economy, where he was involved in post-war reconstruction planning. In 1946, however, he became Director of Studies and Research in the United Nations Secretariat, working with the Economic and Social Council in New York.

The pull of the academic life, however, was too great, and Gottmann returned to France to continue his scholarly work. From the 1940s to the 1960s he held chairs in Paris and America concurrently and also continued membership at the institute at Princeton. During this time, he also published several books in both English and French. These books included *L'Amérique* (1949), *A Geography of Europe* (1950), *Politique des États et Leur Géographie* (1952), and *Virginia at Mid-Century* (1955).

In 1956 Gottmann was invited to do a large-scale metropolitan study of urban problems in the United States for the Twentieth Century Fund. He had always been fascinated by the long string of cities along the eastern seaboard of the United States from Boston to Washington, D.C. His study focused on this region, which he called a "megalopolis." The result of the study was a book, *Megalopolis* (1961), that was to have a worldwide effect on urban studies. According to Patten (1983:xv), "It was a monumental achievement and ranks as one of the most important single geographical ideas of the mid-twentieth century."

Gottmann's interests were not only confined to the Franco-American axis. He frequently lectured on and studied urban problems in a variety of places including Belgium, Israel, Italy, the Netherlands, Switzerland, Great Britain, and Central and South America. In the 1970s he expanded his interests to Japan.

In 1968 he was given a Professorship of Geography in the School of Geography at the University of Oxford and he remains a Fellow of Hertford College, University of Oxford. He has received honorary degrees from the University of Wisconsin and from Southern Illinois University and the Palmes Academiques Chevalier de la Legion d'Honneur of France and the Victoria Medal from the Royal Geographical Society.

Selected Bibliography

1933   "La Premiere Année du Deuxième Plan Quinquennal de l'U.R.S.S." *Annales de Géographie* 42:551–52.

1934   "Une Nouvelle Route au Turkestan Russe." *Annales de Géographie* 43:336.

            "La Situation Economique de l'Uzbekistan." *Annales de Géographie* 43:445–46.

1936   "Orient et Occident: Problèmes Palestiniens." *L'Information Geographique* 1:5–12.

            "Une Carte de L'Aridité en Palestine." *Annales de Géographie* 45:430–33.

1938   "L'Homme, la Route et l'Eau en Asie Sud-Occidentale." *Annales de Géographie* 47:575–601.

1942   "Laterization in Africa: Acaetta's Work on Its Cause and Cure." *Geographical Review* 32:319–21.

            "The Background of Geopolitics." *Military Affairs, Journal of the American Military Institute* 6:197–206.

1943   "Nature and Men in French North Africa." *The Yale Review* 32:474–92.

"Economic Problems of French North Africa." *Geographical Review* 33:175–96.

1944   "Vauban and Modern Geography." *Geographical Review* 34:120–28.

"Recent Contributions to the Geography of the Sahara." *Geographical Review* 34:147–50.

1945   "Raw Materials in the Western Pacific." *Ninth Conference of the Institute of Pacific Relations*, Hot Springs, Virginia, French Paper No. 1.

"The Isles of Guadeloupe." *Geographical Review* 35:182–203.

1946   "French Geography in Wartime." *Geographical Review* 36:80–91.

1948   "De La Methode d'Analyse en Géographie Humaine." *Annales de Géographie* 56:1–12.

"Jacques Weulerosse: Obituary." *Geographical Review* 37:507.

1949   *L'Amérique*. Paris: Hachette.

1950   "Social Motives in Geographical Analysis." *Geographical Review* 40:146–48.

"Geography and the United Nations." *Scottish Geographical Magazine* 66:129–34.

1951   *A Geography of Europe*. New York: Henry Holt.

1952   "The Political Partitioning of Our World: An Attempt at Analysis." *World Politics* 4:512–19.

1955   "Problèmes d'Israel." *Geographia*, 32–38.

Virginia at Mid-Century. New York: Henry Holt.

1957   "Megalopolis, or the Urbanization of the Northeastern Seaboard." *Economic Geography* 33:189–200.

1958   "Regional Planning in France: A Review." *Geographical Review* 48:257–61.

1959   "Revolution in Land Use." *Landscape* 8:15–21.

1961   *Megalopolis: The Urbanized Northeastern Seaboard of the United States*. New York: The Twentieth Century Fund.

1962   *Economics, Esthetics and Ethics in Modern Urbanization*. New York: The Twentieth Century Fund.

1963   "Henri Baulig: An Obituary." *Geographical Review* 53:611–12.

1964   "Great Capitals in Evolution." *Geographical Review* 54:124–27.

"Incidences Politiques de l'Évolution Agricole Moderne." *Politique Étrangère* 29:181–92.

1966   "The Ethics of Living at High Densities." *Ekistics* 21:141–45.

"Why the Skyscraper?" *Geographical Review* 54:190–212.

1967   With R. Harper. *Metropolis on the Move: Geographers Look at Urban Sprawl*. New York: Wiley.

1969   *Virginia in Our Century*. Charlottesville: University Press of Virginia.

1970   "Urban Centrality and the Interweaving of Quarternary Activities." *Ekistics* 29:322–31.

1971   "Office Growth and Decentralization: The Case of London." *Geographical Review* 61:136–38.

1973   *The Significance of Territory*. Charlottesville: The University Press of Virginia.

1974   "The Evolution of Urban Centrality—Orientations for Research." *Research Papers, Oxford School of Geography*. No. 8.

          "The Dynamics of Large Cities." *Geographical Journal* 140:254–61.

1975   "The Evolution of Urban Centrality." *Ekistics* 40:220–28.

          "The Evolution of the Concept of Territory." *Social Science Information* 14:29–47.

1977   "The Role of Capital Cities." *Ekistics* 44:240–43.

1978   "The Mutation of the American City: A Review of the Comparative Metropolitan Analysis Project." *Geographical Review* 68:201–8.

          "How the Central City Works: The Case of New York." *Geographical Journal* 144:301–4.

1980   "Planning and Metamorphosis in Japan: A Note." *Town Planning Review* 51:171–76.

          "Spatial Partitioning and the Politician's Wisdom." *International Political Science Review* 4:432–55.

1981   "Managing Megalopolis in Europe." *Geographical Journal* 147:85–87.

          "Japan's Organization of Space: Fluidity and Stability in a Changing Habitat." *Ekistics* 48:258–65.

1982   "The Basic Problem of Political Geography: The Organization of Space and the Search for Stability." *Tijdschrift voor Economische en Sociale Geografie* 73:340–49.

Chronology

1915   Born in Kharkov, U.S.S.R.

1917   Both parents killed and Gottmann taken to Paris.

1934   Received Diplôme d'Études Supérieures in geography and history from the Sorbonne.

1937   Received his Licencié ès Lettres in geography and history.

1942   Fled France during Nazi occupation; went to New York.

1943   Positions at the Institute for Advanced Study in Princeton and at Johns Hopkins University.

1945   Returned to Paris to serve on the staff of the minister of the national economy.

1946   Appointed Director of Studies and Research in the United Nations Secretariat in New York.

1949	Published *L'Amérique*.
1950	Published *A Geography of Europe*.
1955	Published *Virginia at Mid-Century*.
1956	Invited by the Twentieth Century Fund in New York to do a large-scale metropolitan study of urban problems in the United States.
1961	Published *Megalopolis*.
1968	Appointed Professor of Geography in the School of Geography at the University of Oxford.

Reference

Patten, John, ed. 1983. *The Expanding City*. New York: Academic.

Arnold Henry Guyot

Arnold Henry Guyot was one of the many geographers who emigrated to the United States from Europe. Born in Boudevilliers, a small Swiss village near Neuchatel, on September 28, 1807, he received his early education in Switzerland, where he was especially interested in both the natural sciences and religion. Guyot eventually focused on science but retained an interest in religion for the rest of his life. In 1829, he went to study at the University of Berlin, and in 1835 he received a Doctor of Philosophy degree.

While in Berlin, Guyot became part of the intellectual ferment of the time. Many famous scholars, including the philosophers G. W. Hegel and Friedrich Schleiermacher, were also in Berlin. Although Guyot took courses from these men, he was primarily influenced by the geographers *Carl Ritter and *Alexander von Humboldt. His dissertation on the natural classification of lakes was dedicated to both Ritter and Humboldt.

Guyot's first teaching position at the Academy of Neuchatel, which he took after several years of tutoring and travelling, was in both geography and history. In 1839, the academy was made a university, and Guyot was appointed Professor of Physical Geography and History. While at Neuchatel, he also spent his summers doing fieldwork on the mountain system of the Alps. His research focused on glacial action by looking at the placement of erratic rocks. Along with Louis Agassiz, another scientist interested in glaciers, he studied the glaciers of the Aar, Gries, and Rhone valleys. He also made hundreds of temperature and depth observations in Lake Neuchatel and Lake Morat from which he made bathymetric maps of the lake basins. "As a follower of Humboldt and Ritter, he sought to describe in detail and to systematize what was known of the vertical nature of the surface of the earth, to make geographical information three-dimensional by determining the heights of mountains . . . and the depths of lakes and oceans" (Ferrel, 1981:66).

From the beginning of his research career, Guyot was interested in scientific methodology. He believed that efforts should be focused on finding patterns or laws. In his book *Earth and Man*, he admonished geographers to "rise to the courses" by developing theories and then to "descend to the consequences" through the gathering of empirical data (p. 20). In his article on geography published in Johnson's encyclopedia in 1875, he states that geography "seeks to understand the relations of mutual dependence which bind natural phenomena together as cause and effects into a vast system, into one great individual mechanism which is the territorial globe itself, with all it contains" (Vol. 2, Part 1, p. 479).

In March 1848, political strife in Switzerland brought about the closing of the Academy at Neuchatel. Although Guyot was offered several teaching positions at the time, his friend Louis Agassiz urged him to spread the geographic ideas of Ritter and Humboldt by moving to the United States. Although he was forty-one years old and the sole supporter of his mother, two sisters, and a nephew, he decided to take the advice of Agassiz.

In January and February of 1849, Guyot was invited to give a series of lectures through the Lovell Institute in Boston. The lectures focused on physical geography and how it related to human history. Originally given in French, the lectures were translated into English and later gathered into a book, *Earth and Man*. The book brought fame to Guyot, and between 1849 and 1910, it was revised and reprinted seven times. It was popular with both the scientific community and the educated public.

Guyot's first full-time employment in the United States was with the Massachusetts Board of Education. The board was interested in the teaching of geography in public schools and had heard that Guyot was familiar with European teaching techniques that were superior to pedagogical methods used in the United States. He was asked to lecture and conduct teacher's institutes at the state normal schools.

Guyot had developed his teaching philosophy from his interaction with the educationalist Johann Pestalozzi, as well as from Ritter, Agassiz, Humboldt, and others. His ideas were expressed in his 1866 book *Introduction to the Study of Geography*, where he states:

The nature of our mind is such that the acquisition of knowledge is always gradual. That gradual progress, whatever be the object of our study, has three main stages. We first take a general outside view of the object, or of the field to be studied; we then fairly go into the study of all its parts; last of all we derive from this thorough analyses the means of rising to the knowledge of the laws and principles which regulate and pervade the whole. (P. iii)

Guyot called the first stage the "perceptive stage," the second the "analytic stage," and the third the "synthetic stage."

Maps also played a major role in Guyot's geographic instructional techniques.

"He believed that map study should precede book study, and a geography textbook without maps was of little use. He frowned on the use of ornate maps for illustrative purposes in books, because in his plan the map should be the subject of the text and the focus of the whole study" (Anstey, 1958:446–47).

Since the types of geographic materials necessary to implement Guyot's ideas in schools were not available, he was asked to provide them for teachers. As a result, the *Guyot Geographic Series* of graded textbooks were developed, and according to W. B. Scott (1884:263), they revolutionized the approach to geographical study in the United States. This geography series was widely accepted, and Guyot prepared special state supplements describing the geography of New York, Ohio, Indiana, Illinois, Michigan, Vermont, and Massachusetts.

Guyot continued to be involved with a variety of research projects while developing his teaching materials. In 1850 he was asked by the Smithsonian and New York's State Board of Regents to develop a workable network of weather stations in New York. His "Directions for Meteorological Observation" (1854), published by the Smithsonian, gave practical information to those who would staff these stations. According to Ferrell (1981:65), "This same effort lead to Guyot's editing a series of *Meteorological Tables* to be used as pocket calculators in processing the data, and as each edition was revised, expanded and published by the Smithsonian, they became known among scientists around the world for their convenience."

In 1854, the Trustees of the College of New Jersey, now called Princeton University, asked Guyot to help them improve the quality of science teaching and offered him an endorsed chair as Professor of Physical Geography and Geology. This appointment is considered by many to be a major landmark in the development of university-level geography in the United States. Guyot stayed at Princeton for the next thirty years although he also taught at the State Normal School at Trenton, the Union Theological School and Columbia University in New York City, and at Princeton Theological Seminary.

In addition to writing and teaching, Guyot also did a considerable amount of travelling. Shortly after the completion of the transcontinental railroad in 1869, he visited the western United States. This trip laid the foundation for the First Princeton Transcontinental Excursion in 1877. These excursions became an important part of scientific study at Princeton and involved the collection of a plethora of mineral fossils, and other types of artifacts. In order to house all of these collected materials, Guyot established a teaching museum in geology and archaeology at Princeton that was modelled after the Museum of Comparative Zoology at Harvard, established by his friend and colleague Louis Agassiz.

From all accounts, Guyot was an interesting and inspiring teacher. An article in *Science* (1884:218–19) outlines these characteristics: "He avoided the snare of routine which entraps so many of the college professors of this country; but, by always proposing to himself new lines of inquiry and new subjects of investigation, he kept his mind perpetually fresh so that, until the infirmities of old age attacked him, he was younger than many of his juniors." His textbooks were used in many school systems and accounts of his lectures appeared on the front page of the *New York Times* (December 8, 1854).

Guyot received numerous honors and awards for his geographic work. At one time he had a glacier, a species of animal, a landform, a crater on the moon, and four mountains named after him. The noted paleontologist Edward Cope named *Artiodactyla hyopotamus guyotianus* in his honor, and the term *guyot* was coined by Harry Hess in 1946 to denote a flat-topped undersea mount. Guyot Hall was built in Princeton in 1909 and is the home of the geology and biology departments. Guyot had a strong influence on many scholars, most notably *William Morris Davis, a pioneer in the development of landform studies and the Association of American Geographers. According to Anstey (1958:449), "Guyot's greatest influence in American geography must be stated in terms of the hundreds of students which he instructed, many of whom became teachers and passed on the geographic knowledge which he introduced to the country." He died on February 8, 1884.

Selected Bibliography

1848   "On the Distribution of the Different Species of Rocks in the Erratic Basin of the Rhone." *Edinburgh New Philosophical Journal* 44:249–71.

                "On the Erratic Basin of the Rhine." *Edinburgh New Philosophical Journal* 45:20–27.

                "Topography of the Pennine Alps, and the Primitive Site of the Principal Series of Rocks Found in the Basin of the Rhone." *Edinburgh New Philosophical Journal* 44:319–29.

1849   *Earth and Man: Lectures on Comparative Physical Geography, in Its Relation to the History of Mankind.* Translated from the French by C. C. Felton, Boston.

                "On the Erratic Phenomena of the Central Alps." *Proceedings of the American Association for the Advancement of Science* 2:311–21.

                "On the Erratic Phenomena of the White Mountains." *Proceedings of the American Association for the Advancement of Science* 2:308–11.

1851   "On the Progress of the System of Meteorological Observations Conducted by the Smithsonian Institution, and the Propriety of Immediate Extension Throughout the American Continent." *Proceedings of the American Association for the Advancement of Science* 6:167–68.

1852   "On the Concordance of the Mosaic Account of the Creation with That Given by Modern Science." *Evening Post* (New York). Abstract of a series of lectures at the Springler Institute, New York City, March 6, 12, 15, and 23.

                A Collection of Meteorological Tables, Washington, D.C.: Smithsonian Institution.

1854	"Directions for Meteorological Observations." *Smithsonian Institution, 10th Annual Report*, 215–44.
1859	"Address of Professor Guyot: Humboldt Commemoration." *Journal of the American Geographical and Statistical Society* 1:242–45.
1861	"On the Appalachian Mountain System." *American Journal of Science and Arts* 81:157–85.
1863	"Notes on the Geography of the Mountain District of Western North Carolina." *North Carolina Historical Review* 11:251–318.
1866	*Introduction to the Study of Geography.* New York: Scribner's.
1869	"Artesian Well at Terre Haute, Indiana." *American Journal of Science and Arts* 48:270–71.
1871	*New Illustrated Family Atlas of the World . . . with Descriptions Geographical, Statistical, and Historical.* Edited by Alvin Jewett Johnson. New York.
1880	"On a New Map of the Catskill Mountains, with Remarks on the Physical Geography and Hypsometry of That Region." *Appalachia* 2:97–108.
	"On the Physical Structure and Hypsometry of the Catskill Mountain Region." *American Journal of Science and Arts* 119:429–51.
1883	"On the Existence in Both Hemispheres of a Dry Zone, and Its Causes." *American Journal of Science and Arts* 126:161–66.
1884	*Creation; or the Biblical Cosmogony in the Light of Modern Science.* New York.

Chronology

1807	Born in Boudevilliers, Switzerland, on September 28.
1835	Doctorate from University of Berlin.
1839	Appointed Chair of History and Physical Geography at the Academy of Neuchatel.
1848	Came to the United States.
1849	Delivered Lowell Institute Lectures at Boston. Publication of *Earth and Man*.
1850	Invited by Smithsonian Institution to help develop a system of meteorological observations for North American continent.
1854–84	Chair of Physical Geography and Geology at Princeton.
1859	On the council of American Geographical Society.
1863	Original member at formation of National Academy of Sciences.
1866–75	Published series of textbooks.
1867	Elected to American Philosophical Society.
1873	Received Medal of Progress from World's Exhibition at Vienna for textbook series.
1877	First Princeton Transcontinental Excursion.

1878   Received gold medal for textbook series at Exposition Universelle, Paris.

1884   Died on February 8.

References

Anstey, Robert L. "Arnold Guyot, Teacher of Geography." *Journal of Geography* 57:441–49.

Ferrell, Edith H. 1981. "Arnold Henry Guyot." *Geographers Biobibliographical Studies* 5:63–71.

Scott, W. B. 1884. "Arnold Henry Guyot." *The Popular Science Monthly* 25:263.

Peter Haggett

For the past thirty-five years, Peter Haggett has held teaching and research positions at universities around the world. He was born on January 23, 1933, in Somerset, England. Although the primary school he attended from age five to eleven was an old "two-roomer," he believed he received a first-class primary education because of the dedication and interest expressed by his teachers. He passed an examination at age eleven and entered grammar school, which was a big school, compared to his primary school, with 250 boys. According to Haggett (Browning, 1982:41), "Geography was well taught; the headmaster was an old Cambridge geographer who had written a number of books on the geography of 'the empire,' as it was called then."

Haggett's decision to focus on geography, however, occurred at the age of sixteen when he was hospitalized for an injury suffered as the result of a rugby match. While spending several months in an orthopaedic hospital, he came across a book entitled *The Geomorphology of New Zealand* by *Charles Cotton. At the time he was uncertain as to which subject to study at university, but according to Haggett (1990:2), "Cotton's diagrams of finely-etched landforms and the problems which their morphology and origin posed made up my mind. I resolved to take forward the study of 'physiography' by whatever route was open to me."

In 1951 he was offered a scholarship from St. Catharine's College at Cambridge University. He was one of a group of seven students in that class who were geographers. His mentor was Gus Caesar, and he was impressed with Caesar's ability to critically and logically analyze his written work, yet still be able to show him how to reassemble it into something more meaningful. He also came into contact with William Vaughan Lewis, the person who had the greatest impact on his mathematical ideas. While at Cambridge, his work was in both physical and economic geography. He wrote a bachelor's thesis dealing with the historical geography of the area around the Quantoch Hills.

Upon graduation with a bachelor's degree from Cambridge in 1954, Haggett decided to stay there when offered a research scholarship. The following year he accepted an offer from University College, London, as an assistant lecturer in geography. After two years at University College, the head of the Cambridge geography department offered him a position, and he returned to Cambridge in 1957 at the age of twenty three.

Although Haggett's interests were primarily in location analysis, he was expected to teach a course on Latin America. In order to fulfill these duties, he went to Brazil several times in the late fifties and early sixties. As a result, he produced four or five papers on various Latin American topics during this time. Once he had the chance, however, he concentrated on the area of locational analysis. This work resulted in the publication of his first book, *Locational Analysis in Human Geography*. Although the book was primarily a description of work that had been done in the United States and on the continent, and contained little of Haggett's own original research, it was an elegant synthesis of a variety of important ideas. At nearly the same time, he published another book, coedited with Richard Chorley, entitled *Frontiers in Geographical Teaching*. Both books were widely read in both Britain and the United States.

In 1966 Haggett accepted a position as Professor of Urban and Regional Geography at the University of Bristol. Three years later, in 1969, he was awarded a Ph.D. from Cambridge. He was elevated to Head of Department at Bristol in 1975, Dean of the Faculty of Social Sciences in 1972; Pro-Vice-Chancellor in 1979; and Acting Vice-Chancellor for a year in 1984. He has also been a visiting professor at many universities throughout the world.

Haggett continued to write many books and research journal articles. Among his most important books were *Models in Geography, Network Analysis in Geography, Geography: A Modern Synthesis, Processes in Physical and Human Geography, Spatial Diffusion: An Historical Geography of Epidemics in an Island Community, Spatial Aspects of Influenza Epidemics*, and *The Geographer's Art*. His current work deals with epidemiological problems and their geographical aspects associated with AIDS and measles.

Besides receiving a plethora of research grants, Haggett has been an editor for several geographical journals including *Cambridge Geographical Monographs, Environment and Planning: International Journal of Urban and Regional Research, Geographical Analysis, Progress in Physical Geography*, and *Progress in Human Geography*.

Haggett's contributions to geography have been recognized by his peers, and he received many awards for his work, including the Philip Lake Prize for Geography from Cambridge (1953), the Gill Memorial Award from the Royal Geographical Society (1966), the Cullum Gold Medal from the American Geographical Society (1969), and the Patron's Gold Medal from the Royal Geographical Society (1986). Honorary degrees have been received from the University of Bristol (1986) and the University of Durham (1989).

Selected Bibliography

1959   "The Bahia-Goa Route in the Dispersal of Brazilian Plants to Asia."
            American Antiquity 25:267–68.

1961   "Land Use and Sediment Yield in an Old Plantation Tract of the Serro
            Do Mar, Brazil." *Geographical Journal* 127:50–59.

1963   "Regional and Local Components in the Distribution of Forested Areas
            in South-East Brazil: A Multivariate Approach." *Geographical Journal*
            130:365–78.

1964   "Towards a Statistical Definition of Ecological Range: The Case of Quer-
            cus Suber." *Ecology* 45:622–25.

            With Kusuma Gunawardena. "Determination of Population Thresholds for
            Settlement Functions by the Reed-Muench Method." *Professional Geog-
            rapher* 4:6–9.

            With Christopher Board. "Rotational and Parallel Traverses in the Rapid
            Integration of Geographic Areas." *Annals of the Association of American
            Geographers* 54:406–10.

1965   Edited with Richard J. Chorley. *Frontiers in Geographical Teaching: The
            Madingley Lectures*. London: Methuen.

            With R. Chorley and D. R. Stoddart. "Scale Standards in Geographical
            Research: A New Measure of Areal Magnitude." *Nature* 205:844–47.

            Locational Analysis in Human Geography. London: Edward Arnold.

            With Richard Chorley. "Trend-Surface Mapping in Geographical Re-
            search." *Transactions of the Institute of British Geographers* 37:47–67.

1967   "Three Pioneers in Locational Theory: A Review." *Geographical Journal*
            133:357–59.

            Edited with Richard Chorley. *Models in Geography*. London: Methuen.

            "An Extension of the Horton Combinatorial Model to Regional Highway
            Networks." *Journal of Regional Science* 2(2):281–90.

1969   "Geographical Research in a Computer Environment." *Geographical
            Journal* 135:500–509.

            With Richard Chorley. *Network Analysis in Geography: Exploration in
            Spatial Structure*. London: Edward Arnold.

            "New Regions for Old." *Geographical Magazine* 52:210–17.

1970   "On the Efficiency of Alternative Aggregations in Region-Building Prob-
            lems." *Environment and Planning* 2:285–94.

1972   *Geography: A Modern Synthesis*. New York: Harper and Row.

1975   With A. D. Cliff, J. K. Ord, K. Bassett, and R. B. Davies. *Elements of
            Spatial Structure: A Quantitative Approach*. Cambridge: Cambridge Uni-
            versity Press.

            With R. G. Peel and M. D. Chisholm. *Processes in Physical and Human
            Geography*. London: Heinemann.

1976   "Hybridizing Alternative Models of an Epidemic Diffusion Process."
        Economic Geography 52:136–46.

1977   "Geography in a Steady State Environment." *Geography* 62:159–67.

1980   With A. D. Cliff. "Changes in the Seasonal Incidence of Measles in
        Iceland, 1896–1974." *Journal of Hygiene* 10:1–7.

1981   With A. D. Cliff, J. K. Ord, and G. R. Versey. *Spatial Diffusion: An
        Historical Geography of Epidemics in an Island Community*. Cambridge:
        Cambridge University Press.

1982   "Methods for the Measurement of Epidemic Velocity from Time-Series
        Data." *International Journal of Epidemiology* 11:82–89.

1984   With A. D. Cliff. "Island Epidemics." *Scientific American* 250:138–47.

1986   With A. D. Cliff and J. K. Ord. *Spatial Aspects of Influenza Epidemics*.
        London: Pion.

1988   With A. D. Cliff. *Atlas of Disease Distributions: Analytic Approaches to
        Epidemiological Data*. Oxford: Blackwell Reference Series.

1990   *The Geographer's Art*. Oxford: Blackwell.

Chronology

1933   Born January 23 in Somerset, England.

1954   Graduated from Cambridge (B.A.) with first class honors.

1955   Took position as Assistant Lecturer in Geography at University College,
        University of London.

1957   Offered position as University Demonstrator in Geography at Cambridge
        University.

1959   First publications dealing with Brazil.

1965   Published *Frontiers in Geographical Teaching* and *Locational Analysis in
        Human Geography*.

1966   Took position as Professor of Urban and Regional Geography at the Uni-
        versity of Bristol.

        Received the Gill Memorial Award from the Royal Geographical Society.

1967   Published *Models in Geography*.

1969   Awarded the Ph.D. from Cambridge. Published *Network Analysis in
        Geography*.

        Received the Cullum Gold Medal from the American Geographical Society.

1972   Published *Geography: A Modern Synthesis*.

1975   Appointed head of the Department of Geography at the University of
        Bristol.

1979   Appointed Pro Vice-Chancellor at the University of Bristol.

1982   Published *Spatial Diffusion: An Historical Geography of Epidemics in an
        Island Community*.

1986   Published *Spatial Aspects of Influenza Epidemics*. Received the Patron's
            Gold Medal from the Royal Geographical Society. Received an Honorary
            LL.D. from the University of Bristol.

1989   Received an Honorary D.Sc. from the University of Durham.

Reference

Browning, Clyde E. 1982. *Conversations with Geographers: Career Pathways and Research Styles*. Studies in Geography No. 16, Chapel Hill, N.C.: University of North Carolina, Department of Geography.

Chauncy D. Harris

The past five decades have seen significant advances in the fields of urban geography and the geography of the Soviet Union, much of which can be attributed to the work of Chauncy D. Harris. Born in Logan, Utah on January 31, 1914, he was the son of Estella Spilsbury Harris and Franklin Stewart Harris, who was the most important influence on his life. Franklin had a Ph.D. in Agronomy from Cornell University and was a productive research scientist. He later became president of Brigham Young University and Utah State University. He also had a keen geographic sense and when Chauncy, at the age of eight, decided to become a geographer, he was encouraged by his father. According to Harris (1990:406):

My father had a copy of the *World Almanac*, which had population figures for cities in the United States. I became curious about why some cities were larger than others and what were the activities that supported the population in larger cities. . . . At that time I decided to become a geographer. Many years later in my doctoral dissertation I returned to this question.

Harris attended Brigham Young University and received an A.B. degree in 1933. The degree was awarded with "high honors," and he was valedictorian of his graduating class. He later spent two years at Oxford University and a year at the London School of Economics as a Rhodes Scholar. He graduated with a B.A. in 1936 and an M.A. in 1943 from Oxford. While a Rhodes Scholar, he also spent time living with both French and German families, which led to an improved facility with those two important scientific languages.

Upon arrival at the University of Chicago as a graduate student in the summer of 1933, Harris met Harold M. Mayer and *Edward L. Ullman. All three were interested in Urban Geography, as was professor Charles C. Colby. According to Harris (1990:405), "The simultaneous presence of three youngsters all deeply curious about urban phenomena heralded a new period in which an initial critical mass was reached.'' Colby took particular interest in Harris and was his ''most influential teacher, dissertation supervisor, friend, counsellor and colleague'' (Personal correspondence, December 7, 1990).

Harris's doctoral dissertation, *Salt Lake City: A Regional Capital*, was completed in 1940 and analyzed this regional capital and the activities associated with its basic support. Although initially interested in the growth of cities, Harris changed his focus in the early forties and began to look at the classification of cities. He presented his first paper, ''A Functional Classification of Cities in the United States,'' at a meeting of the Association of American Geographers in New York City in 1941. The publication of this paper was well-received at the time and is today considered by many to be a classic paper in the field of urban geography. Some of the data collected for his functional classification paper was used as the basis for another study on suburbs that was published in the *American Journal of Sociology* a year later. This work on city and suburb classifications was recognized by both sociologists and political scientists, as well as by geographers. These first few papers established Harris's reputation as an important scholar in the emerging field of urban geography.

In 1945 The American Academy of Political and Social Science decided to publish a special volume on the city in its *Annals*. Harris was invited to prepare an article and decided to work with Ullman as a coauthor. This article, ''The Nature of Cities,'' looked at the multiple-nuclei pattern of urban development and has since become a classic paper on urban patterns. These original ideas of Harris and Ullman have been expanded in a variety of new ways in social-area analysis or factorial ecology (Larkin and Peters, 1983:168–70).

During this early period of his career, Harris was an Assistant Professor of Geography at the University of Nebraska and then returned to the University of Chicago in 1943 to become an Assistant Professor there. He also worked under Stephen Jones in the Office of the Geographer at the U.S. Department of State during 1942 and 1943 and then went to the Far East Division, Research and Analysis Branch, of the Office of Strategic Services from 1944–45.

During these wartime years, Harris became interested in the Soviet Union while working for the Department of State. Despite the paucity of data available, he was able to write and publish two important papers, which were published by the *Geographical Review* in 1945. One paper looked at both regional and functional aspects of urban growth in the Soviet Union and the other was devoted to the ethnic complexity of cities in the southern and western fringes of the Soviet Union.

The next major project by Harris dealing with the Soviet Union was what Allan Rodgers calls ''a truly monumental study'' (1984:3), the translation of Balzak, Vasyutin, and Feigin's text on the *Economic Geography of the U.S.S.R.* Among Harris's responsibilities were the addition of maps, appendices, and numerous explanatory footnotes, as well as the function of editing the volume.

In 1962 Harris had a similar task as editor of the English-language edition of *Soviet Geography: Accomplishments and Tasks*, published by the American Geographical Society.

Harris's publications in the Soviet field fall into two categories: those on geography as a research and teaching discipline in the Soviet Union, and those on its industrial and agricultural resources. As a result of his many visits to the Soviet Union and his exchanges with scholars from centers of Soviet studies, Harris wrote a series of articles about teaching and research in geography in the Soviet Union. In the late sixties and early seventies Harris returned to his studies of Soviet cities and wrote both book chapters and journal articles dealing with this topic. He also published a monograph entitled *Cities of the Soviet Union* published by the Association of American Geographers. According to Rodgers (1984:7), "the scholarship demonstrated in this volume evidenced an extraordinary knowledge of Soviet urban and population geography. Despite its seeming regional specificity, this volume would rank among the very best scholarly studies produced by our profession in recent history." Chauncy Harris made significant contributions to both urban geography and the geography of the Soviet Union. He also was actively involved in a variety of scholarly organizations. He was both Secretary and President of the Association of American Geographers, Vice President of the American Geographical Society, Vice President, Secretary-General, Treasurer, and Editor of the International Geographical Union, President of the American Association for the Advancement of Slavic Studies, Vice President of the Regional Science Association, and an active member in many other scholarly organizations.

As a result of his work, Harris was awarded many honors, including the Distinguished Service Award for the Geographic Society of Chicago (1965); the Honors Award from the Association of American Geographers (1976); the Laureat d'Honneur from the International Geographical Union (1976); the *Alexander von Humboldt Gold Medal, *Gesellschaft für Erdkunde zu Berlin* (1978); the Award for Distinguished Contributions to Slavic Studies from the American Association for the Advancement of Slavic Studies (1978); the Cullum Geographical Medal from the American Geographical Society (1985); the Master Teacher Award from the National Council for Geographic Education (1986); and the Victoria Medal from the Royal Geographical Society (1987). He also received honorary degrees from the Universidad Catolica de Chile (1956) and Indiana University (1979).

Selected Bibliography

1941   "Electricity Generation in London, England." *Geographical Review* 31:127–34.

            "Location of Salt Lake City." *Economic Geography* 17:204–12.

1942   "Ipswich, England." *Economic Geography* 18:1–12.

"Growth of Larger Cities in the United States 1930–1940." *Journal of Geography* 41:313–18.

1943   "A Functional Classification of Cities in the United States." *Geographical Review* 33:86–99.

"Suburbs." *American Journal of Sociology* 49:1–13.

1945   "The Cities of the Soviet Union." *Geographical Review* 35:107–21.

"Ethnic Groups in Cities of the Soviet Union." *Geographical Review* 35:466–73.

With Edward Ullman. "The Nature of Cities." *Annals of the American Academy of Political and Social Science* 242:7–17.

1946   "The Ruhr Coal-Mining District." *Geographical Review* 36:194–221.

1949   *Economic Geography of the USSR*. Edited by Chauncy D. Harris. New York: Macmillan.

1950   With Jerome D. Fellmann. "Geographic Serials." *Geographical Review* 40:649–56.

1952   "Geographical Literature on the Soviet Union: A Discussion." *Geographical Review* 42:615–27.

1953   "The Refugee Problem of Germany." *Economic Geography* 29:10–25.

1954   "Geography of Manufacturing." In Preston E. James and Clarence F. Jones, eds., *American Geography: Inventory and Prospect*. Syracuse, N.Y.: Syracuse University Press.

"The Market as a Factor in the Localization of Industry in the United States." *Annals of the Association of American Geographers* 44:315–48.

1955   "Growing Food by Decree in Soviet Russia." *Foreign Affairs* 33:268–81.

1956   "Soviet Agricultural Resources Reappraised." *Journal of Farm Economics* 38:258–73.

"The Pressure of Residential-Industrial Land Use." In William L. Thomas, Jr., ed., *Man's Role in Changing the Face of the Earth*. Chicago: University of Chicago Press, 881–95.

1958   "Geography in the Soviet Union." *Professional Geographer* 10:8–13.

1959   "English, French, German, and Russian as Supplementary Languages in Geographical Serials." *Geographical Review* 49:387–405.

1961   "Current Geographical Serials, 1960." *Geographical Review* 51:284–89.

1962   *Soviet Geography: Accomplishments and Tasks*. English edition edited by Chauncy D. Harris. New York: American Geographical Society.

1964   "Methods of Research in Economic Regionalization." *Geographia Polonica* 4:59–86.

1966   "Charles C. Colby, 1884–1965." *Annals of the Association of American Geographers* 56:378–82.

1968   "City and Region in the Soviet Union." Chapter 11 in R. P. Beckinsale and J. M. Houston, eds., *Urbanization and Its Problems: Essays in Honour of E. W. Gilbert*. Oxford: Blackwell.

1970   "Urbanization and Population Growth in the Soviet Union, 1959–1970." *Geographical Review* 61:102–24.

1972   *Cities of the Soviet Union: Studies in Their Functions, Size, Density, and Growth*. Chicago: Rand McNally.

1973   With Jerome D. Fellmann. "Current Geographical Serials, 1970." *Geographical Review* 63:99–105.

1976   *Bibliography of Geography*. Part 1: *Introduction to General Aids*. Chicago: University of Chicago, Department of Geography, Research Paper No. 179.

1977   "Edward Louis Ullman, 1912–1976." *Annals of the Association of American Geographers* 67:595–600.

1979   "Geography at Chicago in the 1930's and 1940's." *Annals of the Association of American Geographers* 69:21–32.

1981   With Jerome D. Fellmann. "Current Geographical Serials 1980." *Geographical Review* 71:83–90.

1982   "The Urban and Industrial Transformation of Japan." *Geographical Review* 72:50–89.

With Richard L. Edmonds. "Urban Geography in Japan: A Survey of Recent Literature." *Urban Geography* 3:1–21.

1987   "Theodore Shabad, 1922–1987." *Soviet Geography* 28:376–85.

1988   "Alfred H. Meyer, 1893–1988." *Journal of Geography* 29:653–57.

1990   "Urban Geography in the United States: My Experience of the Formative Years." *Urban Geography* 11:403–17.

"Unification of Germany in 1990." *Geographical Review* 8:170–82.

Chronology

1914   Born January 31 in Logan, Utah.

1933   Received an A.B. (with high honors, valedictorian) from Brigham Young University.

1934–37   Received a Rhodes Scholarship to study at Oxford University and the London School of Economics. Awarded a B.A. in 1936 and an M.A. in 1943 from Oxford.

1939–41   Instructor in Geography at Indiana University.

1940   Awarded a Ph.D. in geography from the University of Chicago.

1941–43   Assistant Professor of Geography at the University of Nebraska.

1942–45   Worked in the Office of the Geographer at the U.S. Department of State and in the Far East Division of the Office of Strategic Services during World War II.

1943	Assistant Professor of Geography at the University of Chicago. Published "A Functional Classification of Cities in the United States."
1945	Published "The Nature of Cities," with Edward Ullman, and "The Cities of the Soviet Union."
1947	Promoted to full Professor at the University of Chicago.
1949	Edited *Economic Geography of the USSR*.
1954–60	Appointed Dean of the Division of the Social Sciences at the University of Chicago.
1956	Received an Honorary D.Econ. from Universidad Catolica de Chile.
1956–64	Vice President of the International Geographical Union.
1957–58	President of the Association of American Geographers.
	Appointed Vice President for Academic Resources at the University of Chicago.
1962	Edited *Soviet Geography: Accomplishments and Tasks*.
1976	Received the Honors Award from the Association of American Geographers and the Laureat d'Honneur from the International Geographical Union.
1978	Received the Alexander von Humboldt Gold Medal from the Gesellschaft für Erdkunde zu Berlin.
1979	Received an Honorary LL.D. from Indiana University.
1985	Received the Cullum Geographical Medal from the American Geographical Society.
1986	Received the Master Teacher Award from the National Council for Geographic Education.
1987	Received the Victoria Medal from the Royal Geographical Society.

References

Larkin, Robert P., and Gary L. Peters. *Dictionary of Concepts in Human Geography*. Westport, Conn.: Greenwood Press.

Rodgers, Allan. 1984. "The Contributions of Chauncy Harris to Geographical Studies of the Soviet Union: An Appreciation," Chapter 1 in George J. Demko and Roland J. Fuchs, *Geographical Studies of the Soviet Union: Essays in Honor of Chauncy D. Harris*. Research Paper No. 211, University of Chicago, Department of Geography, 1–11.

David W. Harvey

One of Britain's foremost geographers is David W. Harvey of Oxford University, who was born in Kent, England, on October 31, 1935. He attended the Gillingham Grammar School for Boys in Kent, and his interest in geography started at around age eleven or twelve. According to Harvey, "I think it had a lot to do with a notion of romance with what was out there in the rest of the world, so I used to read all these books about the rest of the world. I also used to bicycle around the Kent countryside a lot. I think getting a bicycle was one of the first things that got me into the idea of actually appreciating landscape" (Peake and Jackson, 1988:6). At the age of sixteen, Harvey discovered historical maps of the British landscape and was intrigued with the process of the historical transformation of geographical landscapes. Another interesting aspect of his childhood remembrances is that he always had an urge to run away from home. "I think that all good geographers," he said, "try to run away from home!"

After passing A-levels in Geography, English Literature, and History in 1953, Harvey enrolled in St. John's College, Cambridge, the following year. He originally was interested in reading English literature at Cambridge but his ideas changed when it became evident to him that when one went to university one did not read English literature, one read critics. He said, "I always figured it was easier to read the books on your own . . . so I shifted more into geography after that" (Peake and Jackson, 1988:6).

Harvey graduated from Cambridge in 1957 with a B.A. in geography. He stayed on at Cambridge to study for a Ph.D., which he completed in 1961 with a dissertation titled "Aspects of Agricultural and Rural Change in Kent, 1800–1900." Upon leaving Cambridge in 1961, he accepted a position as Assistant Lecturer in the Department of Geography at the University of Bristol. His publications in this early part of his career focused on his previous research in Kent and on problems associated with agricultural land use. The position at Bristol was upgraded to Lecturer in 1964, and Harvey remained there until 1969.

After eight years at Bristol, Harvey decided to move on. Since the Geography Department at Bristol was one of the best in Britain, he found it very hard to think of moving from a place like Bristol to somewhere else in Britain. At the same time, he was married to an American and was tired of commuting across the Atlantic; thus he decided to take a position in the United States. In 1969 he was offered an Associate Professorship at Johns Hopkins University in Baltimore, which interested him because it had an interdisciplinary program heavily oriented towards both environmental engineering and urban problems.

In 1969 his first book was published. *Explanation in Geography* was very well received and established Harvey as one of the foremost thinkers on the philosophy and methodology of geography. While at Johns Hopkins, Harvey concentrated on issues in urban geography, as well as trying to outline his own ideas on Marxist geography. He published a variety of books and journal articles on these topics. Foremost among his books were *Social Justice and the City, The Limits to Capital, The Urbanisation of Capital*, and *Consciousness and the Urban Experience*. He looked with some skepticism on the so-called ''quantitative revolution'' in geography and the ''unfortunate gap between the scholarly studies of historical geographers and the burgeoning analytical techniques of human geographers concerned with contemporary distributions'' (Harvey, 1989:211). He was also concerned that Marx and Marxism were ''scarcely to be found in geography,'' and, therefore, tried to ''keep the flame of Marxian scholarship alive'' with his work.

Harvey remained at Johns Hopkins for eighteen years, but in 1987 was offered the position of *Halford Mackinder Professor of Geography at the University of Oxford, an offer he could not resist. In 1989 Harvey published *The Condition of Postmodernity* and is currently involved with issues of postmodernism in urban systems.

Harvey's work has brought him a variety of awards and honors. In 1960 he received a Leverhulme European Scholarship to study at Uppsala University, and in 1976 he was awarded a Guggenheim Memorial Fellowship to study the French urbanization experience in the twentieth century. He was given the Gill Memorial Award from the Royal Geographical Society (London) in 1972 for his contributions to theoretical geography, the Honours Award from the Association of American Geographers in 1980, and the Anders Retzius gold medal of the Swedish Society for Anthropology and Geography in 1989.

Selected Bibliography

1963   "Locational Change in the Kentish Hop Industry and the Analysis of Land Use Patterns." *Transactions of the Institute of British Geographers* 33:123–24.

1964   "Fruit Growing in Kent in the Nineteenth Century." *Archaeologia Cantiana* 79:95–108.

1966   "Theoretical Concepts and the Analysis of Agricultural Land-Use Patterns." *Annals of the Association of American Geographers* 56:361–74.

"Geographical Processes and the Analysis of Point Patterns: Testing Models of Diffusion by Quadrat Sampling." *Transactions of the Institute of British Geographers* 40:81–95.

1967   "Models of the Evolution of Spatial Patterns in Human Geography." In R. J. Chorley and P. Haggett, *Models in Geography*. London: Methuen.

"The Problem of Theory Construction in Geography." *Journal of Regional Science* 7:1–6.

1968   "Pattern, Process and the Scale Problem in Geographical Research." *Transactions of the Institute of British Geographers* 45:71–78.

1969   *Explanation in Geography*. London: Edward Arnold.

1970   "Social Processes and Spatial Form: An Analysis of the Conceptual Problems of Urban Planning." *Papers of the Regional Science Association* 25:47–69.

1972   "On Obfuscation in Geography: A Comment on Gale's Heterodoxy." *Geographical Analysis* 41:323–30.

1973   *Social Justice and the City*. London: Edward Arnold.

1974   With Lata Chatterjee. "Absolute Rent and the Structuring of Space by Governmental and Financial Institutions." *Antipode* 6:22–36.

"Class-monopoly Rent, Finance Capital and the Urban Revolution." *Regional Studies* 8:239–55.

"What Kind of Geography into What Kind of Public Policy." *Transactions of the Institute of British Geographers* 63:18–24.

1975   "Some Remarks on the Political Economy of Urbanism." *Antipode* 7:54–61.

"The Geography of Capitalism Accumulation: A Reconstruction of the Marxian Theory." *Antipode* 7:9–21.

1976   "The Marxian Theory of the State." *Antipode* 8:80–89.

1978   "On Countering the Marxian Myth—Chicago Style." *Comparative Urban Research* 6:28–45.

1979   "Monument and Myth." *Annals of the Association of American Geographers* 69:362–81.

1982   *The Limits of Capital*. Oxford: Basil Blackwell.

1983   "Owen Lattimore: A Memoire." *Antipode* 15:8–11.

1984   "On the History and Present Condition of Geography: An Historical Materialist Manifesto." *Professional Geographer* 36:1–11.

1985   *The Urbanisation of Capital*. Oxford: Basil Blackwell.

Consciousness and the Urban Experience. Oxford: Basil Blackwell.

1987   "The Representation of Urban Life." *Journal of Historical Geography* 13:317–21.

"Three Myths in Search of a Reality in Urban Studies." *Society and Space* 5:367–86.

"The World Systems Trap." *Studies in Comparative International Development* 22:42–47.

1988 "The Production of Value in Historical Geography." *Journal of Historical Geography* 14:305–06.

1989 "From Models to Marx." In W. MacMillan, ed., *Remodelling Geography*. Oxford: Basil Blackwell.

The Urban Experience. Oxford: Basil Blackwell.

The Condition of Postmodernity. Oxford: Basil Blackwell.

Chronology

1935 Born on October 31 in Kent, England.

1954 Enrolled at St. John's College, the University of Cambridge.

1957 Graduated from Cambridge with a B.A. in Geography and entered the Ph.D. program.

1961 Completed his Ph.D. with a dissertation titled "Aspects of Agricultural and Rural Change in Kent, 1800–1900." Appointed as an Assistant Lecturer in the Department of Geography at the University of Bristol.

1963 Published first article, "Locational Change in the Kentish Hop Industry and the Analysis of Land-Use Patterns."

1969 Appointed Associate Professor of Geography at Johns Hopkins University. Publication of first book, *Explanation in Geography*.

1972 Received the Gill Memorial Award of the Royal Geographical Society (London) for contributions to theoretical geography. Promoted to Professor of Geography at Johns Hopkins.

1973 Published *Social Justice and the City*.

1980 Received the Honours Award from the Association of American Geographers.

1982 Published *The Limits to Capital*.

1985 Published *The Urbanisation of Capital* and *Consciousness and the Urban Experience*.

1987 Appointed Halford Mackinder Professor of Geography at the University of Oxford.

1989 Awarded the Anders Retzius gold medal of the Swedish Society for Anthropology and Geography. Published *The Urban Experience* and *The Condition of Postmodernity*.

Reference

Peake, Linda, and Peter Jackson. 1988. "The Restless Analyst: An Interview with David Harvey." *Journal of Geography in Higher Education* 12:5–20.

Karl Haushofer

Karl Haushofer is a tragic figure in the historical development of geography. He is considered the father of German geopolitics, and his association during World War II with the regime of Adolf Hitler led many geographers to discount his ideas and influence during the postwar era.

Haushofer was born in Munich on August 27, 1869. He came from a conservative Bavarian aristocratic family. His grandfather, father, and uncle were all professors, and he was brought up in a stimulating intellectual environment. He was the only son of Max and Adelheld Haushofer. Karl's father was a professor of political economy at the Technical University of Munich, and his Uncle Karl, after whom he was named, was a professor of mineralogy at the same university.

In 1887, Haushofer graduated from the gymnasium and commenced a career in the military. In 1889, he became an officer in the regiment of Prince-Regent Luitpold of Bavaria. In 1896, he married Martha Mayer Doss, who became a major influence in both his professional and private life. She was a highly educated, strong-willed woman who was primarily responsible for his eventual decision to have an academic career. She was also his primary scientific collaborator and contributed to his extraordinary productivity.

Haushofer took a series of courses at the Bavarian War Academy between 1895 and 1897, and after various postings with military units, he became an instructor of modern military history in 1904. In 1906 after his first publication was critical of one of his commanders, he was reprimanded and transferred to the 3rd Division at Landau. In order to escape from this difficult situation, Haushofer took an opportunity to be posted to Japan in 1909.

According to Weigert (1942), Haushofer's stay in East Asia was the determining experience for his career as a geopolitician and geographer. As a result of his short stay in Japan, he and his wife produced their first book, *Dai Nikon*, in 1913. The book was a geographical analysis and assessment of Japan's military capability and rise toward world-power status. They produced the four hundred-page text in less than four months.

In 1913, the forty-four-year-old major enrolled as a doctoral student at the University of Munich, where he studied under the supervision of Professor Erich von Drygalskie. Haushofer obtained his doctorate a mere seven months later and graduated summa cum laude in geography, geology, and history. His dissertation was titled, "The German Contribution to the Geographical Investigation of Japan and the Sub-Japanese Region."

His studies were interrupted by active service on the Western Front during World War I, but he returned to Munich in December of 1918 and began work on the geographical development of the Japanese empire. He retired from the military in October 1919, at fifty years of age, with the rank of major general. It was also in 1919 that Haushofer met and established a friendship with Rudolf Hess. Hess became both a student and assistant of Haushofer and eventually, as Hitler's deputy, became Haushofer's patron and primary link to the Nazi regime.

In 1921, Haushofer was involved in preparing confidential reports for the German Ministry of Defense on East Asian current affairs and became recognized as Germany's foremost expert on Japan. Three years later, his career as a geographer was greatly enhanced when he became editor of *Zeitschrift für Geopolitik* and published his first book, *Geopolitics of the Pacific Ocean*.

Haushofer's concept of geopolitics was derived from the ideas of three scholars: the Swedish political scientist Rudolf Kjellen, the German geographer *Friedrich Ratzel, and the British geographer *Halford J. Mackinder. The term *geopolitik* was taken from the work of Kjellen; from Ratzel, he adopted the concepts of living space (*Lebensraum*) and "state organisms"; and from Mackinder, he adopted the idea of the seas as the source of a nation state's greatness.

According to Heske and Wesche (1988:98), "In Haushofer's analysis, the fact that Germany had slid into World War I against both the principal oceanic powers and the foremost continental power indicated an inadequate political-geographical awareness of world-scale power relationships on the part of his countrymen and their leaders." In order to educate the German people and their leaders, Haushofer developed the discipline of geopolitics and after 1919, published several hundred articles and over forty books.

Geopolitics, as defined by Haushofer in his book *Building Block of Geopolitics* (1928:27), is

the science of the conditioning of political processes by the earth. It is based on the broad foundation of geography, especially political geography, as the science of political space organisms and their structure. The essence of regions as comprehended from the geographical point of view provides the framework for geopolitics within which the course of political process must proceed if they are to succeed in the long term. . . . Geopolitics wants to and must become the geographical conscience of the state.

In order for his ideas to become the "geographical conscience of the state," it became imperative for Haushofer to popularize his ideas with both the leaders and the masses of the German people.

An important subfield of geopolitics was what Haushofer called "defense geography." In his book *Defense Geopolitics* (1932:12), he defined *defense geography* as the

science of the capability of a life form to assert itself to the extent that it relates to the earth's surface, its horizontal and vertical dimension, and its environmentally determined life, insofar as defensive capability is supported by the character of the country, its climate and manifestations determined by man, and insofar as the defense commitment shapes the landscape.

These ideas were to eventually lead to the mental mobilization for war of Nazi Germany. The idea of military strength as an important instrument of state politics is found throughout his writings.

Although Haushofer advocated the idea of a "Greater Germany" that would incorporate ethnic German areas, he said in his 1946 article on the "Defense of German Geopolitics" that he advised Hitler against further expansion after 1938. During the Nazi period, Haushofer's concepts of geopolitics were introduced into the German school system as part of the history and geography curriculum. Geopolitics also became an examination subject in German universities. His influence, however, was limited, and he deluded himself about his ability to influence the Nazi leadership. "In effect the Nazi leadership used him and his name to promote an expansionist outlook in Germany and to serve the scientific justification of German territorial claims abroad, only to limit his role after 1938 when he was no longer convenient" (Heske and Wesche, 1988:101).

Haushofer's declining years were marked by his rapidly fading influence and his increasing disillusion with the Nazi regime. He returned from the university in 1939, the same year the Nazis embarrassed and humiliated him by banning one of his books that dealt with boundaries. He came under suspicion and was interrogated by the secret state police. He was eventually placed under detention at Dachau for four weeks, and his sons were imprisoned in Berlin. His oldest son, Albrecht, was murdered by the SS in 1945. Although not arraigned at the Nuremburg Trials, Haushofer was put under pressure to apologize for his works. In 1946 he wrote "Defense of German Geopolitics" in which he tried to justify his work, and on March 10 of that year, along with his wife, he committed suicide.

Selected Bibliography

1911   "The Geographical Foundations of the Japanese Armed Forces" (Die Geographischen Grundlagen der Japanischen Wehrmacht). *Mitteilungen der Geographischen Gesellschaft in Munchen* 6:166–68.

1913   *Dai Nikon*. Berlin: E. S. Mittler.

1920   "Basic Geographical Directions in the Development of the Japanese Em-
            pire, 1854–1914" (Die Geographischen Grundrichtungen in der Entwick-
            lung des Japanischen Reiches von 1854–1914). *Geographische Zeitschrift*
            26:8–25.

1921   *The Geographical Development of the Japanese Empire*. Vienna: L. W.
            Seidel.

1924   *Geopolitics of the Pacific Ocean* (Geopolitik des Pazifischen Ozeans).
            Berlin: Kurt Vowinckel.

1928   *Building Blocks of Geopolitics* (Bausteine zur Geopolitik). Berlin: Kurt
            Vowinckel.

1929   "The State Issue in East Asia and Its Lessons for Europe" (Die Länderfrage
            in Ostasien und ihre Lehre für Europa). *Zeitschrift für Geopolitik* 6:1081–
            92.

1931   *Geopolitics of Pan-Ideas* (Geopolitik der Pan-Ideen). Berlin: Zentral.

1932   *Defense Geopolitics* (Wehr-Geopolitik). Berlin: Junker und Dünnhaupt.

1946   "Defence of German Geopolitics." In E. A. Walsh, *Total Power*. Garden
            City, N.Y.: Doubleday.

Chronology

1869   Born in Munich, August 27.

1887   Graduated from Royal Maxmillian Gymnasium; joined the regiment of
            Prince-Regent Luitpold of Bavaria.

1906   Published first article, which analyzed a military maneuver.

1913   Published first book, *Dai Nikon*; enrolled at the University of Munich and
            completed a doctorate in geography (summa cum laude).

1921   Became Honorarprofessor (extraordinary professor) at the University of
            Munich.

1924   Publication of *Geopolitik des Pazifischen Ozeans*; visited Hess and met
            Hitler in Landsberg prison.

1930   Became Fellow of the American Geographic Society.

1931   Publication of *Geopolitik der Pan-Ideen*.

1932   Publication of *Wehr-Geopolitik*.

1934–37   President of the Germany Academy.

1938   Participated in the Munich Conference and claimed to have counseled Hitler
            against further expansion.

1944   Was interrogated by the Gestapo after the plot on Hitler's life and was
            temporarily imprisoned, as were his sons.

1946   Karl and Martha Haushofer committed suicide at their country estate,
            Hartschimmelhof, March 10.

References

Heske, Henning, and Rolf Wesche. 1988. "Karl Haushofer." *Geographers Biobiblio-graphical Studies* 12:95–106.
Weigert, H. W. 1942. "Haushofer and the Pacific." *Foreign Affairs* 20:732–42.

Herodotus

Herodotus was born in Halicarnassus [known now as Bodrum] on the Aegean coast of Turkey in 484 B.C., and was possibly of mixed Carian-Greek descent. His father's name was Carian, and the family seems to have been in good standing in the community. His parents were called Lyxes and Dryo, and he had a brother, Theodoros. Halicarnassus was on the edge of the Greek world at the time, so it was in many ways influential on the views of history and geography that Herodotus would develop. As Evans (1982:3) commented, "Yet to be born in Halicarnassus was probably to be something of an outsider. The city was a Dorian foundation, but not a member of the Dorian Pentapolis."

After some problems with a failed *putsch* in which Herodotus was involved, he began a period of exile on Samos, where he probably began his serious historical research. Rich in engineering works and historical interest, Samos apparently provided a stimulus that had been missing before in Herodotus's life. After his stay on Samos, he returned to Halicarnassus and expelled Lygdamis, the tyrannical ruler, only to leave again as a result of his own unpopularity. According to Evans (1982:4), "He was now a Greek without a state, and when the colony of Thurii was founded in south Italy, he went there, and became a citizen." It is possible, though not known with certainty, that he later died there.

However, and of particular significance for geographers, we know that Herodotus travelled widely, visiting such places as Egypt, Babylon, the Ukraine, and Italy, always observing and reflecting on what he saw. Though generally identified as a historian, his work must also be considered part of classical geography. His *History* begins with the Greek struggle with the barbarians and ends with the Greek capture of the Hellespont.

In addition to its historical content, the work is rich in descriptions of places and local cultures, however, giving it its geographical dimension. Kish (1978) provides several examples of Herodotus's geographical writings. Herodotus was also aware, at least to some degree, of the operation of physical processes on the landscape. For example, he wrote of how the Nile delta must have been built and hypothesized that winds tended to blow from cooler to warmer places. His use of logic to establish and test ideas about natural processes was exceptional, even though some of his ideas may have been subsequently refuted by more accurate scientific methods.

One puzzling event contemplated by Herodotus, among many earlier writers and thinkers, was the regularity of summer floods in the Nile River. The Nile would rise quickly in May, reach a peak flow in September, then decline to its lowest flow during the following April, completely out of phase with the behavior of other known rivers of the time, including the Tigris and Euphrates. After rejecting all of the explanations that he could find to date for this phenomenon, Herodotus offered his own hypothesis, based on the widely accepted idea of symmetry in the order of the natural world. If the Danube had its course in western Europe, then, he believed, the source of the Nile must also be far to the west of what was then called Libya. Given these relative locations of rivers, he argued that in winter the sun's more southerly course put it more directly above the Nile, causing substantial evaporation and decreased flow during the winter months. During the summer, however, as the sun moved northward to diminish the flow of the other known rivers, the Nile, now cooler, could flourish and reach its annual peak. Though not quite the way a physical geographer might explain this to a class today, it shows Herodotus's ability to employ logic in the solution of a problem within the limited observations of his day.

Selected Bibliography

429 B.C.   *History of the Persian Wars.*

Chronology

484 B.C.   Born in Halicarnassus, in what is now known as the town of Bodrum, on the Aegean coast of Turkey.

454–450 B.C.   Exiled to island of Samos.

440–444 B.C.   Returned to Halicarnassus and expelled tyrant, Lygdamis. Finding he was unpopular in the city, he left.

443 B.C.   Travelled to the new colony of Thurii, in southern Italy, which promised citizenship and a land grant.

430–424 B.C.   Publishes his *History*. Written after his journeys, from memories and notes.

424 B.C.   Died.

References

Evans, J.A.S. 1982. *Herodotus*. Boston: Twayne.
Kish, George, ed. 1978. *A Source Book in Geography*. Cambridge, Mass.: Harvard University Press.

Alfred Hettner

Alfred Hettner was an important figure in the development of geography in Germany and was probably the only geographer of his generation to enter the university with the intention of becoming a geographer. He was born in Dresden on August 6, 1859, one of fourteen children. His father, Hermann Hettner, was a renowned historian of art and literature. He was a gifted child and easily passed through the gymnasium, finishing at the top of his class with an ''outstanding'' designation.

Hettner entered the University at Halle in 1877, where he studied under Alfred Kirchoff, who gave him his first introduction to geography. While at Halle, he also studied with the geologist K. von Fretsch and the philosopher Rudolf Haym. Hettner was the first student in Germany to enter the university with the goal of becoming a geographer. After only a year at Halle, Hettner transferred to the University of Bonn. It was there that he came under the influence of Theobald Fischer, who encouraged him to do research on the climate of Chile. In 1879, he transferred once again, this time to work on his doctoral studies at Strassburg to study with Georg Gerlard. He took his doctorate in 1881 for a thesis entitled, ''The Climate of Chile and West Patagonia.''

In 1882, Hettner was offered the position of private tutor in the home of the British Ambassador to Colombia, but the ambassador did not like Bogotá, and after having paid Hettner a considerable sum, returned to England in March 1883 leaving Hettner with over a year, until August 1884, to travel in South America. After extensive trips in South America and a brief stay in the eastern United States, he returned in September 1884 to Germany. The results of these excursions in South America were published as the book *Travels in the Colombian Andes* (1888) as well as appearing in a variety of scientific articles.

For the next four years, Hettner lived in Dresden and Leipzig. For his prospective professorial dissertation, or *habilitation*, he submitted the results of research on the geomorphology of the Saxon highlands. Hettner's research was supervised by *Friedrich Ratzel, and his degree was granted in 1887.

After having completed his work for Ratzel and having taught at Leipzig for only one semester, Hettner returned to extensive travels in South America to work for the famous German ethnologist Adolf Bastran. Hettner was to collect items for the Ethnological Museum in Berlin. This time his journeys lasted more than two-and-a-half years, and he reported the progress of his trip in letters to *Ferdinand von Richthofen, which were published in the *Proceedings of the Geographical Society in Berlin* from 1888 to 1890. Unfortunately, Hettner suffered a setback due to health problems; he suffered hardship and sickness in his journeys and contracted atrophy of the leg muscles, which affected his walking ability for the rest of his life.

Hettner returned to Leipzig in 1891, where he taught a course on South America and where he remained until 1897. In 1895, he accepted an offer by the B. G. Teubnes Press to be editor of a geographical journal, the *Geographische Zeitschrift*. In January 1895, the first of twelve yearly issues appeared, and in the foreword Hettner wrote:

It (the journal) will serve first of all scientific research, but will contain no specialized work which can only be understood by specialists and is of interest only to them. Rather, it will deal only with basic questions and summarize the results of scientific research in generally comprehensible and entirely fluent presentation. (Vol. 1, 18–19)

In 1897, Hettner undertook one of several field tours in Europe. His first trip, a journey through Russia to the Caucasus resulted in the publication of his book *European Russia* (1905), which was translated into Russian several times and underwent four editions in Germany. Trips outside of Europe also took him to a variety of places, in "1908 to Egypt, in 1911 to Algeria and Tunisia, and . . . in 1913 to Asia" (Plewe, 1982:58).

In 1899, Hettner accepted a position as an associate professor at the University of Heidelberg. He founded the Geographical Institute and was awarded the rank of full professor in 1906. His research progressed on a variety of fronts. World War I made him focus on political geography. According to Plewe (1982:58), "In his work Hettner had always been concerned with political problems of the contemporary world and now he devoted himself almost entirely to political geography, on which he wrote numerous articles." In 1916, Hettner founded the series *Theatres of the War*, enlarged his old work to include the Russian Empire (1916), wrote a book on *England's World Dominance and the War* (1915), and another on *The Peace and Germany's Future* (1917). Hettner also emphasized regional studies. A large regional volume on Europe had been published in 1907. This book was a compromise between a textbook and a handbook. Hettner did not resume publications on regional studies until 1923, when he reduced his old work on Europe and began similar volumes on non-European regions. Hettner's procedure for studying and writing about regions was quite straightforward. "His arrangement of material moves from general to specialized elements, i.e., from the continent as a whole to its major regions, and then finally to the individual component regions. For each section Hettner supplies brief statements about the history and the current state of research, as well as reference to the most important literature and maps" (Plewe, 1982:58). As a result of these regional studies, Hettner brought attention to, and recognition of, the chorological, or spatial, principle in geography.

According to Plewe (1982:58), however, the "work which created for Hettner his unmistakable place in the history of geography—*Geography: Its History, Its Nature, and Its Methods* (1927)—grew out of numerous articles in the *Geographische Zeitschrift*." Hettner maintained that geography was concerned with the spatial arrangement of terrestrial things, which is unlike the systematic sciences that are based on separate categories of things, or the historical sciences, which focus on separate categories of things or sequences of human events.

Although Hettner returned from the University at Heidelberg in 1928, he continued his research and publication efforts. Unfortunately, because he was ostracized as a "quarter-Jew" under the Third Reich, he was not allowed to continue to publish. After his death in 1941, however, several of his works were published posthumously. These works included *A Geography of Man*, which was published in three volumes as *General Human Geography* (1947) and *Transport Geography* (1952) both edited by H. Schmitthenner, and *Economic Geography* (1957) edited by E. Plewe.

Also as a result of his contributions to geography, Hettner was awarded the Collum Gold Medal by the American Geographical Society in 1929. The inscription on the medal said, "Alfred Hettner for regional studies that are admirably proportioned and informed with experience as explorer, editor, and teacher." In 1935, Hettner was made an honorary member of the Geographical Society in Dresden.

Hettner also had a profound influence on his students and developed close personal relationships with many of them. Out of some thirty men who took their doctorates under him, eleven became professional geographers and several others attained chairs in related fields, particularly geology. Hettner's contributions are eloquently summed up by Plewe (1982:59): "If one attempts to express Hettner's significance in a single sentence, the following could be said: he consolidated geography as a science, he sought out its place in the system of sciences and placed it there solidly with his own work and work which he inspired."

Selected Bibliography

1885   "The Sierra Nevada of Santa Marta." *Petermanns Geographischen Mitteilungen* 31:92–97.

1888   "The Cartographic Results of a Trip to the Colombian Andes." *Petermanns Geographischen Mitteilungen* 34:104–12.

1891   "The Southernmost Part of Brazil: Rio Grande do sul." *Zeitschrift der Gesellschaft für Erdkunde Berlin* 26:85–144.

1893   "The Andes of Western Colombia: An Orographical Sketch." *Petermanns Geographischen Mitteilungen* 39:129–36.

1905   *European Russia: A Study in Human Geography*. Leipzig-Berlin.

1915   *England's World Domination and the War*. Leipzig.

1917   *The Peace and Germany's Future*. Stuttgart.

1927   *Geography: Its History, Its Nature and Its Methods*. Breslau.

1929   "Geopolitics and Political Geography: And the Position and Methods of Economic Geography." *Geographische Zeitschrift* 35:332–45.

1930   *The Climates of the Earth*. Leipzig.

1933   *Comparative Regional Geography*. Vol. 1: *The Earth, Land, Ocean, the Structure and Major Formations of the Earth*. Leipzig.

        Comparative Regional Geography. Vol. 2: *The Surface of the Earth*. Leipzig.

1934   *Comparative Regional Geography*. Vol. 3: *The Water Bodies of the Earth; The Climates of the Earth*. Leipzig.

        Comparative Regional Geography. Vol. 4: *The Plant World; The Animal World; Mankind; World Regions*. Leipzig.

Chronology

1859   Born in Dresden, August 6.

1879   Went to Strasbourg to study for his doctorate.

1882–84   Travelled in South America.

1884   Returned to Leipzig to study with Richthofen and later with Ratzel.

1888   Returned to South America; travelled in Peru, Chile, Argentina, Uruguay, and southern Brazil.

1890   Appointed as an assistant professor in Leipzig and promoted in 1894 to "extraordinary" professor.

1895   Became editor of the new journal *Geographische Zeitschrift* and wrote part of the text for the Spamer atlas.

1899   Accepted appointment as Associate Professor at the University of Heidelberg.

1905   Publication of *European Russia: A Study in Human Geography*.

1915   Publication of *England's World Dominance and the War*.

1917   Publication of *The Peace and Germany's Future*.

1927   Publication of *Geography: Its History, Its Nature and Its Methods*.

1930   Publication of *The Climates of the Earth*.

1933–35   His four-volume *Comparative Regional Geography* series was published.

1935   Forced by the National Socialist Nazi government to relinquish his work as editor of the *Geographische Zeitschrift*.

1941   Died August 31 at Heidelberg.

Reference

Plewe, Ernst. 1982. "Alfred Hettner." *Geographers Biobibliographical Studies* 6:55–63.

Alexander von Humboldt

Alexander von Humboldt, who, together with *Carl Ritter, founded modern geography in Germany in the nineteenth century, was born in Berlin on September 14, 1769. His father, Major Alexander Georg von Humboldt, an officer in the Prussian army, died only ten years later. Young Alexander and his older brother Wilhelm were left to be raised by their mother.

Alexander and Wilhelm received their early education from tutors, who gave the brothers an excellent foundation in classical languages and mathematics, and young Alexander looked forward to a career in the army. Gradually, however, he developed an interest in the sciences and decided to further his education, urged on by a mother who protested his interest in a military career. His first university experience began in 1789 at the University of Göttingen, where he met Georg Forster, who had just returned for a voyage around the world with *Captain James Cook. In 1790 the two travelled together down the Rhine and across to England, a trip that undoubtedly stimulated Humboldt's interest in geography. He took numerous notes along the journey, and published from them a book, *Mineralogische Beobachtungen über einige Basalte am Rhein*, in that same year.

Humboldt decided that minerals interested him, so he went to study at the School of Mines in Freiberg (1791–92), where he studied under well-known geologist A. G. Werner. In 1792 Humboldt was appointed ''Assessor cum voto'' in the Prussian Department of Mines, where he continued to be fascinated with geology and landforms. He worked his way up to supervisor-in-chief in 1795, and along the way was able to travel to Italy and Switzerland. However, after his mother died in 1796, Humboldt gave up his position to pursue his interest in natural science. Aided by a small inheritance, he was free to travel and study.

Humboldt's first major overseas voyage was to South America in 1799 with a French botanist, Aimé Bonpland. They travelled first to Venezuela, then some 1,700 miles up the Orinoco River. Along the way Humboldt prepared maps, made measurements of latitude and longitude, collected specimens, and took notes. The two travelled along the Andes in Colombia, Ecuador, and Peru; went north to Mexico; sailed on to Cuba; and finally visited the United States. After five years of travel, they headed back to Europe on June 30, 1804.

Humboldt returned to Berlin, but after Napoleon defeated the Prussians in the Battle of Jena in 1806, he decided to move on, first to Italy and then to Paris. There he stayed for nearly two decades, working to publish the results of his five years of field studies in the Americas. The work grew into thirty volumes, published between 1805 and 1834 under the general title *Voyage aux Régions Équinoxiales du Nouveau Continent*. This work impressed the scholarly world of the day considerably, especially the last few volumes. According to *Preston James and Geoffrey Martin (1981:121):

*Charles Darwin said later that he had read and reread this account of scientific travels and that it had changed the whole course of his life. . . . For a world emerging from the first shock produced by the impact of the discoveries, Humboldt's books were like a fresh breeze because they were filled not only with the excitement of travel in strange places, but also with the reports of careful scientific investigation, the seeking of answers to questions about the interconnections among the phenomena grouped together in rich diversity on the face of the earth.

Humboldt returned to Berlin in 1827, where he secured a position as chamberlain in the court of the Prussian king. In 1827–28 he gave a series of lectures, the *Kosmos* lectures, at the University of Berlin. These lectures were accepted enthusiastically by the audiences. In the following year, he travelled in Russia and Siberia from April until nearly the end of December, and he was received with enthusiasm wherever he went. Among other observations, he was fascinated with temperatures during this trip, and discovered permafrost as well.

During the last years of his life Humboldt was committed to producing his greatest work, a summing up of what he had learned, written in such a way that it would have broad appeal. The plan had been developed earlier in the *Kosmos* lectures. This vast work, *Kosmos: Entwurf einer Physischen Weltbeschreibung*, was published in four volumes. The first volume was published in 1845, when Humboldt was already seventy-six years old, and the last appeared posthumously in 1862. In his introduction, he wrote, "The most important aim of all physical science is this: to recognise unity in diversity, to comprehend all the single aspects as revealed by the discoveries of the last epochs, to judge single phenomena separately without surrendering to their bulk, and to grasp nature's essence under the cover of outward appearances" (cited in Dickinson, 1967: 29).

Though his earlier health had been excellent, as was evidenced by his rigorous travels, Humboldt had a stroke in 1857, then died on May 6, 1859. According to Dickinson (1967:31):

Specialists have recognised Humboldt's important contributions to their particular fields. What has not been so generally recognised among English-speaking scholars, is Humboldt's insistence on the areal associations of diverse categories of physical and human phenomena. This is his contribution to geographic knowledge and the discipline of geography. In this respect he was a pioneer and well ahead of his times and resources.

Selected Bibliography

1811–22   *Political Essay on the Kingdom of New Spain*. Translated by J. Black. 4 vols. London.

1815   *Researches Concerning the Institutions and Monuments of the Ancient Inhabitants of America*. Translated by H. M. Williams. 2 vols. London.

1818–23   *Personal Narrative of Travels to the Equinoctial Regions of the New Continent During the Years 1799–1804*. Translated by H. M. Williams. 7 vols. London.

1823   *A Geognostical Essay on the Superposition of Rocks in Both Hemispheres*. Translated from French. London.

1845–62   *Cosmos: Sketch of a Physical Description of the Universe*. Translated by E. Sabine. 4 vols. London.

1847   *Views of Nature*. Translated by E. C. Otté and H. G. Bohn. London.

1849   *Aspects of Nature*. Translated by E. Sabine. 2 vols. London.

1852–69   *Personal Narrative of Travels to the Equinoctial Regions of America During the Years 1799–1804*. Translated by T. Ross. 3 vols. London.

1871–83   *Cosmos*. Translated by E. C. Otté and others. London.

Chronology

1769   Born in Berlin.

1789   Attended University of Göttingen, studying physics, philology, and archaeology.

1790   Began a hiking trip down the Rhine to the Netherlands and then took a ship to England.

1791   Attended School of Mines at Freiberg in Saxony, where he studied physics, chemistry, geology, and mining.

1792   Appointed inspector and later director of mines in the Prussian state of Franconia.

1793   First scientific paper published.

1797   Resigned from his government position in preparation for travelling. On June 4 sailed from Spain to visit South America. This trip lasted five years.

1800   Mapped 1725 miles of the Orinoco River.

1801   Arrived in Colombia to begin exploration of the Andes of Colombia, Equador, and Peru. For the first time, established altitudes with an aneroid barometer and recorded temperatures with a thermometer.

1802	Climbed to the 19,286-foot level of Mt. Chimborazo (alt. 20,561 feet), the highest altitude that had been reached by humans. This record held for twenty-nine years.
1803	Arrived in Acapulco. Updated population figures for Mexico by consulting parish priests.
1804	Sailed to Havana, Cuba. Arrived in Philadelphia in May. From June 1 to 13, he was in Washington, D.C., where he had many meetings with Thomas Jefferson. Sailed for France on June 30. Lived in Paris until 1827.
1827	Moved to Berlin. Post as Chamberlain to the King of Prussia.
1828	Lectured at the Royal Academy of Sciences in Berlin.
1829	Travelled by coach to Siberia at the invitation of the czar to explore the mineral resources. Urged the czar to set up a network of climate stations across the continent, where data could be recorded. (By 1835, this was done from St. Petersburg to an island off Alaska.)
1834	Began outline of *Cosmos*.
1845	Publication of the first two volumes of *Cosmos*.
1859	Died.

References

Dickinson, Robert E. 1969. *The Makers of Modern Geography*. New York: Praeger.
James, Preston E., and Geoffrey J. Martin. 1981. *All Possible Worlds: A History of Geographical Ideas*. 2d ed. New York: Wiley.

Ellsworth Huntington

One of the most controversial figures in the development of geographical thought in America was Ellsworth Huntington. He lived and worked during the formative years of geography in the United States. The author of 28 books, parts of 29 others, and over 240 scholarly articles, Huntington was one of the most prolific American geographers. He has been severely criticized both during his time and since his death, but *Chauncy D. Harris was probably correct when he said, "Most people who criticize him have never read his work."

Huntington was born in Galesburg, Illinois, on September 16, 1876, the third of six children born to Henry Strong and Mary Lawrence Huntington. His father was an ordained minister of the Congregational Church and had a great influence on his son. Huntington attended grade school in Gorham, Maine, and from all accounts was an excellent student. At the age of twelve, his father moved to Milton, a suburb of Boston, to become a pastor at a local church. Huntington attended Milton High School and graduated near the top of his class in 1893. On July 18, 1892, he passed the Harvard entrance examinations in elementary Latin and Greek, advanced Latin and Greek, French, and Plane Geometry. Although he had planned on entering Harvard, his family could not afford the cost of a Harvard education and sent him instead to Beloit College in Wisconsin, where he could live with his aunt, Theresa Gaytes.

Huntington started his undergraduate career at Beloit in September 1893, one of eighteen members of the class of 1897. He was an excellent student at Beloit and was influenced by his much-travelled cousin, Frederic Gulliver, who was a geologist and a founding member of the Association of American Geographers. Although Beloit did not offer any geography courses, the college had a very good geology program. Huntington graduated in the fiftieth graduating class from Beloit with a Bachelor of Arts degree in 1897. According to Professor Collie (Martin, 1973:10), he "took high rank as a student here, especially in science. At graduation he ranked among the first scholars of his class."

On September 24, 1897, Huntington was offered a position as assistant to the president of Euphrates College, in Harpoot, Turkey. Euphrates College, a religious school associated with the American Board of Commissioners for Foreign Missions, had seven hundred students and twenty faculty. Huntington taught English and the Christian religion, as well as geology and geography. He also conducted research on the geology of the Harpoot Group of Mountains in Turkey and maintained a regular meteorological station at the college, from which the data was used to publish two articles in the *Monthly Weather Review*. He continued to pursue his mapmaking interests and, in April 1901, satisfied his desire to travel, when he floated 190 miles down the Euphrates River on a raft.

A few weeks after his trip down the Euphrates, Huntington was notified that he had been awarded a Harvard University Townsend Scholarship. He entered Harvard University in 1901 and took courses toward a Master of Arts degree in the Division of Geology. During that year he also published two articles about his trip on the Euphrates. His principal mentor at Harvard was *William Morris Davis, and with his encouragement, Huntington earned the Master of Arts degree. After spending a couple of years travelling and doing research in Asia, Huntington was awarded the Edward William Hooper Fellowship to continue his studies at Harvard under Davis. Although the results of his research in Asia were published in a variety of geographical and geological journals, Huntington still had to write a thesis. Huntington passed his preliminary examinations for the Ph.D. with a unanimous vote, but on May 25, 1907, when he took his final examination, he failed. Although he had established himself as one of the most published and travelled men in the history of American geography, one member of his Ph.D. committee at Harvard was not satisfied with Huntington's work, which was the reason for the failure.

Fortunately for Huntington, he was offered a position as instructor at Yale University in 1907. During that same year, his first book, *The Pulse of Asia*, was published and was very well received. The dedication of the book read "To William Morris Davis, First of Modern Geographers." During these early years at Yale, Huntington made formal application for the Ph.D. degree and it was conferred upon him in June 1909.

Besides teaching courses such as "Geography of Europe," "Anthropogeography," and "Geographic Controls in History," Huntington was also an active scholar. From 1905 to 1917, he published three books, *The Pulse of Asia, Palestine and Its Transformation*, and *Asia: A Geography Reader*, and many journal articles and gave numerous public addresses and papers before the Association of American Geographers. According to his biographer, Geoffrey Martin (1973:77):

During these years Huntington formulated, analyzed, and developed two ideas which were destined to become associated with his life's work. The first of these ideas was that of the occurrence of climatic pulsations within historic time. . . . The second of his very large ideas developed at this time involved the notion that there exists a climatic optimum for the human being, regardless of that being's race.

In 1912 Huntington requested a promotion to a professorship at Yale. For a variety of reasons, the promotion was denied but his appointment was extended for two years. In 1915 he severed his connection with Yale University and returned to his parents' home in Milton, Massachusetts. At the age of thirty-nine, and probably at the height of his creativity, he was unemployed. He wrote several human geography textbooks, specifically for the high school and college audience, in order to have some financial support.

After the outbreak of World War I, Huntington was commissioned a captain in the Military Intelligence Division. The primary work of his division was to gather information about the countries where the United States might have to conduct military operations. He left the Military Intelligence Division after the war, in 1919, to accept a research associate position in geography at Yale University.

Upon his return to Yale, Huntington was offered a very small salary. He had been offered professorships at several major universities, including Michigan, Wisconsin, and Minnesota, that would have included a much higher salary than he was offered at Yale, but he decided to return to Yale and try to develop a geography department within the university—a formidable task that was ultimately unsuccessful.

During the twenties, Huntington was a prolific scholar authoring or coauthoring ten books and seventy-five articles or chapters of books. His contributions to the development of geographic science were quite substantial (Martin, 1973:237):

He was one of the first geographers in the United States to insist upon the worth of the isopleth, to investigate cycles effectively, to insist upon mathematical measurement rather than inaccurate generalization, and to use the correlation coefficient extensively. He authored the first substantial textbook concerning the principles of human geography in the United States; he provided four textbooks enabling the field of economic geography to take hold; and authored several other books dealing with the general principles of geography, the effects of climate,and the nature and causes of climatic change.

Huntington's books were widely used throughout the United States at the high school and university levels.

Huntington was a founding member of the Association of American Geographers and was elected its president in 1923. Between 1904 and 1941, he delivered a total of eighteen papers at the association's annual meetings. He contributed more articles to *The Geographical Review* than any other geographer between 1902 and 1922. Besides teaching at Yale for forty years, he taught in summer schools at Chicago (1931), Clark (1932), and Harvard (1940).

Huntington had many critics, particularly those who attacked his "deterministic" views and the fact that he ventured into fields other than his own. According to Martin (1973:250), "It is probably not too much to say that Huntington was the most controversial figure in United States geography in the first half of the twentieth century." Although Huntington has been labeled as an "environmental determinist," a careful reading of his works reveals that he did not think climate was nearly all-determining. In the preface to *The Human Habitat* (1927:vi) Huntington wrote, "Physical environment never compels man to do anything: the compulsion lies in his own nature. But the environment does say that some courses of conduct are permissible and others impossible." Six years later in *Economic and Social Geography* (1933:16), he states that "geographic environment merely offers opportunities to man. Man's own will determines which of the various opportunities he will accept, and how far he will go in using them."

Huntington continued to publish during the thirties and early forties. One of his major works, *Mainsprings of Civilization*, was published in 1945. After a heart attack in October 1946, Huntington returned to work by January 1947, but he died on October 17 of that year.

Selected Bibliography

1898	"On the Road in Turkey." *The Round Table* 19:184–86; 193–96.
1900	"Electric Phenomena in the Euphrates Valley," *Monthly Weather Review* 28:286–87.
	"The Climate of Harpoot, Turkey in Asia." *Monthly Weather Review* 29:250–53.
1902	"Through the Great Canon of the Euphrates River." *The Geographical Journal* 20:175–200.
1903	"The Hittite Ruins of Hilar, Asia Minor." *Records of the Past* 2:131–40.
1905	"With a Minbashi in Turkestan." *Appalachia* 11:17–27.
	"The Mountains of Turkestan." *The Geographical Journal* 25:22–40, 139.
	"The Mountains and Kibitkas of Tian Shan." *Bulletin of the American Geographical Society* 37:513–30.
1907	*The Pulse of Asia*. Boston: Houghton Mifflin.
1910	"The Fringe of Verdure Around Asia Minor." *National Geographic Magazine* 21:761–75.
1912	"The New Science of Geography." *Yale Review* 2:82–96.
1913	"Changes of Climate and History." *American Historical Review* 18:213–32.
1915	*Civilization and Climate*. New Haven: Yale University Press.
1919	*The Red Man's Continent*. New Haven: Yale University Press.
	"The Future of Palestine." *Geographical Review* 7:24–35.
1920	With Sumner W. Cushing. *Principles of Human Geography*. New York: Wiley.
1922	With Frank E. Williams. *Business Geography*. New York: Wiley.

1927	*The Human Habitat*. New York: Van Nostrand.
1932	"Capacity and Heredity." *Eugenical News* 17:78–80.
1933	With F. E. Williams and Samuel Van Valkenburg. *Economic and Social Geography*. New York: Wiley.
1935	"Climatic Pulsations." *Geografiska Annaler* 16:571–607.
	"On Boundaries." *Annals of the Association of American Geographers* 25:134–35.
	Tomorrow's Children: The Goal of Eugenics. New York: Wiley.
1940	*Principles of Economic Geography*. New York: Wiley.
1943	"The Geography of Human Productivity." *Annals of the Association of American Geographers* 33:1–31.
1945	*Mainsprings of Civilization*. New York: Wiley.

Chronology

1876	Born in September 16 in Galesburg, Illinois.
1893	Graduated from Milton High School.
1897	Awarded the B.A. from Beloit College and took position as assistant to the president at Euphrates College, Harpoot, Turkey.
1898	Published first two articles in *Monthly Weather Review*.
1901	Entered Harvard University in the M.A. program in geology.
1907	Failed Ph.D. exam at Harvard University and published *The Pulse of Asia*.
1913	Elected First Vice President of the Association of American Geographers.
1916	Elected President of the Ecological Society of America.
1923	Elected President of the Association of American Geographers.
1927	Published *The Human Habitat*.
1933	Published *Economic and Social Geography*.
1934	Elected President of the American Eugenics Society.
1942	Received the Distinguished Service to Geography Award from the National Council of Geography Teachers.
1945	Published *Mainsprings of Civilization*.
1946	Awarded Honorary Doctorate of Science from Beloit College.
	Awarded Honorary D.Litt. from Clark University.
1947	Died on October 17.

Reference

Martin, Geoffrey J. 1973. *Ellsworth Huntington: His Life and Thought*. Hamden, Conn.: Archon Books.

Preston Everett James

Preston James was one of the strongest and most colorful influences in American geography during the middle of the twentieth century. Born in Brookline, Massachusetts, on February 14, 1899, he came from a well-to-do family where education was considered very important. He enrolled at Miss Pierce's Elementary School in Brookline and in 1911 was sent to the Noble and Greenough Preparatory School, where he received a classical education. Upon graduation from this school he was awarded the Edward Revere Little Medal for outstanding achievement.

In September 1916, James entered Harvard University, where he was planning to study English with the noted Shakespearean scholar George Kittredge. After taking a course in physiography from *Wallace W. Atwood, however, James changed his mind and decided to prepare for a career in geography. During his summers at Harvard, he participated in several geological field excursions. He graduated from Harvard in 1920 with a B.A. in geology and the following year was awarded the M.A. in climatology.

In 1921 James left Harvard to enroll in the geography program at Clark University. Atwood, his teacher at Harvard, had been appointed President and Director of the newly formed Graduate School of Geography at Clark, and James decided to do his doctoral work there. Atwood insisted that students in geography at Clark should have a regional specialization, and in response, James went on an extensive field reconnaissance trip to Latin America. This journey was to provide him with his dissertation topic, "Geographic Factors in the Development of Transportation in South America," and several articles that were soon published in geographical journals. According to Martin (1987:64), "This seems to have been the first dissertation from a geography department in the United States which dealt with the whole of Latin America."

James completed his doctoral degree in 1923 and accepted a position on the geography faculty at the University of Michigan, where his primary duty was to teach the introductory class. Armed with notes on such a class developed by *Carl Sauer, James proved to be an enthusiastic teacher. In 1924, along with R. B. Ball, he published *Outline for a Course on the Principles of Geography*, and by 1929 this work had evolved into his book *Regional Geography: A Chorographical Study of the World*, which was followed by *An Outline of Geography*, published in 1935.

While at Michigan, James also became involved in a variety of field research projects, including trips to Trinidad (1924), Canada (1926), Brazil (1930), Central and South America (1930–31), Brazil (1938), Portugal, France, and England (1938), and Mexico (1940). Numerous publications came out of these trips, mostly dealing with Latin America or the regional concept. James was also extensively involved with the work of the Association of American Geographers during these years. He was elected Councillor (1934–35) and Secretary (1936–41). Besides travelling in the summer, he taught at Clark University (1928), Stanford University (1933), the University of Wisconsin (1937), the University of Texas (1940), and Harvard University (1941).

During World War II, James was called to Washington to become part of the Research and Analysis Branch of the Office of Strategic Services (O.S.S.). He was appointed as Chief of the Latin American Division until 1943, and then Chief of the Geographic Division of the Europe-Africa section. During this time he also published a textbook on Latin America. With this book, according to Jensen (1986:274):

James achieved international renown with his monumental *Latin America*, published in 1942, a book long considered the best regional geography textbook in English. It was the product of nearly twenty years of field observation and reading by the first geographer to adopt a continental-scale approach to understanding Latin America. That the fifth edition should have appeared at the end of 1985, just a month before his death, is eloquent testimony to the book's success in interpreting the region for more than four decades.

In 1945, James was invited by *George Cressey to join the geography department at Syracuse University. During his twenty-three years at Syracuse, James published sixteen books and approximately seventy articles and helped build the geography program. He continued to be involved with the affairs of the Association of American Geographers (A.A.G.) and served as President in 1951 and Honorary President in 1966. In order to celebrate the fiftieth anniversary of the A.A.G., James was asked, along with C. F. Jones, to edit a volume on the evolution of geography in the United States. This volume, *American Geography: Inventory and Prospect*, has become a classic.

James served as chairman at Syracuse from 1950 to 1968 and retired in 1969. As an Emeritus Professor, he continued his scholarly pursuits. He turned his attention to the historical development of geography from classical to modern times. As a result, he published *All Possible Worlds, A History of Geographical Ideas*, which capped his long scholarly career.

James received numerous awards for his contributions to geography from the American Geographical Society, the Royal Geographical Society, the Association of American Geographers, the National Council for Geographic Education, and the Pan American Institute of Geography and History. He was elected an honorary member of the Geographical Society of the U.S.S.R. and received honorary degrees from Eastern Michigan University (1967), Clark University (1968), Syracuse University (1973), and the University of Michigan (1974).

In 1971 *D. W. Meinig edited *On Geography: Selected Writings of Preston E. James*, which had twenty-two of James's writings and included a bibliography of his works. In 1980, D. J. Robinson edited *Studying Latin America: Essays in Honor of Preston E. James*, which included six essays by Latin American scholars as well as a biographical assessment of James. In the introduction to *On Geography*, Richard Hartshorne summed up James's contributions, "As one who has experienced with him a half-century in the profession, I can testify that during that period his role has been outstanding, his total impact second to none." Preston E. James died on January 5, 1986, in his eighty-seventh year at Honolulu.

Selected Bibliography

1922   "The Geographic Setting of the Tacna-Arica Dispute." *Journal of Geography* 121:339–48.

1924   "The Possibilities of Cattle Production in Venezuela." *Bulletin of the Geographical Society of Philadelphia* 22:45–46.

1925   "Geographic Factors in the Development of Transportation in South America." *Economic Geography* 1:247–61.

1927   "Iquique and the Atacama Desert." *Scottish Geographical Magazine* 43:203–15.

1929   *Regional Geography: A Chorographical Study of the World.* 2 vols. Mimeographed by Edward Brothers, Ann Arbor, Mich.

1932   "The Coffee Lands of Southeastern Brazil." *Geographical Review* 22:225–44.

1933   "Rio de Janeiro and Sao Paulo." *Geographical Review* 213:271–98.

1934   "The Terminology of Regional Description." *Annals of the Association of American Geographers* 24:78–86.

1935   *An Outline of Geography.* Boston: Ginn.

1937   "The Distribution of People in South America." In C. C. Colby, ed., *Geographic Aspects of International Relations.* Chicago: University of Chicago Press, 217–40.

1938   "The Changing Patterns of Population in Sao Paulo State, Brazil." *Geographical Review* 28:353–63.

1941   "The Process of Pastoral and Agricultural Settlement on the Argentine Humid Pampas." *Journal of Geography* 40:121–37.

1942	*Latin America*. New York: Odyssey.
1946	*Brazil*. New York: Odyssey.
1951	"The Cultural Regions of Brazil." In T. Lynn Smith and Alexander Marchant, *Brazil: Portrait of Half a Continent*. New York.
1952	"Toward a Further Understanding of the Regional Concept." Presidential Address. *Annals of the Association of American Geographers* 42:195–222.
1954	With C. F. Jones. *American Geography: Inventory and Prospect*. Syracuse, N.Y.: Syracuse University Press.
1963	"A New Look at Latin America—How Bright the Future," *U.S. News and World Report* 15:72–83.
1964	*Introduction to Latin America*. New York: Odyssey.
1972	*All Possible Worlds: A History of Geographical Ideas*. New York: Wiley.
1977	With E. C. Mather. "The Role of Periodic Field Conferences in the Development of Geographical Ideas in the United States." *Geographical Review* 67:446–61.
1978	With G. J. Martin. *The Association of American Geographers: The First Seventy-Five Years, 1904–1979*. Washington, D.C.: The Association of American Geographers.

Chronology

1899	Born in Brookline, Massachusetts, February 14.
1920	Graduated with a B.A. in geology from Harvard.
1923	Completed Ph.D. degree in geography at Clark University and became a member of the geography department at the University of Michigan.
1929	Publication of *Regional Geography: A Chorographical Study of the World* (two volumes).
1935	Publication of *An Outline of Geography*.
1936	Elected secretary of the Association of American Geographers.
1942	Publication of *Latin America*.
1949	Publication of *A Geography of Man*. More field work in Brazil.
1951	President of the Association of American Geographers.
1954	Coauthored and contributed two chapters to *American Geography: Inventory and Prospect*.
1966	Honorary president of the Association of American Geographers.
1970	Cofounder, Archive and Association History Committee.
1978	Coauthored *The Association of American Geographers: The First Seventy-Five Years, 1904–1979*.
1986	Died in Honolulu on January 5.

References

Jensen, Robert G. 1986. "Preston Everett James, 1899–1986." *Journal of Geography* 86:273–74.

Martin, Geoffrey. 1987. "Preston Everett James." *Geographers Biobibliographical Studies* 11:63–70.

Meinig, D. W., ed. 1971. *On Geography: Selected Writings of Preston E. James*. Syracuse, N.Y.: Syracuse University Press.

Mark Jefferson

Mark Jefferson had a critical influence on the development of American geography during the first half of the twentieth century. As a professor of geography for almost forty years at the Michigan State Normal College, he was instrumental in the development of teacher education programs that focused on geography. He was also an active scholar who had a great influence on geography with both his written and oral presentations.

Mark Jefferson was born on March 1, 1863, in Melrose, Massachusetts, the seventh child born to Daniel and Mary Jefferson. During his childhood, he loved the outdoors and liked to identify flora and fauna in the nearby woods. He also had a noticeable interest in reading, and at an early age started writing letters and notes to himself.

Jefferson entered Boston University as a member of the eleven-man class of 1884, where he studied for three years. He was particularly good at languages and became proficient in Greek, Latin, German, Italian, French, and Spanish. During his third year at Boston University, he was offered and accepted a position as an assistant to the director of the National Observatory of the Argentine Republic at Cordoba.

Jefferson worked at the observatory for the next three years, first as an assistant, and then, after promotions, as third and later, second, astronomer. He was enthusiastic about his work and because of his proficiency in mathematics and his working knowledge of six foreign languages, he was promoted quickly, While in Argentina, he seized every opportunity to travel and become familiar with the region. In 1889 Jefferson left Argentina to return to Boston to complete his university education and receive his bachelor's degree. During the same year, he re-commenced a courtship with Theodora Bohnstedt, and two years later they were married.

During the summer of 1890, Jefferson accepted a position as a teacher at Mitchell Boys School in Billerica, Massachusetts. While at Mitchell he taught

French, Latin, English, Spanish, Mathematics, and Geography. The following year he resigned his job at Mitchell to accept a position as principal of the Turners Falls High School. He was asked to teach a course in physical geography at Turners Falls and in order to prepare himself, he enrolled in an intensive six-week summer course in earth science at Harvard. During this course, he met *William Morris Davis who was to become his geographic mentor.

In 1896 Jefferson received an inheritance from his wife's aunt that enabled him to resign his teaching position and enroll at Harvard where he studied both geology and geography from September 1896 to July 1898. He was awarded an A.B. degree in 1897 and an A.M. degree the following year. Perhaps more important than receiving these degrees was the chance to study with William Morris Davis. These two years at Harvard constituted the only formal education in geography received by Jefferson.

After completion of his work at Harvard in 1898, Jefferson was appointed submaster at the Brockton High School. He continued to keep in close contact with Davis, and when a special program for Cuban teachers was set up at Harvard for the summer of 1900, Davis recommended Jefferson for the geographer's post. He accepted the position and developed a series of eighteen lectures and twelve field excursions for the program. The following year Jefferson was offered and accepted a professorship in geography at the Michigan State Normal School in Ypsilanti.

Jefferson was to spend the most productive years of his life, the next forty-eight years, at Ypsilanti. According to his biographer, Geoffrey Martin (1968:62), "It was here that his life as a devoted geographile began. On campus his task was to teach geography; off campus his self-imposed task was that of further geographic study. He ensconced himself in his study, began a contribution which was to effect a shift in the direction of American geographic thought in the first half of the twentieth century." During this same time, he was also deeply involved in a variety of civic duties and for many years constituted a one-man city planning commission for Ypsilanti.

His early research focused on rivers and the processes associated with meander belts. His deep concern for teachers led him to develop and publish his first textbook, *Teachers Geography*, in 1906. He was also one of the original forty-six charter members who gathered at Philadelphia in 1904 to establish the Association of American Geographers.

Jefferson had a close relationship with the American Geographical Society; he published 31 papers between the years 1909 and 1941 in their publication. During this same time period, he published almost 150 book reviews for the Society.

The 1920s were Jefferson's most prolific years. Besides publishing many scholarly articles, he also became involved in the making of maps. "By the end of the 1920s, Jefferson had produced and copyrighted approximately 18 base maps, of countries, continents, states, and the world, that were selling throughout the U.S.A." (Martin, 1968:74).

Although Jefferson was known for his prodigious output of scholarly work in geography, he also had a tremendous impact on geographic education through his teaching at Michigan State Normal College. During his thirty-eight years as head of the geography department, he personally offered sixty-two different courses in geography and introduced scores of teachers to geographic issues. Stephen Visher (1949:307) described Jefferson's success in the classroom in the following words:

During his earlier years at Ypsilanti he started on their geographic careers three men who later became presidents of the Association of American Geographers and two others who have risen high in the Association. . . . Indeed, few major universities with departments of geography and with large numbers of students, fine equipment, and graduate school opportunities have approached that record, of starting in geography as many men who subsequently rose high in the profession.

In the summer of 1937, Jefferson was asked to retire against his will because of a rule the Michigan State Board of Education had passed, decreeing that teachers over the age of seventy should retire from the classroom. Jefferson was hurt and embittered that his institution had afforded him little respect after a long and distinguished career. Although no longer employed at Ypsilanti, Jefferson remained active in the Association of American Geographers and served as chairman of the nominating committee in 1940–41, prepared three papers for the Association of American Geographers' meetings between 1940 and 1949, and evaluated several manuscripts for the *Annuals*, Jefferson died on August 6, 1949.

Jefferson's work was recognized with a variety of honors and awards, including the Cullum Medal of the American Geographical Society (1931), the Helen Culver Medal of the Chicago Geographical Society (1931), and the Distinguished Service Award from the National Council of Geography Teachers.

Selected Bibliography

1897   "The Antecedent Colorado." *Science* 138:293–95.

1898   "Mean Sea Level." *The Journal of School Geography* 2:113–14.

            "Atlantic Estuarine Tides." *National Geographic Magazine* 9:400–409.

1902   "Limiting Width of Meander Belts." *National Geographic Magazine* 13:373–84.

1903   "The Geography of Lake Huron at Kincardine, Ontario." *Journal of Geography* 2:144–55.

1905   "Out of Door Work in Geography." *Journal of Geography* 4:49–57.

1906   *Teachers Geography: A Notebook and Syllabus.* Ypsilanti.

1907   "The Distribution of People in South America." *Bulletin of the Geographical Society of Philadelphia*, 1–11.

1911   "The Culture of the Nations." *Bulletin of the American Geographical Society* 43:241–65.

1912   "Distribution of Schooling in the United States." *American Schoolmaster* 6:255–63.

1913   "The Anthropography of North America." *Bulletin of the American Geographical Society* 45:161–80.

"A New Density of Population Map of Europe." *Bulletin of the American Geographical Society* 45:667–70.

1915   "How American Cities Grow." *Bulletin of the American Geographical Society* 47:19–37.

1916   "Utah, the Oasis at the Foot of the Wasatch." *Geographical Review* 1:346–58.

"The Distribution of People in Japan in 1913." *Geographical Review* 2:368–72.

1921   "On Population Estimates and the Case of Constantinople in Byzantine Days." *Geographical Review* 11:616–18.

1924   *Man in Europe: Here and There*. New York: Harcourt Brace.

1925   "Looking Back at Malthus." *Geographical Review* 15:177–89.

1926   *Principles of Geography*. New York: Harcourt Brace.

"Actual Temperatures of South America." *Geographical Review* 16:443–66.

1928   "The Civilizing Rails." *Economic Geography* 4:217–31.

1929   "The Geographic Distribution of Inventiveness." *Geographical Review* 19:675–77.

1933   "Great Cities of 1930 in the United States with a Comparison of New York and London." *Geographical Review* 23:90–100.

1939   "The Law of the Primate City." *Geographical Review* 29:226–32.

1941   "The Great Cities of the United States, 1940." *Geographical Review* 31:479–87.

Chronology

1863   Born in Melrose, Massachusetts, on March 1.

1880   Entered Boston University.

1883   Left Boston University for a position at the National Observatory of the Argentine Republic at Cordoba.

1889   Returned from Argentina to Boston University to finish work for his B.A.

1896   Enrolled at Harvard to study both geology and geography with William Morris Davis.

1897   Awarded the A.B. degree from Harvard.

1898   Awarded the A.M. degree from Harvard and appointed submaster at Brockton High School.

1901   Accepted a professorship in geography at the Michigan State Normal
             School in Ypsilanti.

1906   Published first textbook, *Teachers Geography*.

1907   Elected President of the Michigan Academy of Sciences.

1916   Elected President of the Association of American Geographers.

1926   Published *Principles of Geography*.

1931   Awarded the Cullum Medal of the American Geographical Society and
             the Helen Culver Medal of the Chicago Geographical Society.

1939   Awarded the Distinguished Service Award from the National Council of
             Geography Teachers and published "The Law of the Primate City."

1949   Died on August 6.

References

Martin, Geoffrey. 1968. *Mark Jefferson: Geographer*. Ypsilanti, Mich.: Eastern Michigan
      University Press.
Visher, Stephen. 1949. "Mark Jefferson, 1863–1949." *Annals of the Association of
      American Geographers* 34:307–10.

Immanuel Kant

Immanuel Kant, a monumental figure in the history of philosophy, also played an important role in the development of geographic thought. He was instrumental in freeing geography from its close relationship with theology.

Kant was born in Königsberg, East Prussia, on April 22, 1724. The son of a craftsman, a harness-maker, he lived in modest circumstances, although his parents made him follow a strict pietistic creed. He received his elementary education at the suburban hospital school, which was followed by eight years (1732–40) at the *Collegium Fridericianum*. Kant was especially good at Latin and decided to study classical philology.

He entered the University of Königsberg on September 24, 1740. Although he studied primarily with the philosophy faculty and majored in both philosophy and mathematics, he was also interested in physics and attended lectures given by J. G. Teske, a follower of Newton's natural philosophy. From all accounts, Kant had little interest in theology, although he may have preached a few sermons at one time. Upon completion of his studies at the university, he probably spent several years as a private tutor for wealthy families in the Königsberg area. He also used that period to further acquaint himself with the philosophical literature.

Kant received a doctorate on June 12, 1755, from the philosophy faculty in Königsberg. His treatise, *On Fire*, was favorably received by his teacher. At the age of thirty-one, he was recognized as a lecturer after writing an essay titled *New Treatment of the First Principles of Metaphysical Knowledge*. A third treatise, *Disputation on the Treatise "Monadologis Phisica,"* was successfully defended on April 10, 1756, and led towards a professorship.

Professors at Königsberg were poorly paid and Kant had to supplement his income as an assistant librarian in the Royal Library and from fees he received for lectures. He lectured on a wide variety of subjects, including physics, natural science, mechanical science, hydrostatics, hydrokinetics, military engineering, pyrotechnics, and mathematics. During his third term (1756–57), he probably introduced his lectures on physical geography. According to Buttner and Hoheisel (1980:56), "Altogether he scheduled and held forty-seven four-lesson lectures on physical geography during his teaching period of 82 semester terms. On the average he managed to deliver these lectures to relatively numerous audiences of 30 to 50 freshmen."

Although he was offered professorship positions at Erlangen and Jena that would have paid more, Kant refused their offers because he wanted a full professorship from the University of Königsberg, which he was awarded finally in 1770. Kant enjoyed Königsberg a great deal and although it only had thirty or forty thousand inhabitants, it was a cosmopolitan city with broad-ranging commercial connections with England, Denmark, Sweden, and Poland. Kant is reported to have said that Königsberg was a place where one could find out a great deal about the world without having to travel. This gave inspiration to Kant, especially in his search for a global view. In his physical geography, as in his natural science, Kant followed his basic philosophical hope of creating a uniform, self-contained and self-sufficient world system and world concept.

After being appointed a full professor, Kant resigned his position at the library. In 1780 he was appointed to the board of governors at the university and elected rector at the university in the summer of 1786. He never was especially interested in administrative work and disliked attending meetings. From all accounts, he was a good teacher interested in the well-being of his students. He became ill in the final years of his life and delivered his last lecture in 1796. He died on February 12, 1804, and was entombed in 1880 in a chapel near the cathedral at Königsberg.

When compared to the abundance of his philosophical writings, little is left of his geographical writings. Most of what we know about his geographical ideas is based on his lectures. Kant believed the human element was an integral part of geography and claimed physical geography to be "a summary of nature," and the basis for history and "all the other possible geographies." In an essay on Kant, George Kish points out the differences between the classical Ptolemaic definitions of geography and Kant's ideas (1978:398):

There was an essential difference between his work and that of the classical scholars. The latter laid primary emphasis on the areal divisions of the earth and the business of systematically describing their distinctive content. Kant, on the other hand, was not so much concerned with composite terrestrial units of different orders, but with the orderly investigation of particular areally differentiated phenomena.

Kant believed that geography could be divided into three sections ("Physical Geography," 1802: Vol. 1, Part 4):

This discipline will thus be divided into physical, moral, and political geography. Within it will first be discussed the characteristics of nature. . . . It is this part, which also deals with the natural relationships of all lands and seas and their interconnections, that is the true foundation of all history, which otherwise would hardly differ from fairy tales.

The second segment considers man on earth, in terms of the variety of his natural characteristics and the moral differences that exist. . . . Finally the conditions of states, which we can view as a result of the mutual influences of the forces discussed previously, and of the peoples of the earth will be considered.

Kant made an enormous impact on the thinking of geographers in the nineteenth and twentieth centuries. *Alexander von Humboldt was directly influenced by Kant, and many statements by Humboldt about the methods of geography are very similar to those proposed by Kant. The ideas of Kant can also be found in the works of *Carl Ritter and *Alfred Hettner. The legacy of Kant was stressed by Buttner and Hoheisel (1980:55): "The latest research has revealed that the history of geography should bed divided into two periods: before Kant and after Kant—we are still in the latter period."

Selected Bibliography

1755   "General Natural History and Theory of the Heavens." *Kants Gesammelte Schriften* 1:215–368.

1757   "Outline and Announcement of a Course of Lectures on Physical Geography." *Kants Gesammelte Schriften* 2:3–10.

1763   "The Only Possible Ground for a Proof of the Existence of God." *Kants Gesammelte Schriften* 2:63–163.

1765   "Report of the Arrangement of the Lectures for the Winter Session, 1765–1766." *Kants Gesammelte Schriften* 2:312–13.

1775   "On the Various Races of Man: Announcement of the Lectures on Physical Geography for Summer 1775." *Kants Gesammelte Schriften* 2:427–43.

1781   "Critique of Pure Reason." *Kants Gesammelte Schriften* 4:1–252.

1788   "On the Use of Teleological Principles in Philosophy." *Kants Gesammelte Schriften* 8:157–84.

1790   "Critique of Judgement." *Kants Gesammelte Schriften* 5:165–485.

1794   "Remarks on the Influence of the Moon on the Weather." *Kants Gesammelte Schriften* 8:315–24.

1802   "Physical Geography." *Kants Gesammelte Schriften* 9:151–436.

Chronology

1724   Born at Königsberg, April 22.

1740   Matriculated at the University of Königsberg.

1755   Qualifies for, and becomes lecturer at, the University of Königsberg. Publication of "General Natural History and Theory of the Heavens."

1756   Begins lecturing on geography at Königsberg.

1763   Publication of "The Only Possible Ground for a Proof of the Existence of God."

1770   Receives the ordinary professorship in philosophy.

1781   Publication of "Critique of Pure Reason."

1790   Publication of "Critique of Judgement."

1798   Publication of "The Strife of the Faculties."

1802   Publication of "Physical Geography."

1804   Death at Königsberg after six years of chronic ill health, February 12.

References

Buttner, Manfred, and Karl Hoheisel. 1980. "Immanuel Kant." *Geographers Biobib-liographical Studies* 4:55–67.
Kish, George, ed. 1978. *A Source Book in Geography*. Cambridge, Mass.: Harvard University Press.

Wladimir Köppen

Wladimir Köppen, the renowned German climatologist, was born on September 25, 1846, in St. Petersburg in what at the time, of course, was the Russian Empire. Wladimir's grandfather had been invited to Russia from Germany by Catherine the Great and had remained in Russia as a physician to the czar. Wladimir's father, Peter von Köppen, was employed as a geographer and statistician at the Academy in St. Petersburg, where his success was ultimately rewarded by promotion to Academician, the highest attainable academic rank in the empire (*The New Encyclopaedia Britannica*, 1989).

Without doubt, Wladimir's father had considerable influence on his own intellectual training and choice of career. Wladimir attended the equivalent of secondary school in Simferopol, in the Crimea, from about 1858 to 1864, and there became interested in the local region's natural environment, from its physiography to its flora, fauna, and climate. The seeds of geographical awareness were sowed in his mind during those years, and a long and successful career in climatology was in its incipient phase.

Following his years in secondary school, Köppen went to study at the University of St. Petersburg, where, among other things, he became increasingly curious about the environmental differences between there and the Crimea and about the causes of those differences, especially with respect to vegetation. Such comparisons and contrasts would remain an enduring interest.

At the age of twenty, Köppen set off to study at the University of Heidelberg in Germany, where he completed a doctoral dissertation in 1870. The focus of that study was on the relationship between temperatures and plant growth. After a stint with the ambulance corps during the Franco-Prussian War, Köppen headed back to Russia, where he took a position as an assistant at the Central Physical Observatory in St. Petersburg. Building on the experience gained in that position, he moved on to become the head of an emerging meteorology program at the German Naval Observatory in Hamburg.

In 1884 Köppen produced his first major geographical contribution, a temperature map of the world based on monthly temperature deviations from selected mean values. It was not until 1900, however, that his initial climate classification system was introduced. Subsequently he continued to improve his approach, publishing a major revision in 1918, which considered annual variations in both temperature and rainfall, and a final version in 1936. Köppen observed many of the regularities that occurred on world climate maps and demonstrated those regularities by plotting them on a generalized hypothetical continent, an idea still employed in most physical geography texts today. His mathematical system of classification, using temperature and rainfall data, was of such importance that it remains as an influence on many of the subsequent classification systems that have been devised, including Trewartha's, with which most geography students today are familiar, and still, after more than ninety years, it is given credit in virtually all physical geography texts as the basis for climate classification, a considerable tribute to an enduring work.

Though Köppen is remembered now almost exclusively for his contributions to climatology, his awareness and appreciation of geography extended well beyond those boundaries. Though he has been described as modest and retiring, he is known to have been keenly interested in the ideas of his time and in the predicament of humankind as well. Though he never travelled widely, his interest in places was keen. Additionally, he was concerned with land-use changes and reform and was an advocate of Esperanto, the international language.

In 1919 Köppen retired from his position in Hamburg and in 1924 moved to Graz, Austria, where he worked with another major figure in climatology, Rudolph Geiger, to produce the multivolume *Handbuch der Klimatologie*. Köppen died in Graz on June 22, 1940.

Selected Bibliography

1884   "Die Warmezonen der Erde, nach der Dauer der heissen, gemassigten und kalten Zeit, und nach der Wirkung der Wärme auf die organische Welt betrachtet." *Meteorologische Zeitschrift* 1:215–26.

1900   "Versuch einer Klassification der Klimate, vorzugsweise nach ihren Beziehungen zur Pflanzenwelt." *Geographische Zeitschrift* 5:593–611.

1918   "Klassification der Klimate nach Temperatur, Niederschlag, und Jahreslauf." *Petermanns Geographische Mitteilungen* 64:243–48.

1931   *Grundriss der Klimakunde*. Berlin.

1936   *Das Geographischen System der Klimate*.

1940   *Handbuch der Klimatologie* (Handbook of Climatology). Edited with Rudolph Geiger. Berlin: Gebruder Borntraeger.

Chronology

1846	Born September 25, in St. Petersburg.
1864	Began studies at University of St. Petersburg, specializing in botany.
1867	Transferred to University of Heidelberg.
1870	Received doctoral degree.
1871	Served during the Franco-Prussian War in the ambulance corps.
1879	Meteorologist of the German Naval Observatory in Hamburg.
1884	Produced a world map of temperature belts.
1900	Introduced his mathematical system of climate classification.
1919	Retired from his position at the observatory in Hamburg.
1924	Moved to Graz, Austria.
1940	Died June 22, in Graz.

Reference

Anonymous. 1989. *The New Encyclopaedia Britannica*. Vol. 6, 15th ed. Chicago: Encyclopaedia Britannica.

Pyotr Kropotkin

Pyotr Kropotkin is well known for his revolutionary ideas and theories relative to the development of anarchism in Russia. He also made significant contributions in the area of physical geography.

Kropotkin was born in Moscow on November 27, 1842, into a distinguished family of princes. He studied at the Pages School from 1857 to 1862 and after school, to the surprise of many friends, chose to join the Amur Cossack Army. He served as a "troubleshooter" in the army under the governor general of Eastern Siberia.

In 1864 Kropotkin embarked on an expedition to unchartered regions in Northern Manchuria. After crossing the Big Khingan mountains, he discovered a group of tertiary volcanoes in the Ilkhuri-Alin range. In another expedition in the same year, along the Sungari River, he made a series of meticulous meteorological observations. In the summer of the following year he organized and paid for an expedition to the Irkutsk gubernia to study ice sediments. During his travels on the northern slopes of the Eastern Sayan mountains, he found evidence of continental glaciation.

Kropotkin's most important trip, however, took place during the spring of the following year. With support from a local gold-mining entrepreneur and the Russian Geographical Society, he did a study of the area between the Lena gold fields and the city of Tchyta. He studied several mountain ranges as well as the Patomskoye and Vitimskoye plateaus. The amount and quality of geographical and geological information he collected on this trip was recognized by the Russian Geographical Society, and as a result, he was awarded a gold medal.

These early studies in geology, geography, botany, and physics were undertaken with a great sense of purpose, but Kropotkin realized his own shortcomings, primarily because he had little formal education in these areas. In the fall of 1867, he decided to enroll in St. Petersburg University to study physics and mathematics. At the same time, he worked for the Statistical Committee of the Ministry of the Interior under the geographer P. P. Semenov.

In the later part of the 1860s and the early 1870s Kropotkin was actively involved with the Russian Geographical Society and in 1871 was elected secretary of its physical geography department. In the early 1870s, Kropotkin was one of the first scientists to study the causes of glaciation in Europe. He was sent to Finland and Sweden by the Geographical Society in 1871 to study the structure of alluvial glacial ridges called *eskers*.

According to Olga Alexandrovskaya (1983:59), "Pyotr Kropotkin is rightfully regarded as a founder of the so-called 'glacial theory', i.e., the theory of the Quaternary continental glaciation." He analyzed the dynamic movement of glacial ice and determined that this movement was the result of the plastic flow of the ice. In addition, he also analyzed the results of glacial action and determined the origins of glacial erosional landforms such as *cirques* and *roches moutonnees*. This work provided a good framework for further researchers who studied glacial action.

Throughout the early 1870s, Kropotkin increasingly turned his attention to social problems. As a result of his revolutionary and anarchist activities, he was jailed in 1874. In 1876, however, he made a daring flight from prison and emigrated to Western Europe. He spent the next forty years of his life in exile. In 1877 he settled in Switzerland and two years later founded *Le Revolte*, an anarchist newspaper. In 1881 he was banished from Switzerland and went to France. After being sentenced to a five-year prison term in France, he was granted amnesty and went to Great Britain, where he remained for the next thirty years. During his time in Britain, Kropotkin wrote a series of articles on how economic activity ought to be organized. He was also responsible for the Russian geography section in the *Encyclopaedia Britannica*. A look at his writings between 1890 and 1900 reveals varied interests in many topics. His most famous work, *Anarchism: Its Philosophy and Ideals*, was published in London in 1896.

In 1917 Kropotkin was given permission to return to Russia. Although he was seventy-five, he continued to engage in creative activities. His last work was a book on ethics that was published after his death. He died on February 8, 1922, and was buried in Moscow.

Selected Bibliography

1865   "Two Trips to Manchuria in 1864" (Dve Poezoki v Manchzhuriju, 1864 goda). *Zapiski Sibirskogo Otdelenia Russkogo Geographicheskogo Obshchestva* 8.

1867   "Okinsky Karaul." *Zapiski Sibirskogo Otdelenia Russkogo Geographichskogo Obshchestva* 10.

1868   "The Olekminsko-Vitimskaya Expedition." *Izvestiya Russkogo Geographichskogo Obshchestva* 4.

1869	"Issledovania ob Erraticheskikh Valunakh i o Delyuvialnikh Obrazova-niyakh." *Izvestiya Russkogo Geographichskogo Obshchestva* 5.
1871	"Five Letters from Finland." *Izvestiya Russkogo Geographichskogo Ob-shchestva* 5, 6, 7.
	An Expedition to Study the Russian Northern Seas (Ekspeditsiya dlya Issledovania Russkikh Severnikh Morei). St. Petersburg.
1873	"The Olekminsko-Vitimskaya Expedition of 1868." *Zapiski SibiRusskogo Geographicheskogo Obshchestva po Obshchei Geografii* 3.
1875	"A General Review of the Orography of Eastern Siberia" (*Obshchi Ocherk Orografiyi Vostochnoi Sibiri*). *Zapiski SibiRusskogo Geographicheskogo Obshchestva po Obshchei Geografii* 7.
1904	"The Desiccation of Eur-Asia." *Geographical Journal* 23:722–41.
1909	*La Grande Revolution*. Paris.
1913	*Modern Science and Anarchism*. Philadelphia.

Chronology

1842	Born in Moscow November 27.
1867	Became a member of the mathematics department of St. Petersburg University and served on the statistical committee of the Ministry of the Interior.
1868	Elected as a member of the Russian Geographical Society and worked on the problems of the northern seas and Russia. Published "The Olekminsko-Vitimskaya Expedition."
1869	Published an important paper on erratic boulders.
1871	Secretary of the physical geography section of the Russian Geographical Society and worked on glacial deposits in Sweden and Finland. Published "Five Letters from Finland" and "An Expedition to Study the Russian Northern Seas."
1879	Founded the newspaper *Le Revolte* in Geneva (published in Paris from 1881).
1890–96	Wrote a series of papers on evolution in the *Nineteenth Century* magazine.
1893	Became a member of the British Association for the Advancement of Science.
1899	Published *Fields, Factories and Workshops*.
1904	Published "The Desiccation of Eur-Asia" in the *Geographic Journal*.
1909	Published *La Grande Revolution* in Paris.
1913	Published *Modern Science and Anarchism* in Philadelphia.
1922	Died at Dmitrov on February 8.

Reference

Alexandrovskaya, Olga. 1983. "Pyotr Alexeivich Kropotkin." *Geographers Biobiblio-graphical Studies* 7:57–62.

Halford John Mackinder

Halford J. Mackinder was both an academic geographer and a practicing politician, and through his efforts, the academic discipline of geography was revived in British universities in the early twentieth century. He was born in Gainsborough on February 15, 1861. His family was well-off; he was on the son of a medical practitioner and had the benefit of a French governess as an early teacher. He attended the Gainsborough Grammar School and then went to Epsom College, a public school that had a good program in the sciences. He enrolled at Christ Church College at Oxford in October 1880 and won a five-year "junior studentship" in physical science.

Mackinder was an excellent student and received a first-class honors degree in physical science. During his last two years at Oxford, he concentrated on courses in history, law, and geology. He was also active in the Oxford Union, where he frequently gave speeches and made acquaintances with many people who would later help him in his efforts at educational reform.

It is unclear how Mackinder developed his interest in geography, since it was not a subject then taught at the universities. Almost immediately after graduation, on November 17, 1885, he gave his first University Extension lecture on physical geography. By May 1886, he was appointed University Extension lecturer in natural science and economic history.

After being appointed University Extension lecturer, Mackinder planned a series of lectures to develop a synthetic geography that ran from the physical sciences to the humanities, calling this set of concerns and the lectures "The New Geography" (Kearns, 1985:71). Mackinder was called to the bar in 1886 but decided to abandon his work as a barrister and devote himself to university work.

Mackinder crystallized his ideas about geography in "The Scope and Methods of Geography," a paper that he delivered to the Royal Geographical Society in 1887 and that was widely regarded as the centerpiece in the fight to reform the teaching of geography. He believed that physical and human geography were really only one subject, two stages of one investigation. By combining both the sciences and humanities, geography, according to Mackinder (1887:160), was "the common element in the culture of all men, a ground on which the specialists could meet." He believed (1887:143) that the central theme of geography was "to trace the interaction of man in society and so much of his environment as varies locally." He went on to declare (1887:159) that "on lines such as I have sketched, a geography may be worked out which shall satisfy at once the practical requirements of the statesman and merchant, the theoretical requirements of the historian and scientist, and the intellectual requirements of the teacher."

As a result of Mackinder's efforts to promote geography, the Royal Geographical Society persuaded Oxford University to appoint him as Reader in Geography in 1887. He was a natural orator and preached his geographical gospel with zeal and fervor (Gilbert, 1951:23). He continued to give University Extension lectures and was given a fellowship at Christ Church in 1892. During the same year, he accepted the position of Principal of the new University Extension College at Reading. A few years later, he took on the added duties of a part-time lecturer at the London School of Economics. As a result of his efforts, the University of Oxford established the Oxford School of Geography in 1899.

In 1902 Mackinder published one of his most important works, *Britain and the British Seas*. In this book he emphasized his ideas about a "New Geography." The book, according to Kearns (1985:73),

possessed two qualities all too rare in books intended primarily as teaching aids: it followed a coherent argument, and it presented an original synthesis. Beyond that there was the vivid language. Mackinder's phrases evoke hands moving over maps and globes, tracing discontinuities, balancing complementarities and drawing the underlying geographical structure through the wealth of detail to the surface.

In 1903 Mackinder dropped his University Extension work and left Reading to become director of the London School of Economics and Political Science. He believed this position would enable him to have a more direct impact on both political decisions and the development of geography.

In 1904 Mackinder presented a paper to the Royal Geographical Society entitled "The Geographical Pivot of History." In this paper, he described the central part of Eurasia as "the pivot area," a term he later changed to the "heartland." His central thesis (1904:423) was that since the advent of steam navigation, the world had become one closed political system and "the pivot region of the world's politics" was "that area of Euro-Asia which is inaccessible to ships." He went on to argue that if one agreed that the world were a closed political system, then combinations of power were "likely to rotate round the pivot state, which is always likely to be great, but with limited mobility as compared with the surrounding marginal insular powers." According to *Preston

James and Geoffrey Martin (1981:259), "Mackinder's Heartland theory was nothing less than a model to place the broad sweep of world history on the stage provided by global geography." Although Mackinder mentioned "heartland" only once in his 1904 paper, he used the term extensively in his elaboration of the paper in his book *Democratic Ideals and Reality*, which was published in 1919 and in which he summarized his view of global strategy with the now-famous saying:

> Who rules East Europe commands the Heartland,
> Who rules the Heartland commands the World Island,
> Who rules the World Island commands the World.

In 1910, at the age of forty-nine, Mackinder started his political career and entered Parliament as a Liberal Unionist M.P. from the Camlachie Division of Glasgow. He held this seat for twelve years, until 1922, when he lost the seat to the Labour Party. He was sixty-two when he left Parliament, and his last quarter century was marked by several honorary posts related to geography as well as to government. From 1920 to 1945, he served as chairman of the Imperial Shipping Committee, and from 1925 to 1930, he was chairman of the Imperial Economic Committee. In 1920 he also took charge of a special temporary mission as British High Commissioner for South Russia, at the completion of which he was knighted.

Mackinder had a lasting impact on the development of geography. According to *Laurence Stamp (1947:530), his ideas became "absorbed as an essential part of geography as it is now studied throughout the universities of Britain." The impact of Mackinder's paper on the "heartland" was also far-reaching. It is claimed to have inspired the Swedish political scientist Rudolf Kjellen and the German geographer *Karl Haushofer in their studies of geopolitics and was indirectly associated with the Nazi policy of conquest. According to the American political geographer Norman Pounds (1972:426), "Few papers presented to a learned society have been more significant than this one."

In recognition of Mackinder's outstanding contributions to geography, he received the Patron's Medal, the highest award from the Royal Geographical Society; the Charles P. Daly medal was presented to him in 1944 from the American Geographical Society. Mackinder died at eighty-six on March 6, 1947, in Dorset.

Selected Bibliography

1887   "The Scope and Methods of Geography." *Proceedings of the Royal Geographical Society* 9:141–60.

1890   "The Physical Basis of Political Geography." *Scottish Geographical Magazine* 6:78–84.

1895   "Modern Geography, German and English." *Geographical Journal* 6:367–79.

1902   *Britain and the British Seas*. Oxford.

1904   "The Development of Geographical Teaching out of Nature Study." *Geography Teacher* 2:191–97.

            "The Geographical Pivot of History." *Geographical Journal* 33:462–76.

1911   "The Teaching of Geography from an Imperial Point of View, and the Use Which Should Be Made of Visual Instruction." *Geography Teacher* 6:79–86.

1913   "The Teaching of Geography and History as a Combined Subject." *Geography Teacher* 7:4–19.

1917   "Some Geographical Aspects of International Reconstruction." *Scottish Geographical Magazine* 33:3–11.

1919   *Democratic Ideals and Reality: A Study in the Politics of Reconstruction*. Oxford.

1921   "Geography as a Pivotal Subject in Education." *Geography Journal* 57:376–84.

1931   "The Human Habitat." *Scottish Geographical Magazine* 47:321–35.

1935   "Progress of Geography in the Field and in the Study During the Reign of His Majesty King George the Fifth." *Geography Journal* 86:1–12.

1942   "Geography, an Art and a Philosophy." *Geography* 27:122–30.

1943   "The Round World and the Winning of the Peace." *Foreign Affairs* 21:595–605.

Chronology

1861   Born at Gainsborough, Lincolnshire, February 15.

1883–84   First-class honors B.A. degree in physical science, 1884 obtained a second-class degree in history, began reading for a law degree.

1886   Appointed University Extension lecturer in Natural Science and Economic History.

1887   Appointed Reader in Geography at Oxford and published "The Scope and Methods of Geography."

1902   Appointed full-time lecturer in economic geography at the London School of Economics and published *Britain and the British Seas*.

1903   Appointed Director of the London School of Economics and Political Science.

1904   Published "The Geographical Pivot of History."

1910   Elected to Parliament.

1913–46   Chairman of the Geographical Association.

1916   President of the Geographical Association.

1919	Publication of *Democratic Ideals and Reality: A Study in the Politics of Reconstruction*.
1920	Appointed chairman of the Imperial Shipping Committee and took charge of a special temporary mission as British High Commissioner for South Russia.
1922	Elected honorary member of the Hungarian Geographical Society.
1923	Given a personal chair in Geography at London University.
1928	President of the Human Geography section of the International Geographic Union.
1932–36	Vice President of the Royal Geographic Society.
1944	Awarded the Charles P. Daly Medal by the American Geographic Society.
1945	Awarded the Patron's Medal of the Royal Geographic Society.
1947	Died March 6, at Parkstone, Dorset.

References

Gilbert, E. W. 1951. "Seven Lamps of Geography: An Appreciation of the Teaching of Sir Halford J. Mackinder." *Geography* 36:21–41.

James, Preston E., and Geoffrey J. Martin. 1981. *All Possible Worlds: A History of Geographical Ideas*. 2d ed. New York: Wiley.

Kearns, Gerry. 1985. "Halford John Mackinder." *Geographers Biobibliographical Studies* 9:71–86.

Pounds, Norman J. G. 1972. *Political Geography*. New York: McGraw-Hill.

Stamp, L. Dudley. 1947. "The Right Honorable Sir Halford Mackinder, P.C." *Nature* 159:530–31.

George Perkins Marsh

George Perkins Marsh was born in 1801 in Woodstock, Vermont, a tiny settlement on a branch of the Connecticut River. Before even reaching school age, Marsh often spent time in the woods with his father, who awakened in George a keen interest in landscape and the processes of nature. He graduated from Dartmouth in 1820, passed his bar examination, and set up a small law practice in Burlington, Vermont. He was also elected to Congress by the Whig Party in 1843.

Marsh's childhood interests in the forest stayed with him, and later he began to look at forests much differently than he had earlier, recognizing that not only in Vermont but in numerous other places in the growing United States as well, people were modifying the environment, cutting the forests, exhausting the soils, and overgrazing the slopes. Marsh worked in the forest industry in Vermont and was a careful observer of the changing landscape there. In a speech to the Agricultural Society of Rutland County in September 1847 (cited in Lowenthal, 1953:209) he said, in referring to the interaction between deforestation, soil changes, and stream erosional patterns: "The changes, which these causes have wrought in the physical geography of Vermont, within a single generation, are too striking to have escaped the attention of any observing person. The signs of artificial improvement are mingled with the tokens of improvident waste."

Marsh cited the work of European foresters in conserving the rate at which forests there were being cut, but he was already beyond their simple measures in his thinking. As Lowenthal (1953:209–10) noted, "Like so many other Americans of his time, Marsh approached problems with a decidedly utilitarian bias; with him theory was at once translated into action, and scholarship was mere antiquarianism unless it could be turned to practical account. . . . His interest in geography led him to promote the cause of conservation."

Marsh's view of people and nature was conditioned by his religious convictions. As Lowenthal (1953:211) pointed out, "The reverberating intricacies of cause and effect obsessed Marsh; he was overwhelmed by the realization of the moral consequences of the fact that every action, even every thought, left an indelible record in nature and in the mind of God." Among geographers, it was *Alexander von Humboldt who most influenced Marsh; other influences on his geographic thinking came from far afield, from the works of Goethe, Wordsworth, and others who were looking anew at the relationship between people and nature. Romanticism affected him greatly, though it was countered, at least to some degree, by nationalism. He was unsatisfied with the geographic works of *Carl Ritter and *Arnold Guyot and rejected their teleological underpinnings. To Marsh, the essence of geography was to be found in the interactions between people and the natural environment.

In 1849, after losing a bid for reelection to Congress, Marsh was appointed the U.S. minister to Turkey, and in 1861 President Lincoln designated him as minister plenipotentiary to Italy. These positions gave him time to live abroad, and he held the latter position until his death.

Marsh's premier work made its first appearance in 1864 under the title *Man and Nature, or Physical Geography as Modified by Human Action*. In the introduction to the book (1864:iii), which represented the climax of Marsh's conservation efforts, he wrote about what he envisioned as his purpose, namely,

to indicate the character and, approximately, the extent of the changes produced by human action in the physical conditions of the globe we inhabit; to point out the dangers of imprudence and the necessity of caution in all operations which, on a large scale, interfere with the spontaneous arrangements of the organic and of the inorganic worlds; to suggest the possibility and the importance of the restoration of disturbed harmonies and the material improvement of wasted and exhausted regions; and, incidentally, to illustrate the doctrine that man is, in both kind and degree, a power of a higher order than any of the other forms of animated life, which, like him are nourished at the table of bounteous nature.

Lowenthal (1958:334) noted that, "Marsh sought no fame from his scholarly work and did not think he deserved any. He wrote because he had something interesting and useful to say, not to gain acclaim." He also noted (Lowenthal, 1958:335) that, "Marsh's virtue as a scholar was his ability to see scientific and social problems from fresh viewpoints." Certainly that was one of the successful elements of *Man and Nature*. In all of his works, from his writings to his diplomatic work, he remained realistic and pragmatic, dedicated to understanding how human actions were affecting the earth and why people should be concerned about it. Marsh's book was published in a revised edition in 1874 with the title *The Earth as Modified by Human Action: A New Edition of Man and Nature* and again in 1885 with the title *The Earth as Modified by Human Action: A Last Revision of Man and Nature*.

Marsh died in Italy in 1882, with his wife, Caroline, at his side. He was buried in Rome's Protestant Cemetery, not far from where Shelley and Keats were laid to rest.

Selected Bibliography

1848   Remarks on slavery in the territories of New Mexico, California, and
            Oregon; delivered in the House of Representatives, August 3, 1848. Bur-
            lington, Vt.: *Burlington Free Press* office print.

1862   *The Origin and History of the English Language and the Early Literature
            It Embodies.* New York: Scribner's.

1864   *Man and Nature, or Physical Geography as Modified by Human Action.*
            New York.

1874   *The Earth as Modified by Human Action: A New Edition of Man and
            Nature.* New York: Scribner's.

1885   *The Earth as Modified by Human Action: A Last Revision of Man and
            Nature.* New York: Scribner's.

Chronology

1801   Born in Woodstock, Vermont.

1820   Graduated from Dartmouth and passed bar examination.

1843   Elected to Congress from Vermont by Whig Party.

1849   Defeated for reelection. Appointed as the U.S. Minister to Turkey.

1861   President Lincoln appointed him minister plenipotentiary to the Kingdom
            of Italy. Held this position until his death.

1882   Died.

References

Lowenthal, David. 1953. "George Perkins Marsh and the American Geographical Tra-
        dition." *Geographical Review* 43:207–13.
———. 1958. *George Perkins Marsh.* New York: Columbia University Press.

Matthew Fontaine Maury

Matthew F. Maury was born in Spotsylvania County, Virginia, on January 14, 1806. He attended a rural school and the Harpeth Academy in Williamson County, Tennessee. He entered the United States Navy in 1825, and, except for a little education he received in the Navy, he had no further formal education.

Maury served on a variety of vessels from 1826 to 1829 and then went on the voyage of the *Vincennes*, the first U.S. Navy ship to sail around the world. According to *Preston James and Geoffrey Martin (1981:150), "At an early age Maury had developed an insatiable curiosity concerning all matters that lay beyond his immediate horizon. His voyage around the world left him with many unanswered questions concerning the characteristics of the oceans." From 1831 to 1834, he sailed off the west coast of South America and on his return completed the writing of *A New Theoretical and Practical Treatise on Navigation*, which was published in 1836. In 1839, while returning to New York after visiting his parents in Tennessee, the stagecoach in which he was riding turned over, and his right leg was badly broken. During his long convalescence, Maury wrote several articles that were very critical of the Navy, and, upon returning to active duty in 1842, he was appointed director of the Navy Depot of Charts and Instruments (which was later to become the United States Naval Observatory and Hydrographic Office).

Maury devoted much of his time in this new position to the charting of observations of winds and currents, and he devised a blank form on which ships' captains could record specific observations about them. These observations were located by latitude and longitude, then the data was sent back to Washington where it was plotted on maps. The information was published in Maury's *Wind and Current Charts*. Although the recording of this data was mandatory for United States Navy ships, many merchant vessels also provided data in exchange for the *Charts* and *Sailing Directions* Maury wrote. As a result of Maury's work, the international maritime conference held in Brussels in 1853 adopted a uniform system of recording observations modelled after Maury's ideas. This conference also brought recognition to Maury as an international expert.

Maury was also responsible for the development of new instruments used for sounding ocean depths. As a result of this work, the first map of the floor of the North Atlantic Ocean was produced. This map was valuable in the planning of the route for the first transatlantic cable. Since Maury had access to good information about winds and currents, there was a demand by ships' captains for more accurate sailing directions. "Maury was able to advise ships' captains concerning the best routes to follow. His sailing directions cut the trip from New York to Rio de Janeiro by ten days" (James and Martin, 1981:151).

Collecting data was not enough for Maury. He wanted to develop a generalized picture of the surface winds of the earth. As a result, he developed a "diagram of the winds." The diagram was a circular figure that showed wind belts and areas of calm on a meridianal hemisphere. Also included was a cross-section that illustrated the vertical components of atmospheric circulation. This diagram appeared in his book, *The Physical Geography of the Sea*, which was published in 1855, and in which Maury was very explicit about his ideas concerning the development of a generalized model of the movements of water and air (1855: xv): "I am wedded to no theories, and do not advocate the doctrines of any particular school. Truth is my object. . . . In every instance that theory is preferred which is reconcilable with the greatest number of known facts."

Maury's career as both a geographer and a naval officer abruptly ended in 1861 when, on the secession of Virginia, he resigned his commission to join the Confederacy. He was commissioned in the Confederate Navy and was sent to England to purchase and outfit ships. He was in England when the Confederacy collapsed, and since he was in need of money to support his family, he decided to write a series of geography textbooks. These books for elementary schools were revised and renamed several times and remained in print into the 1930s. In 1873 Maury published another book entitled *Physical Geography*, which was one of the major physical geography textbooks published in the United States in the 1870s.

Maury returned to the United States in the summer of 1868. He accepted a professorship position at the Virginia Military Institute and the superintendency of a Physical Survey of Virginia. The remaining years of his life were spent writing, lecturing at the Institute, and giving speeches to the public. According to Leighly (1977:60), Maury's most significant contributions to geographical studies were "(1) a first attempt at drawing a bathymetrical chart of the North Atlantic Ocean, principally from deep-sea soundings made under Maury's direction, (2) a map of isotherms for March and September of the surface water of the Atlantic, and (3) information on deep-sea sediments brought up by a sounding apparatus invented by one of Maury's subordinates." He died on February 1, 1873, in Lexington, Virginia.

Selected Bibliography

1834   "On the Navigation of Cape Horn." *American Journal of Science* 26:54–
            63.

1836   *A New Theoretical and Practical Treatise on Navigation*. Philadelphia.
            Rev. eds. entitled *Elementary, Practical and Theoretical Treatise on Nav-
            igation*. Philadelphia. 1843; 1845.

1844   "The Gulf Stream and Currents of the Sea." *American Journal of Science*
            47:161–81.

1847–60   *Wind and Current Charts*, 70 sheets.

1850   "On the Currents of the Atlantic Ocean." *Proceedings of the American
            Association for the Advancement of Science* 3:74–80.

1851   "On the Currents of the Atlantic and Existence of the North-West Pas-
            sage." *Edinburgh New Philosophy Journal* 51:51–55.

1853   "Valley of the Amazon." *De Bow's Review* 14:449–60, 556–67; 15:36–
            43.

1855   *The Physical Geography of the Sea*. New York.

1864   *Physical Geography for Students and General Readers*. London.

1868   *First Lessons in Geography*. New York.

1870   *Manual of Geography*. New York.

1873   *Physical Geography*. New York.

Chronology

1806   Born January 14 in Spotsylvania County, Virginia.

1825   Appointed Midshipman, U.S. Navy.

1836   Promoted to Lieutenant, U.S. Navy. Publication of *A New Theoretical and
            Practical Treatise on Navigation*.

1847   Publication of first *Wind and Current Charts*.

1851   Publication of *Explanations and Sailing Directions to Accompany Wind
            and Current Charts*.

1855   Publication of *The Physical Geography of the Sea*.

1858   Promoted to Commander, U.S. Navy.

1861   Resigned from U.S. Navy and commissioned in Confederate Navy.

1866   Contracts with New York publisher to write series of textbooks in
            geography.

1868   Appointed Professor of Physics and Superintendent of Physical Survey of
            Virginia, Virginia Military Institute, Lexington; and publication of *First
            Lessons in Geography*.

1870   Publication of *Manual of Geography*.

1873   Died at Lexington, Virginia, February 1. Publication of *Physical
            Geography*.

References

James, Preston E., and Geoffrey J. Martin. 1981. *All Possible Worlds: A History of Geographical Ideas*. 2d ed. New York: Wiley.
Leighly, John. 1977. "Matthew Fontaine Maury." *Geographers Biobibliographical Studies* 1:59–63.

Donald W. Meinig

Historical geography in America has been greatly influenced by the work of Donald W. Meinig. He was born in Palouse, Washington, November 1, 1924, on a small farm. His father was the son of German immigrants who had farmed for a few years in Iowa before coming to Palouse. These agricultural and rural roots had an influence on Meinig's interests in historical geography. He states, in regard to his development of an interest in geography (1989:4):

All I know is that we lived on a hill with an extensive view of the town about a mile to the north, of several half-bald buttes and a long line of forested mountains in Idaho on the east, and the endless rolling hills to the south and west. As far back as I can remember I was fascinated by that panorama. I wanted to know the names of all those features, I wondered what lay beyond.

As a schoolboy, geography was Meinig's favorite subject and "fired" his imagination. He was particularly interested in maps and the insights they give as to the nature of places. Instead of having imaginary playmates or imaginary adventures as many other children had, he had "imaginary geographies."

Upon graduation from high school, Meinig took a few courses in geography at the University of Washington but then spent the next three years in the United States Army. With the war over, and the G.I. Bill available, he decided to enter the School of Foreign Service at Georgetown University. He graduated with a degree in Foreign Service in 1948, but because of the dark clouds surrounding Foreign Service Officers as a result of the witch hunts of Senator Joseph McCarthy, he decided to forego a career in that area. He decided he wanted to be a professor and a historical geographer, something he knew little about. With little advice about where to go to graduate school, he decided to enter the graduate program at the University of Washington. He graduated with an M.A. in geography in 1950 and then took a position as an instructor in the Department of Geography at the University of Utah. While teaching at Utah, he also worked on a dissertation topic that dealt with the Palouse Country of Washington. He completed his dissertation on the Walla Walla area and was awarded the Ph.D. in 1953.

During the early years of his career at Utah, Meinig published a variety of articles that focused on issues in historical geography. His primary interest, however, was to "create a literature that would at once exemplify something of the character and value of the geographical approach to history and the historical approach to regional study" (1989:9). The result of this interest was the publication of his first book, *The Great Columbia Plain: A Historical Geography, 1805–1910*, which was published by the University of Washington Press. Meinig's nine years in Utah heightened his interest in social groups and led him to focus on communities that were characteristic of various regions. As a result, he wrote his classic paper, "The Mormon Culture Region: Strategies and Patterns in the Geography of the American West," which was published in the *Annals of the Association of American Geographers*.

In 1959 Meinig took a position at Syracuse University where he was to stay for the rest of his career. He continued his interest in the western United States and published a small book on Texas in 1969 (*Imperial Texas: An Interpretative Essay in Cultural Geography*) and two years later another book on the southwest.

Meinig spent the 1973–74 academic year at the University of St. Andrews in Scotland and in Israel at the Hebrew University of Jerusalem. As a result of these experiences, he began to take a broader view of America and its historical geography. In recent years, he has worked on a two-volume work, *The Shaping of America: A Geographical Perspective on 500 Years of History*. The first volume, *Atlantic America, 1492–1800*, was published in 1986 by the Yale University Press. He is currently working on the second volume that will be entitled *Continental America*.

While at Syracuse University, Meinig rose through the academic ranks and became chairman of the department in 1968. He held that position until 1973, when he was made Maxwell Professor of Geography, and in 1990 he became Maxwell Research Professor of Geography. He has held temporary appointments at a variety of universities including the University of Adelaide, the University of Colorado, the University of Cincinnati, the State University of New York at Brockport and Cortland, the Hebrew University, St. Andrews University, Ohio State University, the University of Idaho, and Washington State University. He has given special lectures or guest lectures at many universities throughout the world.

Meinig thoroughly enjoys being a geographer and has eloquently written about these pleasures (1989:25):

The born-geographer lives geography; that is to say, every scene, every place is of interest; every place is full of clues about history and culture, about values, tastes and fashions. Every place generates comparisons, prompts mental images of other places, similar in some way, different in others and every report of events, past or present, local or distant, is immediately "placed" in geographic context and conjures some mental images of its particular setting. Geography is a way of making sense of the world and an inexhaustible source of interest and pleasure.

I was one of the lucky ones. . . . It has been such a richly satisfying thing that when I reflect upon my life . . . it seems as if from the moment I first looked out in wonder across the hills of Palouse I have lived happily everafter.

Meinig's accomplishments have been recognized by his colleagues with a variety of honors and awards. He received an award "for meritorious contribution to the field of geography" from the Association of American Geographers (1965), the Award of Merit from the Seattle Historical Society (1968), the Award of Merit from the American Association for State and Local History (1969), the Charles P. Daly Medal from The American Geographical Society (1986), and the Master Teacher Award from the National Council for Geographic Education (1986).

Selected Bibliography

1954   "The Evolution of Understanding an Environment: Climate and Wheat Culture in the Columbia Plateau." *Yearbook of the Association of Pacific Coast Geographers* 16:25–34.

              "Wheat Sacks Out to Sea: The Early Export Trade of the Walla Walla Country." *Pacific Northwest Quarterly* 45:13–18.

1955   "The Growth of Agricultural Regions in the Far West: 1850–1910." *The Journal of Geography* 54:221–32.

              "Isaac I. Stevens, Practical Geographer of the Early Northwest." *Geographical Review* 45:542–58.

1956   "Culture Blocs and Political Blocs: Emergent Patterns in World Affairs." *The Western Humanities Review* 10:203–22.

1959   "Colonization of Wheatlands: Some Australian and American Comparisons." *The Australian Geographer* 7:205–13.

1961   "Goyder's Line of Rainfall: The Role of Geographic Concept in South Australian Land Policy and Agricultural Settlement." *Agricultural History* 35:207–14.

1962   *On the Margins of the Good Earth: The South Australian Wheat Frontier, 1869–1884.* Chicago: Rand McNally.

1965   "The Mormon Culture Region: Strategies and Patterns in the Geography of the American West, 1847–1864." *Annals of the Association of American Geographers* 55:191–220.

1967   "Cultural Geography." *Introductory Geography: Viewpoints and Themes.* Commission on College Geography Publications No. 5, Association of American Geographers.

1968   *The Great Columbia Plain: A Historical Geography, 1805–1910.* Seattle: University of Washington Press.

1969	*Imperial Texas: An Interpretative Essay in Cultural Geography.* Austin: University of Texas Press.
1971	*On Geography: Selected Writings of Preston E. James.* Edited by Meinig. Syracuse, N.Y.: Syracuse University Press.
	Southwest: Three Peoples in Geographical Change 1600–1970. Oxford: Oxford University Press.
1972	"American Wests: Preface to a Geographical Interpretation." *Annals of the Association of American Geographers* 62:159–84.
1976	"The Beholding Eye: Ten Versions of the Same Scene." *Landscape Architecture* 66:47–54.
1978	"The Continuous Shaping of America: A Prospectus for Geographers and Historians." *The American Historical Review* 83:1186–1217.
1979	*The Interpretation of Ordinary Landscapes.* Edited by Meinig. Oxford: Oxford University Press.
1983	"Geography as an Art." President's Guest Lecture. *Transactions of the Institute of British Geographers* 8:314–28.
1986	*The Shaping of America: A Geographical Perspective on 500 Years of History.* Vol. 1: *Atlantic America, 1492–1800.* New Haven: Yale University Press.
1989	"Cliffard Darby: An American Memoir." *Journal of Historical Geography* 15:20–33.
	"A Geographical Transect of the Atlantic World, *ca.* 1750." In Eugene D. Genovese and Leonard Hochberg, eds., *Geographical Perspectives in History: Essays in Honor of Edward Whiting Fox.* Oxford: Basil Blackwell.
	"The Historical Geography Imperative." *Annals of the Association of American Geographers* 79:79–87.

Chronology

1924	Born on November 1 in Palouse, Washington.
1948	Graduated with a B.S. in Foreign Service from Georgetown University.
1950	Graduated with an M.A. in Geography from the University of Washington and took a teaching position in the Department of Geography at the University of Utah.
1953	Awarded a Ph.D. from the University of Washington.
1954	First publication of "The Evolution of Understanding an Environment."
1959	Appointed Associate Professor at Syracuse University.
1965	Published "The Mormon Culture Region" and received the award "for meritorious contribution to the field of geography" from the Association of American Geographers.
1968	Publication of first book, *The Great Columbia Plain*; appointed chairman of the Department of Geography, Syracuse University.

1971	Publication of *Southwest: Three Peoples in Geographical Change 1600–1970*.
1973	Appointed Maxwell Professor of Geography, Syracuse University.
1986	Publication of *Atlantic America, 1492–1800*; given "Master Teacher Award" from the National Council for Geographical Education and the Charles P. Daly Medal from the American Geographical Society.
1990	Appointed Maxwell Research Professor of Geography.

Hugh Robert Mill

Hugh Robert Mill was born in Thurso, Scotland, on May 28, 1861, one of eleven children. His father worked at three occupations—as doctor, farmer, and magistrate.

Hugh Mill went to an infant school in 1866, then on to Free Church School in 1870. Tuberculosis ended his formal schooling while he was just a youth, though his interest in reading and education stimulated him to a life of learning. His special interests were literature, natural history, and physical science. His sisters helped teach him, and students were brought into the Mill home to help him learn subjects in which his siblings could not instruct him. After his father died, his mother moved to Edinburgh in 1877. There he attended night classes at the Watt Institution and worked to prepare himself for entry into the University of Edinburgh, where he matriculated in 1880 and graduated three years later with a Bachelor of Science degree.

After graduation Mill took his first job, as a scientist at the Scottish Marine Station in Granton on the Firth of Forth. A fellowship allowed him to continue his education as well, and he studied the salinity of sea water in the Firth of Forth for his doctoral thesis. He was awarded his doctorate in 1886 by the University of Edinburgh and stayed on at Granton until 1888. However, his doctoral work had introduced him to geography, and in 1887 he began working as a lecturer in geography and physiography at the Heriot-Watt College, which gradually expanded its programs and achieved university status. Mill also began giving lectures for university extensions, lecturing in towns in Scotland and northern England (Freeman, 1977).

After ending his work at Granton in 1888, Mill supplemented his income by publishing school texts, beginning with *Elementary Commercial Geography* and then *The Realm of Nature*, which was to be used for half a century as a basic text in physical geography. Mill married Frances MacDonald in 1889, and in 1892 took a job as Librarian for the Royal Geographical Society. In 1895 he was joint secretary with John Scott Keltie for the Sixth International Geographical Congress, which was held in London. From 1893 to 1900, he served as Recorder for the Geography section of the British Association for the Advancement of Science, and in 1901 he served as President.

During the late 1890s, Mill and his wife, along with Edward Heawood and A. J. Herbertson, began a series of bathymetric studies of lakes in the Lake District in northern England. They went on to do similar studies of some lakes in Scotland soon after the turn of the century with Sir John Murray and others. In 1896 he developed a plan for using the Ordnance Survey sheets to map land quality and land use in the British Isles, and provided samples to show how pragmatic such a project could be, though it was not be done (Wrigley, 1950).

In 1899 Mill edited *International Geography*, a mammoth work that included the works of seventy authors and covered more than a thousand pages. In 1901 he became joint director of the British Rainfall Organization, which had grown from an organization of some 450 observers in 1861 to one with more than 3,500 observers by 1900. The collected observations were published annually in *British Rainfall* and in *Symons's Monthly Meteorological Magazine*. In 1903 Mill and his wife moved to London, the location of the British Rainfall Organization's headquarters. There he began to organize scientific studies of the accumulated weather data and to establish more recording stations. His work was meticulous, as illustrated by his study of rainfall at the Ben Nevis observatory between 1883 and 1904.

Mill worked on other projects as well, including his book *The Siege of the South Pole*, which had been stimulated earlier by the International Geographical Congress in 1895. Despite his interest in the polar world, however, he was never able to visit there.

Failing eyesight led him to contemplate retirement as early as 1912, but he postponed it until 1919, the year in which the British Rainfall Organization was merged with the Meteorological Office of the Air Ministry. Retirement neither slowed his curiosity nor ended his scientific contributions to geography. At the request of Lady Shackleton, he wrote another book. *Life of *Ernest Shackleton*, which allowed him to return to his interest in the polar realm, and *Life Interests of a Geographer*, which was later published in London as *Hugh Robert Mill: An Autobiography*.

Beyond that, Mill's main interest became the climate of the British Isles, and he wrote at length on that topic for a chapter in Ogilvie's *Great Britain: Essays in Regional Geography*, which was issued in 1928 by the International Geographical Congress in Britain.

Hugh Robert Mill died in East Grinstead, in Sussex, on April 5, 1950, after thirty years of retirement.

Selected Bibliography

1888   *Elementary Commercial Geography.*
1891   *The Realm of Nature.*

1896   "Proposed Geographical Description of the British Islands Based on the Ordinance Survey." *Geographical Journal*, April.

1899   *International Geography*. Edited by Mill.

1900   "A Fragment of the Geography of England: South-west Sussex." *Geographical Journal*. March and April.

             "The Development of Habitable Lands." *Scottish Geographical Magazine* March.

             The New Lands.

1901   *British Rainfall*. Edited by Mill (until 1918).

1911   Editor of the Geographical Section. *Encyclopaedia Britannica*.

1923   *Life of Sir Ernest Shackleton*.

1928   Chapter on climate and weather in *Great Britain: Essays in Regional Geography*.

1930   *The Record of the Royal Geographical Society*.

1931   "Herbertson Memorial Lecture." *Geographical Teacher* 11.

1933   "Flashlights on Geography—Featuring Scotland." *Geography* 19.

1944   *Life Interests of a Geographer*. Issued in typescript.

1951   *Life Interests* reappeared as *Hugh Robert Mill: An Autobiography*.

Chronology

1861   Born May 28 at Thurso, Scotland.

1880   Entered Edinburgh University.

1883   B.Sc., Edinburgh.

1884   Chemist and physicist, with the Scottish Marine Station at Granton.

1886   D.Sc., Edinburgh. First visit to London.

1887   Lecturer in geography and physiography at Heriot-Watt College, Edinburgh, until 1892.

1888   First book: *Elementary Commercial Geography*.

1892   Librarian of the Royal Geographical Society.

1895   Joint Secretary of the sixth International Geographical Congress, London.

1900   Honorary LL.D., St. Andrews University. Resigned from his post at the Royal Geographical Society.

1901   Director of the British Rainfall Organization. Began publication of annual issues of *British Rainfall*. Editor of *Symons's Monthly Meteorological Magazine*.

1903   Rainfall expert to the Metropolitan Water Board, London (until 1919).

1907   President of the Royal Meteorological Society (until 1909).

1911   Editor of the Geographical Section, *Encyclopaedia Britannica*.

1917	Chairman of the Research Committee, Royal Geographical Society (until 1920).
1921	Advised Sir Ernest Shackleton on "Quest" expedition to Antarctic.
1926	Member of the Management Committee, Scott Polar Research Institute (until 1939).
1928	Centenary of German Geographical Society, Berlin.
1931	President of the Geographical Association.
1937	Retired from Council of the Royal Geographical Society.
1941	Wrote an account of his experiences in the Royal Meteorological Society's *Quarterly Journal*.
1950	Died April 5 at East Grinstead.

References

Freeman, T. W. 1977. "Hugh Robert Mill." *Geographers Biobibliographical Studies* 1:73–78.

Wrigley, Gladys M. 1950. "Hugh Robert Mill: An Appreciation." *Geographical Review* 40:657–60.

John Muir

John Muir, the eldest son of Daniel and Ann Gilrye Muir, was born on April 21, 1838, in the small Scottish coastal town of Dunbar, near Edinburgh. He was one of eight children. His father served in the British Army and then owned a grain shop in Dunbar. Daniel Muir, a fanatic Calvinist, played an important, and mostly negative, role in shaping John's attitudes and ideas. Life as a child in the Muir household was grim and austere. There was little laughter or frivolity; John's father ruled the household with the proverbial "iron fist." John revealed later that his father thrashed him almost every evening.

John's early school years were spent similarly. School was grim, and he hated it. According to Muir, Scotland's whole educational system was "founded on leather." Even when he was quite young, however, people noticed that he had some extraordinary talents and interests.

It was only in the outdoors that Muir found refuge from much of the rigidity of his childhood. He loved to play outdoors with his friends, and, long afterward, at the age of seventy-five, commented in his autobiography (*The Story of My Boyhood and Youth*, 1913:2): "With red-blooded playmates, wild as myself, I loved to wander in the fields to hear the birds sing, and along the seashore to gaze and wonder at the shells and seaweeds, eels and crabs. . . . When I was a boy in Scotland I was fond of everything that was wild, and all my life I've been growing fonder and fonder of wild places and wild creatures."

An important force in Muir's life was the family's decision to move to Wisconsin when he was eleven. With no formal schooling available, Muir taught himself algebra, geometry, and trigonometry and developed an insatiable appetite for reading. His favorite writers included Shakespeare, Milton, and *Alexander von Humboldt, and he was especially delighted by the geographic exploits of Humboldt.

Juxtaposed with reading, his other passion was inventing and building things. He devised a stream-powered sawmill and made a thermometer, a barometer, and a variety of other odd, but useful, inventions. One of his inventions won first prize at the agricultural fair in Madison, Wisconsin, in 1860. Perhaps more important, however, his inventions caught the eye of the wife of a professor at the University of Wisconsin, who immediately recognized Muir's genius and invited him to become a student at the university.

Muir was at first enthralled with the University of Wisconsin, which at that time had only three buildings and a tuition cost of $32 a year. He moved into a dorm, set up his own chemistry lab in his room, and conducted chemistry and biological experiments. Other students, as well as professors, were amazed at his creativity and inventiveness. He was especially delighted to work with Professor Ezra Carr, a science professor at the university, who taught Muir about the emerging science of glaciology and shared his personal library with him. The works of Wordsworth, Emerson, Thoreau, Humboldt, and Agassiz were of special interest.

In his junior year, Muir decided to leave the university and start "wandering." Ironically, John Muir never received his bachelor's degree from the university, but thirty-four years later, he was given an honorary doctorate. After wandering around much of southeast Canada and the north-central United States, working in a variety of industrial jobs and almost losing his eyesight in an industrial accident, he decided that he would follow in the footsteps of Humboldt and go to South America.

On September 1, 1867, at twenty-nine Muir headed south from an area near Indianapolis, Indiana, to the Gulf of Mexico. Only two years after the American Civil War, it was a harrowing time for a "northerner" to travel in the South, but Muir eventually made it to Cedar Keys in Florida. An account of this journey and the environmental observations made by Muir were eventually published in his essay "A Thousand-Mile Walk to the Gulf."

Muir's original intention of following in the footsteps of Humboldt were thwarted when he contracted malaria and was forced by poor health to abandon his South American journey. Instead, Muir decided to head west to California; in 1868 he arrived in San Francisco and then went on to the Yosemite area of the Sierras. While in Yosemite, he became fascinated with the region's geology and ecology. The unity of nature focused his thoughts, and he solidified his belief that "when we try to pick out anything by itself, we find it hitched to everything else in the universe" (Wolfe, 1945:124).

While in Yosemite, he also remembered Dr. Carr's lessons on glaciology and studied the evidence of glacial action in the Yosemite region. As a result, Muir published several articles on the region's glacial evolution. They were not well-received by much of the scientific community. Josiah Whitney and Clarence Starr King, leaders in the emerging field of geology and geomorphology, looked scornfully on Muir's ideas and ridiculed him as a "mere sheepherder" and "ignoramus," though he gained support from others, including Louis Agassiz, Joseph LeConte, John Tyndall, and even Ralph Waldo Emerson.

During the early 1870s Muir continued his studies of the Sierras but broadened them somewhat to include more ecological variables. He was far better equipped to observe and interpret than he had been during his first summer because many able scientists of the day (John Tyndall, Asa Gray, John Torrey) visited him and provided him with an on-site graduate faculty. He now wanted to elucidate what he called "the mystery of harmony." These observations, dealing with life forms in relation to altitude and other phenomena, were the first systematic observations of life zones in the Sierra Nevada and among the earliest made anywhere in the world.

During the mid-1870s Muir turned his attention to the giant sequoias. In a paper for the American Association for the Advancement of Science, he concluded that the big trees, rather than seeking wet areas, actually created such areas by capturing water that would normally come roaring downslope in destructive floods. He also became concerned with the practices of lumber companies and sheepmen and their influence on the environment. He presented a paper on the urgency of protecting the Sierra forest before the American Association for the Advancement of Science at its twenty-fifty annual meeting and it was published in its proceedings.

Throughout the later 1870s, he travelled in the west (Oregon, Washington, Utah). Little more than a decade had passed since the United States had purchased Alaska from the czar of Russia and little was known about it except that it was very cold and dangerous. The lure of Alaska proved to be too great, and Muir postponed his engagement to Louie Wanda and left San Francisco for Alaska in May 1879 on the first of his five trips to Alaska. On that first trip, he sailed into a small unchartered bay that did not even appear on the charts of Captain Vancouver made ninety years earlier. The bay, later named Glacier Bay because of its tidewater glaciers, enthralled Muir.

The first glacier that Muir encountered in Alaska he later named after the famous Scottish geologist *James Geikie. Just beyond the point where the northwest fork of Glacier Bay begins, Muir encountered a large glacier a-mile-and-a-half wide and seven-hundred-feet high in places. This was the first recorded sighting of the glacier that later was to bear Muir's name.

Although the 1880s and 1890s brought financial prosperity and independence for Muir, he continued his writing and advocacy for environmental causes. He made additional trips to Alaska, and during one trip through the Bering Straits he observed the landscape on both the Alaskan and Siberian coastlines. From that observation, he concluded that the Asian and North American continents had at one time been connected by a land bridge. Though generally accepted today, such an idea had not even been considered in the 1880s.

The 1890s were a decade of activism for Muir. In early 1890, he wrote two articles about Yosemite that were published by *Century* in August and September. They called for the preservation of the Yosemite region and made the case that if citizens wanted to keep the country they loved habitable they would have to fight for its preservation. By this time Muir had published some sixty-five articles and had a considerable number of followers. His strong advocacy for forest preservation gave rise to the often-repeated statement (Clarke, 1984:265) that Muir was "the father of the American National Forests." In 1892 he met informally with friends and drafted the articles of incorporation for the Sierra Club, which has become one of the most influential environmental organizations.

Muir believed that the only way to save the wilderness was for people to come to love it. He was encouraged by friends to change his writing genre from articles to books. Thus, in 1894 Muir's first book, *The Mountains of California*, was published. A biogeorahic study of the Sierra Nevada, it was an instant success—the first printing sold out within weeks of publication. It was followed in 1901 by Muir's second book, *Our National Parks*.

Following a strenuous world tour that he made in 1903 at age sixty-five, Muir actively campaigned for the preservation of Hetch-Hetchy Valley. To Muir, a plan to drown Hetch-Hetchy Valley, northeast of Yosemite Valley, was an outrage to all Americans. Although a National Park since 1890, the increasing demand for water by the growing city of San Francisco put utilitarian interests above those of conservation and preservation. The effort by Muir and his followers to preserve this region was the first example of a nationwide wilderness preservation campaign anywhere in the world (Hall, 1987:100), and this campaign acted as a catalyst for the creation of the United States National Park Service (Jones, 1965). Unfortunately, Muir lost his battle and a dam was built across Hetch-Hetchy Valley.

In 1911 Muir's third book, *My First Summer in the Sierra*, was published, and at the age of seventy-three, Muir embarked on his long-deferred South American expedition. Finally he was able to walk in the footsteps of Humboldt and fulfill his boyhood dream.

Muir's fourth book, *The Story of My Boyhood and Youth*, was published in 1913, the same year in which he received an honorary doctorate from the University of California at Berkeley—his third such degree.

In the latter part of 1914, Muir developed pneumonia and was hospitalized in Los Angeles. On Christmas Eve, with proof sheets of his newest book, *Travels in Alaska*, spread out on his hospital bed, he quietly died.

Selected Bibliography

1877   "On the Post-Glacial History of Sequoia gigantea." American Association for the Advancement of Science, *Proceedings* 25:242–53.

1884   "On Glaciation of the Arctic and Subarctic Regions . . . in the Year 1881." 48th Congress, 1st Session, Senate Report, Vol. 8, 135–47.

1888   *Picturesque California and the Regions West of the Rocky Mountains from Alaska to Mexico.* Edited by Muir. San Francisco: J. Dewing.

1893   "Alaska." *American Geologist* (May): 287–99.

1894   *The Mountains of California.* New York: Century.

1901   *Our National Parks.* Boston: Houghton Mifflin.

1909	*Stickeen*. Boston: Houghton Mifflin.
1910	"The Hetch-Hetchy Valley: A National Question." *American Forestry* 16:263–69.
1911	*Henry Edward Harriman*. New York: Doubleday, Page.
	My First Summer in the Sierra. Boston: Houghton Mifflin.
1912	*The Yosemite*. New York: Century.
1913	*The Story of My Boyhood and Youth*. Boston: Houghton Mifflin.
1915	*Letters to a Friend*. Edited by Jeanne C. Carr. Boston: Houghton Mifflin.
1917	*Works: The Sierra Edition*. Edited by William F. Badé. 10 vols. New York: Houghton Mifflin.
1938	*John of the Mountains: The Unpublished Journals of John Muir*. Edited by Linnie Marsh Wolfe. Boston: Houghton Mifflin.

Chronology

1838	Born April 21 in Dunbar, Scotland.
1849	Muir family moved to a homestead near Portage, Wisconsin.
1861	Enrolled at University of Wisconsin.
1863	Left University of Wisconsin. Began a series of odd jobs.
1867	Decided to explore the wilderness as a vocation.
1869	First summer in the Sierra mountains, herding sheep.
1870	In the Yosemite with LeConte geological expedition.
1871	Development of his theory on the glacial origins of Yosemite.
1879	First trip to Alaska.
1890	Yosemite National Park Bill passed, largely as a result of his article in *Century Magazine*.
1893	Visited Europe.
1899	Member of the Harriman-Alaska expedition (fourth trip).
1914	Died December 24, in Los Angeles.

References

Clarke, James M. 1984. *The Pathless Way*. Madison: University of Wisconsin Press.
Hall, Colin Michael. 1987. "John Muir in New Zealand." *New Zealand Geographer* (October): 99–103.
Jones, H. R. 1965. *John Muir and the Sierra Club*. San Francisco: Sierra Club Books.
Wolfe, Linnie M. 1945. *The Life of John Muir*. Madison: University of Wisconsin Press.

Lewis Mumford

Lewis Mumford was born on October 19, 1895, in Flushing, New York. After an uneventful trip through grammar school, he entered Stuyvesant High School in 1909 with an eye toward an engineering career. Along the way, however, that goal gave way to his interest in writing, and in 1912 he enrolled in the City College of New York to begin his preparation for a career as a writer (Miller, 1989).

A turning point in Mumford's education occurred in 1915, when he discovered the works of Patrick Geddes and subsequently began to explore New York City on foot as a student whose classroom had become that metropolis. Those explorations were not only to set the direction in which his writings would take him, but also to cultivate in him a geographical sense as well. Though never formally educated as a geographer, his writings certainly had an influence on urban geographers and planners, especially in the United States.

After a brief sojourn in the United States Navy during 1918 and 1919, Mumford briefly joined the staff of *The Dial*. In 1920 he moved to London, where he became editor of *Sociological Review* for a short while, after which he returned to New York and began to write for *The Freeman*. The following year he married Sophia Wittenberg.

With his wife, Mumford took up residence in New York's Greenwich Village and in 1922 published *The Story of Utopias*. In that same year they moved to Brooklyn Heights, and the following year he became a cofounder of the Regional Planning Association of America. In 1924 Mumford published his first book on architecture, *Sticks and Stones*. In July 1925 his son, Geddes, was born. Mumford lectured abroad, in Geneva and Edinburgh, where he met with Patrick Geddes. With their new son, he and Sophia moved to Sunnyside Gardens, in Queens, an area planned by the Regional Planning Association of America.

In 1926 Mumford spent his first summer in Amenia, New York, an old iron-making center. It was a location that would be of considerable importance for him. He continued to write, travel, and lecture, and in 1928 worked on the Regional Planning Association of America development of a plan for Radburn, in Fair Lawn, New Jersey.

His publications were beginning to demonstrate the breadth of his intellectual interests; from the subject of architecture he went on to write *Herman Melville* and, 1931, *The Brown Decade*. In that same year he joined the staff of *The New Yorker*, where he wrote columns such as "The Sky Line" and "The Art Galleries."

In 1934 Mumford published what perhaps was the first book that had an impact more directly on geography, *Technics and Civilization*. He also became a member of the New York City Board of Higher Education. In the following year, his daughter, Alison, was born, and the year after that the Mumford family moved to Amenia.

Amenia proved to be an excellent place for Mumford to live and work, and he began to put together another influential book on urban affairs, *The Culture of Cities*, which was published in 1938. By then, as World War II began, he was getting actively involved in opposing American neutrality, an issue over which he lost such notable friends as Frank Lloyd Wright.

In 1942 he took a position at Stanford University in Palo Alto, California, where he helped design a new program in the humanities. Only two years later, however, he resigned his post and moved back to Amenia. There he published *The Condition of Man*.

Tragedy struck the Mumford family in September, 1944, when Geddes was killed in combat in Italy. After that, the family moved to Hanover, New Hampshire, and Mumford began writing *Green Memories*, a biography of his son Geddes, and began actively campaigning against the use of nuclear weapons.

After living for another four years in New York City, Mumford took a position as a visiting professor at the University of Pennsylvania, beginning a relationship that lasted for a decade, during which *Art and Technics*, *The Transformations of Man*, and *The City of History* appeared. After the latter won the National Book Award, he went as a visiting lecturer to the University of California at Berkeley. In 1962 Mumford again returned to his beloved Amenia to work on an autobiography and on his history of technology and human development, which ultimately led to two volumes, *The Myth of the Machine*. Vol. 1: *Technics and Human Development*, published in 1967, and *The Myth of the Machine*. Vol. 2: *The Pentagon of Power*, published in 1970. In between publication of those two volumes, he found time to publish *The Urban Prospect*. All of these volumes had an influence on geography and geographers, as well as on many other social sciences.

In 1982, after having earlier published *My Works and Days*, Mumford finally published his autobiography, *Sketches from Life*, which was nominated for an American Book Award. Four years later he received the National Medal of Arts.

Though Mumford dabbled in the world of academia, from Stanford to the

University of Pennsylvania, his was by-and-large the world of letters and the craft of writing. He died january 26, 1990, in Amenia, New York.

Selected Bibliography

1922   *The Story of Utopias*. New York: Boni and Liveright.

1924   *Sticks and Stones: A Study of American Architecture and Civilization*. New York: Boni and Liveright.

1926   *The Golden Day: A Study in American Experiences and Culture*. New York: Boni and Liveright.

1928   *Herman Melville*. New York: Harcourt, Brace.

1931   *The Brown Decades: A Study of the Arts in America, 1865–1895*. New York: Harcourt, Brace.

1934   *America and Alfred Stieglitz: A Collective Portrait*. Edited by Lewis Mumford, Dorothy Norman, Paul Rosenfeld, and Harold Rugg. Garden City, N.Y.: Doubleday, Doran.

         Technics and Civilization. New York: Harcourt, Brace.

1938   *The Culture of Cities*. New York: Harcourt, Brace.

         Wither Honolulu? A Memorandum Report on Park and City Planning. Prepared by Lewis Mumford for City and County of Honolulu Park Board. Honolulu.

1939   *Regional Planning in the Pacific Northwest: A Memorandum*. Portland, Ore.: Northwest Regional Council.

1940   *Faith for Living*. New York: Harcourt, Brace.

1943   *The Social Foundations of Post-War Building*. Rebuilding Britain Series No. 9. London: Faber and Faber.

1944   *The Condition of Man*. New York: Harcourt, Brace.

1945   *City Development: Studies in Urban Disintegration and Renewal*. New York: Harcourt, Brace.

         The Plan of London County. Rebuilding Britain Series. No. 12. London: Faber and Faber.

1946   *Values for Survival: Essays, Addresses, and Letters on Politics and Education*. New York: Harcourt, Brace.

1947   *Green Memories: The Story of Geddes Mumford*. New York: Harcourt, Brace.

1951   *The Conduct of Life*. New York: Harcourt, Brace.

1952   *Art and Technics*. New York: Columbia University Press.

1955   *The Brown Decades: A Study of the Arts in America, 1865–1895*. Rev. ed. New York: Dover.

         Sticks and Stones: A Study of American Architecture and Civilization. Rev. ed. New York: Dover.

1956	*The Transformations of Man*. New York: Harper & Brothers.
1961	*The City in History: Its Origins, Its Transformation, and Its Prospects*. New York: Harcourt, Brace and World.
1962	*The Story of Utopias*. Rev. ed. New York: Viking.
1967	*The Myth of the Machine*. Vol. 1: *Technics and Human Development*. New York: Harcourt, Brace and World.
1968	*The Golden Day: A Study in American Literature and Culture*. New York: Dover.
	The Urban Prospect. New York: Harcourt, Brace and World.
1970	*The Myth of the Machine*. Vol. 2: *The Pentagon of Power*. New York: Harcourt Brace Jovanovich.
1972	*The Transformations of Man*. New York: Harper & Row/Torchbook.
1975	*Findings and Keepings: Analects for an Autobiography*. New York: Harcourt Brace Jovanovich.
1979	*My Works and Days: A Personal Chronicle*. New York: Harcourt Brace Jovanovich.
1982	*Sketches from Life: The Autobiography of Lewis Mumford*. New York: Dial.

Chronology

1895	Born in Flushing, New York on October 19.
1912	Decides to become a writer, enrolls in City College of New York.
1918	Joins U.S. Navy.
1919	Mustered out of the Navy.
1922	Publishes his first book: *The Story of Utopias*.
1923	Cofounder of the Regional Planning Association of America.
1924	Publishes his first book on architecture, *Sticks and Stones*.
1929	Begins visiting professorship at Dartmouth College.
1934	Appointed to New York City Board of Higher Education.
1940	Joins Committee to Defend America by Aiding the Allies.
1942	Joins faculty of Stanford University, California.
1944	Resigns from Stanford.
1946	Visits England as an advisor on post-war urban planning.
1951	Visiting professor at University of Pennsylvania.
1957	Visiting professorship at MIT.
1961	Visiting professor at University of California, Berkeley.
1964	Drafts city plan for Oxford, England. Presidential Medal of Freedom.
1972	Awarded the National Medal for Literature.

1986   Awarded the National Medal of Arts.

1990   Died in Amenia, New York, January 26.

Reference

Miller, Donald L. 1989. *Lewis Mumford: A Life*. New York: Weidenfeld and Nicholson.

Sebastian Münster

Sebastian Münster was born on January 20, 1488, in the little village of Niederingelheim, near Mainz, in Germany. Though not much is known about Münster's family, they seem to have been middle class, and his early education was probably typical of the time. In 1505 he entered the Franciscan Order in Heidelberg, Germany, and began studies in logic, philosophy, and cosmology. Two years later he went to Louvain, where he studied mathematics, astronomy, and geography. From Louvain he went on to study at Freiburg under Gregorius Reisch, a Hebrew scholar and geographer, as well as a theologian.

In 1509 he went to Rufach, where he pursued the same subjects under the tutelage of Conrad Pellikan, who was said to have warned the young Münster of concentrating too much on geography at the expense of philosophy and theology. In 1511 Münster went to the Franciscan monastery in Pforzheim, along with Pellikan, and in the following year he was ordained.

In 1514, again in conjunction with Pellikan, Münster became a lecturer in philosophy and theology at Tübingen, where he also ended up studying geography with Johannes Stöffler. Four years later he moved to Basel, Switzerland; Pellikan came a year later, and they renewed their studies in theology together.

In 1520 Münster took a lecturer position at the University of Heidelberg and published a Hebrew grammar. Four years later, he became a professor of Hebrew there and began to concentrate more of his studies on languages and linguistics. However, he also developed a friendship with Beatus Rhenanus, who renewed Münster's interest in cosmography.

In 1529 he moved to Basel again, where he took a position as professor of Hebrew. He left the Franciscan order and married that year as well. His teaching of Hebrew brought considerable recognition to the University of Basel, and he went on to become Professor of Old Testament Theology there, and later still, Rector of the university in 1546–48.

To Münster, theology and geography, especially cosmography, were of a single cloth, interwoven and inseparable. In his geographical works, which comprise only a small portion of his total intellectual output, he wrote on the aims and methods of geography. He argued (Büttner and Burmeister, 1979:101) that "geography sheds light on the Bible . . . gives ordinary people who are unable to travel widely a realization of the creation and rule of the world by God." Münster believed that cosmography treated as a science, would help people assimilate the ideas that geography could provide.

Given his theological training, Münster began his work with a discussion of the Creation, but his real focus was on the earth's surface during that process. According to Büttner and Burmeister (1979:101), "He was seeking a compromise between Greek thought, the biblical account of creation, and the theology of the Reformation by directing attention to the surface of the earth." Münster's major geographical work, *Cosmography*, was influenced both by his own studies in philosophy and theology and by the work of *Ptolemy. It was the first major geographic publication after the first early voyages of discovery. Though strongly based in the theological picture of the day in some ways, his geographical views nevertheless were of considerable interest. He had a clear awareness of scale and looked at places from the largest and most general to the smallest and most particular. Surface features and climate, as well as agricultural potential and population distribution, attracted his attention.

The *Cosmography* was divided into two parts, general (Part 1) and special (Part 2), in a manner similar to some of its predecessors. Unlike them, however, Münster's special geography delved more deeply into the study of regions, from Germany to the British Isles. Part 1 contained only three maps, one of which showed a combination of biblical and Greek thought in geographic studies. In Part 2, however, maps appeared in a variety of orientations, and Münster through this work is thought to have pioneered the development of street maps. Most of his theological themes are found in Part 1.

Münster's work was the most popular geographic work published during the sixteenth century; it enjoyed forty-six editions and was published in six different languages. It was influential on a number of subsequent geographers and cartographers, including Mercator, Keckermann, and *Immanuel Kant. According to Büttner and Burmeister (1979:103), "To a great extent the fascination of Münster's work lies in the relation of his geography to the theological and philosophical outlook of his time, and his influence on those who were concerned to place geography in a universal system of thought was considerable."

About four years after he ended his career as Rector of the University of Basel, Münster contracted the plague. He died on May 26, 1552.

Selected Bibliography

1520   "Epitome Hebraicae Grammaticae." Basel.

1523   "Dictionarium Hebraicum." Basel.

1524   "Institutiones Grammaticae in Hebraeam Linguam." Basel.

1525	"Instrument der Sonnen." Oppenheim.
	"Grammatica Hebraica Absolutissima Eliae Levitae." Basel.
	"Composita Verborum et Nominum Hebraicorum Eliae Levita Autore Editum." Basel.
1526	*Kalender of die Jahre* 1527, 1533, 1549. Basel.
1527	"Chaldaica Grammatica." Basel.
	"Dictionarium Chaldaicum." Basel.
	"Capitula Cantici Autore Eliae Levita." Basel.
	"Compendium Hebraicae Grammaticae." Basel and Paris.
1528	"Erklärung des Instruments der Sonnen." Oppenheim.
1529	"Instrument über den Mondslauf." Worms.
	"Erklärung des Instruments über den Mond." Worms.
1530	"Germaniae Descriptio." Basel.
	"Dictionarium Trilingue." Basel.
1531	"Compositio Horologiorum." Basel.
1532	"Weltkarte su Simon Grynaeus." Basel: Novus Orbis.
1534	"Instrumentum Novum." Basel.
	"Canones Super Novum Instrumentum Luminarium." Basel.
	"Hebraica Biblia Latina." 2 vols. Basel.
1535	"Isagoge Elementalis in Hebraican Linguam." Basel.
1536	*Mappa Europae*. Frankfurt. 2d ed., 1537.
	"Organum Uranicum." Basel.
1537	"Evangelium Secundum Matthaeum in lingua Hebraica." Basel.
1538	Edition and translation into Latin of "Aegidius Tschudis Rhaetia." Basel.
	Edition of "Solin and Mela." Basel.
1539	"Accentuum Hebraicorum Liber ab Eliae Iudaeo Editus." Basel.
1540	Edition and translation into Latin of *Geographica universalis Claudii Ptolemaei*. Basel. 4th ed., 1552.
1542	"Opus Grammaticum Consummatum." Basel.
1544	*Cosmographia*. 4th ed. Small German edition, Basel.
1546	Edition of *Shaera Mundi by Abraham bar Chija*. Basel.
1550	*Cosmographia*. 17th ed. Large German edition, Basel, 1628.
1551	"Rudimenta Mathematica." Basel.

Chronology

1488	Born January 20 in Niederingelheim, a town near Mainz, Germany.
1505	Entered Franciscan Order in Heidelberg.
1507	Studied mathematics, geography, and astronomy in Louvain.

1512	Ordained as a priest.
1514	Lectured at the Ordensstudium in Tübingen. A student of Stöffler.
1520	Sympathizes with Martin Luther's ideas.
1522	Lecturer in Hebrew at the Ordensstudium in Heidelberg.
1524	Professor of Hebrew at Heidelberg University.
1529	Professor of Hebrew at Basel University. Left the Franciscan Order and married.
1542	Professor of Old Testament Theology at Basel.
1544	Published *Cosmography*.
1546	Rector of Basel University.
1552	Died of the plague, May 26 in Basel.

Reference

Büttner, Manfred, and Karl H. Burmeister. 1979. "Sebastian Münster." *Geographers Biobibliographical Studies* 3:99–106.

Fridtjof Nansen

Fridtjof Nansen was born in Store-Froen, Norway, a small town near Christiania [now Oslo], on October 10, 1861. His early schooling took place in Christiania, and in 1880 he passed the entrance exams for admittance into the university, where he took up the study of zoology. He knew that he wanted to be able to pursue an occupation that would allow him to spend time outdoors. Nansen was an athletic young man, accomplished as a skier, skater, and hunter. His athleticism served him well in later life, when the rigors of Arctic exploration would test his endurance to the limit.

In 1882 Nansen signed on to a sealing vessel, the *Viking*, for a voyage that took him into the waters around Greenland, where he first saw, and was captivated by, the Greenland ice sheet. In that same year, he became zoology curator at the Bergen museum, where he worked on several papers on zoology and histology. For one of those papers, ''The Structure and Combination of Histological Elements of the Central Nervous System,'' published in 1887, he received his doctoral degree from the University in Christiania.

In May 1888, six years after first seeing it, Nansen led an expedition to Greenland to cross the ice sheet, a crossing that was made between August 15 and September 26. Afterward, he and his followers wintered over on the west coast of Greenland, where he began collecting information about the Eskimos there, material that he later used in his first book, *Eskimo Life*, which was published in 1891.

Nansen returned to Norway in 1889, and in 1890, while finishing his book on the Eskimos, presented to the Norwegian Geographical Society a plan for building a ship, which he proposed to allow to freeze in the waters off eastern Siberia and be carried across the Arctic Ocean to Spitsbergen by oceanic currents. Though Nansen's plan was criticized by many, the Norwegian government decided to fund much of the project, and the remainder of the funds were raised from other sources, including private donations. His new ship, the *Fram*, built to withstand the pressures of frozen ice and buffeting seas and winds, set off from Christiania on June 24, 1893, and in September of that year was frozen solidly into the growing Arctic ice, allowing the drift to begin.

On March 14, 1895, having determined that the vessel could indeed withstand the pressures and successfully finish its voyage, Nansen left the *Fram* to set out northward. With one companion, dogsleds, and kayaks, he reached slightly beyond 86 degrees north latitude, the furthest north that anyone had reached at the time, before turning back. This exploration put to rest forever the idea that there was an open polar sea at those high latitudes.

Nansen and his companion then returned to Franz Josef Land. They wintered on Frederick Jackson Island in a stone hut covered with walrus hides, which they had built themselves. In the spring of 1896 they headed toward Spitsbergen, and on the way ran into Frederick Jackson, the island's namesake. Jackson was returning from another Arctic expedition at the time, so Nansen and his companion returned to Norway with Jackson, and the *Fram* reached Christiania in September 1896. Nansen recorded these expeditions in a two-volume work, *Farthest North*, which was published in 1897.

Nansen next took a position as professor of zoology, which had been established especially for him at the university at Christiania. In 1900 he went for a cruise in the Norwegian Sea aboard the *Michael Lars*. Later his interests drifted from zoology to oceanography, and in 1908 his position became professor of oceanography. During the following years, he worked on numerous scientific projects, including the analysis of information that he had collected on his earlier Arctic explorations, and went on sojourns by sea to Spitsbergen, the Azores, through the Barents Sea, the Kara Sea, and around Siberia.

In 1917 Nansen was appointed to lead a Norwegian commission to the United States, where he successfully negotiated government support of the provision of essential supplies to Norway as World War I was getting under way. In 1920 he headed the Norwegian delegation to the first assembly of the League of Nations.

In April of that year the League appointed him as the high commissioner responsible for repatriation of some half million prisoners of war from Russia, who had been in the German and Austro-Hungarian armies and were being held by the Russian government, which would not recognize the League of Nations. Nansen successfully negotiated the release and repatriation of more than 400,000 prisoners in September 1922.

During the time that he was serving in that high commission position, Nansen was also asked by the Red Cross to lead an effort to relieve some of the famine problems that were affecting Russia in 1921. He convinced Moscow to allow him to open an office there of the "International Russian Relief Executive," which was finally funded by private donations. In 1922 he initiated an international agreement signed in Geneva that allowed displaced persons to have an identification card. In that same year, Nansen received the Nobel Peace Prize.

Nansen died on May 13, 1930, and in 1931, in his honor, the Nansen International Office for Refugees was established in Geneva. In writing about Nansen's life, Finley (1930:534) ended his comments by noting: ''And not only will Northern skalds [ancient Scandinavian poets] sing of his adventures in rune and epic, but peoples in the South whom he has helped in their misery will remember him gratefully as some Promethean Titan who sought to give them succor, as one who defied powers that seemed omnipotent, and who hoped till hope created 'from its own wreck' the thing it contemplated.''

Selected Bibliography

1887   ''The Structure and Combination of Histological Elements of the Central Nervous System.''

1891   *Eskimo Life.*

1897   *Farthest North.* Vols. 1 and 2. London: Macmillan.

1911   *Northern Mists.* Vols. 1 and 2. London: W. Heinemann.

1927   *Adventure and Other Papers.* Freeport, N.Y.: Books for Libraries Press. Reprinted in 1967.

Chronology

1861   Born October 10 near Oslo, Norway.

1880   Passed entrance examination for university. Studied zoology.

1882   Sailed on sealing ship *Viking* to waters off Greenland. Appointed curator of zoology at the Bergen museum.

1888   Crossed Greenland ice sheet for the first time.

1893   Voyage to open polar sea aboard the *Fram*. Voyage lasted three years.

1896   Professor of zoology at Christiania University.

1900   Oceanographic voyage aboard *Michael Lars* to Norwegian Sea.

1906   Appointed first minister from Norwegian monarchy to London.

1908   Appointed Professor of Oceanography at Christiana University in Oslo, Norway.

1910   Voyage through the northeastern North Atlantic.

1912   Voyage aboard his yacht *Veslemoy* to waters near Spitsbergen.

1913   Travelled through the Barents Sea and Kara Sea to mouth of the Yenisey River and back through Siberia.

1914   Oceanographic cruise to Azores.

1917   Appointed head of Norwegian commission to the United States. Negotiated an agreement on importing essential supplies into Norway.

1920   Norwegian representative to League of Nations; negotiated with Russia on repatriation of 500,000 prisoners of war held from the former German and Austro-Hungarian armies.

1922   On Nansen's initiative, an international agreement was signed in Geneva introducing the identification card for displaced persons known as the ''Nansen Passport.'' Awarded Nobel Peace Prize for his relief work after World War I.

1926	Rector of St. Andrew's University, Scotland.
1930	Died, May 13.

Reference

Finley, John H. 1930. ''Fridtjof Nansen.'' *Geographical Review* 20:533–34.

James J. Parsons

James J. Parsons is one of this century's foremost Latin Americanist and Iberianist geographers. He was born in Cortland, New York, on November 15, 1915. After attending public schools in Monrovia and Pasadena, California, he went to Pasadena Junior College from 1933 to 1935. From junior college, he went to the University of California at Berkeley and graduated with an A.B. degree in 1937. His undergraduate training at Berkeley was in economics, and much of his later geographic work also had an emphasis on economic issues.

After completing his undergraduate degree, Parsons took a position as News Editor at the *Ukiah Redwood Journal*. According to his friend and graduate school colleague, Robert C. West (Denevan, 1989:xxvi), his experience as a journalist "may well have enhanced his ability to produce the precise, facile prose that characterizes his professional writings. His simple, direct English, unencumbered by jargon, makes all of his works a delight to read."

Parsons decided to change his academic specialty when he entered the graduate-level geography program at Berkeley. He was greatly influenced by his mentor *Carl Sauer, who instilled in him an appreciation for the historical evolution of landscapes and for the relationship between people and the physical environment. Sauer also emphasized the importance of field work in geographical research, an idea Parsons enthusiastically adopted and one that is evidenced in Parsons' later work. Parsons completed his M.A. in geography at Berkeley in 1939, and his thesis was titled "The California Hop Industry: Its Eighty Years of Development and Expansion." In this work he developed the themes of agricultural diffusion and colonization, ideas that were to appear in many of his later works. His first published work, based on this thesis, was "Hops in Early California Agriculture," published in *Agricultural History* in 1940.

It was during this time, however, that Parsons started to develop his interest in Latin America. During the semester break, from December 1940 to January 1941, he took a trip into northern Mexico with West, his fellow student and friend. The two of them took a trip across the Sierra Madre Occidental over the colonial "Topia Road." According to West (Denevan, 1989:xxviii), "The trip across the Sierra took ten exhausting days of travel by mule and foot. . . . This may have been Jim Parson's first fieldwork in Latin America, and perhaps it whetted his desire to continue geographical investigations in that part of the world."

Upon completion of this journey, West and Parsons submitted an article about their experiences to the *Geographical Review*, where it was published as "The Personality of Mexico" the following year.

During World War II, Parsons served in the United States Army and rose through the ranks from private to major. He returned to Berkeley after the war to work on his Ph.D., which he completed in 1948. He had been appointed Instructor of Geography at Berkeley in 1946 and spent the rest of his academic career at that institution rising through the academic ranks to Assistant Professor (1948), Associate Professor (1952), and Full Professor (1960). At various times he has also served as Chairman of the Department of Geography and Chairman of the Center for Latin American Studies.

The primary emphasis of Parson's geographic research has been on Latin American topics, especially on how humans impact vegetation. This work has included studies on the anomalous pine savanna in Nicaragua and easternmost Honduras, the grasslands of northern Colombia, the *Llanos* of Colombia and Venezuela, and the pastures of Central America. "In the various places he knows well and is well known, such as Colombia, the western Caribbean, and the Canaries, local scholars have no difficulty locating him in the tradition of those who have gone before: [*Alexander von] Humboldt, [*Alfred] Hettner, and Sapper" (Denevan, 1989:xxxii).

In 1959 Parsons received a Guggenheim Fellowship for a year's study and travel in Portugal and Spain, which became the catalyst for a variety of studies in that region dealing with such topics as the historical development of the exploitation of natural resources, innovative farming techniques, and architecture. His recent work has focused on the Canary Islands and the role those islands have played in the transfer of artifacts and lifeways to the New World.

Although most of Parsons' work has dealt with Latin America, he has also had a long-time interest in the regional geography of California. He has authored over fifteen studies dealing with various issues in California's regional geography, including economic studies of agriculture, home-building and residential location, energy use, and manufacturing.

Besides his five books and monographs, and over one hundred articles and notes in a wide variety of journals, Parsons has also been a mentor to numerous geographers interested in Latin American and non–Latin American topics. While at Berkeley, he has supervised thirty-four Ph.D. dissertations and has been a source of encouragement to numerous geographers.

Parsons has been deeply involved in the work of the Association of American Geographers and served as both its Vice President (1973–74) and President

(1974–75). He has also served as President of the Association of Pacific Coast Geographers (1954–55). He has been on the editorial boards of *Hispanic-American Historical Review*, *Latin American Research Review*, *Ibero-Americana*, *Journal of Interamerican Studies*, *Progress in Geography*, and *Oxford University Press Research Series in Geography*.

Honors awarded include an honorary degree, *Doctor honoris causa*, University de Antioquia (Medellin, Colombia; 1965); ARCO Award for Achievement from the California Council for Geographic Education (1977); Outstanding Contribution Award from the Conference of Latin Americanist Geographers (1978); Honors from the Association of American Geographers (1983); David Livingstone Memorial Medal from the American Geographical Society (1985); and the Pedro Justo Berrio Medal from the Department of Antioquia in Colombia (1987).

Perhaps the best tribute to Parsons comes from his former student Kent Mathewson (Denevan, 1989:xxxv):

In describing the man himself, this remarkable spirit of generosity may be the single attribute that will come to mind most quickly. Those who have been fortunate in knowing James Parsons in the field, in the classroom, at conferences, as a colleague, or simply as admirers of his work, will attest that his contagious sense of affinity for all sorts of people and a multiplicity of remarkable places is something that is impossible not to share.

Selected Bibliography

1940   "Hops in Early California Agriculture." *Agricultural History* 14:110–16.

1941   With Robert C. West. "The Topia Road: A Trans-Sierran Trail of Colonial Mexico." *Geographical Review* 31:406–13.

1945   "Coffee and Settlement in New Caledonia." *Geographical Review* 35:12–21.

1949   *Antioqueno Colonization in Western Colombia*. Berkeley: University of California Press.

            "California Manufacturing." *Geographical Review* 39:229–41.

1950   "Recent Industrial Development in the Gulf South." *Geographical Review* 40:67–83.

            "The Geography of Natural Gas in the United States." *Economic Geography* 26:162–78.

1952   "The Settlement of the Sinu Valley of Colombia." *Geographical Review* 42:67–86.

1956   *San Andres and Providencia: English-Speaking Islands in the Western Caribbean*. University of California Publications in Geography, No. 12.

1957   *San Francisco*. Garden City, N.Y.: Doubleday.

            "Bananas in Ecuador: A New Chapter in the History of Tropical Agriculture." *Economic Geography* 33:201–16.

1960	"Starlings for Seville." *Landscape* 10:28–31.

1962   "The Cork Oak Forests and the Evolution of the Cork Industry in Southern Spain." *Economic Geography* 38:195–214.

The Green Turtle and Man. Gainsville: University of Florida Press.

1967   Coeditor with S. V. Ciriacy-Wantrup. *Natural Resources: Quality and Quantity*. Berkeley: University of California Press.

Antioquia's Corridor to the Sea: An Historical Geography of the Settlement of Uraba. Berkeley: University of California Press.

With William M. Denevan. "Pre-Columbian Ridged Fields." *Scientific American* 217:92–100.

1971   With David R. Radell. "Realejo: A Forgotten Colonial Port and Ship-building Center in Nicaragua." *Hispanic American Historical Review* 51:295–312.

1975   "The Historical Preconditions of Industrialization—Medellin Reconsidered." *Proceedings of the Conference of Latin Americanist Geographers* 5:119–24.

1977   "Geography as Exploration and Discovery." *Annals of the Association of American Geographers* 67:1–16.

1980   Coeditor with William V. Davidson. *Historical Geography of Latin America: Papers in Honor of Robert C. West*. Baton Rouge: Louisiana State University.

1981   "Human Influences on the Pine and Laurel Forests of the Canary Islands." *Geographical Review* 71:253–71.

1983   "The Migration of Canary Islanders to the Americas: An Unbroken Current Since Columbus." *The Americas* 39:447–81.

1986   "A Geographer Looks at the San Joaquin Valley." *Geographical Review* 76:371–89.

1987   "The Origin and Dispersal of the Domesticated Canary." *Journal of Cultural Geography* 7:19–33.

1988   "Hillside Letters in the Western Landscape." *Landscape* 30:15–23.

"The Scourge of Cows." *Whole Earth Review* 58:7–11.

1991   "Giant American Bamboo in the Vernacular Architecture of Colombia and Ecuador." *Geographical Review* 81:131–53.

Chronology

1915   Born November 15 in Cortland, New York.

1933–35   Attended Pasadena Junior College.

1937   Graduated with an A.B. degree from the University of California at Berkeley.

1940   First publication, "Hops in Early California Agriculture."

1941–45   In the United States Army.

1948	Awarded Ph.D. in Geography from the University of California at Berkeley and appointed Assistant Professor at Berkeley.
1949	Publication of first book, *Antioqueno Colonization in Western Colombia*.
1960	Appointed Full Professor and Chairman of the Department of Geography at Berkeley.
1965	Awarded honorary degree from the University de Antioquia in Medellin, Colombia.
1974–75	Elected President of the Association of American Geographers.
1978	Received the Outstanding Contribution Award from the Conference of Latin Americanist Geographers.
1983	Received the "Honors" awarded from the Association of American Geographers.
1985	Received the David Livingstone Memorial Medal from the American Geographical Society.

Reference

Denevan, William M., ed. 1989. *Hispanic Lands and Peoples: Selected Writings of James J. Parsons*. Boulder, Colo.: Westview.

Albrecht Penck

Albrecht Penck was born on September 25, 1858, in Leipzig-Readnita. For the most part his schooling began and ended in Leipzig, where he entered the university in 1875 before his seventeenth birthday to study various sciences with Hermann Kolbe, August Schenk, and Hermann Credner.

As a youngster, Penck had been interested in the natural environment around Leipzig and had even collected *glacial erratics*. This interest led directly to his first scientific publication, in 1877, "Nordische Basalte im Diluvium von Leipzig," which was only the first in what became a long and impressive series of geomorphological studies.

Credner, a geologist, helped Penck get a job as an assistant with the Saxony geological survey, which was working on maps of the area around Leipzig Bay, an experience that not only provided financial assistance to Penck while he was finishing his doctorate, but also illustrated his field abilities. In 1878 Penck finished his dissertation, *Studien über lockere vulkanische Auswürflinge*.

In 1881 Penck moved to Berlin to study paleontology under Karl Zittel. In Berlin Penck wrote his *habilitation* treatise, *Die Vergletscherung der Alpen*, which was finished in 1882. This work expanded his reputation and led to job offers in Königsberg and Vienna. Penck accepted the offer in Vienna, where the department of geography was chaired by Friedrich Simony, whose main interest was human geography. Penck was enthusiastic with his assignment in Vienna and quickly began to expand his own interest in geography. He was involved in the development of thematic and topographic maps and encouraged the view that field study should be on a par with books and lectures as a means of attaining and expanding geographical knowledge. In Vienna, according to Meynen (1983:102), "In student circles he—at first simply professor and excursion leader—became a loved teacher, and was transformed from a geologist to a complete geographer."

As this geographical polish was being added to the young geologist's character,

Penck began to look seriously at regional geography, and in 1887 published a volume on the regional geography of Germany, *Das Deutsches Reich*. Regional geographies of Belgium, the Netherlands, and Luxemberg followed. In Vienna he also continued working as editor of *Jahrsberichte der Geographische Gesellschaft*, a position that he had accepted while he was still in Munich. He also began working as editor for *Berichte der Vereines der Wiener Geographen*, and in 1886 he founded *Geographischen Abhandlungen*.

In 1894 Penck published his celebrated *Morphologie der Erdoberfläche*, or *Morphology of the Earth's Surface*, in which he distinguished his concern with *geomorphology*, a term that he apparently coined, as distinct from other branches of geology. Volume 1 dealt with metric measurement of surface features and processes involved in their evolution, concentrating on the agents of erosion and deposition—weathering, mass wasting, running water, glaciers, wind, and waves—and internal processes. The second volume dealt with actual landform complexes: mountains and valleys, hills and plains, residual landforms, basins and lakes, volcanoes, and coastal landforms were topics, along with more detailed localized landscape features. Penck emphasized both the description of landforms and an understanding of the processes that have shaped them. His landform-classification system, however, was based on form rather than process. He distinguished six "topographic" forms: plains, scarps, mountains, valleys, hollows, and caverns. Assemblages of landforms were distinguished as well, since the forms above did not occur in isolation. The major structural forms that Penck identified were the following: plains with horizontal strata, slightly folded strata, fault blocks, strongly folded areas, basalt flows, and intrusive igneous masses.

In 1897 Penck made his first trip abroad, visiting Canada and the United States. While there, he attended several scientific meetings, including a meeting of the American Association of Science in Michigan. In 1904 he returned to the United States, where he attended a meeting of the International Geographical Union in Washington, D.C., and went on a guided field trip with *William Morris Davis. During the first decade of the twentieth century, Penck also published a series of works on the Alps, under the general title *Die Alpen im Eiszeitalter*.

In 1906 Penck left his position in Vienna and replaced *Ferdinand von Richthofen at Berlin University, where he immediately became editor of a series of texts, *Bibliothek Geographischer Handbüchler*, which had originally been established by *Friedrich Ratzel. He also founded another series, *Bibliothek Länderkundliche Handbüchler* in 1906 and still another, *Meereskunde: Sammlung Volkstümlicher Vorträge*, in the following year. In the academic year 1908–9, Penck went to teach at Columbia University for a year, and William Morris Davis went to Berlin University in his place.

In 1921 Penck was awarded the order Pour le Mérite, civilian class. By that time he was a member of scientific organizations of every sort, from the Austrian Academy of Science and the Prussian Academy of Science to the Berlin *Montags Gesellschaft* and *Mittwoch* club. In 1928, as chair of the Berlin Geographical

Society, Penck was responsible for organizing the centenary celebration for that group. Meynen (1983) described this as the "high point" of Penck's career, and after it, he was sought by government ministries for advice on every matter imaginable.

Soon after reaching the age of eighty, Penck retired to Mittenwald, a favorite village in Bavaria, where he lived from 1940 until 1942, at which time ill health forced him and his wife to return to Berlin. His wife died soon after the move, and he died in a sanatorium in Prag-Reuth on April 2, 1945.

Selected Bibliography

1877   "Nordische Basalte im Diluvium von Leipzig" (Northern Basalts in Diluvium from Leipzig). *Neues Jahrbuch für Mineralalogie, Geologie und Paläontologie*, 243–50.

1878   "Studien über lockere vulkanische Auswürflinge" (A Study of Loose Unsorted Volcanic Materials). *Zeitschrift der Deutschen Geologischen Gesellschaft* 30:97–129.

1879   "Die Geschiebeformation Norddeutschlands" (The Unstratified Deposits in North Germany). *Zeitschrift der Deutschen Geologischen Gesellschaft* 31:117–203.

1882   *Die Vergletscherung der Deutschen Alpen, die Ursachen, periodische Wiederkehr und ihr Einfluss auf der Bodengestaltung* (The Glacial Formations of the German Alps, Their Periodical Oscillations and Influence on the Surface Topography). Gekrönte Preisschrift Univ. München, Leipzig.

"Eustatische Schwangungen des Meeresspiegels" (Eustatic Oscillations of Sea Level). *Jahresbericht der Geographischen Gesellschaft München* 7(1881–82): 47–120.

Die Formen der Erdoberfläche. (The Form of the Earth's Surface). Sammlung gemeinnützige. . . . No. 70. Prague.

1883   "Einfluss das Klimas auf die Gestalt der Erdoberfläche" (The Influence of Climate on the Earth's Surface). *Verhandlungen der 3 Deutschen Geographentages Frankfurt*, 78–92.

1884   "Geographische Wirkungen der Eiszeit. Mit einer Höhenkarte der Schneelinie in Europa während der Gegenwart und der Eiszeit" (Geographical Effects of the Ice Age with an Altitudinal Map of the Snow Line in Europe at the President Time and During the Ice Age). *Verhandlungen der 4 Deutschen Geographentages München*, 66–84.

"Mensch und Eiszeit" (Man and Ice Age). *Archiv für Anthropologie* 15:211–28.

"Über Periodizität der Thalbildung" (On Periodicity in Desert Accumulation). *Verlandlungen der Gesellschaft für Erdkunde Berlin* 11:1–21.

1887   "Physikalische Skizze von Mittleeuropa" (Physical Outline of Central Europe). *Länderkunde Erdteil Europe*. Edited by A. Kirchhoff. 1:89–113.

"Über Denudation der Erdoberfläche" (On the Denudation of the Earth's Surface). *Schriften der Vereins zur Verbreitung natur-wissenschaftlicher Kenntnisse in Wien*. 27:431–57.

1888   "Die Bilding der Durchbruchthäler." *Schriften der Vereins* 28:433–84.

1889   "Das Endziel der Erosion und Denudation" (The End-Product of Erosion and Denudation). *Verhandlungen der 8 Deutschen Geogrentages Berlin*, 91–100.

"Oberflächenbau" (Upper Level Surfaces). *Anleitung zur Deutschen Landes-Volksforschung Stuttgart*, 1–66.

"Das Konigreich der Niederlande. Das Konigreich Belgien. Das Grossherzotum Luxemburg." *Länderkunde Europe*. Edited by A. Kirchhoff. Stuttgart, 421–581.

1890   "Die Glazialschotter in Ostalpen" (Glacial Stone Deposits in the Eastern Alps). *Mitteilungen des Deutschen und Österreichisches Alpenvereins* 16:289–92.

1891   "Die Formen der Landoberfläche" (The Form of the Land Surface). *Verhandlungen der 9 Deutschen Geographentages Wien*, 28–37.

1892   "Die Herstellung einer einheitlichen Weltkarte im Masstabe von 1:1,000,000" (The Construction of a Uniform World Map on the 1:1,000,000 Scale). *International Geographical Congress, Bern* 5:191–98.

1894   *Morphologie der Erdoberfläche* (Morphology of the Earth's Surface). In F. Ratzel, ed., *Bibliothek Geogr. Handbuch*. 2 vols.

1895   "Die geographische Lage von Wien" (The Geographical Situation of Vienna). *Schriften der Vereins zur Verbreitung natur-wissenschaftlicher Kenntnisse in Wien* 35:673–706.

1896   "Die Geomorphologie als genetische Wissenschaft. Eine Einleitung über geomorphologische Nomenklatur" (Geomorphology as a Genetic Science. An introduction to a Geomorphological Nomenclature). *International Geographical Congress Rep. London* 6:735–47.

1899   "Über Geländedartstellung auf Karten des Hochgebirges" (On Cartographic Methods of Representing High Mountains). *Verhandlungen der Gesellschaft Deutscher Naturforscher und Ärxte 71 Vers* 2(1):33–35.

"Austria-Hungary," 189–301; "Austria," 302–15; and "Bosnia-Herzegovina," 324–26. *International Geography*. Edited by H. R. Mill. 2d ed., 1900; 3d ed., 1903.

1901   "Die Übertiefung der Alpen-Thäler" (On the Depth of Alpine Valleys). *International Geographical Congress Berlin (1899)*, 232–40.

With Eduard Brückner. *Die Alpen im Eiszeitalter* (The Alps in the Ice Age). Leipzig. 3 vols. 1901–9.

1905   "Climatic Features in the Landscape." *American Journal of Science* 4:173–84.

1908   "Das Alter des Menschengeschlechts" (The Antiquity of the Human Race). *Zeitschrift Ethnologie* 40:390–407, 428–36.

1910	*Die Hafen of New York* (The Harbors of New York). No. 37.
1912	"Die Lage der deutschen Grosstädte" (The Situation of Major German Cities). *Städtebauliche Vorträge* 5(5):35pp.
1914	"The Shifting of the Climatic Belts." *Scottish Geographical Magazine* 30(5):281–93.
1916	"Das Krieg und das Studium der Geographie" (The War and Geographical Study). *Zeitschrift der Gesellschaft fur Erdkunde Berlin* 51:158–76, 222–48.
1921	"Der Grossgau im Herzen Deutschlands" (The Major Provinces of Inner Germany). *Leipzig*.
1924	"Das Antlitz der Alpen" (The Face of the Alps). *Naturwissenschaften* 12:1000–7.
1926	"Deutschland als geographische Gestalt" (Germany as a Geographical Expression). *Leopoldina* 1:72–81.
	"Die Morphologie der Klimazonen" (The Morphology of the Climatic Zones). *Naturwissenschaften* 62:482–508.
1930	"Central Asia." *Geographical Journal* 76:477–87.
1933	"Eustatische Bewegungen des Meeresspiegels während der Eiszeit" (Eustatic Changes of Sea Level during the Ice Age). *Geographische Zeitschrift* 39:329–39.
	"Über den Löss." *Sitzungsberichte der Preussischen Akademie der Wissenschaften Berlin*.
1942	"Die Stärke der Verbreitung des Menschen" (The Varied Density of Population Distribution). *Mitteilungen der Österreicheschen Geographischen Gesellschaft in Wien* 85:241–69.

Chronology

1858	Born September 25 in Leipzig-Readnita.
1875	Entered the university in Leipzig.
1877	Published first paper, on glacial deposits.
1878	Worked on doctoral thesis and also worked for the geological survey of Saxony.
1881	Went to Munich to study paleontology. Continued work on geological mapping.
1885	Moved to University of Vienna.
1891	First advocated the 1:1,000,000 map at Bern International Congress.
1897	Travelled in Canada and the United States.
1906	Moved to Berlin University, as successor to Ferdinand von Richthofen.
1908	Exchange professor at Columbia University.
1940	Retired.
1945	Died at Prag-Reuth on April 2.

Reference

Meynen, Emil. 1983. "Albrecht Penck." *Geographers Biobibliograhical Studies* 7:
      101–8.

John Wesley Powell

John Wesley Powell was born on March 29, 1834, in Mt. Morris, New York, a small town on the Genesee River not far from Rochester. His father, a travelling minister for the Methodist Episcopal Church, continuously moved westward with his family, and by 1838 they lived in southern Ohio. The small frontier towns in which they lived made schooling difficult for John, though he was fortunate enough to receive tutoring from some who stimulated in him a lifelong commitment to reading and learning, and George Crookham especially encouraged in young John not only a habit of reading, but also a love of the outdoors. According to *Preston James (1979:117), when John was only ten, "the two examined some nearby Indian mounds, looking for Indian artifacts, and also went out with the State Geologist to identify and map mineral resources."

The Powell family's westward movement continued, and in 1846 it took them to a farm in southern Wisconsin, where Powell had to accept, in his father's frequent absences, the task of running the farm at the age of fourteen. From there, the family moved to Wheaton, Illinois, in 1852, where he entered the local college. He did not find that experience challenging and began teaching in a local school. During subsequent summers, he took lengthy boat trips on the Illinois and Mississippi rivers, collecting shells and plants.

With the approach of the Civil War, John began studying map-making and military tactics. In 1861 he joined the Illinois Volunteer Infantry, where he was quickly commissioned and began to move up the officer's ranks. As a captain, he commanded a battery of troops in the Battle of Shiloh, where his right arm was struck by a bullet and later amputated. Powell went on to lead troops in battle at Vicksburg, was promoted to major, and served as Chief of Artillery in the Battle of Nashville, before leaving the army in 1865.

After short stints as professor of geology, first at Illinois Wesleyan University, then at Illinois Normal College, Powell left academic life in search of something more exciting. With a group of volunteers, he went to climb mountains in

Colorado and after that began expeditions sponsored to some extent by the
government. On May 24, 1869, Powell launched four boats into the Green River
in Wyoming and began a journey that would bring him considerable notoriety.
From Green River Junction, the trip took him through the Uinta Mountains on
the Green River and then on down the Colorado River through the Grand Canyon.
For Powell this was not only a great adventure, but also the beginning of a
decade of productive research and writing about the Uinta Mountains and the
Colorado Plateau, work that led to a deeper understanding of the role of running
water and erosional processes in the shaping of landscapes in the arid western
United States. His work utilized the "base level" concept in fluvial erosion,
setting the stage for William Morris Davis's work on peneplains. Additionally,
he worked to classify landforms and streams, and added to the literature the
concepts of antecedent, consequent, and superimposed streams. At the same
time that he was working on ideas about landforms and fluvial processes, he
was also collecting information about the Native Americans in the area and their
languages, not only so that he could communicate with them, but also in order
to ease their transition into the changing world that was being created around
them by frontier settlement expansion.

In the summer of 1870, the Department of the Interior began to support, with
congressional approval, the Geographical and Topographical Survey of the Colorado River of the West and its Tributaries, and subsequently The United States
Geographical and Geological Survey of the Rocky Mountain Region. Work on
this survey convinced Powell that the western United States was indeed different
and needed to be treated differently. According to James (1979:118), "He recognized that here was a vast, little-known country about to be occupied by
miners, lumbermen, cattlemen, and farmers who had little idea of the physical
character of the land."

Thus, Powell argued with Congress for the necessity of inventorying this area
in advance of settlement and classifying the land according to its capacity for
utilization. During the 1870s he worked with *Grove K. Gilbert, who went on
to introduce the concept of the graded stream, for which Gilbert gave much
credit to discussions that he had had with Powell about fluvial processes. In
1877 Illinois Wesleyan University, where he had taught briefly before, awarded
him both M.A. and Ph.D. degrees.

Published in 1878, Powell's *Report on the Lands of the Arid Region of the
United States* demonstrated the breadth of knowledge gained by a decade of
work. It also clearly demonstrated an understanding of the western United States
as a region that needed to be dealt with differently by the federal government.
He argued against the use of the rectangular land survey in the west, supported
a land management plan that would utilize his intimate knowledge of the area
as settlement increased, and recognized the overwhelming importance of water
to the region. His ideas were opposed immediately by lumbermen, cattlemen,
and the politicians that catered to them, much to the ultimate harm of the region.

That his understanding of this vast region was sound is still appreciated today, as exemplified by the many references to him in Marc Reisner's influential *Cadillac Desert: The American West and Its Disappearing Water*. As James (1979:119) noted, "No part of Powell's life is more spectacular than his heroic efforts to preserve the public domain from pillage for private gain." His ideas were basic influences in the conservation movement in the United States, and he was instrumental in having the Bureau of Reclamation established under President Theodore Roosevelt. That much of his advice about the problems of settling the arid western United States went unheeded was certainly no fault of his. Unfortunately, as Reisner (1986:503) has noted, following a brief litany of the settlement of the western United States, "The cost of all this, however, was a vandalization of both our natural heritage and our economic future, and the reckoning has not even begun." To Powell this would be no surprise.

In 1879 four different surveys of the western United States, including the one headed by Powell, merged to form the United States Geological Survey, whose task was to explore and map the western United States. Clarence King became the first Director of the new Geological Survey, and at the same time Powell became director of the newly established Bureau of Ethnology, which had just been established at the Smithsonian. Two years later King resigned, and for the next thirteen years Powell was the director of both agencies.

Powell retired from the Geological Survey in 1894, though he remained director of the Bureau of Ethnology for two more years. In 1896 he retired to Haven, Maine, with his wife. He died there on September 23, 1902, nearly penniless.

Selected Bibliography

1867   "Exploration of the Valley of the South Platte, Colorado and Ascent of Pike's Peak, Scientific Expedition to the Rocky Mountains." *Illinois State Board of Educational Proceedings*, 9–13.

1873   "Some Remarks on the Geological Structure of a District of Country Lying to the North of the Grand Canyon of the Colorado." *American Journal of Science and Arts* 5:446–65.

1875   "Explorations of the Colorado River of the West and Its Tributaries." Washington, D.C.: Government Printing Office.

1876   *Report on the Geology of the Eastern Portion of the Unita Mountains and a Region of Country Adjacent Thereto.* Washington, D.C.: Government Printing Office.

              "Types of Orographic Structure." *American Journal of Science and Arts*, Ser. 3. 12:414–28.

1877   "Introduction to the Study of Indian Languages" Washington, D.C.: Government Printing Office. 2d ed., 1880.

1878   "Report of the Lands of the Arid Region of the United States." Washington, D.C.: Government Printing Office. Second printing 1879 with a more detailed account of Utah.

"The Philosophy of the North American Indians." *Journal of the American Geographical Society* 8:251–68.

1881   "Sketch of the Mythology of the North American Indians" and "On the Evolution of Language. . . . " *Smithsonian Institution Bureau of Ethnology 1st Annual Report*, 17–56, 71–86.

1883   "Human Evolution." *Transactions of the Anthropological Society of Washington* 2:176–208.

1884   "On the Fundamental Theory of Dynamic Geology." *Science* 3:511–13.

1886   "The Causes of Earthquakes." *Forum* 2:370–91.

1888   "Methods of Geologic Cartography in Use by the United States Geological Survey." *International Geological Congress*, Berlin.

1891   "Hydrography, Engineering, the Arid Lands and Irrigation Literature." *U.S. Geological Survey 11th Annual Report*, Part 3, 1–289, 345–88.

        "Indian Linguistic Families of America North of Mexico." *Smithsonian Institution Bureau of Ethnology 7th Annual Report*, 1–142.

1892   "The North American Indians." *The United States of America: A Study of the American Commonwealth*. New York. 1:190–272.

1893   "The Geologic Map of the United States." *Transactions of the American Institute of Mining Engineers* 21:877–87.

        "General Work in Taxomony." *U.S. Geological Survey 14th Annual Report*, Part 1.

1895   "Physiographic Processes." *National Geographic Monographs* 1:1–32.

1896   "Relation of Primitive People to Environment, Illustrated by American Examples." *Smithsonian Institution Annual Report*, 625–37.

1898   "An Hypothesis to Account for the Movement in the Crust of the Earth." *Journal of Geology* 6:1–9.

Chronology

1834   Born March 29 at Mt. Morris, New York.

1838   Moved to Ohio.

1846   Moved to Wisconsin.

1852   Moved to Illinois and taught in a country school.

1858   Curator of Conchology, Illinois Natural History Society.

1860   Principal of Hennepin Public Schools.

1861   Became a captain in artillery.

1862   Lost his right arm below the elbow at the battle of Shiloh.

1863   After recovering, rejoined his unit and took part in the seige of Vicksburg under General Grant.

1864   Promoted to major. Chief of Artillery in the Battle of Nashville.

1865   Discharged from the army. Began teaching geology.

1866	Professor of Geology in Illinois. Began explorations with expedition to Pike's Peak, Colorado.
1869	Joined the Geographical and Geological Survey, Rocky Mountain region. Grand Canyon trip, studied cliff dwellers.
1871	Second Grand Canyon trip.
1873	Moved to Washington, D.C. Survey of Plateau region of Arizona, Nevada, and Utah.
1877	Illinois Wesleyan University awarded him the M.A. and Ph.D. degrees.
1879	Helped found the U.S. Geological Survey with Clarence King. Became the director of Bureau of Ethnology in the Smithsonian Institution.
1881	Became Director of U.S. Geological Survey (until 1894). L.L.D. degree from Columbia University.
1889	President, American Association for the Advancement of Science.
1902	Died September 23 at Haven, Maine.

References

James, Preston E. 1979. "John Wesley Powell." *Geographers Biobibliographical Studies* 3:117–24.

Reisner, Marc. 1986. *Cadillac Desert: The American West and Its Disappearing Water.* New York: Penguin.

Ptolemy

Ptolemy, actually known in his own time as Claudius Ptolemaeus, made notable contributions to geography and cartography, as well as to mathematics and astronomy. Though the times of his birth and death are not known, according to Kish (1978), it is believed that he lived between approximately A.D. 100 and 170. He was native to Hellenistic Egypt, and it was there that he lived and worked.

Somewhat better known are the times within which Ptolemy made his various contributions to astronomy, around 127 to 151, and to geography, around 150 to 160 (Dickinson, 1969). Ptolemy was influenced by, and built upon, the works of earlier geographers, including Marinus of Tyre and Hipparchus.

The written works of Ptolemy have survived, so we know much more directly of his work than that of earlier geographers. His major astronomical work was the *Almagest*, which became a standard work on the celestial bodies until the time of *Copernicus. Ptolemy agreed with *Aristotle that the earth was a sphere around which the various celestial bodies orbited, though he did not admit an acceptance of either the earth's rotation on its axis or its revolution around the sun.

As Ptolemy turned his attention to geography and to the compilation of his eight-volume *Guide to Geography (Geographike Syntaxis)*, he carried on with earlier work begun by Marinus of Tyre, his teacher. Marinus had gathered data on places in order to revise earlier maps of the known world. Ptolemy was able to take advantage of knowledge collected during the second century by Roman explorers and merchants and to utilize this knowledge in updating the work of Marinus. Ptolemy's work on geography did not become known in the West until early in the fifteenth century, when it was translated into Latin.

Ptolemy's cartography built upon the work of Hipparchus, from whom he took especially the use of a grid comprising lines of latitude and longitude. Dividing each of these lines into 360 segments, he had a grid system along which any place could be located precisely. However, his work was still fraught with errors, partly because there was no accurate way at the time for measuring longitude, and his choice of a "prime meridian" was suspect, partly because he accepted Poseidonius's erroneous estimate of the circumference of the earth—18,000 miles. The latter error alone would mean an error of some 100 miles for every ten degrees along a meridian. Dickinson (1969:36) wrote:

As an example of the errors resulting from Ptolemy's attempt at exactitude in positions, there may be instanced the parallel of 36 degrees N. in the Mediterranean area, which was taken to pass through not only the Straits of Gibraltar and Rhodes, as approximately it does, but also through Sardinia and Sicily, while Carthage and that part of the African coast were placed south of it, not north as they are.

Dickinson goes on to identify numerous other specific errors and problems with Ptolemy's works, as well as to note some of the earlier misconceptions—many of which had been introduced earlier by Hipparchus—that were corrected by Ptolemy. For example, Hipparchus had believed that Byzantium and Massilia were on the same line of latitude, which Ptolemy showed not to be the case. In addition to some of the errors cited already, Ptolemy also placed the equator too far north. Given his methods, however, as Dickinson (1969:34) has also noted, "Ptolemy and his predecessors, longing for scientific precision, confused the appearance of it with probabilities or something less; we may praise, commiserate, or blame them as we will." Ptolemy's collection of errors helped lead Columbus, many centuries later, to conclude that Asia was much nearer to Europe than it really was.

Ptolemy's *Guide to Geography* was composed of an initial volume on cartography, including map projections; six volumes of tables of latitudes and longitudes; and a final volume of maps of various regions of the world. Thus, the work was essentially cartographic. In his own words, cited in Kish (1978:107), Ptolemy wrote:

It is the prerogative of Geography to show the known habitable earth as a unit in itself, how it is situated and what is its nature; and it deals with those features likely to be mentioned in a general description of the earth, such as the larger towns and the great cities, the mountain ranges and the principal rivers. Besides these it treats only of features worthy of special note on account of their beauty.

Selected Bibliography

127–151   *Almagest* (a work on classical astronomy).

150–160   *Geographike Syntaxis*. Translated by Edward Luther Stevenson as *The Geography of Ptolemy*. New York: New York Public Library, 1932.

            Tetrabiblos. Translated by F. E. Robbins, Loeb Classical Library. London: William Heinemann, 1940.

Cosmographia: Theatrum Orbis Terrarum.
Geographia: Theatrum Orbis Terrarum.
Harmonica.

Chronology

100	Approximate date of birth in Egypt.
127–150	Worked at the library at Alexandria.
150–160	Published *Geographike Syntaxis*.
170	Approximate date of death.

References

Dickinson, Robert E. 1969. *The Makers of Modern Geography*. New York: Praeger.
Kish, George, ed. 1978. *A Source Book in Geography*. Cambridge, Mass.: Harvard University Press.

Friedrich Ratzel

Friedrich Ratzel, the youngest of four children, was born in Karlsruhe, Germany, on August 30, 1844. His mother was a servant in the court of the Grand Duke of Baden, and his boyhood was spent primarily on the grand-ducal estate on which his family lived. Though he showed an early interest in nature and a passion for reading, his family guided him toward a career in pharmacy.

In preparation for that career the young Ratzel began an apprenticeship, and after three years passed the qualifying examination for becoming a pharmacist. Subsequently he worked as a pharmacist for about three years, though during that time he continued to pursue his own interest in natural science. He studied the classical language necessary for university entrance at that time, and finally, in 1866, with the reluctant approval of his parents, entered the polytechnic university at Karlsruhe and then the university at Heidelberg, where he received a doctorate in zoology in 1868.

In the following year, Ratzel attended lectures given by Haeckel, who had been considerably influenced by the publication of *Charles Darwin's *Origin of the Species* a decade earlier. "Within this context," Bassin (1987:124) has perceptively noted, "the particular fascination presented by the study of natural science may well be understood, for it offered nothing less than the fundamental key to an understanding of the universe. It was in such an intellectual climate that Ratzel received his most important intellectual development."

Peschel and *Ferdinand von Richtofen had already set down the basic methods for a systematic geographic study of the earth's physical features. Ratzel focused his attention on the study of geology, paleontology, and zoology, and Haeckel's influence on his thinking quickly became apparent as well. Ratzel's first book, published in 1869, was *Sein und Werden der organischen Welt*, or *The Nature and Development of the Organic World*, described by Bassin (1987:124) as "a popular presentation of the new scientific *Weltanschauung* . . . based largely on Haeckel's *General Morphology*." As Bassin (1987:124) also pointed out, "It is much to Ratzel's credit that he was to reject this excess in his mature work, and distance himself explicitly from leading Social Darwinists such as Haeckel.''

Along with the natural sciences, Ratzel was attracted also to journalism. While still at the university in Heidelberg, he wrote articles for the *Kölnische Zeitung*, science articles that enjoyed increasing popularity. The unification of Germany in 1871 extended some of Ratzel's interests as well. As *Preston James and Geoffrey Martin (1981:168) noted, following that event, ''His strong sense of national pride drew his attention away from academic studies to field observation of the ways Germans lived and made use of resources.'' Travel was more important to him than ever, and in 1873–74 the *Kölnische Zeitung* even sent him to North America as a correspondent. There he travelled from New York all the way to San Francisco via a circuitous route, and from there by boat to Mexico. According to Bassin (1987:124), that trip was highly influential on Ratzel's future development because ''the example of a maturing and visibly expanding society in North America impressed and overwhelmed him, and had the effect of shifting his most fundamental interest away from the natural organic world to human society itself.'' Ratzel's background in natural science and his enthusiasm for writing, coupled with his travels to North America, led him to the doorway of geography, where he subsequently entered and gained a stature shared by few in the pantheon of great geographers.

Ratzel returned to Germany in 1875 and was appointed as a *Privatdozent* in geography at the Technical University in Munich, his first teaching position. There he moved quickly to establish full academic credentials in geography with the completion of his *Habitation* thesis on out-migration from China and the establishment of Chinese enclaves in other lands, his first excursion into anthropogeography. Soon thereafter, at the age of thirty-two he was appointed *ausserordentlicher Professor*, or special professor, a considerable accomplishment in so short a time.

In 1877 Ratzel married Marie Wingens, whom he had met four years earlier in England, and over the next four years they had two daughters. Though he was now travelling less, he was beginning to do more writing on geography. Having had time to consider his observations on his trip through North America, he published a two-volume study, completed in 1880, *Die Vereinigten Staaten von Nord-Amerika*, a major regional geography of North America. In that work he began to develop some of the themes in human geography that were brought to maturity in the first volume of his classic work on human geography, *Anthropogeographie oder Grundzüge der Anwendung Der Erdkunde auf die Geschichte*, published in 1881. The second volume, *Anthropogeographie: Die geographische Verbreitung des Menschen*, however, did not appear until 1891.

Ratzel increasingly turned his attention to political issues and the creation of political geography as we recognize it today. Applying many of the same principles that shaped his earlier works, Ratzel published his *Political Geography* in 1897. Though it was a large and exhaustive work, he followed it with a number of articles that developed some of the themes in even more depth; the most detailed of these additional works was the publication in 1901 of *Der Lebensraum: Eine Biogeographische Studie*. As did many of his contemporaries, Ratzel viewed the political state as a biological organism, one constantly growing and evolving, one constantly in need of an expanding territory in which to survive.

According to Bassin (1987:127): this territory

Ratzel termed the *Lebensraum*, and maintained that the state had to expand physically as its population grew or it would exhaust its available sustenance base and decline. . . . He interpreted the contemporary contest among the European powers for colonial acquisitions in Africa and Asia in terms of this quest for *Lebensraum*.

His work had a major impact on the subsequent development of human geography in the twentieth century.

Friedrich Ratzel died on August 9, 1904, while on holiday in southern Germany.

Selected Bibliography

1869   *Sein und Werden der organischen Welt* (The Nature and Development of the Organic World). Leipzig: Gebhardt & Reisland.

1872   "Ernst Häeckel." *Meyers Deutsches Jahrbuch* 1:555–58.

1876   *Die Chinesische Auswanderung* (Chinese Emigration). Breslau: F. U. Kern.

1878   "Die Beurteilung der Völker" (The Judging of Peoples). *Nord und Sud: Eine deutsche Monatsschrift* 6:177–200.

          Die Vereinigten Staaten von Nord-Amerika (The United States of North America). 2 Vols. Munich: Oldenbourg.

1880   "Über geographische Bedingungen und ethnographische Folgen der Völkerwanderungen" (On the Geographical Conditions and Ethnographic Consequences of the Great Migrations). *Verhandlung Gesellschaft Erdkunde Berlin* 7:295–324.

1882   *Anthropogeographie oder Grundzüge der Anwendung der Erdkunde auf die Geschichte* (Anthropogeography, or the Basic Elements of the Application of Geography to History). Stuttgart: Englehorn.

1884   *Wider der Reichsnörgler. Ein Wort zur Kolonialfrage aus Wählerkreisen* (Against the Grumblers in the Reich. A Word about the Colonial Question from the Electorate). Munich: Oldenbourg.

1885   "Entwurf einer neuen politischen Karte von Afrika" (A Draft of a New Political Map of Africa). *Petermanns Geographischen Mitteilungen* 31:245–50.

          Völkerkunde (General ethnography). 3 vols. Leipzig: Bibliographisches Institut.

1887   "Die geographische Verbreitung des Bogens und der Pfeile in Afrika"

(The Geographical Distribution of the Bow and Arrow in Africa). *Ber. Verh. K. Sächsischen Gesell. Wiss. Leipzig Philolog. Hist. Kl.* 34:233–52.

1888   "Über die Anwendung des Begriffs Oekumene auf geographische Problem der Gegenwart" (On the Application of the Concept of the Ecumene to Contemporary Geographical Problems). *Ber. Verh. K. Sächsischen Gesell. Wiss. Philolog. Hist. Kl.* 40:137–80.

1891   *Anthropogeographie: Die geographische Verbreitung des Menschen* (The Geographical Distribution of Mankind). Vol. 2. Stuttgart: Engelhorn.

1892   "Über allgemeine Eigenschaften der geographischen Grenzen und über die politische Grenze" (On the General Characteristics of Geographical Boundaries and on Political Boundaries). *Ber. Verh. K. Sächsischen Gesell. Wiss. Leipzig Philolog. Hist. Kl.* 44:53–104.

1895   "Studien über politische Räume" (Studies on political spaces). *Geographische Zeitung* 1:286–302. "Die deutsche Landschaft" (The German Landscape). *Halbmonatshefte der Deutschen Rundschau* 4:407–28.

1896   "Die Gesetze der räumlichen Wachtums der Staaten" (The Laws of the Spatial Growth of States). *Petermanns Geographische Mitteilungen* 42:97–107.

"The Territorial Growth of States." *Scottish Geographical Magazine* 12(7):351–61.

"Moritz Wagner." *Allgemeine Deutsche Biographie* 40:532–43.

The History of Mankind. Translation of *Völkerkunde* by A. J. Butler. 3 vols. London: Macmillan.

1897   *Politische Geographie* (Political Geography). Leipzig: Oldenbourg.

"Studies in Political Areas." *American Journal of Sociology* 3(3):297–313. 3(4):449–63.

1898   *Deutschland: Einführung in die Heimatkunde* (Germany: An Introduction to the Study of the Homeland). Leipzig: Grunow.

"Politisch-geographische Rückblicke." (Political-Geographical Retrospective). *Geographische Zeitung* 4:14–156, 211–44, 268–74.

"Der Ursprung und das Wandern der Völker geographisch betrachtet." Vol. 1: "Zur Einleitung und Methodisches" (The Origin and the Migrations of Peoples Studied Geographically. Vol. 1: Introduction and Methodology). *Ber. Verh. Sächsischen Gesell. Wiss. Leipzig Philolog. Hist.Kl.* 50:1–75.

1900   *Das Meer als Quelle der Völkergrösse* (The Sea as a Source of the Greatness of People). Munich: Oldenbourg.

"Der Ursprung und das Wandern der Völker geographisch betrachtet. II. Geographische Prüfung der Tatsachen über den Ursprung der Völker" (The Origin and the Migrations of Peoples Studied Geographically. II. A Geographical Examination of the Facts about the Origins of Peoples). *Ber. Verh. K. Sächsischen Gesell. Wiss. Leipzig Philolog. Hist. Kl.* 52:23–147.

1901   "Der Lebensraum. Eine Biogrographische Studie" (Lebensraum: A Bio-
            Geographical Study). *Festgaben für Albern Schäffle zur siebenzigsten
            Wiederkehr seines Geburtstags am 24 Februar 1901*. Edited by K. Bücher.
            Tübingen: Verlag der Laupp'schen Buchhandlung.

            "Der Geist, der über den Wassern Schwebt" (The Spirit That Floats over
            the Waters). *Deutsche Monatschrift* 1:42–53.

1902   *Die Erde und das Leben: Eine Vergleichende Erdkunde* (The Earth and
            Life: A Comparative Geography). 2 vols. Vienna: Bibliographisches
            Institut.

            "Man as a Life Phenomenon on the Earth's Surface." *The History of the
            World*. Edited by H. F. Helmolt. New York: Dodd, Mead, 61–106.

1903   "Nationalitäten und Rassen" (Nationalities and Races). *Türmer-Jahrbuch*:
            43–77. Also in *Kleine Schriften* 2 (1906):462–87.

1904   *Über Naturschilderung* (On the Description of Nature). Munich:
            Oldenbourg.

1905   *Glückinseln und Traüme: Gesammelte Aufsätze aus den Grenzboten* (Is-
            lands of Happiness and Dreams: Collected Articles from Die Grenzboten).
            Leipzig: Grunow.

1906   *Kleine Schriften* (Collected Shorter Writings). Edited by H. Helmolt. 2
            vols. Berlin: Oldenbourg.

1966   *Jugenderinnerungen* (Memories of Childhood and Youth). Munich: Kösel.

1975   "The Earth, Society and the State." *Monadnock* 49:78–90.

Chronology

1844   Born August 30, in Karlsruhe, Germany.

1866   Entered University at Karlsruhe, later moved to Heidelberg.

1868   Ph.D. in Zoology.

1869   Worked as a naturalist and a newspaper correspondent.

1870   Served in the Franco-Prussian War and received a head injury.

1873   Travelled in U.S.A. and Mexico as a newspaper correspondent.

1875   Accepted teaching appointment at the Technical University, Munich.

1880   Promoted to Professor.

1886   Accepted Chair in Leipzig.

1904   Died August 9 in southern Germany.

References

Bassin, Mark. 1987. "Friedrich Ratzel." *Geographers Biobibliographical Studies*
        11:123–32.
James, Preston E., and Geoffrey J. Martin. 1981. *All Possible Worlds: A History of
        Geographical Ideas*. 2d ed. New York: Wiley.

Ernst Georg Ravenstein

Ernst Georg Ravenstein was born in Frankfurt-am-Main, Germany, on December 30, 1834. He spent his boyhood in Frankfurt, where he went to the local *Gymnasium* and the *Stadelsche Kunstinstitut*.

In 1852 he emigrated to London, where he studied under Dr. August Petermann. In 1855 he took a job as a cartographer in the Topographic Department of the War Office. During his work with the War Office he also began writing about geographical topics and published works in both English and German. At the same time, he made several contributions to cartography, including maps of Abyssinia, Equatorial Africa, British East Africa, and India. In 1858 he married an English woman, Ada S. Parry, who was from Kent.

Ravenstein was interested in exploration as well, especially the Russian explorations of the Far East and North America and various explorations of Africa. In 1861 Ravenstein published his first book, *The Russians on the Amur*. His interests in African exploration led him to study African climatology, and he served as a member of the Committee of the British Association, which provided meteorological instruments to missionaries in Africa. Data collected from them were used by Ravenstein and others to extend knowledge about African climates. He was also interested in topography and travel and made an important contribution to nineteenth-century geography by translating and editing *Universal Geography*, the work of *Élisée Reclus.

Between 1862 and 1871, Ravenstein served as President of the German Gymnastic Society, and in 1872 he retired from the War Office. Subsequently during the 1870s, Ravenstein continued to work on various projects and began to develop and deepen his interest in population studies, especially migration. It was here that he was to make his most lasting and important contributions to geography.

Ravenstein's interest in population may have first been stimulated by his studies with Petermann, who had worked with the 1851 census in Britain. At the time, German statistical studies of population data were more advanced than those in

Britain. During the 1870s, Ravenstein published articles on the British census of 1871 and the first of "laws of migration," which are still cited today in migration studies. The first of three articles on the "laws of migration" appeared in *Geographical Magazine* in 1876, followed by two others in the *Journal of the Royal Statistical Society* in 1885 and 1889. During that interval, Ravenstein also managed to publish (1881) a twenty-five-sheet map of East Africa. He published other population studies as well, including a statistical study of Roman Catholics in Great Britain, published in *Geographical Magazine* in 1874; a study of the populations of Turkey and Russia in the *Journal of the Royal Statistical Society* in 1877; and an interesting look at the lands left for European settlement, which appeared in the *Scottish Geographical Magazine* in 1890.

Aside from his works on migration, however, Ravenstein has had little impact on modern geography, even though his methodological approach, with its focus on the development of general laws rather than purely descriptive studies of places, foresaw approaches that would not become popular in geography until the mid-twentieth century. As Grigg (1977:79) noted, "He deserves to rank as one of the founders of theoretical geography, but has received little or no credit for his achievement." Even his "laws of migration" were not particularly influential until their "rediscovery" by demographers and geographers in the 1950s and 1960s.

In an influential article on migration in 1966, Lee (1966:47) noted that "Ravenstein's papers have stood the test of time and remain the starting point for work in migration theory." Subsequently, Lee built on a framework laid down by Ravenstein's generalizations. More recently, and as a continuing tribute to the importance of Ravenstein's work on migration, Weeks (1989:189) commented, "Over time the most frequently heard explanation for migration has been the so-called push-pull theory. . . . This idea was first put forward by Ravenstein. . . . He concluded that pull factors were more important than push factors."

Ravenstein identified several laws at work in creating migration patterns in nineteenth-century England, including the influence of distance on migration, the relationship between technology and migration, the flow of migrants up the urban hierarchy by stages, the interplay of currents and countercurrents of migration, and the selectivity of migration. Probably his most important observation (1889:276), however, was that

bad or oppressive laws, heavy taxation, an unattractive climate, uncongenial social surrounding, and even compulsion (slave trade, transportation), all have produced and are still producing currents of migration, but none of these currents can compare in volume with that which arises from the desire inherent in most men to 'better' themselves in material respects.

Along with his work on population during the 1880s, Ravenstein spent a year as a Professor of Geography at Bedford College in London. In 1891 he became President Section E of the British Association for the Advancement of Science.

In 1898 Ravenstein published *The Journal of the First Voyage of Vasco da Gama*, which he translated and edited. He went on to publish *The Strange Adventures of Andrew Battell* in 1901, and in 1902 he received the Victoria Gold Medal from the Royal Geographical Society, primarily for his work in population and cartography.

In 1908 he published *Martin Behaim*, his major work on cartography, for which he received an honorary doctorate from the University of Göttingen in 1909. After spending most of his adult life in England, Ravenstein died in Hofheim, Germany, on March 13, 1913.

Selected Bibliography

1856   *Handbuch der Geographie und Statistik von Ost und Nord Europa*. Leipzig.

1861   *The Russians on the Amur*. London.

1870   *Denominational Statistics of England and Wales*. London.

            Reisenhandbuch für London, England und Schottland. Hildburghausen, Bibliographisches Institut.

1874   "Statistics of Roman Catholicism in Great Britain." *Geographical Magazine* 1:103–6.

1876   "Census of the British Isles, 1871: Birthplaces and Migration." *Geographical Magazine* 3:173–77, 201–6.

            "Laws of Migration: Counties and General." *Geographical Magazine* 3:229–33.

            London, England, Schottland und Irland. Leipzig: Bibliographisches Institut.

            The Universal Geography, Élisée Reclus. Edited and translated by Ravenstein. London.

1877   "The Populations of Russia and Turkey." *Journal of the Royal Statistical Society* 40:433–59.

1878   *Cyprus: Its Resources and Capabilities, with Hints for Tourists*. London.

1879   "On the Celtic Languages in the British Isles: A Statistical Survey." *Journal of the Royal Statistical Society* 42:579–636.

1885   "The Laws of Migration." *Journal of the Royal Statistical Society* 40:167–227.

1889   "The Laws of Migration." *Journal of the Royal Statistical Society* 52:241–301.

1890   "The Lands of the Globe Still Available for European Settlement." *Scottish Geographical Magazine* 6:541–46.

            In *The Development of Africa*, Arthur S. White. 14 maps by Ravenstein. London: G. Philip and Son.

1891   "Colonization and Its Limitations." *Journal of the Royal Society of Arts*

39:269–75.

"The Field of Geography." *Scottish Geographical Magazine* 7:536–48.

1898   *A Journal of the First Voyage of Vasco da Gama*. Translated and edited by Ravenstein. No. 99. London: The Hakluyt Society.

1901   With H. R. Mill and H. N. Dickson. "The Climatology of Africa." *Scottish Geographical Magazine* 17:582–95.

The Strange Adventures of Andrew Battell of Leigh in Angola. London: The Hakluyt Society.

1908   *Martin Behaim: His Life and His Globe*. London.

Chronology

1834   Born December 30 in Frankfurt-am-Main, Germany.

1852   Emigrated to London. Became a student of Dr. August Petermann.

1855   Worked with Topographic Department, War Office.

1872   Retired from the War Office.

1877   Served on the Council of the Royal Statistical Society (until 1892).

1882   Professor of Geography, Bedford College, London.

1894   Served on Council of the Royal Geographical Society (unitl 1896).

1909   Received an honorary Ph.D. from University of Göttingen.

1913   Died March 13, at Hofheim, Germany.

References

Grigg, David B. 1977. "Ernst Georg Ravenstein." *Geographers Biobibliographical Studies* 1:79–82.

Lee, Everett. 1966. "A Theory of Migration." *Demography* 3:47–57.

Weeks, John R. 1989. *Population: An Introduction to Concepts and Issues*. 4th ed. Belmont, Calif.: Wadsworth Publishing.

Élisée Reclus

Élisée Reclus was born on March 5, 1830, in the small town of Sainte-Foy-la-Grande in southwestern France. He was one of fourteen children in the Reclus family, a family dominated by the strong convictions of his father, a Calvinist pastor. Though many of his character traits, including the attitudes that he had toward others, came from his father, he inherited from his mother, a teacher, the ability and desire to write.

After an unsuccessful stint at the Theology Faculty of Montauban in 1848, Élisée and his older brother, Élie, went to Germany. In 1851 they entered Berlin University, where they took a course from *Carl Ritter. Two years later, after the successful coup d'état of Napoleon III, they joined a number of other French exiles in England. Later in the same year, 1853, Élisée sought refuge in the United States, where he settled in New Orleans and earned a living as a tutor.

With little income and few opportunities to travel in the United States, Reclus moved to New Grenada, now Colombia, where he engaged in an unsuccessful farming enterprise that left him destitute by 1857. At that point he returned to France, where he took up residence in Paris and hoped to find work in journalism or geography, a field in which he had continued to be interested.

His political convictions continued to deepen. According to Giblin (1979:125), by the time of his return to Paris "gradually he moved towards an anarchist outlook. . . . He held the view that liberty was always antithetical to authority and that immorality came from the denial of liberty."

Though Reclus's earlier exposure to Ritter had undoubtedly whetted his appetite for geography, most of his subsequent learning in that field came from his own reading and his travels. While in Paris he sent some articles that he had written on geographical topics to the secretary of the Paris Geographical Society, Malte-Brun. Impressed by Reclus's work, Malte-Brun in turn sponsored Reclus for membership in the Société de Géographie in 1858.

Reclus had also begun working for the Hachette firm in Paris, publishers of the *Guides Joanne*. He travelled around France and other parts of Europe for the next decade or so and published several geographic articles, including publications in *La Terre, Bulletin de la Société de Géographie*, and *Revue Germanique*.

His growing stature in geography helped him escape deportation in 1871, when he was actively involved in the Commune of Paris, though he did end up in exile in Switzerland and elsewhere until 1889. During those years he travelled to Austria, Hungary, Egypt, Tunisia, Algeria, Italy, Spain, and Portugal, among others. Finally he did return to Paris, and in 1892 he was awarded the gold medal by the Paris Geographical Society for his *Nouvelle géographie universelle*, which also garnered for him recognition by the Royal Geographical Society in London and was a major contribution to nineteenth century geographic knowledge. As Giblin (1979:126) has commented, "Reclus's *Universal geography* includes some fine analytical work. . . . Reclus was not content merely to describe but wished also to explain."

In his last major work, *L'homme et la terre*, Reclus complements his earlier work and extends and clarifies his own thinking about geography. Reclus focused on population within a broad context of historical development, and this work was one of social geography, one that stepped beyond his previous works to include the responses that people make to the environments within which they find themselves. According to Giblin (1979:127), "All this means that determinism is discarded; for identical physical characteristics do not result in identical economic and social responses."

Reclus's social geography did not have the influence that he expected it to have on French geography, primarily because rural and regional geographies were mainstays of the French geographic repertoire at the time. Only later would his attempts to integrate sociology, economics, and cultural studies into a geographic framework that viewed social evolution over time come to have an impact.

Reclus had an interest in cartography as well. He was careful to maintain high quality in the maps that appeared in his works, and in 1895 he conceived the idea of making a giant globe on the scale of 1:1,000,000. Though people were interested, the cost was estimated to be beyond anything reasonable.

Despite his stature in French geography, Reclus never taught in France, and he ran into problems when he tried to teach in Belgium at the University of Brussels because of his past political activities. Finally Reclus and a small band of colleagues went to the Université Libré Nouvelle in Brussels, though the Belgian government refused to allow students from the new university to become candidates for degrees. In 1898 Reclus established the *Institut géographique*.

Though the number of students was small because of the government decision, Reclus continued to teach in the new university in Brussels until his death on July 4, 1905.

Selected Bibliography

1859   "Étude sur les fleuves." *Bulletin de la Société de Géographie* (Sér. 4)
            18:69–104.

            Préambule à 'De la Configuration des Continents' de Carl Ritter." *Revue
            Germanique* 8:241–67.

            "Quelques mots sur la Nouvelle-Grenade." *Bulletin de la Société de Géo-
            graphie* (Sér. 4) 17:11–41.

1860   *Guide du voyageur à Londres.* In *Collection Guide Joanne.* Paris.

1861   *Voyages à la Sierra Nevada de Ste. Marthe. Paysage de la vie tropicale.*
            Paris.

1862   "Le littoral de la France." *Revue des Deux Mondes* (December 15): 901–
            36; (August 1, 1863): 673–702; (November 15, 1863): 460–91; (September
            1, 1864): 191–217.

            "Le coton et la crise américaine." *Revue des Deux Mondes* (January 1):
            176–208.

            With G. Hickel. *Intinéraire descriptif et historique de l'Allemagne.* 2d ed.

            Allemagne de Nord. In *Collection Guide Joanne.* Paris.

1863   "Les Noirs américains depuis la guerre civile." *Revue des Deux Mondes*
            (March): 315–40.

1864   With P. Joanne. *Stations d'hiver de la Méditerranée: Nice, Hyères,
            Cannes, Monaco, Menton, Bordighera, San Remo.* Paris.

            "De l'acrion humaine sur la géographie physique. L'homme et la nature."
            Review of *Man and Nature* by G. P. Marsh. *Revue des Deux Mondes*
            (December 1):762–71.

1865   "Les oscillations du sol terrestre." *Revue des Deux Mondes* (January 1):
            57–84.

            "Études sur les dunes." *Bulletin de la Société de Géographie* 9:193–221.

            "L'histoire du peuple américain." Review of work by A. Carlier. *Bulletin
            de la Société de Géographie* (Sér. 5) 9:143–64.

1866   "Les républiques de L'Amérique du Sud, leurs guerres et leur projet de
            fédération." *Revue des Deux Mondes* (October):953–80.

1867   "L'Océan, étude de physique maritime." *Revue des Deux Mondes* (August
            15):963–93.

            "Les Basques. Un peuple qui s'en va." *Revue des Deux Mondes*
            (March):315–40.

1868   *La terre. Description des phénomènes de la vie du globe.* 2 vols. Paris.

            "L'election présidentielle de la Plata et la guerre du Paraguay." *Revue
            des Deux Mondes* (August 15): 891–910.

1869   *Histoire d'un ruisseau.* Paris: Hachette.

1873   "Les pluies de la Suisse." *Bulletin de la Société de Géographie* (Sér. 6)
            5:88–91.

"Note relative à l'histoire de la mer d'Aral." *Bulletin de la Société de Géographie* (Sér. 6) 6:113–18.

1874 "Voyage aux régions minières de la Translyvanie occidentale." *Tour du Monde*. Paris. 704. *Nouvelle géographie universelle. La Terre et les hommes*. 19 vols. Paris. (Through 1894)

"Hégémonie de l'Europe." *La Société Nouvelle* (10 année) 1(112):433–43. April.

1880 *Histoire d'une montagne*. Paris: J. Hetzel.

1894 "Leçon d'ouverture du cours de géographie comparée dans l'espace et dans le temps." Brussels.

1895 "Project de construction d'un globe terrestre à l'échelle du cent millième." *La Société Nouvelle*.

1901 *L'enseignement de la géographie, globes, disques globulaires et reliefs*. 2d ed., 1902. Brussels.

1902 With Onésime Reclus. *L'empire du milieu. Le climat, le sol, les races, la richesse de la Chine*. Paris.

1903 "Le panslavisme et l'unité russe." *Revue des Deux Mondes* (November 1): 273–84.

1905 *Nouvelle introduction au dictionnaire géographique et administratif de la France*. 7 vols. (1890–1905). The introduction is in a special volume.

L'homme et la terre. 6 vols. Paris.

1908 *Les volcans de la terre*. Société Belge d'Astronomie. (Published posthumously)

Chronology

1830 Born March 5 at Ste.-Foy-la-Grande in southwestern France.

1848 Passed examinations allowing him to leave school.

1851 Became student of Carl Ritter.

1853 Moved to New Orleans.

1857 Returned to France.

1858 Joined Paris Society of Geography.

1871 Arrested and imprisoned for participation in Paris Commune.

1872 Exile in Switzerland.

1882 Traveled to Hungary and Asia Minor.

1884 Traveled to Egypt, Tunisia, and Algeria.

1885 Toured Spain and Portugal.

1889 Returned to Paris. Visited Canada and United States.

1892 Gold Medal from Geographical Society of Paris.

1894 Professor at the Université Libré Nouvelle in Brussels.

1905 Died July 4 in Belgium.

Reference

Giblin, Beatrice. 1979. ''Élisée Reclus.'' *Geographers Biobibliographical Studies* 3:125–32.

Ferdinand Freiherr von Richthofen

Ferdinand Freiherr von Richthofen was born into a noble family on May 5, 1833, in Karlsruhe, Germany. As a youngster, he grew up in a rural environment amid the natural riches of the landscape around Karlsruhe, where he found an interest in everything from the rocks beneath his feet to the plants and animals that he encountered on his expeditions.

After attending local schools, he entered the university in Breslau in 1850, where he pursued further his earlier interests in geology. He was interested in chemistry and physics as well and was influenced by the great chemist Bunsen. Unhappy with the way things were at Breslau, Richthofen decided, in 1854, to transfer to the University of Berlin where he found the professors more stimulating, and where he discovered the elderly *Carl Ritter, who was still lecturing there. In Berlin he found other students who shared his interest in the natural sciences along with his newly developed interest in Asia. Though pragmatism forced Richthofen to finish his thesis on melaphyritic rocks, which he completed in 1856, his real desire by that time was to travel to Asia to observe first hand the Asian landscapes about which Ritter had so admirably written. Instead, however, he went to work. The Imperial Geological Office in Vienna needed help compiling geological maps of the Austro-Hungarian region, so Richthofen took advantage of an opportunity to be involved in those explorations. According to Kolb (1983:110), "In this early stage of his career, Richthofen showed several of his special talents, notably his extraordinary aptitude for basic analytical observations, large-scale comparison and synthetic synopsis." His geological work in Austria led to his *habilitation* degree in geology at the University of Vienna, after which he went to Berlin in 1860.

Out of his fieldwork in Austria came a publication, as well, *Geognostische Beschreibung der Umgegend von Predazzo, Sankt Cassian und der Seisser Alpe in Süd-Tirol*, which appeared in 1860. In that same year, the Prussian government selected Richthofen to accompany an expedition to eastern Asia. Led by Count

Eulenberg, its purpose was to establish commercial treaties with Japan, China, and Siam [Thailand], as well as to study the land and resources of the region. Richthofen was able to use his knowledge of geology to good purpose on this expedition, seeing tropical geomorphic processes, such as soil formation, for the first time.

Richthofen travelled to Ceylon, Japan, Hong Kong, and China, where the Taiping rebellion made any scientific fieldwork impossible for him. With his interest in tropical environments piqued, he was able to spend time in the field in Java. When negotiations were finally finished, he did not head immediately back with the delegation; rather, he returned by a circuitous route that included a crossing of the Burma mountain ridge and that took him as far afield as California.

In the summer of 1862, with the gold rush still in full swing, Richthofen travelled through California, where he ended up staying for six years, mainly to study the magnificent Sierra Nevada, and where he met and became friends with a number of American geologists. Two useful publications came out of his California experience, *The Comstock Lode*, published in 1865, and *Principles of the Natural System of Volcanic Rocks*, published in 1867.

In 1868 he returned to study China, where he worked when he could until 1872. Difficulties were many, however, and so in 1872 Richthofen decided to return to Berlin, where he began plans for a five-volume study of China, along with an atlas of China. The Prussian Ministry of Culture supported his China studies and, in 1875, offered him a chair at the University in Bonn from which he could have a leave of absence in order to finish work on the second volume of his China study. In the 1879–80 academic year, Richthofen gave his first geography lectures at Bonn, where he remained until 1883.

Though his past work in the field was not coupled with teaching, his philosophy of geography and its importance had been evolving for many years. As *Preston James and Geoffrey Martin (1981:167) noted about Richthofen:

To reach useful and reliable conclusions, he believed, a geographical study of any part of the face of the earth must start with a careful description of the physical features and then must move on to an examinations of the relationships of other features of the earth's surface to the basic physical framework. . . . The highest goal of geography is the exploration of the relationship of man to the physical earth and to the biotic features that are also associated with the physical features.

From Bonn, Richthofen accepted a chair in Leipzig, where he remained for three years before accepting a position in physical geography in Berlin in 1886. During his time in Leipzig, he completed his China atlas and *A Guide for Research Expeditions*, which was published in 1886.

Berlin appealed to Richthofen. Though he was sought out by the government as a recognized authority on China, and though he continued his research and writing on that area as well, he accomplished many other things in addition. In

1899 he was elected to the Academy of Sciences in Berlin, and in 1900 he founded the Institute for Oceanography in Berlin and became its first director. He enthusiastically supported polar expeditions and polar studies and was an active member of the Geographical Society of Berlin.

In 1903 Richthofen became rector of the university in Berlin, and two years later, on October 6, 1905, he died in Berlin. Following his death, two major collections of his works appeared, one, edited by Tiessen, focused mainly on China, and the other, edited by Schlüter, contained his works on transportation and settlement.

Selected Bibliography

1860   *Geognostische Beschreibung der Umgegend von Predazzo, Sankt Cassian und der Seisser Alpe in Süd-Tirol* (A Geognistic Description of the Region of Predazzo, Sanct Cassian and the Seisser Alps in Southern Tirol). Gotha.

1864   "Die Metall-Produktion Californiens und der angrenzenden Länder" (Metal Production in California and Adjacent Regions). *Petermanns Geographische Mitteilungen Ergänz* 3(14).

1865   *The Comstock Lode*. San Francisco.

1867   *Principles of the Natural System of Volcanic Rocks*. San Francisco.

1876   "Über den Seeverkehr nach und von China im Altertum" (On Oceanic Traffic to and from China in Antiquity). *Verhandlungen der Gesellschaft für Erdkunde, Berlin* 3:168–78.

1877–1912   *China. Ergebnisse eigener Reisen und darauf gegründeter Studien* (China: The results of my own travels and studies based on these). Vol. 1, Berlin 1877. Vol. 2, Berlin, 1882. Vol. 3, Postum, edited by E. Tiessen, Berlin, 1912. Vol. 4, Berlin, 1883. Vol. 5, edited by F. Frech, Berlin, 1911.

1883   *Aufgaben und Methoden der heutigen Geographie* (The Tasks and Methods of Modern Geography). Lecture given at Leipzig University on April 27.

1885   *Atlas von China, Das nördliche China*. (Atlas of China. Northern China). Berlin.

1886   *Führer für Forschungsreisende. Anleitung zu Beobachtungen über Gegenstände der Physischen Geographie und Geologie* (A Guide for Research Expeditions: An Introduction to Observations on Physical Geography and Geology). Leipzig.

1894   "China, Japan and Korea." *Geographical Journal* 4:556–61.

1895   "Der Friede von Shimonoseki in seinen geographischen Beziehungen" (The Peace of Shimonoseki in Its Geographical Significance). *Geographische Zeitschrift* 1:19–39.

1898   "Kiautschou, seine Weltstellung und voraussichtliche Bedeutung" (Kiautschou, Its Place in the World and Its Foreseeable Significance). *Preussische Jahrbücher*.

1900   "Geomorphologische Studien aus Ostasien. Über Gestalt und Gliederung einer Grundlinie in der Morphologie Ostasiens'' (Geomorphological Studies from East Asia: On the Shape and Classification of the Main Features in the Morphology of East Asia). *Sitzungsberichte der Preussischen der Akademie der Wissenchaften, Berlin*, 888–925.

1901	"Geomorphologische Studien aus Ostasien. Gestalt und Gliederung der ostasiatischen Küstenbogen'' (Geomorphological Studies from East Asia. The Shape and Classification of the East-Asiatic Coastline). *Sitzungsberichte der Preussischen Akadameie der Wissenschaften, Berlin*, 782–808.
1902	"Geomorphologische Studien aus Ostasien. Die morphologische Stellung von Formosa und den Diukiu-Inslen'' (Geomorphological Studies from East Asia: The Morphological Position of Formosa and the Riukiu Islands). *Sitzungsberichte der Preussischen Akademie der Wissenschaften, Berlin*, 944–75.
1903	"Geomorphologische Studien aus Ostasien. Über Gebirgskettungen in Ostasien, mit Ausschluss von Japan'' (Geomorphological Studies from East Asia. On the Mountain Chains of East Asia, Excluding Japan) and "Gebirgskettungen im Japanischen Bogen'' (Mountain Chains in the Japanese Bend). *Sitzungsberichte der Preussischen Akademie der Wissenschaften, Berlin*, 867–918.
1904	*Das Meer und die Kunde vom Meer* (The Ocean and Oceanography). Lecture at Berlin University.
1905	*Ergebnisse und Ziele der Südpolarforschung* (Aims and Results of South Polar Research). Berlin.
1907	*Tagebücher aus China* (China diaries). Edited by E. Tiessen. 2 vols. Berlin.
1908	*Vorlesungen über allgemeine Siedlungs und Verkehrsgeographie* (Lectures on General Settlement and Transportation Geography). Edited by O. Schlüter. Berlin.
1912	*Das südliche China* (Southern China). Edited by M. Groll. Berlin.

Chronology

1833	Born May 5 in Karlsruhe, Upper Silesia, Germany.
1850	Entered University of Breslau.
1854	Moved to University of Berlin.
1856	Presented first thesis on melaphyritic rocks. Went to work in Vienna (until 1860).
1860	Joined the Prussian government expedition to Japan.
1862	Travelled to California, remained until 1868.
1868	Travelled to China.
1870	Visited Japan.
1872	Returned to Berlin, Germany. Began writing on Asia.
1875	Worked at Bonn University (until 1883).
1883	Professor of Geography, Leipzig University.

1886	Professor of Physical Geography, University of Berlin.
1899	President of seventh International Geographical Congress, Berlin. Elected as member of Academy of Sciences, Berlin.
1900	Founded the Institute of Oceanography, Berlin; became its first Director.
1903	Rector of Berlin University.
1905	Died October 6 in Berlin.

References

James, Preston E., and Geoffrey J. Martin. 1981. *All Possible Worlds: A History of Geographical Ideas*. 2d ed. New York: Wiley.

Kolb, Albert. 1983. "Ferninand Freiherr von Richthofen." *Geographers Biobibliographical Studies* 7:109–15.

Carl Ritter

Carl Ritter was born on August 7, 1779, in the small town of Quedlinburg in Germany's Harz Mountains. His father, Johann Friedrich, was a court physician, and he and his wife, Dorothea, had a total of six children, of which Carl was the fourth (Kramer, 1959).

Carl's father died in 1784 at a relatively young age, leaving Carl's mother with six children to raise. Fortunately, an educator and philanthropist, Christian Gotthilf Salzmann, had established a school in Schnepfenthal, and he was willing to take in Carl, only five, as a student on a non-fee-paying basis. Carl's brother Johannes went to Schnepfenthal as a student as well, and the family's longtime tutor, GutsMuths, went to work as a tutor under Salzmann.

Carl Ritter's education at Schnepfenthal had a lasting impact on his thinking and learning. According to Linke (1981:99), "A particularly important feature of the school's teaching as a whole was the strong emphasis laid on stimulating and concept-based learning, with close contact between teacher and pupil." Ritter reluctantly left Schnepfenthal in 1796 and registered at the University of Halle to study the management of state properties, though he found numerous opportunities to study geographical topics.

In 1798 Ritter moved to Frankfurt to work as a tutor for the children of a wealthy banker, Bethmann-Hollweg. There he pursued his geographical inclinations as well, taking his students on trips of interest in the local region and working on thematic maps and his first major geographic work, *Europa: ein geographisch-historisch-statistisches Gemälde*, which was published in two volumes, one in 1804 and the other in 1807. A supplemental atlas, *Sechs Karten von Europa*, was published in 1806 to accompany the two-volume "portrait." According to Linke (1981:100), "This work reflected the major characteristic of all Ritter's subsequent geographical works: the presentation of geography in an intellectually stimulating form rather than as a mere cataloguing of facts for memorization."

In 1807 Ritter had his first meeting with Johann Heinrich Pestalozzi in Switzerland, and he was very impressed with the well-known educator. In that same year, Ritter also met *Alexander von Humboldt, who had thoroughly established his own credentials as a geographer by that time. In the next few years Ritter had opportunities to travel to Switzerland and Italy, and to meet again with Pestalozzi.

Ritter went to Göttingen in 1813, where he was able to commit himself to his geographical studies on a full-time basis. Out of that time came the first two volumes of his *Erdkunde*, published in 1817 and 1818. In 1819 he took a position as professor of history in Frankfurt, and married Lilli Kramer, a woman from Duderstadt.

In 1820 Ritter moved to Berlin to take positions both at the university there, the first chair in geography in Germany, and at the Prussian Military Academy. In that same year, he published *Die Vorhalle europaischer Volkergeschichte*, and in the following year he received his official doctorate. According to *Preston James and Geoffrey Martin (1981:127) "Ritter was a brilliant and influential lecturer . . . his lectures were clear and well organized. . . . He was a master of the art of using the blackboard to illustrate his ideas." Between 1822 and 1859, *Die Erdkunde* occupied much of his attention. Revisions of the first two volumes, which had been published a few years earlier, were followed by seventeen additional volumes. As James and Martin (1981:130) commented, "In contrast to the clarity of his lectures, Ritter's published works are often obscure. Scholars have struggled to find suitable translations for some of his passages. . . . many of his assertions of relationships have never been and could never be subjected to rigorous verification." Linke (1981:101) described *Die Erdkunde* as "one of the most comprehensive works ever undertaken by one individual."

In 1822 Ritter was elected to the Prussian Academy of Sciences, and in 1824 he became a corresponding member of the Société Asiatique de Paris. In the following year, he became a professor of regional geography, history, and ethnology at the University of Berlin. In 1828 he established the *Gesellschaft für Erdkunde zu Berlin* (the Berlin Geographical Society). In the 1830s and 1840s, he travelled widely in Europe. Many of these trips lasted for weeks at a time, allowing him to absorb firsthand the landscapes and peoples of the countries that he visited, from England and Ireland in the west, to Turkey in the east, though he never visited Russia. His visits included meetings with both scientists and artists.

Given the extent of Ritter's teaching commitments and travels, it is not surprising that some of the ideas and areas that he had envisioned as additions to *Die Erdkunde* were never completed. On May 6, 1859, Humboldt, with whom Ritter had established an important relationship, died. Only a few months later, on September 29, 1859, Ritter himself died. Thus, in one year, Germany and the world lost two of its most important geographers. James and Martin (1981:130) noted, "So these two great scholars, who died in the same year in Berlin, each in his own way attempted to establish a 'new geography.' Each tried to embrace the knowledge of mankind concerning the earth as the home of man. . . . both had confidence that continued use of proper geographical methods would eventually bring to light the inner meaning of the universe.''

One measure of Ritter's importance can be seen in the observation that his chair in geography was not filled again until 1874, when H. Kiepert, who had worked with Ritter on latter parts of *Die Erdkunde*, was hired to fill it.

Selected Bibliography

1804   *Europa: ein geographisch-historisch-statistisches Gemälde*. Vol. 1, Frank-furt-am-Main. Vol. 2, Frankfurt-am-Main, 1807.

1817   *Die Erdkunde im Verhältniss zur Natur und zur Geschichte des Menschen.* 2 vols. 2d ed., 1822–59.

1862   *Comparative Geography*. Allgemein erdkunde, Berlin.

1863   *Europa Vorlesungen an der Universität zu Berlin gehalten von Carl Ritter.* Edited by H. A. Daniel. Berlin.

1866   *The Comparative Geography of Palestine on the Sinaitic Peninsula.* Trans-lated by William L. George. New York: Appleton.

1875   *Carl Ritter: Ein Lebensbild nach seinem handschriftlichen Nachlass.* Ed-ited by G. Kramer. Halle. (Vol. 2 is a collection of letters by Carl Ritter.)

Chronology

1779   Born August 7 in Quedlinburg, located in Germany's Harz Mountains.

1785   Went to Schnepfenthal to attend school.

1796   Began studies at Halle University.

1798   Began career as a tutor, in Frankfurt-am-Main.

1811   Travelled in Switzerland.

1813   Visit to Göttingen.

1820   Moved to Berlin. Appointment to University of Berlin and the Prussian Military Academy.

1821   Awarded Ph.D.

1825   Professor of Regional Geography, Ethnology and History at University of Berlin.

1834   Travelled to Vienna and eastern Alps.

1837   Visited Constantinople, Greece, and southeast Europe.

1839   Travelled to Switzerland, Italy, and southern France.

1840   Travelled to Denmark, Norway, and Sweden.

1845   Visited Belgium, Paris, the Pyrenées, and southern France.

1856   Curator of Royal Cartographic Institute (Prussia).

1859   Appointed supervisor of the Map Room of the Royal Library. Died September 29.

References

James, Preston E., and Geoffrey J. Martin, 1981. *All Possible Worlds: A History of Geographical Ideas*. 2d ed. New York: Wiley.
Kramer, Fritz L. 1959. "A Note on Carl Ritter." *Geographical Review* 49:406–9.
Linke, Max. 1981. "Carl Ritter." *Geographers Biobibliographical Studies* 5:99–108.

Arthur H. Robinson

One of the scholars responsible for the development of cartography in America is Arthur H. Robinson. He was born in Montreal, Canada, to American parents on January 5, 1915. His early education was in Northfield, Minnesota, but he later moved to Oxford, Ohio, where his father was a professor of history. He also spent a year, during his teens, in England where he attended the Friend's School Saffron Walden.

In 1932 Robinson entered Miami University in Oxford, Ohio. After four years, he graduated with a Bachelor of Arts degree in January 1936, with a major in history and a minor in geography. The following fall he entered the graduate program in the Department of Geography at the University of Wisconsin in Madison. He worked with Professors V. C. Finch, G. T. Trewartha, and J. R. Whitaker, who stimulated his interest in cartography. In June 1938, he was granted a Master of Arts degree.

In September 1938, Robinson entered the Ph.D. program in geography at Ohio State University at Columbus where he studied primarily under Professors G. H. Smith and R. Peattie. His specialty was cartography, but his minor field was geomorphology in the Department of Geology. Later on in that year he married Mary Elizabeth Coffin. While pursuing his graduate work at Ohio State, he began doing free-lance cartographic work and was the cartographic author for Peattie's *Geography in Human Destiny* and Sears, Quillen, and Hanna's book *This Useful World*.

Robinson had to interrupt his Ph.D. work during World War II. He went to Washington, D.C. in October 1941 and some months later was named Chief of the Cartography Section of the Geography Division and later the Chief of the Map Division of the Office of Strategic Services (O.S.S.). Among his many tasks was the preparation of most of the strategic maps for the Joint Chiefs of Staff and the base materials for the daily situation maps for the Operations

Division of the War Department. While in the O.S.S., Robinson was commissioned captain and eventually rose to the rank of major in the U.S. Army.

After the war, in the summer of 1945, Robinson accepted a position as assistant professor in the Department of Geography at the University of Wisconsin at Madison. During his first two years of teaching at Madison, he also finished work on his Ph.D. dissertation, and the degree was awarded by The Ohio State University in 1947. Although he wrote a few short works that were published in the *Geographical Review* during the war, his first major work was *The Look of Maps: An Examination of Cartographic Design*, published by the University of Wisconsin Press in 1952. During the forties and fifties, Robinson rose through the academic ranks at Wisconsin from assistant, to associate, to full professor. In 1966 he was named Chair of the Department of Geography, as well as Director of the University of Wisconsin Cartographic Laboratory. In 1967 he was named Lawrence Martin Professor of Cartography.

During his thirty-five years at Wisconsin, Robinson was instrumental in the development of the instructional program in cartography. Through his efforts, a small mapmaking establishment in the 1940s grew to become the official University of Wisconsin Cartographic Laboratory. He was also responsible for the development of both a bachelor's and master's degree in Cartography.

Robinson has been an active scholar throughout his career. He has been the author or coauthor of sixteen books and monographs. His *Elements of Cartography*, originally published in 1953, has undergone many revisions and is a classic textbook for the teaching of cartography. He has written more than fifty professional papers that have appeared in a variety of journals including *Geographical Review*, *Annals of the Association of American Geographers*, *Surveying and Mapping*, *Professional Geographer*, *The Cartographic Journal*, *The American Cartographer*, and *Social Education*. He has also written numerous reviews and encyclopedia articles, and produced maps.

Robinson has held a variety of positions in professional organizations. He was President of the International Cartographic Association (1972–76); a member of the Board of Directors and Chairman of the Cartographic Division of the American Congress on Surveying and Mapping; editor of *The American Cartographer* during its first three years; and President of the Association of American Geographers (1963–64).

As a result of his work, Robinson has received numerous honors and awards. He has received the Legion of Merit from the United States Army (1946); the Citation for Meritorious Contributions from the Association of American Geographers (1953); and the Distinguished Service Award and the Helen Culver Gold Medal from the Geographic Society of Chicago (1959, 1983). He also was awarded two Guggenheim Foundation Research Fellowships (1964, 1978); the Earle J. Fennell Award and the Cartography Division Award for Meritorious Service from the American Congress on Surveying and Mapping (1977, 1979); and the Carl Mannerfelt Medal from the International Cartographic Association (1981). Robinson is also the recipient of two honorary degrees, a Doctor of

Letters from Miami University of Ohio (1966) and a Doctor of Science from The Ohio State University (1984).

Selected Bibliography

1940   With J. A. Barnes. "A New Method for the Representation of Dispersed Rural Population." *Geographical Review* 30:134–37.

1941   With S. McCune. "Notes on a Physiographic Diagram of Tyosen." *Geographical Review* 31:653–58.

1946   "A Method for Producing Shaded Relief from Areal Slope Data." *Annals of the Association of American Geographers* 36:248–52.

1950   "The Size of Lettering for Maps and Charts." *Surveying and Mapping* 10:37–44.

1951   "The Use of Deformational Data in Evaluating Map Projections." *Annals of the Association of American Geographers* 41:58–74.

1952   *The Look of Maps: An Examination of Cartographic Design.* Madison: University of Wisconsin Press.

1953   *Elements of Cartography.* New York: Wiley.

1954   "Geographic Cartography." In Preston James and Clarence Jones, eds., *American Geography: Inventory and Prospect.* Syracuse, N.Y.: Syracuse University Press. 553–77.

1957   With V. C. Finch, G. T. Trewartha, and E. H. Hammond. *Elements of Geography.* New York: McGraw-Hill.

            With R. A. Bryson. "A Method of Describing Quantitatively the Correspondence of Geographical Distributions." *Annals of the Association of American Geographers* 47:379–91.

            With N.J.W. Thrower. "A New Method of Terrain Representation." *Geographical Review* 47:507–20.

1961   With G. T. Trewartha and E. H. Hammond. *Fundamentals of Physical Geography.* New York: McGraw-Hill.

1962   "Mapping the Correspondence of Isarithmic Maps." *Annals of the Association of American Geographers* 52:414–25.

1965   "The Future of the International Map." *The Cartographic Journal* 2:23–26.

1970   With M. L. Hsu. *The Fidelity of Isopleth Maps.* Minneapolis: University of Minnesota Press.

            "Erwin Josephus Raisz, 1893–1968." *Annals of the Association of American Geographers* 60:189–93.

1974   With J. B. Culver. *The Atlas of Wisconsin.* Madison: University of Wisconsin Press.

1976   With B. Petchenik. *The Nature of Maps: Essays Toward an Understanding of Maps and Mapping.* Chicago: University of Chicago Press.

1979	"Geography and Cartography Then and Now." *Annals of the Association of American Geographers* 69:97–102.
1982	*Early Thematic Mapping in the History of Cartography*. Chicago: University of Chicago Press.
1990	"Rectangular World Maps—No!" *Professional Geographer* 42:101–4.

Chronology

1915	Born in Montreal, Canada, January 5.
1936	Awarded a B.A. degree with a major in history and a minor in geography from Miami University in Oxford, Ohio.
1938	Awarded an M.A. degree in Geography from the University of Wisconsin.
1942–45	Chief of the Map Division of the Office of Strategic Services, Washington, D.C.
1945	Accepted position as Assistant Professor in the Department of Geography at the University of Wisconsin at Madison.
1947	Awarded a Ph.D. from Ohio State University.
1952	First book published, *The Look of Maps*.
1953	Received a citation for meritorious contributions to geography from the Association of American Geographers; published *Elements of Cartography*.
1957	Published *Elements of Geography*.
1966	Named Chair of the Department of Geography and Director of the University of Wisconsin Cartographic Laboratory; awarded an honorary Litt. D. from Miami University of Ohio.
1967	Named Lawrence Martin Professor of Cartography.
1974	Published *The Atlas of Wisconsin*.
1977	Awarded the Earle Fennel Award of the American Congress on Surveying and Mapping.
1981	Awarded the Carl Mannerfelt Medal from the International Cartographic Association.
1988	Received the Master Mentor Award from the National Council for Geographic Education and the John Oliver LaGorce Medal from the National Geographic Society.

Richard Joel Russell

Richard Joel Russell was born on November 16, 1895, in Hayward, California, and moved to Hawaii with his family in 1899. After a few years, they returned to California, then moved frequently to other places while young Richard was growing up. His family was descended from early New Englanders, and the travelling he did with his parents apparently instilled in him a love for travel and observation.

In high school his interest in the natural world was stimulated both by his teachers and by the outdoor activities in which he liked to participate, including hiking, hunting, and camping. During one summer he even drove one of his high school teachers to watch an eruption of Lassen Peak in northeastern California.

Russell entered the University of California at Berkeley in 1915, planning to study agriculture, though he switched to geology once he was there. After interrupting his education for a stint as an officer in the Navy during World War I, Russell returned to Berkeley to finish his degree in vertebrate paleontology. He graduated with honors in 1920 and went on to study structural geology under Andrew Lawson and George Louderback at Berkeley. While working toward his doctorate in geology, he worked as a teaching assistant in both geology and geography, where the latter department was composed of two people, *Carl Sauer and John Leighly.

Russell taught a variety of geography classes for Sauer and Leighly, and in the process learned a considerable amount about geography and the geographic perspective. Despite his growing interest in geography, however, when he received his doctorate in geology, in 1925, he sought a position in a geology department. His first job was as an associate professor of geology at Texas Technological College in Lubbock, where he taught during the academic years 1926–27 and 1927–28. Unimpressed with life in Lubbock, he accepted a position at Louisiana State University (L.S.U.) in Baton Rouge in the fall of 1928, where he was given the task of developing a geography program within the department of geology. The challenge proved irresistible, and Baton Rouge remained Russell's home for the rest of his life.

Russell worked first with H. V. Howe and then with Fred Kniffen to build the combined geography and geology program at L.S.U. At the same time he continued to do fieldwork in California, studying the Sierra Nevada and Basin and Range provinces. His earliest publications, in the late 1920s, were all focused on California. They included studies of the Hayward Fault, California climates, and the Warner Range. These interests, both geological and climatological, occupied Russell's attention throughout his lifetime, though his regional focus shifted from California to Louisiana, then on to the Caribbean, Europe, and elsewhere. He considered himself a geomorphologist and treated climatology more as an avocation, a hiatus from serious fieldwork. Paradoxically for Russell, as Kniffen (1973:242) commented, "Much to his chagrined surprise, the climatic studies were readily accepted and praised, whereas those in geomorphology, each of which had required much study in the field, gained limited attention." Despite the broad regional interests that are apparent in some of his work, Russell concentrated increasing attention after 1930 on his work in Louisiana, where he was slow to find geomorphic problems of interest in a landscape so much less dramatic than that of the Sierra Nevada. He focused on alluvial studies, first in Louisiana, where he also was interested in the geosynclinal structure that was catching alluvial deposits and sinking under their weight, then along other rivers, from the Rhône and Rhine in Europe to the Amazon. He also became fascinated with beaches, both their composition and their formation. An interest in beach rock led him to places as far away as Mauritius and Australia.

In 1936 Russell became chair of the geography department, and in subsequent years he achieved many other things as well. In 1937 he received the first [*Wallace W.] Atwood Award from the Association of American Geographers, for example, and in 1939 he became associate editor of *Zeitschrift für Geologie*. In 1943 he was recognized as a distinguished professor by the Association of American Geographers; five years later, he became president of that organization and, in the same year, a Special Fellow of the Belgian-American Educational Foundation. His administrative abilities continued to be recognized as well, as Russell became the acting director of the school of geology in 1944 and Dean of the Graduate School at Louisiana State University in 1948, a position that he held until 1961, during which time he also served as editor of the *LSU Studies*. In 1953 he was president of the Council of Deans of Southern Graduate Schools. During his tenure as dean, he found time to be director of L.S.U.'s Coastal Studies Institute for several years as well, and to serve terms as chairman of the National Research Council's Division of Earth Sciences and president of the Geological Society of America.

After leaving his dean's position, Russell became Boyd Professor of Geography at L.S.U. until 1966. In 1967 he received a distinguished service award

from the United States Navy. Russell died on September 17, 1971, in Baton
Rouge.

Selected Bibliography

1926   "Recent Horizontal Offsets along the Hayward Fault." *Journal of Geology*
            34:507–11.

            "Climates of California." *Publications in Geography* 2:73–84.

1927   "Landslide Lakes of the Northwestern Great Basin." *Publications in Ge-
            ography* 2:231–54. Berkeley, University of California.

            "The Landforms of Surprise Valley, Northwestern Great Basin. *Publi-
            cations in Geography.* 323–58.

1928   "Basin Range Structure and Stratigraphy of the Warner Range, North-
            eastern California." *Geological Science Bulletin* 17:387–496. Berkeley,
            University of California.

1931   "Dry Climates of the United States." Vol. 1: "Climatic Map." Vol. 2:
            "Frequency of Dry and Desert Years 1901–1920." *Publications in Ge-
            ography* 5:1–41, 254–74.

1932   "Landforms of San Gorgonio Pass, Southern California." *Publications in
            Geography* 6:23–121.

1933   "Alpine Landforms of Western United States." *Bulletin of the Geological
            Society of America* 44:927–50.

1934   "Climatic Years." *Geographical Review* 24:92–103.

1935   With H. V. Howe and J. H. McGuirt. *Physiography of Coastal Southwest
            Louisiana.* Geological Bulletin No. 6. Baton Rouge, Louisiana, Depart-
            ment of Conservation, 1–72.

            "Cheniers of Southwestern Louisiana. *Geographical Review* 25:449–61.

1936   "The Desert-Rainfall Factor in Denudation." *Report of the 16th Inter-
            national Geological Congress* 2:753–63. Washington, D.C.

            "Physiography of the Lower Mississippi River Delta." In *Reports on the
            Geology of Plaquemines and St. Bernard Parishes.* Geological Bulletin
            No. 8. Baton Rouge, Louisiana, Department of Conservation, 3–86.

1938   "Quaternary Surfaces in Louisiana." *Comptes Rendus International Geo-
            logical Congress* 2 (Sect. F):406–12. Amsterdam.

            "Physiography of Iberville and Ascension Parishes." *Reports of the Ge-
            ology of Plaquemines and St. Bernard Parishes.* Geological Bulletin No.
            13. Baton Rouge, Louisiana, Department of Conservation, 3–86.

1939   "Morphologie des Mississippi Deltas." *Geographische Zeitschrift 45 Jah-
            resbericht* 8:281–93.

1940   "Quaternary History of Louisiana." *Bulletin of the Geological Society of
            America* 51:1199–1234.

            "Gulf Coast Geosyncline: America's Great Petroleum Reserve." *Comptes
            Rendus 17th International Geological Congress* 4:269–72. Moscow.

1941   "Climate Through the Ages." *1941 Yearbook of Agriculture*. Washington, D.C.: U.S. Dept. of Agriculture, 67–97.

1942   "Geomorphology of the Rhône Delta." *Annals of the Association of American Geographers* 32:149–254.

1944   *The Mississippi River*. Bureau of Educational Material, Louisiana State University, Baton Rouge.

            "Origin of Loess." *American Journal of Science* 242:447–50.

            "Lower Mississippi Valley Loess." *Bulletin of the Geological Society of America* 55:1–40.

1945   "Climates of Texas." *Annals of the Association of American Geographers* 35:37–52.

            "Post-War Geography." *Journal of Geography* 44:301–12.

1948   "Coast of Louisiana." *Bulletin de la Société Belge de Geologie, Paleontologie et Hydrologie* 57:380–94.

1949   "Geographical Geomorphology." *Annals of the Association of American Geographers* 39:1–11.

1951   *Louisiana, Our Treasure Ground*. Bureau of Educational Materials, Louisiana State University, Baton Rouge.

            With Fred B. Kniffen. *Culture Worlds*. New York: Macmillan.

1953   "Coastal Advance and Retreat in Louisiana." *Comptes Rendus 19th International Geological Congress* (Sect. 4) 4:109–18. Algiers.

1954   "Alluvial Morphology of Anatolian Rivers." *Annals of the Association of American Geographers* 44:363–91.

1956   With H. O'R. Steinberg. "Fracture Patterns in the Amazon and Mississippi Valleys." *Proceedings of the 17th International Geographical Congress*. Washington, D.C., 380–85.

1957   "Instability of Sea Level." *American Scientist* 45:414–30.

1958   "Geological Geomorphology." *Bulletin of the Geological Society of America* 69:1–21.

1959   "Caribbean Beach Rock Observations." *Zeitschrift für Geomorphologie*. Band 6. H 3:227–36.

1961   Edited by Russell. "Pacific Island Terraces: Eustatic?" *Zeitschrift für Geomorphologie*. Band 3. Supp.

            With Fred B. Kniffen and E. L. Pruitt. *Culture Worlds* (brief edition). New York.

1963   "Beach Rock." *Journal of Tropical Geography* 17:24–27.

1964   "Duration of the Quaternary and Its Subdivisions." *Proceedings of the National Academy of Sciences* 52:(3)790–96.

1965   "Southern Hemisphere Beach Rock." *Geographical Review* 55:17–55.

            With W. G. McIntyre. "Australian Tidal Flats." Coastal Studies Series No. 12. Baton Rouge: Louisiana State University Press.

With W. G. McIntyre. "Beach Cusps." *Bulletin of the Geological Society of America* 76:307–20.

1966   *River and Delta Morphology.* Coastal Studies Series No. 20. Baton Rouge: Louisiana State University Press.

With W. G. McIntyre. *Barbuda Reconnaissance.* Coastal Studies Series No. 16. Baton Rouge: Louisiana State University Press.

1967   "Origin of Estuaries." In G. H. Lauff, ed. *Estuaries.* No. 83. *American Association for the Advancement of Science*, 93–99.

"Aspects of Coastal Morphology." *Geografiska Annaler* (Ser. A) 49 (2):299–309.

River Plains and Seacoasts. Berkeley: University of California Press.

1968   *Glossary of Terms in Fluvial, Deltaic and Coastal Morphology and Processes.* Coastal Studies Series No. 23. Baton Rouge: Louisiana State University Press.

1970   *Oregon and Northern California Coastal Reconnaissance.* Technical Report No. 86. Coastal Studies Institute, Louisiana State University.

Florida Beaches and Cemented Water-Table Rocks. Technical Report No. 88. Coastal Studies Institute, Louisiana State University.

Beaches and Ground Water Studies of Cape Sable, Florida. Technical Report No. 103. Coastal Studies Institute, Louisiana State University.

1971   "The Coast of Louisiana." In J. A. Steers, ed., *Applied Coastal Geomorphology.* London, 84–97.

"Water-Table Effects on Seacoasts." *Bulletin of the Geological Society of America* 82:2343–48.

Chronology

1895   Born November 16 in Hayward, California.

1914   Graduated from high school.

1918   Ensign in U.S. Navy.

1920   B.S. in Palaeontology, from the University of California, Berkeley.

1923   Associate in Geography, University of California, Berkeley (until 1926).

1925   Ph.D. in Geology from University of California, Berkeley. Associate Professor of Geology, Texas Technological College. First papers on California climates and on the Hayward fault.

1926   Associate Professor of Geography, Louisiana State University. Further fieldwork in Sierra Nevada. Visited by *Albrecht Penck.

1928   Professor of Geography, Louisiana State University. Fieldwork in Europe.

1936   Head of geography department, Louisiana State University.

1937   First Atwood Award, Association of American Geographers.

1938   Fieldwork in Rhône delta and Scandinavia; travelled with Penck.

1939   Associate Editor, *Zeitschrift für Geologie.*

1943	Distinguished Lecturer, American Association of Professional Geographers.
1944	Acting Director, School of Geology, Louisiana State University (until 1963).
1948	President of the Association of American Geographers.
1949	Dean of Graduate School, Louisiana State University (until 1961).
1953	Fieldwork in Morocco and Turkey.
1954	Chairman, Division of Earth Sciences, National Research Council.
1957	President, Geological Society of America. Associate Editor, *Zeitschrift für Geomorphologie*. Fieldwork, Amazon River and in the West Indies.
1960	Outstanding Achievement Award, Association of American Geographers. Honorary Fellow, German Academy of Science.
1962	Vice President, Earth Science Division, American Association of the Advancement of Science.
1964	Chairman, Geomorphology section, International Geographical Union (I.G.U.) Congress. Fieldwork in Australia and Indian Ocean.
1967	U.S. Navy, Distinguished Service Award. Elected to Royal Danish Academy.
1969	Chairman, Graduate Schools Association, southeastern section.
1970	Fieldwork in Florida and on West Coast of U.S.A.
1971	Died September 17, Baton Rouge, Louisiana.

Reference

Kniffen, Fred B. 1973. "Richard Joel Russell." *Annals of the Association of American Geographers* 63:241–49.

Rollin D. Salisbury

Rollin D. Salisbury was born on August 17, 1858, near Spring Prairie in rural Walworth County, Wisconsin. After giving up a career as a schoolteacher in New York, Salisbury's father had moved to Wisconsin to become a farmer, and Salisbury grew up on that farm, learning the value of hard work. He attended local schools when he could and in 1874 went to the Whitewater Normal School.

After finishing his teacher training, he took a teaching position for a year and then decided to go to Beloit College, which was near where he had grown up. Fortunately, he was introduced there to the natural sciences, especially to the work of one instructor, Thomas C. Chamberlin, who was also the state geologist. Chamberlin's combination of instruction, fieldwork, and research appealed to the young Salisbury.

After graduation, Salisbury worked as an assistant for Chamberlin at the United States Geological Survey for a year, gaining experience to go with his education. When Chamberlin left Beloit College, Salisbury replaced him in that position and began a career of teaching and research. Out of the work that he had done with Chamberlin came his first publication, coauthored with Chamberlin, "On the Driftless Area of the Upper Mississippi Valley," published in 1885, which gained Salisbury some attention from other geologists. During the 1887–88 academic year, he was able to go to Heidelberg to study and to observe glacial features in Europe. Once back at Beloit College he worked to develop his teaching and to continue his research activities, publishing an article in 1888, "Terminal Moraines from North Germany," based on fieldwork that he had done while studying abroad.

In the meantime, Chamberlin had moved on to a position as president of the University of Wisconsin, and he asked Salisbury to come there as a geology professor. Salisbury accepted the offer and went to Madison for the 1891–92 academic year, where he was associated with "geographic geology." During that year he began a research project on Pleistocene landforms in New Jersey.

In 1892 Chamberlin moved to the University of Chicago, where Salisbury also accepted a position as professor of geographic geology at Chamberlain's request. He remained at the University of Chicago for the rest of his academic career. He continued the work that he had started in New Jersey and was able to encourage some graduate students to work with him on that project. This work led to several publications on the physical geography and glacial geology of New Jersey.

Along with his continued research and publication during the 1890s, Salisbury also became the managing editor of the new *Journal of Geology*, did summer fieldwork in Greenland, became the first president of the Geographic Society of Chicago, was appointed Dean of the Ogden Graduate School of Science in 1899, and led summer expeditions to study glaciation in the Rocky Mountains. As if these activities were not enough, in 1903 he accepted the chair of the new Department of Geography. According to Visher (1953:4), "The prominent status that Salisbury's department soon attained reflected several influences in addition to its being for years the only full-fledged university department of geography." Among those influences, in addition to Salisbury's contributions both as administrator and geographer, were a staff that included *John Paul Goode, *Walter W. Atwood, Harlan Barrows, Charles Colby, Robert Platt, and others; a close relationship with the department of geology; and the prestigious position of the department within the University of Chicago. The new department awarded its first doctorate to F. V. Emerson in 1907, and *Carl Sauer was a student there in 1910.

Despite his administrative assignments, Salisbury continued to teach, mainly geology, and to do research. As Visher (1953:8) noted, "One of the surprising aspects of his teaching was that he, a world-renowned scientist and high dean, regularly taught classes of freshmen, as well as of upper-classmen and graduate students." In 1907 Salisbury's text, *Physiography*, appeared, and he coauthored works with both Atwood and Barrows. As *Preston James and Geoffrey Martin (1981:311–12) pointed out, "Physiography, for Salisbury, was the scientific study of the stage setting on which the human drama unfolded. But the relation of the stage setting to human action was not a causal one." In 1912 Salisbury was elected President of the Association of American Geographers and coauthored, with Harlan Barrows and Walter Tower, *Elements of Geography*; coauthored *Modern Geography*, again with Barrows and Tower, in 1913; and in the following year coauthored, with Chamberlin, still another text, *Introductory Geology*.

In the years afterward, Salisbury dedicated himself even more to the geography department and its programs. As Pattison (1982:107) noted, "In what could not have been an easy transition, he curtailed his outdoor pursuits while installing himself as elder counsellor and wise presence in the Department, now rededicated as a research enterprise." In 1917 he served as Chair and Vice-President for the

Geology and Geography section of the American Association for the Advancement of Science, and in the following year he assumed editorship of the *Journal of Geology*.

Salisbury resigned his position as head of the department in 1919, after making his last appointment to the department, Robert Platt, and briefly became chair of the geology department. In 1921 he helped establish a graduate program in geography at Clark University under Atwood, who had previously taught at the University of Chicago. In the following year his heart began to fail, and he died in Chicago on August 15, 1922.

Selected Bibliography

1885   With T. C. Chamberlin. "On the Driftless Area of the Upper Mississippi Valley." *U.S. Geological Survey Sixth Annual Report*, 199–322.

1888   "Terminal Moraines from North Germany." *American Journal of Science* 35:401.

1891   With T. C. Chamberlin. "On the Relationship of the Pleistocene to the Pre-Pleistocene Formations of Glaciation." *American Journal of Science* 41:359–77.

1896   "Salient Points Concerning the Glacial Geology of North Greenland." *Journal of Geology* 4:769–810.

1898   "The Physical Geography of New Jersey." *New Jersey Geological Survey Final Report* 4:1–170.

1899   With W. C. Alden. "The Geography of Chicago and its Environs." *Bulletin of the Geographical Society*. No. 1. Chicago.

1900   With W. W. Atwood. "The Geography of the Region about Devil's Lake and the Dells of Wisconsin." *Wisconsin Geological and Natural History Statistical Bulletin*. No. 5. State of Wisconsin, Madison.

1902   With others. "The Glacial Geology of New Jersey." *New Jersey Geological Survey*. Final Report. Vol. 5.

1903   With E. Blackwelder. "Glaciation in the Bighorn Mountains, Wyoming." *Journal of Geology* 11:216–33.

1904–6   With T. C. Chamberlin. *Geology*. 3 vols. New York: Holt. Vol. 1: *Geologic Processes and Their Results*. Vol. 2: *Earth History: Genesis-Paleozoic*. Vol. 3: *Earth History: Mesozoic, Cenozoic*.

1907   *Physiography*. New York.

1908   *Physiography: Briefer Course*. New York.

            With W. W. Atwood. "The Interpretation of Topographic Maps." *U.S. Geological Survey Professional Paper*. No. 60. Washington, D.C.: Government Printing Office.

1909   *Physiography*. 2d rev. ed. New York.

1910   *Elementary Physiography*. New York.

1912   With H. H. Barrows and W. S. Tower. *Elements of Geography*. New York.

1913   With H. H. Barrows and W. S. Tower. *Modern Geography*. New York.

            Studies in Geology: A Laboratory Manual Based on Topographic Maps and Folios of the U.S. Geological Survey. New York.

            Laboratory Exercises in Structural and Historical Geology: A Laboratory Manual Based on Folios of the U.S. Geological Survey. New York.

            The Interpretation of Topographic Maps: A Laboratory Manual . . . to Accompany Beginning Courses in Physiography. New York.

1914   With T. C. Chamberlin. *Introductory Geology*. New York.

1915   "Some Matters of History." Address at dedication of Rosenwald Hall. *University of Chicago Magazine* 7:175–78.

1917   With C. N. Knapp. "The Quaternary Formations of Southern New Jersey." *New Jersey Department of Conservation*. Final Report Series, State Geologist. Vol. 8.

1918   "Geology in Education." *Science New Series* 47:325–35.

1919   *Physiography*. 3d rev. ed. New York.

Chronology

1858   Born August 17 near Spring Prairie, Wisconsin.

1877   Graduated from Normal School and taught in a primary school at Whitewater, Wisconsin.

1878   Entered Beloit College, studied under Thomas C. Chamberlin.

1881   Graduated from Beloit College. Began work at U.S. Geological Survey as assistant to Chamberlin.

1882   Appointed to teaching staff at Beloit College. Taught geology, zoology, and botany.

1887   Studied in Heidelberg during a year's leave from Beloit.

1891   Director of Pleistocene studies for the New Jersey Geological Survey.

1892   Professor of geographic geology at University of Chicago.

1893   Managing Editor for geographic geology of *Journal of Geology*.

1895   During the summer, geologist on the Peary Relief Expedition to Northern Greenland.

1898   First President of the Geographic Society of Chicago.

1899   Appointed Dean of the Ogden Graduate School of Science, University of Chicago.

1903   Became the first head of the Department of Geography, University of Chicago.

1904   Became a charter member of the Association of American Geographers.

1908   First President of the Association of American Geographers.

1912   Again, President of the Association of American Geographers.

1918   Editor of the *Journal of Geology*.

1919   Resigned as head of Department of Geography to become the head of the
              Department of Geology.

1922   Heart attack in May. Retired from all duties at University of Chicago.
              Died August 15.

References

James, Preston E., and Geoffrey J. Martin. 1981. *All Possible Worlds: A History of Geographical Ideas*. 2d ed. New York: Wiley.

Pattison, William D. 1982. "Rollin D. Salisbury." *Geographers Biobibliographical Studies* 6:105–13.

Visher, Stephen. 1953. "Rollin D. Salisbury and Geography." *Annals of the Association of American Geographers* 43:4–11.

Carl Ortwin Sauer

Carl Sauer, probably the most important American geographer, was born on Christmas Eve, 1889, in the little town of Warrenton, Missouri. His German ancestors had been part of a religious group identified as "German Methodists," a sect in which his grandfather had been a minister. The group had a college in Warrenton, Central Wesleyan College, and it was there that Carl's father taught. His upbringing was simple and strict, with a closeness to nature and strong sense of rural communal values. Among his friends and relatives, memories of the frontier were still vivid, and young Carl was fascinated by them and by the place of his family in the sweep of settlement in the United States. As *James Parsons (1976:83) commented, "His roots were sunk deep into midwestern soil. . . . His predilection was for rural life and simple folk, in whose wisdom he put great store."

When only nine, Sauer was sent by his family to study in Germany. Upon his return, he went to Central Wesleyan, where he received a B.A. degree in 1908. While there, his wide reading led him to geology and an interest in landforms, which he decided to pursue further at Northwestern University.

Unhappy with geology there, he soon went on to the University of Chicago, where *Rollin Salisbury was gaining a reputation in the geography department. A graduate program in geography had just been established, and Sauer found the department and university much to his liking. In fact, he remained friends with Salisbury long after he had moved on to his own work. Salisbury's training had been primarily in geology, and he considered himself a physiographer. Under his tutelage, Sauer studied landforms and learned his field techniques, beginning with a summer of fieldwork in the upper area of the Illinois River Valley in 1910. Sauer studied with other experts in Chicago as well, including plant ecology under Henry Cowles and human geography under *Ellen Churchill Semple. His doctoral dissertation was on the regional geography of the Ozark Highland.

In 1913, while still a graduate student at Chicago, Sauer married a young woman from Warrenton, Lorena Schowengerdt, who remained with him until her own death, only a month before his own. He finished his dissertation and received his doctorate in 1915, then accepted an appointment in the Geology Department at the University of Michigan, where the department was expanding to include geography in its curriculum. Within only seven years, Sauer had worked his way up to full professor, and had used the time to develop new courses and do extensive fieldwork and research.

In 1923 Sauer accepted an appointment in the Department of Geography at the University of California at Berkeley, where he was joined in forming a new department by John Leighly and *Richard Russell. His appointment was as full professor, whereas Leighly and Russell were still finishing their doctoral work. He initially worked hard to establish the program as an entity separate from geology, where it had previously existed; curricular changes were especially important at first. Sauer brought in guest lecturers from abroad, mainly from Germany, and aimed at developing a quality department, which he certainly did.

In 1925 Sauer began doing fieldwork in Baja California, and quickly developed an interest in the evolution of landscapes there and in other parts of Mexico. At the same time, he was increasingly questioning the way that he and others were approaching geographical studies, and in 1925 he published one of his most important and influential papers, "The Morphology of Landscape," in which, as Parsons (1976:87) so nicely phrased it, Sauer "largely demolished the environmental determinism that had gained prominence in American geography, urging his associates to think instead of man and the land in terms of cause and result." Having moved off in new research directions and thinking, Sauer published his last "regional" study, that of the Pennyroyal, which had been in preparation already, in 1927.

Sauer remained Chair of the Geography Department at Berkeley until 1954, and during that time profoundly influenced American geography. The "Berkeley school of geography," carried to various places by his students, remains one of the most identifiable in American geography. Thirty-seven students completed dissertations under Sauer during his tenure, and many others were done under Leighly and others, so that the Berkeley influence spread far and wide. Sauer's list of publications grew as well, with highlights that include his 1952 book, *Agricultural Origins and Dispersals*; "The Agency of Man on Earth," in *Man's Role in Changing the Face of the Earth*, published in 1956; *The Early Spanish Main*, published in 1966; and one of his last publications, "The Fourth Dimension of Geography," in 1974.

Three years after stepping down as chair, Sauer retired from the University of California in 1957, though he in no way retired from geography. Actually, his research output may even have increased, as he had more time available for it and fewer other demands on him. Among the many honors bestowed upon him, the most important include the Daly Medal, which he received from the American Geographical Society in 1940, the same year in which he served as president of the Association of American Geographers; the Vega Medal in 1957; and the Humboldt Medal from the Berlin Geographical Society in 1959.

Sauer's scholarship was recognized in areas outside of geography, and he was a true member of the "community of scholars." At the same time, as Leighly (1976:345) commented, "Whatever branch of learning Sauer might have chosen to pursue in his youth, he undoubtedly would have arrived in the end at the same comprehensive, compassionate view of the earth and man that he achieved through geography." By looking at how landscapes evolve over time as people interact with the natural environment, Sauer developed a concern for many problems that are still with us today—the ramifications of uncontrolled industrialization, urbanization, and population growth. This concern was nowhere more aptly summed up than in his speech upon receiving the Victoria Medal from the Royal Geographical Society of London (cited in Parsons, 1976:85):

Civilization in our time has developed a technological dominance that has changed the world and is impoverishing it. It has made an economy based on producing and consuming more and more. We are committed to growth and propose to find our way out of our difficulties by more technology. Biologists are well aware of the limited world. Geographers must not forget it.

Carl Sauer died on July 18, 1975, and as a measure of how well this man had become known in his lifetime, the *New York Times* carried an article on his death and referred to him as the "Dean of Geographers."

Selected Bibliography

1916   "Geography of the Upper Illinois Valley and History of Development." *Illinois Geological Survey Bulletin*. No. 27.

1920   "The Geography of the Ozark Highland of Missouri." *Bulletin of the Geographical Society of Chicago*. No. 7.

1924   "The Survey Method in Geography and Its Objectives." *Annals of the Association of American Geographers* 14:17–33.

1925   "The Morphology of Landscape." University of California *Publications in Geography* 2(2):19–53.

1927   "Geography of the Pennyroyal." *Kentucky Geological Survey* (Ser. 6) 25.

            With Peveril Meigs. "Lower California Studies." Vol. 1: "Site and Culture at San Fernando de Velicata." *University of California Publications in Geography* 2(9):271–302.

            "Recent Developments in Cultural Geography." *Recent Developments in the Social Sciences*. Edited by E. C. Hayes. New York, 154–212.

1929   "Landforms in the Peninsular Range of California as Developed about Warner's Hot Springs and Mesa Grande." *University of California Publications in Geography* 3(4):199–290.

1930   With Donald Brand. "Pueblo Sites in Southeastern Arizona." *University of California Publications in Geography* 3(7):415–59.

"Basin and Range Forms in the Chiricauha Area." *University of California Publications in Geography* 3(6):339–414.

1931   With Donald Brand. "Prehistoric Settlement of Sonora, with Special Reference to Cerros de Trincheras." *University of California Publications in Geography* 5(3):63–148.

1932   With Donald Brand. "Aztatlán: Prehistoric Mexican Frontier on the Pacific Coast." *Ibero-Americana*. No. 1.

"The Road to Cibola." *Ibero-Americana*. No. 3.

1934   "The Distribution of Aboriginal Tribes and Languages in Northwest Mexico." *Ibero-Americana*. No. 5.

1935   "Aboriginal Population of Northwestern Mexico." *Ibero-Americana*. No. 10.

1936   "American Agricultural Origins: A Consideration of Nature and Culture." *Essays in Anthropology Presented to A. L. Kroeber*. Berkeley, 278–97.

1937   "The Discovery of New Mexico Reconsidered." *New Mexico Hist. Rev.* 12:270–87.

1938   "Theme of Plant and Animal Destruction in Economic History." *Journal of Farm Economics* 20:765–75.

1939   *Man in Nature: America before the Days of the White Man: A First Book in Geography*. New York: Scribner's.

1941   "The Credibility of the Fray Marcos Account." *New Mexico Hist. Rev.* 16:233–43.

"Foreward to Historical Geography." *Annals of the Association of the American Geographer* 31:1–24.

1944   "A Geographic Sketch of Early Man in America." *Geographical Review* 34:529–73.

1945   "The Relation of Man to Nature in the Southwest." *Huntington Library Quarterly* 8:116–126.

1947   "Early Relations of Man to Plants." *Geographical Review* 37:1–25.

1948   "Colima of New Spain in the 16th century." *Ibero-Americana*. No. 29.

"Environment and Culture during the Last Glaciation." *Proceedings of the American Philosophical Society* 92:65–77.

1950   "Cultivated Plants of South and Central America." *Handbook of South American Indians, Smithsonian Institute, Bur. Am. Ethnol. Bull. 143* 6:319–44.

1952   *Agricultural Origins and Dispersals*. New York: American Geographical Society.

1956   "The Education of a Geographer." *Annals of the Association of American Geographers* 46:287–99.

"The Agency of Man on Earth." *Man's Role in Changing the Face of the Earth*. Edited by William L. Thomas. Chicago, 49–69.

1957   "The End of the Ice Age and Its Witnesses." *Geographical Review* 47:29–43.

1959   "Age and Area of American Cultivated Plants." *Actas del XXXIII Congr. Intern. de Americanistas, San Jose, Costa Rica, 1958* 1:213–29.

1960   "Middle America as Culture Historical Location." *Actas del XXXIII Congr. Int. de Americanistas, San Jose, Costa Rica, 1958* 1:115–22.

1961   "Sedentary and Mobile Bent in Early Man." In S. L. Washburn, ed., *Social Life of Early Man. Viking Fund.* Also in *Anthropology*, no. 31–258–66. Chicago.

1962   "Fire and Early Man." *Paideuma Mitt. für Kulturkunde* 7:399–407.

1963   "Homestead and Community on the Middle Border." *Land Use Policy in the United States.* Edited by H. W. Ottoson. Lincoln, Neb., 65–85.

         Land and Life: A Selection from the Writings of Carl Ortwin Sauer. Edited by John Leighly. Berkeley: University of California Press.

1964   "Concerning Primeval Habitat and Habit." *Festschr. ad. E. Jensen.* Munich, 513–24.

1966   *The Early Spanish Main.* Berkeley: University of California Press.

         "On the Background of Geography in the United States." *Heidelberger Geogr. Arb., Festgabe Zum 65 Geburtstag von Gottfried Pfeifer* 15:59–71.

1969   *Agricultural Origins and Dispersals: The Domestication of Animals and Foodstuffs.* 2d ed. Cambridge, Mass.: MIT Press.

1970   "Plants, Animals and Man." In R. E. Buchanan, E. Jones, and D. McCourt, eds., *Man and His Habitat.* London, 34–61.

1971   *Sixteenth Century North America: The Land and the People as Seen by the Europeans.* Berkeley: University of California Press.

1977   "Seventeenth Century North America." Berkeley: Turtle Island Foundation.

Chronology

1889   Born in Warrenton, Missouri, December 24.

1908   B.A. from Central Wesleyan College.

1911   First publication: "Educational Opportunities in Chicago."

1913   Map editor, Rand McNally, Chicago.

1915   Ph.D., University of Chicago. Instructor, University of Michigan.

1922   Professor, University of Michigan.

1923   Professor, University of California, Berkeley.

1925   Began fieldwork in Mexico; continued almost annually until 1945.

1934   Member of the Selection Committee, Guggenheim Memorial Foundation (until 1963). Advisor to Soil Conservation Service.

1940   President of Association of American Geographers.

1941	Travelled in South America, from Colombia to Chile.
1955	Phil.D. (h.c.), University of Heidelberg. Honorary President, Association of American Geographers.
1960	LL.D., University of California.
1965	LL.D., University of Glasgow.
1975	Victoria Medal from the Royal Geographic Society, London. Died at Berkeley, California.

References

Leighly, John. 1976. "Carl Ortwin Sauer." *Annals of the Association of American Geographers* 66:337–48.
Parsons, James J. 1976. "Carl Ortwin Sauer." *Geographical Review* 66:83–89.

William Scoresby

William Scoresby was born in England in the tiny Yorkshire village of Cropton on October 5, 1789. His father, also William, worked in the whaling industry and was often at sea, and the family moved to the seaport of Whitby while the younger William was only a few years old to be near the senior William's place of work. At the age of only ten, young William sailed with his father and crew to the Arctic on a whaling expedition, a trip that was to stir in him a love of adventure (Waites, 1980).

After experiencing a mixture of education and adventure, the younger William enrolled at the University of Edinburgh to study both chemistry and natural philosophy, though each summer he continued to make voyages with his father back to the Arctic. He spent a short time in the Royal Navy in 1807 and 1808, where he met Sir Joseph Banks, who was to remain a friend and strong influence on Scoresby's career. After his brief Navy experience, Scoresby returned to the University of Edinburgh and his studies in natural history. One professor there, Robert Jameson, along with Banks, encouraged him to continue his Arctic explorations and observations, and he was elected to the Wernerian Society of Edinburgh as well, where he became an active participant.

When he turned twenty-one, Scoresby was given command of a vessel, the *Resolution*, and set off in charge of an Arctic whaling expedition that proved to be quite successful. He married Mary Lockwood in that same year. Soon he was assigned a better ship, the *Esk*, and made repeated Arctic voyages, each time recording observations about weather, ocean conditions, especially waves and currents, and Arctic geography. Scoresby's greatest contributions to geography, undoubtedly, were in oceanography, where his careful and systematic scientific observations were especially important. He captained other vessels as well, the *Fame* and the *Baffin*, and made trips as far away as Greenland. In 1819 he moved to Liverpool, where the *Baffin* had been built according to his own design. Official rejection forced him, however, to forgo his Arctic voyages after

1823, though by then he had certainly established himself as one of the first, if not *the* first, of the Arctic geographers.

Because Scoresby had continued to write papers presenting his observations, however, he had developed a scientific reputation. In 1819 he was elected a Fellow of the Royal Society of Edinburgh, and in the following year his work, *An Account of the Arctic Regions*, was published, and it was followed in 1823 by *Journal of a Voyage to the Northern Whale-Fishery*. Contained in these volumes were some of the first observations of botanical and geological features ever recorded for parts of Greenland and Spitzbergen [Arctic islands belonging to Norway]. Both were major contributions to Arctic geography. In the following year, he was made a Fellow of the Royal Society of London, and his acceptance as a scientist seemed solid.

After giving up whaling and his beloved Arctic voyages, however, Scoresby decided to follow an entirely different bent, and was ordained as a minister in 1825. In the following year his *Narrative of the Loss of the Esk and Lively, Greenland Whalers* was published. From 1827 until 1832 he served as Chaplain at the Floating Church for Seamen in Liverpool, during which time he also managed to establish the British Association in York, to which he remained a regular contributor of scientific papers throughout his lifetime.

In 1828, six years after the death of his first wife, Scoresby married again. Four years later, he became head Chaplain at Bedford Chapel in Exeter, and in 1835 he founded the Exeter Athenaeum Club. Shortly thereafter he invented the Scoresby Compass Needle. In 1839 he left Exeter to take a position as Vicar of Bradford, in Yorkshire, a post that proved to be problematic for him. That same year the first volume of *Magnetical Investigations* was published, and in the next year he gave several lectures on magnetism at the Royal Institution, where he also was able to demonstrate his new compass needle.

During his years at Bradford, Scoresby continued to work on, and completed, the second volume of *Magnetical Investigations*, which was published in 1843. He also met the famous literary Brontë sisters, and developed an educational scheme for schools in Bradford. In 1844 he made his first tour to North America, and in 1845 published *American Factories and Their Female Operatives*. In the following year he resigned his position in Bradford, and, after a second tour of North America in 1847, and the loss of his second wife in that same year, returned to live in Whitby in 1848.

Scoresby's interest in electro-magnetism continued, and he began to delve into zoistic magnetism as well. In 1849 he married again, and in that same year was elected to the Athenaeum in London. His new wife, Georgiana Ker, was from Torquay, and it was there that he made his home. He continued to write; in 1850 *The Franklin Expedition* was published, followed in 1851 by a volume about the work that his father had done, *Memorial of the Sea: My Father*.

In 1856 he sailed to Australia on the *Royal Charter*, still making scientific observations. He returned in August of that year and began compiling his results. On March 21, 1857, he died in Torquay. His *Journal of a Voyage to Australia and Round the World, for Magnetical Research* was published posthumously in 1859.

Selected Bibliography

1810   "Account of the Baloena Mysticetus or Great Northern Whale, and First Correct Figure of It." *Memoirs of the Wernerian Society* 1:578–86.

1815   "Account of Greenland or Polar Ice." *Memoirs* 2(2):261–338.

1816   "Notes of an Advance to Latitude 81°30'N." *Memoirs* 2:642.

1818   "Narrative of an Excursion on the Island of Jan Mayen with Discoveries Thereon." *Edinburgh Philosophical Journal* 1:121.

1819   "On the Anomaly in the Variation of the Magnetic Needle as Observed on Ship-Board." *Philosophical Transactions of the Royal Society of London*. Part 1:96–106.

1820   *An Account of the Arctic Regions: With a History and Description of the Northern Whale-Fishery*. 2 vols. Edinburgh.

1823   *Journal of a Voyage to the Northern Whale-Fishery: Including Researches and Discoveries on the Eastern Coast of West Greenland Made in the Summer of 1822, in the Ship Baffin of Liverpool*. Edinburgh.

1825   "Polar Regions." *Edinburgh Encyclopedia*. 18:1–40.

1826   *Narrative of the Loss of the Esk and Lively, Greenland Whalers*. Whitby.

1828   "On the Possibility of Reaching the Pole by Trans-Glacial Journey." *Edinburgh Philosophical Journal*.

1835   *Memoirs of the Sea: Sabbaths in the Arctic Regions*. London.

          Memorial of an Affectionate and Dutiful Son: Frederick R. H. Scoresby. London.

1839–43   *Magnetical Investigations*. 2 vols. London.

1845   *American Factories and Their Female Operatives*. London. Reprint in 1968. New York: B. Franklin.

1850   *The Franklin Expedition*. London.

          The Whaleman's Adventures in the Southern Ocean: As Gathered by the Rev. H. T. Cheever. Edited by Scoresby. London.

          Zoistic Magnetism. London.

          "On Atlantic Waves, Their Magnitude, Velocity and Phenomena." *Report of the British Association for the Advancement of Science*. Edinburgh, 26–31.

1851   *Memorial of the Sea: My Father: Being Records of the Adventurous Life of the Late William Scoresby, Esq. of Whitby*. By his son, the Rev. William Scoresby. London.

1852   *Magnetical Investigations on Terrestrial Induction and Iron Ships*. London.

1853   "On the Surface Temperature and Great Currents of the Atlantic." *Report of the British Association for the Advancement of Science*. Hull, 18–22.

"On the Popular Notion of an Open Polar Sea. Is It the Fact?" *Report of the British Association*, 92–96.

1859   *Journal of a Voyage to Australia and Round the World, for Magnetical Research*. London. Posthumous work, edited by Archibald Smith.

Chronology

1789   Born October 5 at Cropton, Yorkshire, England.

1800   Sails to Greenland with his father on the *Dundee*.

1802   Family moves to London.

1803   Apprenticed to his father, a ship's commander, aboard the *Resolution*. Voyage to the Arctic.

1806   Chief mate on the *Resolution*. Arctic whaling voyages during summer. Attends Edinburgh University.

1807   Seaman in the Royal Navy. Charts Balta Sound, Shetland Islands. Visits Copenhagen. Assists Navy in bringing Danish vessels to England.

1808   Returns to Edinburgh University.

1811   First voyage as captain of *Resolution*.

1813   Command of the *Esk*. Invents the Marine Diver.

1815   Charts Spitzbergen.

1817   Visits and surveys Jan Mayen Island.

1820   Command of the *Baffin*, successful Arctic whaling voyage.

1822   Charts and names the east coast of Greenland.

1823   Retires from whaling, last voyage to the Arctic.

1824   Entered as a "ten-year" man, Queen's College, Cambridge.

1825   Ordained at York. Appointed curate at Bessingby.

1827   Elected to Institute of France. First chaplain of the Floating Church for Seamen, Liverpool.

1831   Founder of the British Association in York.

1837   Invents the Scoresby Compass Needle, 1836–39.

1839   D.D., Cambridge. Vicar of Bradford.

1840   Lectures on magnetism at the Royal Institution. Shows improved magnetic apparatus to Prince Consort.

1842   Introduces an educational model for Bradford, model schools opened.

1844   Meets President John Tyler, first North American tour.

1845   Works with J. P. Joule on electro-magnetism.

1846   Resigns as Vicar of Bradford.

1847   Second North American tour.

1848   Elected to American Institute, Philadelphia. Advisor on the Franklin Search.

1851   Consulted on the Franklin Mystery. His magnets displayed at the Great
            Exhibition.

1856   Honorary M.A., University of Melbourne. Sails to Australia in January
            and returns to England August 14.

1857   Died March 21 in Torquay, England.

Reference

Waites, Bryan. 1980. "William Scoresby." *Geographers Biobibliographical Studies*
    4:139–47.

Ellen Churchill Semple

Ellen Churchill Semple, the first influential female geographer in the United States, was born in Louisville, Kentucky, on January 8, 1863. The youngest of seven siblings, she was raised in an environment dominated by females since her older brothers had moved out and were on their own. Her mother encouraged reading among the Semple children, and Semple found that quite satisfying. She attended public schools in Louisville, was additionally educated by private tutors, and then went on to college.

Semple attended Vassar, a women's college in Poughkeepsie, New York. She was only sixteen when she matriculated there, and she graduated four years later. Though geography was not a part of the Vassar curriculum at that time, she received an excellent education in which she learned useful reasoning and analytical skills, along with the ability to express herself orally and in writing. Two European trips during her Vassar years formed the basis for some of her written work, and she graduated with honors, among the top ten in her class (Colby, 1933).

Stimulated by the rigor and excitement of intellectual pursuits at Vassar, Semple found her return to Louisville somewhat boring. As Bushong (1984:88) commented, "For her . . . there was insufficient intellectual stimulation to complement the social events, and what intellectual fare Louisville offered paled beside her Vassar environment." Her struggle against that dissatisfaction, however, turned out to be a lengthy one.

Semple travelled in Europe for awhile, then returned to Louisville in 1883 to begin a career teaching in a Louisville girls' school. She taught Latin, Greek, and history, and by all accounts excelled in the classroom. However, she remained unsatisfied.

Though Semple had been tested in geography at Vassar, no courses had been offered. In 1887 she vacationed in London during the summer, and from a recent American graduate of the University of Leipzig she learned about the work of

*Friedrich Ratzel, who at that time was one of the leading geographers in the world. At summer's end she returned to her teaching and began thinking about furthering her education.

In 1889 she began work on an M.A. degree at Vassar, and in the course of her study began to develop a serious interest in geography, even though her readings were concentrated in sociology and economics. In 1890 she got a copy of Ratzel's famous and highly influential *Anthropogeographie*, read it, and decided that she wanted to study with Ratzel in Germany.

Matriculation in most German universities at that time was barred to females, though instructors could agree to allow individuals into classes. The University of Leipzig was no exception, though Semple did manage to take classes from Ratzel in 1891 and again in 1895, and was allowed in to some other classes as well. Her interest in geography matured under Ratzel, though again she returned to Louisville to continue her teaching.

Semple's enthusiasm about geography would not go away, however, and in 1894 she published her first geographical article. She corresponded with Ratzel, who encouraged her to continue her geographic research and writing. Toward the end of the 1890s, her work in geography intensified. In 1897 she published her first articles in geography journals, and in 1903 her first book, *American History and Its Geographic Conditions*, was published, clearly establishing her reputation among American geographers. She also published a series of reviews of Ratzel's works, making American geographers more aware of the work that was being done in Leipzig.

In 1904 Semple experienced two tragic personal losses with the deaths of her mother and her mentor, Friedrich Ratzel. In that same year, however, her professional career continued to blossom. She became a charter member of the Association of American Geographers, was appointed as an associate editor of the *Journal of Geography*, and began work on her second book. Two years later she accepted an appointment as a lecturer in geography at the University of Chicago. As her own work in geography matured, she rejected Ratzel's ideas about the state being an organism, though she remained strongly influenced by his overall work in anthropogeography.

In 1911 her second book, *Influences of Geographic Environment*, was published. In this work she expressed her own interpretation of anthropogeography— Ratzel distilled through the observations of an American geographer. Semple (1911:1) stated her own case clearly from the outset:

Man is a product of the earth's surface. This means not merely that he is child of the earth . . . but that the earth has mothered him, fed him, set him tasks, directed his thoughts, confronted him with difficulties that have strengthened his body and sharpened his wits, given him his problems of navigation or irrigation, and at the same time whispered hints for their solution.

Semple's work fell clearly into the realm of environmental determinism, where her name is still mentioned along with others such as *Ellsworth Huntington when that topic appears in geographic conversations. Semple was clearly aware, however, that the environment ultimately did not control what people did, as is quite apparent in her statement (p. 2) that "man's relations to his environment are infinitely more numerous and complex than those of the most highly organized plant or animal. . . . Nature has been so silent in her persistent influence over man, that the geographic factor in the equation of human development has been overlooked." The depth of her work was considerable, and her scholarship was of high rank; her central themes emphasized not just environmental factors, but the historical context within which people and places had come together to form landscapes.

In that same year, 1911, Semple left with two friends on a trip around the world. In Japan she was fascinated by her observations of agricultural landscapes, and in the Mediterranean region, she found so much of interest that she would ultimately spend the next twenty years or so studying that region and the adaptations that humans had made to it. Upon her return to work, she immediately began research for her next book, not realizing at the time that its contents would take almost two decades to put together.

During the summer of 1912 she taught at Oxford, and in subsequent years she was a visiting lecturer in several universities, including the University of Colorado, Western Kentucky University, Columbia, and the University of California at Los Angeles. She received the Cullum Medal from the American Geographical Society in 1914, and was elected President of the Association of American Geographers for 1921. In that same year she took a position as Professor of Anthropogeography at Clark University. In 1923 the University of Kentucky bestowed on Semple an honorary law doctorate.

In 1929 she began to have heart problems, and for her remaining years she was plagued by ill health; these problems curtailed her writing and research significantly, though she struggled to maintain an ongoing work schedule. In 1931 her third and final book, *The Geography of the Mediterranean Region: Its Relation to Ancient History*, was published. It was the culmination of nearly two decades of research and writing, a work that drew together her interests in geography with her earlier working knowledge of Greek and history. Her health had deteriorated considerably by the time her book was published, and she died on May 8 of the following year, 1932, in West Palm Beach, Florida, where she had gone in hopes that the climate would be more favorable to her condition.

According to *Preston James and Geoffrey Martin (1981:307–8), "Ellen Semple was an enormously persuasive teacher. . . . It is easy to condemn her for presenting concepts that have not withstood the test of time; but she must be appreciated for kindling among her students an enthusiasm for the broad view of the earth as the home of man."

Selected Bibliography

1894   "The American Mediterranean and the Interoceanic Canal." *Vassar Misc.*
            24:4–64.

1896   "Civilization Is at Bottom an Economic Fact." *Third Biennial General Federation of Women's Clubs*. Louisville, 419–27.

1897   "The Influence of the Appalachian Barrier upon Colonial History." *Journal of School Geography* 1:33–41.

            "Some Geographic Causes Determining the Location of Cities." *Journal of School Geography* 1:225–31.

1898   "The Indians of Southeastern Alaska in Relation to Their Environment." *Journal of School Geography* 2:206–15.

1899   "A Comparative Study of the Atlantic and Pacific Oceans." *Journal of School Geography* 3:121–29, 172–80.

            "The Development of the Hanse Towns in Relation to Their Geographical Environment." *Bulletin of the American Geographical Society* 31:236–55.

1900   "A New Departure in Social Settlements." *Annals of the American Academy of Political Social Science* 15:301–04.

            "Louisville: A Study in Economic Geography." *Journal of School Geography* 4:351–70.

1901   "The Anglo-Saxons of the Kentucky Mountains: A Study in Anthropogeography." *Geographical Journal* 17:588–623. Reprinted in *Bulletin of the American Geographical Society* 42 (1910):561–94.

            "Mountain Passes: A Study in Anthropogeography." *Bulletin of the American Geographical Society* 33:124–37, 191–203.

1903   *American History and Its Geographic Conditions*. New York: Houghton Mifflin.

1904   "Geographic Influences in the Development of St. Louis." *Journal of Geography* 3:290–300.

            "Emphasis upon Anthropogeography in Schools." *Journal of Geography* 3:366–74.

            "The Influence of Geographic Environment on the Lower St. Lawrence." *Bulletin of the American Geographical Society* 36:49–466.

            "North-Shore Villages of the Lower St. Lawrence." *Zu Friedrich Ratzels gedächtnis*. Leipzig, 349–60.

1905   "Mountain Peoples in Relation to Their Soil: A Study in Human Geography." *Geographical Teacher* 3:125–31. Reprinted as "A Study in Human Geography: Mountain Peoples in Relation to Their Soil." *Journal of Geography* 4:417–24.

1911   *Influences of Geographic Environment: On the Bases of Ratzel's System of Anthropogeography*. New York: Russell and Russell.

1912   "Influences of Geographic Conditions upon Japanese Agriculture." *Geographical Journal* 40:589–603.

1913   "Japanese Colonial Methods." *Bulletin of the American Geographical Society* 45:255–75.

1916   "Geographical Research as a Field for Women." *The Fiftieth Anniversary of the Opening of Vassar College, October 10 to 13, 1915; A Record.* Poughkeepise, N.Y., 70–80.

1921   "The Regional Geography of Turkey: A Review of Banse's Work." *Geographical Review* 11:338–50.

1930   "Alzira Ah Fi Buldan Al-Bahr Al-Mutawassit Quadiman" (Agriculture in the Ancient Lands of the Mediterranean Countries). *Al-Kulliyah (Mid. E. Forum)* 16:107–12.

1931   "Promontory Towns of the Mediterranean." *Home Geographical Monthly* 1:30–35.

            The Geography of the Mediterranean Region: Its Relation to Ancient History. New York. Reprint in 1971; New York: AMS Press.

1933   With C. F. Jones. *American History and Its Geographic Conditions.* Boston: Russell and Russell. Rev. ed.

Chronology

1863   Born January 8 in Louisville, Kentucky.

1878   Entered Vassar College.

1882   Received B.A. from Vassar.

1891   Received M.A. from Vassar. Began study with Friedrich Ratzel at University of Leipzig.

1894   First geography writing published.

1904   Became charter member of Association of American Geographers. Became Associate Editor of *Journal of Geography* (until 1910).

1906   Appointed lecturer in geography at University of Chicago (until 1924).

1911   Began trip around the world.

1912   Taught at Oxford University Summer School of Geography.

1914   Taught at Wellesley College in the fall term.

1915   Taught at University of Colorado in the summer term.

1917   Taught at Western Kentucky University in the summer term.

1918   Taught at Columbia University in the summer term.

1921   President of the Association of American Geographers. Appointed Professor of Anthropogeography at Clark University (until 1932).

1922   Taught at Oxford University Summer School of Geography.

1925   Taught at University of California, Los Angeles in the spring term.

1931   Awarded Culver Medal by Chicago Geographical Society.

1932   Died May 8 in West Palm Beach, Florida.

References

Bushong, Allen D. 1984. "Ellen Churchill Semple." *Geographers Biobibliographical Studies* 8:87–94.

Colby, C. C. 1933. ''Memoir of Ellen C. Semple.'' *Annals of the Association of American Geographers* 23:229–40.

James, Preston E., and Geoffrey J. Martin. 1981. *All Possible Worlds: A History of Geographical Ideas*. 2d ed. New York: Wiley.

Ernest Shackleton

Ernest Shackleton was born in Ireland on February 15, 1874. Although a poor student, he left school at the age of sixteen to learn sailing. He was very successful at this enterprise and at the age of twenty-two passed his First Mate exam and two years later passed the exam for Master.

Shackleton volunteered to be part of the British National Antarctic Expedition in 1901. On the boat journey to Antarctica he met the geographer *Hugh Robert Mill who was quite impressed with Shackleton's geographic knowledge. Mill wrote (Huntford, 1986:46):

I was at first surprised and a little alarmed at the ceaseless flow of quotation from the poets called forth by the summer night. . . . Nor was it altogether pleasant to find that this young sailor was already familiar with every reference which rose to my mind from books I had read years before his thoughts had turned that way, and with many which I had never seen.

This first trip to the Antarctic proved to be a near disaster. The leader, Robert Falcon Scott, was ill-prepared, and the expedition encountered a variety of navigational problems and was not prepared for the arduous land journey toward the South Pole. Shackleton was one of two companions Scott selected to venture to the South Pole. They had planned to accomplish the near 1,500-mile journey in ninety-one days, but after two months they had only gone 270 miles. They were forced to turn back after an outbreak of scurvy and the collapse of Shackleton.

Shackleton returned to London where he took a job as a writer for the *Royal Magazine*. A few years later he accepted the position of Secretary of the Scottish Royal Geographic Society. He continued his interest in the Antarctic and organized the British Antarctic Expedition of 1907, whose primary goal was to reach the South Pole. Once again, lack of preparation and illness forced them to turn back. This time, however, they were only 97 miles from the pole. According to Huntford (1986:273), "Shackleton had set a marvelous record. He had beaten Scott's furthest south by 360 miles. He had made the greatest single leap forward to either Pole of the earth that anyone had ever achieved. . . . He had shown the way to the heart of the last continent. Whoever finally reached the Pole would have to follow in his wake."

Upon his return to London after this expedition, Shackleton was welcomed as a hero. Even the headlines in the Dublin *Evening Telegraph* read, "South Pole Almost Reached by an Irishman." As a result of this expedition and his other work, Shackleton was knighted by King Edward VII.

In his epic expeditions to the Antarctic, Shackleton was involved in pioneering work in geology, meteorology, and even biology. Having failed to lead a successful expedition to be the first to claim the South Pole, however, Shackleton was forced to turn his attention to another goal, though the seeds of Antarctic exploration had been clearly sowed in him.

As Shackleton wrote much later (1920:vii), "After the conquest of the South Pole by [*Roald] Amundsen who, by a narrow margin of days only, was in advance of the British Expedition under Scott, there remained my one great main object of Antarctic journeyings—the crossing of the South Polar continent from sea to sea." It was to that end that he then dedicated his life. Some sense of his dedication to a singular goal in life can be gleaned from a speech made in Australia by Shackleton in 1917 and cited by Ralling (1983:256–57) in which he said, in arguing for Australian participation in the war, "Death is a very little thing . . . death scarcely weighs in the scale against a man's appointed task. . . . We will die in the pride of manhood, our eyes on the goal and our hearts beating time to the instinct within us."

Though plans for his expedition were carefully laid in 1913, it was not until August 1914, just at the outbreak of World War I, that Shackleton set sail from England aboard the *Endurance*. As Shackleton himself was to write later on (1920:vii), "We failed . . . but the story of our attempt is the subject for the following pages . . . high adventure, strenuous days, lonely nights, unique experiences . . . records of unflinching determination, supreme loyalty . . . struggles . . . disappointments."

Shackleton married, but, preferring the sea to land, he spent little time with his wife, Emily. In a letter to her, cited in Ralling (1983:258), he wrote, "Sometimes I think I am no good at anything but being away in the wilds just with men . . . I am no use to anyone unless I am out facing the storm in wild lands." In 1918, after his failed voyage to the Antarctic, he was appointed by the British government to take charge of the winter equipment for the North Russian expedition, a task which again took him into the high latitude seas that he loved, in this case to Murmansk.

On a final voyage to the Antarctic, Shackleton sailed from London aboard the *Quest* on September 17, 1921, at the age of forty-seven. He planned to chart the Antarctic coastline and to explore for basic minerals and whaling station sites. The *Quest*, despite some problems, finally reached South Georgia in the first days of 1922, and the crew spotted its first icebergs. There in the surroundings so dear to him, Shackleton's heart failed and he died. Though plans were made to return his body to England, Emily decided that he should be laid to rest on South Georgia.

Selected Bibliography

1909   *The Heart of the Antarctic*. London: William Heinemann.

1919   *South*. London: William Heinemann.

Chronology

1874   Born in Ireland, February 15.

1904   Appointed Secretary of the Scottish Royal Geographical Society.

1909   Led British Antarctic Expedition that came to within 100 miles of the South Pole.

1910   Knighted by King Edward VII.

1914   Expedition aboard the *Endurance* to Antarctic (until 1917).

1917   Relieved Ross Sea Party. Delivered speech in Australia.

1921   Sailed aboard the *Quest* for Antarctica.

1922   Died January, buried on South Georgia Island.

References

Huntford, Roland. 1986. *Shackleton*. New York: Wiley.

Ralling, Christopher. 1983. ''Afterword.'' *Shackleton*. London: British Broadcasting Corporation, 255–63.

Joseph Russell Smith

Joseph Russell Smith was born in 1874 in Lincoln, Virginia, to a Quaker family that made its living primarily in agriculture. Quakerism was to affect Smith in numerous ways throughout his life. According to Rowley (1964:14), "Smith always emphasized and lived his belief that facts and ideas in themselves were valueless; they gained worth only when they were put to practical use . . . the moral and cultural heritage of Quakerism must be taken into account in tracing the factors that influenced Smith."

Smith's parents had been disturbed greatly by the Civil War, and he was influenced by their accounts of the war and its ravages. As a youngster, Smith worked hard on the family farm, learning the value of work and experiencing the natural environment. A closeness to the land permeated his inner being and lasted a lifetime.

Smith's early schooling was in Quaker schools, though he spent a final year away at a prep school in preparation for college. Though he had little formal training in geography during his grade school years, his mother introduced him to maps when he was still at home. When he began considering majors for his college years, geography was not among them; economics was his choice.

In 1893 Smith went off to the Wharton School of Finance and Economy at the University of Pennsylvania, a well-established program in economics that he thought would suit his needs perfectly. After his first year in the Wharton School, however, personal economic considerations forced him to drop from full-time student status, so that he could work in order to fund his education. He accomplished this by teaching full-time in high schools until finally in 1897 he returned full-time to the Wharton School to finish his senior year. In 1898 he received his B.A. degree, along with the Terry Prize, which was given for outstanding scholarship.

As so often is the case, chance intervened after his graduation, altering his career goals forever. In 1899 the Isthmian Canal Commission was established by the federal government and funded by Congress to determine the best route for the Panama Canal. The commission consisted mostly of engineers, but it included one economist, Emory Johnson, a professor at the Wharton School, who hired Smith as his assistant. Together they gathered and analyzed data about costs, alternate routes, projected trade, and whatever other variables seemed worth examining. Much of what they did was more geographic than economic, and Smith found the geographic aspects stimulating.

By the middle of 1901, Smith was convinced that he wanted to be a geographer rather than an economist and quit his job with the commission in July and headed for Leipzig, where he wanted to study under two of the most renowned geographers of the time, *Friedrich Ratzel and Karl Sapper. After a year in Leipzig, Smith returned to the Wharton School, where he accepted a fellowship and worked toward a doctorate in economic geography, which he received in 1903, with an emphasis on applied geography.

Though Smith had worked his way through Wharton earlier by teaching, he now turned to it as a career. Immediately after receiving his doctorate, Smith accepted a position in the Wharton School as Instructor of Commerce, where he quickly moved through the ranks to Full Professor and found himself in charge of the Department of Geography and Industry.

In 1919 Smith accepted a position as Professor of Economic Geography at Columbia in the School of Business. At Columbia his career continued to flower as he developed various courses in economic geography, including regional economic geography, and as he began to publish more of his work. Though his first major book, and one of his most influential works, *Industrial and Commercial Geography*, had been published in 1913, it was already in need of revision. At the same time, Smith's interests had become more diversified and he saw a need for books on numerous different geographic topics. During the 1920s his publications included *Human Geography*, books one and two, published in 1921; a revised edition of *Industrial and Commercial Geography* and *North America*, both published in 1925; and *Home Folks: A Geography for Beginners*, published in 1927.

His interests ranged from applied geography, both in the fields of economic geography and conversation, to the writing of basic geography texts at various levels. Throughout the 1930s and 1940s, he continued to revise former texts and write new ones. Among the new ones were the two books of *Human Use Geography*; *Other World Neighbors: The British Empire, Africa, Asia, Latin America*; *Our Country and Northern Neighbors*; and *Geography*.

In 1941–42 Smith was elected President of the Association of American Geographers. Along with his many texts, he wrote numerous articles as well, on a diversity of subjects from farming to conservation. After Smith's death, on February 25, 1966, Starkey (1967:201) wrote about Smith that, "Smith was one of several founders of modern American geography. . . . If Smith's ideas do not stand the test of time, his position as godfather of a young and growing discipline in America should long receive recognition and honor."

Selected Bibliography

1899   "The Philippine Islands and American Capital." *Popular Science Monthly* 40:186–92.

1901   "Western South America and Its Relations to American Trade." *Annals of the American Academy of Political and Social Science.* 18:446–68.

1903   "The Economic Geography of the Argentine Republic." *Bulletin of the American Geographical Society* 35:130–43.

1904   "The Economic Geography of Chile." *Bulletin of the American Geographical Society* 36:1–15.

           "The British System of Commercial Administration." *Annals of the American Academy of Political and Social Science* 24:507–25.

1905   *The Organization of Ocean Commerce.* Philadelphia: The University of Pennsylvania.

           "The Economic Importance of the Plateaux in Tropic America." *Bulletin of the American Geographical Society* 37:461–68.

1907   "Harbor Facilities of London." *Annals of the American Academy of Political and Social Science* 29:386–89.

1908   *The Ocean Carrier.* New York: G. P. Putnam's Sons.

           The Story of Iron and Steel. New York: Appleton.

1913   *Industrial and Commercial Geography.* New York: Henry Holt.

1914   "Soil Erosion and Its Remedy by Terracing and Tree Planting." *Science* (June 12):858–62.

1915   *The Elements of Industrial Management.* Philadelphia: Lippincott.

1916   *Commerce and Industry.* New York: Henry Holt.

           "The Oak Trees and Man's Environment." *Geographical Review* 1 (January):3–19.

           "Tree Crops for Dry Lands." *Journal of Geography* 15 (December):105–12.

           "Ellsworth Huntington, Geographer." *Bulletin of the Geographical Society of Philadelphia* 14:19–23.

1917   "Food Producing Trees." *American Forestry* 23 (April):228–33.

1918   *The Influence of the Great War on Shipping.* Washington: Carnegie Endowment for International Peace.

1919   *The World's Food Resources.* New York: Henry Holt.

           "The Scientific City and Its Food Supply." *Journal of Geography* 28:121–28.

1921   *Human Geography.* Book One: *Peoples and Countries.* Philadelphia: Winston.

           Human Geography. Book Two: *Regions and Trade.* Philadelphia: Winston.

1922   *The Proper Organization of Geography in American Education.* Philadelphia: Winston.

1924   "The Reindeer Industry in America." *Scottish Geographical Magazine* 40 (March):74–88.

1925   *North America*. New York: Harcourt Brace.

            Geography and the Higher Citizenship. Philadelphia: Winston.

            School Geography and the Regional Idea. Philadelphia: Winston.

1927   *Home Folks: A Geography for Beginners*. Philadelphia: Winston.

1928   *Geography and Our Need of It*. Chicago: American Library Association.

1929   *Tree Crops*. New York: Harcourt Brace.

1930   *Our Neighboring Continents*. Philadelphia: Winston.

            Our State and North America. Philadelphia: Winston.

            World Folks. Philadelphia: Winston.

            World Picture Building: Globe Map Studies in Creative Geography. New York: Parl Garrigue.

1931   "Geography for School Superintendents." *School Executives* 50:478–79.

1932   *American Lands and Peoples*. Philadelphia: Winston.

            Home Folks in Texas. Philadelphia: Winston.

1933   *Foreign Lands and Peoples*. Philadelphia: Winston.

            "How Geography Contributes to General Ends in Education." *The Teaching Geography, Thirty-second Yearbook of the National Society for the Study of Education*. Bloomington, Ill.: Public School Publishing, 29–41.

1934   *Human Use Geography; Book One*. Philadelphia: Winston.

            Human Use Geography; Book Two. Philadelphia: Winston.

            Other World Neighbors: The British Empire, Africa, Asia, Latin America. Philadelphia: Winston.

            Our Country and Northern Neighbors. Philadelphia: Winston.

            Our European Neighbors: Homelands and Outlying Areas. Philadelphia: Winston.

            Our Industrial World. Philadelphia: Winston.

            "The Geography of American Geographers." *Journal of Geography* 33:221–30.

1935   *New Jersey: People, Resources and Industries of the Garden State*. Philadelphia: Winston.

            With co-authors. *Methods of Achieving Economic Justice*. Purcellville, Va.: Blue Ridge Herald Press.

            "Are We Free to Coin New Terms?" *Annals of the Association of American Geographers* 25:17–22.

1936   *Our Industrial World with Pennsylvania Supplement*. Philadelphia: Winston.

            California: Life, Resources and Industries of the Golden State. Philadelphia: Winston.

Human Use Geography. Book Two with *Kansas Supplement*, and another with *Virginia Supplement*. Philadelphia: Winston.

1937   *Men and Resources*. New York: Harcourt, Brace.

1939   "Geographic Education's Contribution to World Citizenship." *Secondary Education* 8:87–91.

"Geography: A Group of People in a Place." *Education* 60:195–200.

1941   *The Devil of the Machine Age*. New York: Harcourt, Brace.

1942   *New York: The Empire State*. Philadelphia: Winston.

"Suggestions for Illustrating Books." *Annals of the Association of American Geographers* 32:316.

"Mackinder: 1942." *New Republic* 152:322–23.

1943   *Geography and World War Two*. Philadelphia: Winston.

1946   *Geography of the Americas for Elementary Schools*. Philadelphia: Winston.

Geography of Europe, Asia, and Africa for Elementary Schools. Philadelphia: Winston.

With M. Ogden Phillips. *Industrial and Commercial Geography*. New York: Henry Holt.

1947   With Frank E. Sorenson. *Neighbors Around the World*. Philadelphia: Winston.

With Frank E. Sorenson. *Our Neighbors at Home*. Philadelphia: Winston.

"What Shall the Geography Teacher Teach in the Elementary School?" *Journal of Geography* 46:101–8.

1948   With Frank E. Sorenson. *Neighbors in the Americas*. Philadelphia: Winston.

1949   "Plan or Perish." *Soil Conservation* 14:71.

"Soil Destruction or Tree Crops in the Tropical Forests." *Journal of Geography* 48:303–5.

1950   With Frank E. Sorenson. *Neighbors Across the Seas*. Philadelphia: Winston.

1951   With Frank E. Sorenson. *Neighbors in the United States and Canada*. Philadelphia: Winston.

1954   "How to Understand a Nation." *Journal of Geography* 53:71–84.

1957   "Geography and World Citizenship." *Social Education* 21:205–6, 208.

Chronology

1874   Born in Lincoln, Virginia, of a middle-class, Quaker, agricultural family.

1893   Entered Wharton School of Finance and Economy of the University of Pennsylvania.

1898   Earned B.A. Degree in Economics from Wharton.

1899   Began working for Isthmian Canal Commission.

1901   Began graduate studies at the University of Leipzig under Friedrich Ratzel.

1903   Received doctorate in economic geography from the Wharton School. Accepted the position of Instructor of Commerce at the Wharton School.

1919   Accepted the position of Professor of Economic Geography in charge of the department at Columbia's School of Business.

1942   President of the Association of American Geographers.

1944   Retired from active teaching.

1966   Died on February 25.

References

Rowley, Virginia M. 1964. *J. Russell Smith: Geographer, Educator and Conservationist.* Philadelphia: University of Pennsylvania Press.

Starkey, Otis. 1967. "Joseph Russell Smith." *Annals of the Association of American Geographers* 56:198–202.

Mary Somerville

Mary Fairfax was born on December 26, 1780, in Jedburgh, Scotland. Her mother was Scottish and her father English—a Vice Admiral in the Royal Navy. Her early formal education was virtually nonexistent, and she was discouraged from pursuing things she found fascinating, especially mathematics and the sciences.

After a failed first marriage, she began to educate herself, following those paths that interested her. In 1812 she married William Somerville, a doctor, and moved a few years later to London, which put her much closer to the center of scientific activities. Her husband was elected to the Royal Society of Surgeons in 1817.

Mary Somerville gradually established relationships with numerous scientists, corresponding with them throughout her life. In addition she published several books of her own, beginning with the publication of *The Mechanism of the Heavens* in 1831. In 1833 she and Caroline Herschel became the first female honorary members of the Royal Astronomical Society, attesting to her wide acceptance among the scientists of her time. The following year, 1834, saw the publication of *On the Connection of the Physical Sciences*, one of two books that put her squarely in the realm of geography. It was sufficiently successful to be translated into French and German.

In 1838, Mary, her ailing husband, and her two daughters moved to Italy, hoping that Dr. Somerville's health would be improved. She continued to write and to correspond with other scientists.

Somerville's most influential contribution to geography, *Physical Geography*, was not published until 1848, though she had been collecting materials for it for more than a decade. According to Oughton (1978:110), "Mary Somerville differs from the authors of previous English geographical texts by being concerned not merely with the distribution of phenomena, country by country, but also with the causes underlying those distributions and with relationships between various physical phenomena." Following closely on the publication of *Alexander von Humboldt's *Kosmos*, Somerville's book represented the first English language text on the subject. She included discussions of landforms, atmospheric processes, biogeography, and the role of people in modifying the physical environment, a topic that attracted the attention of *George Perkins Marsh in Vermont, where he was doing his own work on the role that humans were playing in modifying the environment in America.

Physical Geography went through a series of revisions, each of which incorporated the most up-to-date materials and thinking about physical geography. The last revision was published in 1877, five years after her death, thanks to the work of her daughter and John Murray. Honors continued to accrue to Somerville, and her books found acceptance at such places as Cambridge and Oxford. In 1869 she received the Victoria Gold Medal of the Royal Geographical Society of London, though as a patron and not a full member because at the time females were not allowed membership. In that same year she also received the Victor Emmanuel Gold Medal from the Geographical Society of Florence and was elected to the American Philosophical Society.

Mary Somerville died on November 29, 1872, in Naples. Her papers appear in a collection at the Bodleian Library in Oxford. Somerville College in Oxford, established in 1879, provides a lasting tribute to the work of this outstanding woman, who succeeded against all odds in establishing her reputation among nineteenth-century scientists. It is easy to agree with Sanderson (1974:420) that "Mary Somerville was an outstanding scientist, and we can be proud that she called herself a geographer."

Selected Bibliography

1826   "On the Magnetizing Power of the More Refrangible Solar Rays." *Philosophical Transactions* (Royal Society) 96:132.

1831   *The Mechanism of the Heavens*. London.

1832   *A Preliminary Dissertation on the Mechanism of the Heavens*. (Preface to the previous reference, reprinted and sold as a separate volume.) London.

1834   *On the Connection of the Physical Sciences*. London: J. Murray. Ten editions up to 1877.

1835   "Astronomy—the Comet." *Quarterly Review* 105:195–233.

1836   "Experiments on the Transmission of Chemical Rays of the Solar Spectrum Across Different Media." *Comptes-Rendus Acad. des Sci.* 3:473–76.

1848   *Physical Geography*. London: J. Murray. Six further editions with revisions to 1877.

1869   *On Molecular and Microscopic Science*. 2 vols. London.

Chronology

1780	Born Mary Fairfax, December 26 in Jedburgh, Scotland.
1807	Began serious self-education in mathematics and astronomy.
1812	Married Dr. William Somerville.
1816	Moved to London, became involved in scientific, literary, and social circles.
1838	Moved to Italy. Continued writing.
1848	Published *Physical Geography*, the first geography text in the English language.
1869	Awarded the Patron's Victoria Medal of the Royal Geographical Society.
1872	Died November 29 in Naples.

References

Oughton, Marguerita. 1978. "Mary Somerville." *Geographers Biobibliographical Studies* 2:109–11.

Sanderson, Marie. 1974. "Mary Somerville." *The Geographical Review* 64:410–20.

Laurence Dudley Stamp

Laurence Dudley Stamp was born on March 9, 1898, in Catford, London, the last of seven children. Charles Stamp, his father, was a successful businessman who emphasized to his children the importance of success in life.

From an early age, Stamp expressed considerable interest in the natural environment, collecting rocks, fossils, plants, and seashells. Poor health hindered his formal education, though his natural ability helped to overcome formal deficiencies. At the age of fifteen, he was admitted to King's College in London, where he studied a range of subjects, from the arts to engineering and geology, though it was in geology that he excelled and achieved first-class honors. Out of research done as an undergraduate came his first publication, "The Highest Silurian Rocks of the Clun Forest District (Shropshire)," which was published in 1918.

After joining the Royal Engineers, he was sent to France, where he pursued his geological interests and, from that research, published a series of papers. During his time in the Royal Engineers he managed to complete his Master of Science degree and be elected to the Geological Society. Then, in 1919, he was appointed Layton Research Scholar and Demonstrator in the Department of Geology at King's College, from which he had only recently graduated. The following year he received the Daniel Pidgeon Award from the Geological Society.

Also in 1920 the first of his studies of French geology appeared in print, followed by another in 1921, and still another in 1922. For Stamp, 1921 was important for other reasons as well. He completed his doctoral degree in geology, received an honors degree in geography, became a fellow of the Royal Geographical Society, and accepted a job as a petroleum geologist with a company in Burma. In the following year, he received the Gold and Bronze Medals from the Mining and Geological Institute of India.

With his professional credentials well established, Stamp married Elsa Rea in

1923 and moved to Rangoon, where he took a position as professor of geology and geography at the University of Rangoon. Out of that experience came, among other things, a book, *How to Teach Geography in the Schools of India, Burma and Ceylon*, coauthored with his wife.

In 1926 Stamp returned to London, where he took a position as Sir Ernest Cassel Reader in Economic Geography at the London School of Economics and Political Science. He worked with *Sidney W. Wooldridge at King's College to establish a joint geography program, and set about teaching economic geography. This latter experience prompted the writing of *Intermediate Commercial Geography*, which was published in two parts in 1927 and 1928. In 1927 the first edition of his *The World: A General Geography for Indian Schools* was published as well, and in 1928 he was first involved with producing *Chisholm's Handbook of Commercial Geography*, which appeared in numerous subsequent editions.

Stamp continued to expand his work in geography, along with his teaching. In 1929 he published the first of seventeen editions of *The World: A General Geography*. He also became convinced that a major review of the natural resources of Great Britain was of paramount importance. Thus, working with S. H. Beaver, he produced another book, *The British Isles*, which was published in 1933 and represented not an end but a beginning: he saw the broader need for a complete land-use survey of his native land, which had been started in 1930 with the establishment of the Land Utilisation Survey of Britain at the London School of Economics.

In 1933–34 Stamp travelled widely in the United States, mostly with the idea of land-use surveys foremost in his mind. That work developed well during the 1930s, and in 1936 the first of the county reports was published. In 1938 he attended the Fifteenth International Geographical Congress in Amsterdam, where he was one of the speakers. In 1941, with the war causing problems with the land-use survey project, Stamp was made a member of an advisory group for the Ministry of Works and Buildings, and served as Vice Chair of a panel on land utilization in rural areas. The following year, he was appointed as Chief Adviser on rural land use to the Ministry of Agriculture. In these positions he was able to combine his academic training with practical applications, though in 1945 he returned to a position as Chair of Geography at the London School of Economics (Kimble, 1967).

In the following year, he gave his inaugural lecture, "Applied Geography," became a Fellow of the Royal Society of Arts, and published *Britain's Structure and Scenery*. Subsequently he travelled to Canada, among other destinations, and found the Canadian environment much to his liking. He taught at McGill University in summer and even purchased land in Canada in the hope of retiring there some day, though it was never to happen. In 1948 *The Land of Britain: Its Use and Misuse* was published, and it represented a summary of what had been accomplished by the Land Utilisation Survey.

His next appointment in the London School of Economics, in 1949, was to a chair in Social Geography. He became President of the geography section of the British Association for the Advancement of Science in that same year and gave a presidential address on "Planning of Land Use." He also received the Founders' Medal from the Royal Geographical Society and was elected Vice President of the International Geographical Union (I.G.U.). Before the year was over, he was able to launch the World Land Use Survey as well.

In 1950 Stamp became president of the Geographical Association and was awarded the Daly medal by the American Geographical Society. During the decade of the 1950s, Stamp remained extremely active and received further accolades as well. He published *Land for Tomorrow: The Undeveloped World* in 1952, received the Vega Medal in 1954, and in 1956 became president of the International Geographical Union, which met that year in Rio de Janeiro. He was also president of the Institute of British Geographers during that year, and vice president of the Royal Geographical Society. Before the decade ended, he received the medal of the Tokyo Geographical Society, visited Australia, New Zealand, and Hawaii, and then, in 1958, retired and became Professor Emeritus of London University and an honorary lecturer at the London School of Economics.

Still active, he published his *Applied Geography* in 1960, and served in a number of advisory and editorial positions. He lost his wife, Elsa, in 1962. In 1963 he became president of the Royal Geographical Society and, with W. G. Hoskins, published *The Common Lands of England and Wales*. In the following year, he received a medal from the Royal Scottish Geographical Society and published *The Geography of Life and Death: Some Aspects of Medical Geography*. He was knighted in 1965, and died on August 8, 1966, in Mexico City.

Selected Bibliography

1918   "The Highest Silurian Rocks of the Clun Forest District (Shropshire)."
            Geological Society of London 74:221–24.

1920   "Note on the Determination of the Limit between the Silurian and Devonian
            Systems." *Geological Magazine* 57:164–71.

            "Note sur la géologie du Mont-Aigu et du Mont Kemmel." *Annals of the
            Society of Geology* 44:115–26.

1921   "On Cycles of Sedimentation of Eocene Strata, Anglo-French Basin."
            Geological Magazine 58:108–14, 146–57, 194–200.

            "On the Beds at the Base of the Ypresian (London clay) in the Anglo-
            French-Belgian Basin." *Proceedings from the Geological Association*
            32:57–108.

1922   With co-authors. "The Geology of Burma." *Proceedings from the Geo-
            logical Association* 33:1–38.

            "An Outline of the Tertiary Geology of Burma." *Geological Magazine*
            59:481–501.

1923   "The Base of the Devonian with Special Reference to the Welsh Border-
             land." *Geological Magazine* 60:276–82, 331–36, 367–72, 385–410;
             61:351–55.

             With S. W. Wooldridge. "The Igneous and Associated Rocks of Llanwrtyd
             (Brecon)." *Quarterly Journal of the Geological Society of London* 79:16–
             46.

1925   "Some Remarks on the Tectonics of Burma." *Comptes-Rendus 13 Congr.
             Geol. Int. 1922.* 2:1145–50.

1926   "The Igneous Complex of Green Island and the Amherst Coast (Lower
             Burma)." *Geological Magazine* 63: 399–410.

             With F. G. French. *The Indian Empire*. Parts 2–4: *Peninsular India, North-
             West India, India, Burma and Ceylon*.

1927   "Conditions Governing the Occurrence of Oil in Burma." *Journal of the
             Institute of Petroleum Technology* 13:21–70.

             "Geology of the Oil Fields of Burma." *Bulletin of the American Asso-
             ciation of Petroleum Geology* 11:557–79.

             With Elsa C. Stamp. *How to Teach Geography in the Schools of India,
             Burma and Ceylon*. Bombay.

             An Intermediate Commercial Geography. Part 1: *Commodities and World
             Trade*. Part 2: *The Economic Geography of the Leading Countries*.

1928   "The Connection Between Commercial Oil Deposits and Major Structural
             Features with Special Reference to Asiatic Fields." *Journal of the Institute
             of Petroleum Technology* 14:28–52.

             Chisholm's Handbook of Commercial Geography. 11th–13th eds. revised
             by L. D. Stamp and S. G. Gilmour. 18th ed. entirely rewritten by L. D.
             Stamp.

1929   "The Oilfields of Burma." *Journal of the Institute of Petroleum Tech-
             nology* 15:300–49.

             Asia: An Economic and Regional Geography.

             The World: A General Geography. 17 editions.

1930   "Burma: An Undeveloped Monsoon Country." *Geographical Review*
             20:86–109.

             With Elsa C. Stamp. *The New Age Geographies*. Junior Series. Books 1–
             4.

             A Regional Geography. Part 1: *The Americas*. Part 3: *Australia and New
             Zealand*. Part 4: *Asia*. Also 1931, Part 5: *Europe and the Mediterranean*.

             With A. M. Druitt. *World Geography for Middle Schools in Burma*. Part
             1: *Burma and India*. Part 2: *The Rest of the World*.

1931   "The Land Utilisation of Britain." *Scottish Geographical Magazine*
             47:144–50.

             Secondary School Geography. 4 eds. Calcutta.

             "Modern Geographical Ideas." *An Outline of Modern Knowledge*, 813–
             58.

"Suomi (Finland)." *Geography* 16:284–97.

Agricultural Atlas of Ireland.

1932   "The Land Utilisation Survey of Britain." *Nature* 129:709–11.

With A. J. Newman. *New Age West Indian Geographies.* Books 1–4.

1933   With S. H. Beaver. *The British Isles: A Geographic and Economic Survey.* 5 editions.

The New Age Geographies. Junior Series. Books 5–7.

High School Geography. Calcutta.

1934   "Natural Gas Fields of Burma." *Bulletin of the American Association of Petroleum Geology* 18:315–26.

"Land Utilisation Survey as a School and College Exercise." *Journal of Geography* 33:121–30.

With E. C. Willatts. The Land Utilisation Survey of Britain: An Outline Description of the First Twelve One-Inch Maps.

A Regional Geography. Part 2: *Africa.*

1936   "The Geology and Economic Significance of Burma Oilfields." *World Petroleum* 7:580–92.

Through 1946, *The Land of Britain: The Report of the Land Utilisation Survey of Britain.* 92 parts, edited by and including several contributions from Stamp.

A Commercial Geography.

A Concise Geography of the World.

Longman's Descriptive Geography. Book 1. Calcutta.

"Nationalism and Land Utilisation in Britain."*Geographical Review* 27:1–18.

"The Land Utilisation Survey of Britain." *Journal of the Auctioneers and Estate Agents Institute* 17:186–218.

Longman's Descriptive Geography. Book 2. Calcutta.

1938   "Land Utilisation and Soil Erosion in Nigeria." *Geographical Review* 28:32–45.

"Land Utilisation Maps for India." *Journal of the Madras Geographical Association* 13:95–97.

"Planning the Land of Britain." Part 1. *Scottish Agriculture* 21:1–10.

Physical Geography and Geology.

The Place of Geography in University Studies. Calcutta.

1939   With G.H.T. Kimble. *Geography for Today: Africa, Australasia and the British Isles.*

S. C. Chatterjee, with a revision by L. D. Stamp. *Geography of the World with a Detailed Treatment of India..*

A New Geography of India, Burma and Ceylon. Bombay.

1940 "The Irrawaddy River." *Geographical Journal* 95:329–56.

"Fertility, Productivity and Classification of Land in Britain." *Geographical Journal* 96:389–412.

1942 "Siam Before the War." *Geographical Journal* 99:209–44.

"European Agriculture: A Regional Survey." *Geographical Magazine* 15:105–16.

1943 "Land Utilisation in Britain, 1937–43." *Geographical Review* 33:523–44.

"The Scott Report." *Geographical Journal* 101:16–22.

"The Scott Report: A New Charter for the Countryside." *Geographical Magazine* 15:391–404.

1944 "Agriculture and Planning." *Jour. Town Planning Inst.* 30:131–46.

1946 *Britain's Structure and Scenery*. Collins.

1947 "Wartime Changes in British Agriculture." *Geographical Journal* 109:39–57.

1948 *The Land of Britain: Its Use and Misuse*. 3 eds.

"Britain's Coal Crisis: Geographical Background and Some Recent Literature." *Geographical Review* 38:179–93.

1949 With G.H.T. Kimble. *The World: A General Geography*.

1950 "Planning and Agriculture." *Jour. Town Plann. Inst.* 36:141–51.

1951 "Land Use Surveys with Special Reference to Britain." In G. Taylor, ed., *Geography in the Twentieth Century*, 372–92.

"Applied Geography." *London Essays in Geography: Rodwell Jones Memorial Volume*. Edited by L. D. Stamp and S. W. Wooldridge, 1–18.

The Earth's Crust: A New Approach to Physical Geography and Geology.

1952 *Land for Tomorrow: The Undeveloped World*. American Geographical Society.

Africa: A Study in Tropical Development.

With F. K. Hare. *Physical Geography and Geology for Canada*. Toronto.

With B. G. Nene. *A Text-Book of Geography for Higher Secondary Schools*. Bombay.

1953 *Our Underdeveloped World*. English version of *Land for Tomorrow: The Undeveloped World*.

1954 *Man and the Land*. Collins. 2d ed., 1964.

The Underdeveloped Lands of Britain. The Albert Howell Memorial Lecture of the Soil Association.

"Professor A. G. Ogilvie." *Nature* 173:425.

1956 "Some Aspects of Applied Geography." In W. G. East and W. E. Moodie, eds., *The Changing World: Studies in Political Geography*. London, 1003–19.

1957 "Geographical Agenda: A Review of Some Tasks Awaiting Geographical

Attention." *Transactions of the Institute of British Geographers*, 1–17.

"Derwent Stainthorpe Whittlesey, 1890–1956." *Geographical Journal* 123:132–33.

"Major Natural Regions: Herbertson after 50 years." Herbertson Memorial Lecture. *Geography* 42:201–16.

1958   "Measurement of Land Resources." *Geographical Review* 48:1–15. Presidential address to International Geographical Union (I.G.U.) at 1956 Congress and published in *Comptes-Rendus 18 Congrès International de Géographie*, Rio de Janeiro, 1956, 1:140–54.

"The Geographical Distribution of Common Land." *Report of the Royal Commission on Common Land 1955–58*. 462, 185–267.

1959   "The Scope of Applied Geography." *Proc. I.G.U. Reg. Conf. Japan (1957)*, 89–95.

1960   et al. "Commission on a World Land Use Survey." *IGU Newsletter* 11:1–2, 38–46; 15:35–40.

Applied Geography. London: Penguin Books.

Our Developing World. A new edition of *Our Underdeveloped World*.

1961   Editor of *A History of Land Use in Arid Regions*. Paris: U.N.E.S.C.O.

1963   With W. G. Hoskins. *The Common Lands of England and Wales*. Collins New Naturalist Series.

1964   "The Common Lands and Village Greens of England and Wales." *Geographical Journal* 130:457–69.

The Geography of Life and Death: Some Aspects of Medical Geography. London: Collins Fortana Library.

Some Aspects of Medical Geography. University of London. Heath Clark Lectures, 1962.

"Harry Louis Nathan: First Lord Nathan of Churt." *Geography* 49:57–58.

"Sidney William Wooldridge (1900–1963)." *Geographical Review* 54:129–31.

1965   "Britain's Railway Policy." *Geographical Journal* 131(3):375–79.

"Hawaii—The Fiftieth State." *Scottish Geographical Magazine* 81(2):78–86.

"Planning Problems in the New Forest." *Advmt. Sci.* 22:134–46.

"Sir E. John Russell F.R.S. (1872–1965)." *Geographical Journal* 131:581.

With H. J. Fleure. "Sir E. John Russell (1872–1965)." *Geography* 50:380–81.

1966   "Ten Years On." *Transactions of the Institute of British Geographers* 40:11–20.

"Philatelic Cartography: A Critical Study of Maps on Stamps with Special

Reference to the Commonwealth.'' *Geography* 51(3):179–97.

"Dr. Gilvert Hovey Grosvenor.'' *Geographical Journal* 132:332–33.

Chronology

1898   Born March 9 at Catford, London, England.

1913   Entered King's College, University of London.

1914   Awarded Sambrooke Scholarship, King's College. Elected to the Geolo-
            gists' Association.

1917   Completed full honors course in geology and botany. Gained first-class
            honors in the geology examination. Enlisted in the Artists' Rifles.

1918   Served in France with the Royal Engineers, but given leave to take his
            Master of Science examination.

1919   Appointed as Layton Research Scholar and Demonstrator in the Geology
            Department of King's College.

1921   Received the degree of Doctor of Science in Geology. Took the B.A.
            honors degree examination in Geography, given first-class honors. Became
            a fellow of the Royal Geographical Society. Appointment as an oil geologist
            with a commercial company in Burma.

1922   Awarded the Gold and Bronze medals of the Mining and Geological In-
            stitute of India.

1923   Appointed Professor of Geology and Geography at the University of
            Rangoon.

1926   Returned to London University as Cassel Reader in Economic Geography,
            London School of Economics.

1930   Began organization of Land Utilisation Survey.

1933   Established his own press, Geographical Publications Ltd., to assist the
            publication of the Land Utilisation Survey reports. Founding member of
            the Institute of British Geographers. Began wide travels in United States
            associated with land use.

1936   First of ninety-two county reports, part of Land Utilisation Survey; editor
            of all of them.

1942   Appointed as Chief Advisor on rural land use to the Ministry of Agriculture.

1945   Chair of Geography at London School of Economics.

1949   Appointed to a chair of Social Geography, London School of Economics.
            President of Geography Section of the British Association for the Ad-
            vancement of Science. Elected Vice President of International Geograph-
            ical Union (I.G.U.).

1950   President of Geographical Association. Awarded Daly medal of the Amer-
            ican Geographical Society.

1951   Director of World Land Use Survey.

1952   Elected President of I.G.U. (until 1956).

1956	President of Institute of British Geographers. Vice President of Royal Geographical Society.
1957	Travel to Japan, New Guinea, Australia, and Hawaii.
1958	Retired and appointed Professor Emeritus by London University and an honorary lecturer by the London School of Economics.
1963	President of Royal Geographical Society.
1965	Knighted. Chairman of the National Resources Advisory Committee of the newly formed Ministry of Land and Natural Resource.
1966	Went to the Latin American Regional Conference of I.G.U., but died on August 8 in Mexico City.

Reference

Kimble, George H. 1967. "Laurence Dudley Stamp." *Geographical Review* 57:246–49.

Strabo

Strabo was born circa 64 B.C. in Amasia, in what is now part of central Turkey. His family was relatively well-off, and he received a worthwhile education. He travelled rather widely within the Greek world, lived and studied in Rome for awhile, and spent time in Egypt, where he was able to make a journey up the Nile. Because of his family's wealth, Strabo was able to pursue a scholarly life, dedicating himself to investigations of things that interested him and to literature as well.

Strabo's major work, *Geographica*, was important for at least two reasons. First, it survived, so that from it we can learn what was known in his day about geography. This seventeen-volume work on geography was passed down almost intact, whereas his written work on history was mostly lost.

Second, Strabo's *Geographica* was taken primarily from the works of his predecessors. He chose things to suit himself, taking what he thought important from earlier geographers and leaving what he did not find useful, though, in retrospect, later scholars have shown that his choices were not always sound on either account. For example, whereas Strabo defended Homer's knowledge of geography, he dismissed *Herodotus as a "fable monger" (James and Martin, 1981). As Dickinson (1969:28) noted with respect to Strabo, "His own choice of authorities was neither impeccable nor exhaustive, and on the side of mathematical geography he was definitely ill-equipped."

Strabo wrote for Roman administrators and military leaders, not for "scholars." His approach was generally pragmatic, arguing for the importance of providing detailed descriptions of areas that are inhabited and showing little or no interest in regions beyond those known to be settled. Description, not explanation, was his primary concern, and the books of his *Geographica* are devoted to such descriptions.

Strabo did recognize the need for a strong scientific and mathematical basis for geography and at the same time suggested that the science of geography was a realm for philosophers. Especially important for geographers, according to Strabo, was a working knowledge of geometry and astronomy, which would help improve an understanding of everything from the distribution of climates to the description of landforms.

Strabo's writings described everything from the inhabited portion of the earth as he knew it, to its basic shape and form (spheroidal), to changes that occurred from time to time in its surface form (volcanoes), to climatic zones and regional portraits (India, Arabia). Strabo's impact during his own age seems to have been minimal, however. As *Preston James and Geoffrey Martin (1981:37) have pointed out, "It is interesting that many centuries passed before Strabo's *Geography* was actually read. . . . By the sixth century after Christ, Strabo's *Geography* had been 'discovered' and had become a classic, as indeed it remained for many centuries thereafter." Similarly, Dickinson (1969:30) wrote, "To whatever use Strabo's *Geography* may have been put as a work of reference by those to whom it was particularly addressed, it seems to have received no immediate attention from other writers. . . . It does not appear to have gained a wide reputation until long after."

Strabo died A.D. 20. Because so much else written by the Greeks about geography has been lost, Strabo's work provides us with the greatest single summation of geographic knowledge up until his time.

Selected Bibliography

Geographica (Geography). 17 books.

Chronology

ca. 64 B.C.	Born in what is today central Turkey.
	Family was well-to-do. Received a Greek education. Studied in Rome.
	Worked in Library at Alexandria.
ca. 24 B.C.	At Alexandria, travelled up the Nile as far as Philae.
ca. 20 A.D.	Died.

References

James, Preston E., and Geoffrey J. Martin. 1981. *All Possible Worlds: A History of Geographical Ideas*. 2d ed. New York: Wiley.
Dickinson, Robert E. 1969. *The Makers of Modern Geography*. New York: Praeger.

Thomas Griffith Taylor

Griffith Taylor, as he was generally known, was born on December 1, 1880, in the English village of Walthamstow in Essex. His father, James, was a chemist and metallurgist. Soon after his birth, Griffith's family moved to Serbia, where his sister, Dorothy, was born. The family returned to England in 1884, then went on to Australia in 1893 (Rose, 1964).

Taylor's schooling was not out of the ordinary, though in Sydney he went entirely to private schools. At King's School, Taylor met Frank Debenham, who later became head of the Geography Department at Cambridge. After working for a while, Taylor enrolled at Sydney University in 1899, where he studied mainly physics and geology, receiving his Bachelor of Science degree with honors in 1904. During those years, he first worked with Professor Edgeworth David and developed an interest in field studies that remained with him throughout his life.

In 1905 Taylor finished an additional bachelor's degree in engineering, then became a Demonstrator in geology at Sydney University. In that position he expanded his fieldwork to include South Australia and the Great Barrier Reef. In 1907 he gave the first formal lectures in geography at Sydney University, then accepted a research scholarship to Cambridge University, where he remained until 1910.

Taylor's Cambridge experience was stimulating and important. He met and studied with such important figures as Sir Archibald Geikie, was elected as a Fellow of the Geological Society, and accompanied *William Morris Davis on some field expeditions to study glaciated landscapes in the Alps. In 1910 Taylor joined Robert Falcon Scott aboard the *Terra Nova* for an expedition that he made to the Antarctic as a representative of the Commonwealth Weather Service, for which he was officially a physiographer.

In 1911 Taylor published his first book, *Australia in Its Physiographic and Economic Aspects*, and coauthored another book that was published in that same year, *New South Wales: Historical, Physiographical and Economic*. Following the Antarctic expedition, he continued working for the Commonwealth Weather Service, and, in 1913, published the (coauthored) book *Climate and Weather of Australia*. In the following year, he married Doris Priestley and published *A Geography of Australasia*. He lectured on the Antarctic in places as far away as South Africa as well because the public seemed fascinated with Scott's adventures there. In 1916 he published his account of the Scott expeditions, *With Scott: The Silver Lining*, which received popular acclaim.

For a variety of reasons, Taylor became interested in moving from his work in the meteorology department to an academic appointment and used his contacts to help himself. Finally, he was appointed Associate Professor of the new geography department at Sydney University in 1921. He worked to build that department, and in 1923 was awarded the Livingstone Centenary Medal of the American Geographical Society. His work on Australia continued, though his conclusions about the limitations of aridity on the development of that continent were unpopular. While at Sydney he became the founding president of the Geographical Society of New South Wales, as well as joint editor of its new journal, the *Australian Geographer*. Despite his accomplishments, however, he could not get promoted to full professor at Sydney, and so took an appointment as full Professor of Geography at the University of Chicago in 1929.

In Chicago Taylor continued to broaden his own research interests, though he remained an authority on Australia and Antarctica as well. He was able to meet and work with a number of prominent American geographers at Chicago, including *Wallace W. Atwood, *Ellen Churchill Semple, and Roderick Peattie. In 1931 he became vice president of the geography section of the British Association for the Advancement of Science, and attended the annual meeting in London that year. He also attended the International Geographical Union (I.G.U.) meeting in Paris, and he continued to publish on a number of topics.

However, Taylor was not satisfied with Chicago and began to look elsewhere for a position. He was considered for a position at Cambridge, which he very much wanted, but ended up being offered a position in Toronto in 1935, Foundation Professor of Geography in a new program at Toronto University. In that same year, he acted as an advisor for Admiral Byrd's second Antarctic expedition and did fieldwork in various parts of both the United States and Canada. As he had earlier in Australia, Taylor worked to build the Toronto geography department into one of considerable strength and respect, and at the same time, he viewed the Canadian climate as a major factor in the potential development of that country. Fortunately, his views of Canada were more optimistic than they had been for Australia.

During the late 1920s and 1930s, Taylor published several important books, including *Environment and Race: A Study of Evolution, Migration, Settlement and Status of the Races of Man*, in 1927; *Environment and Nation: Geographical Factors in the Cultural and Political History of Europe*, in 1936; and *Environment, Race and Migration*, in 1937. In 1938 he became President of the geography section of the British Association for the Advancement of Science, and in 1940 he was elected the first non-American president of the Association of American Geographers.

During the 1940s, Taylor continued fieldwork and research, and published *Our Evolving Civilization: An Introduction to Geopacifics* in 1946. Two years later, he was appointed as an Advisor for the Interim Council of the Australian National University, which allowed him to return to Australia for several months, where he visited university campuses. He made a similar tour of British universities in 1950, and in that same year published *Geography in the Twentieth Century*.

In 1951 he retired from Toronto University and became a Professor Emeritus. He served that year as honorary president of the Canadian Association of Geographers, which had just been formed. In 1952 he returned to Australia, where he became a council member of the Royal Society of New South Wales, in Sydney. According to *Preston James and Geoffrey Martin (1981:260), "In Australia he was welcomed as a national hero, for by that time the general public had discovered that he had been right." Two years later, he was elected to the Australian Academy of Science; in 1958 he published his autobiography, *Journeyman Taylor: The Education of a Scientist*, and in 1959 he became the first president of the Institute of Australian Geographers. He continued to write, and in 1961 received the Medal of the Royal Society of New South Wales, as well as an honorary Doctor of Letters degree from Sydney University. He died in Sydney on November 5, 1963.

Soon after his death Marshall (1964:427) wrote, "The quality of greatness is indefinable, but it is unmistakable. With the death of Griffith Taylor . . . geography, and particularly Australian geography, lost a great man."

Selected Bibliography

1910   "The Physiography of the Proposed Federal Territory at Canberra, Australia." *Bulletin in the Bureau of Meteorology*. No. 6. Melbourne.

1911   "The Physiography of Eastern Australia." *Bulletin of the Bureau of Meteorology*. No. 8. Melbourne.

             With A. W. Jose and W. G. Woolnough. *New South Wales: Historical, Physiographical and Economic*. Melbourne: Whitcombe & Tombs.

             Australia in its Physiographic and Economic Aspects. Edited by A. J. Herbertson. Oxford: Clarendon Press.

1913   With H. A. Hunt and E. A. Quayle. *Climate and Weather of Australia*. Commonwealth Bureau of Meteorology, Melbourne.

             "The Western Journeys." *Scott's Last Expedition* 2:182–290. Edited by L. Huxley. London: Smith Elder.

             "A Résumé of the Physiography and Glacial Geology of Victoria Land, Antarctica." *Scott's Last Expedition*, 416–29.

1914   "Mining and Economic Geology." *Oxford Survey*, 21–267.

"Antarctica, the British Sector." *Oxford Survey*, 518–38.

"Physical Features and Their Effect on Settlement." *Oxford Survey*, 34–91.

"Physiography and Glacial Geology of East Antarctica." *Geographical Journal* 44:365–82, 452–67, 553–71.

A Geography of Australasia. Edited by A. J. Herbertson. Oxford: Clarendon Press.

"Evolution of a Capital: A Physiographic Study of the Foundation of Canberra, Australia." *Geographical Journal* 48:378–95, 536–54.

1915   "Climatic Control of Australian Production." *Bulletin of the Bureau of Meteorology.* No. 11. Melbourne.

1916   *With Scott: The Silver Lining.* London: Smith Elder; New York: Dodd Mead, 464 pp.

With O.J.R. Howarth. *The World and Australasia.* Edited by A. J. Herbertson. Oxford: Clarendon Press.

1918   *Atlas of Contour and Rainfall Maps of Australia.* Advisory Council of Science and Industry, Melbourne.

The Australian Environment, Especially as Controlled by Rainfall: A Regional Study of the Topography, Drainage, Vegetation and Settlement and of the Character and Origin of the Rains. Memoir No. 1, Advisory Council of Science and Industry, Melbourne.

"Climatic Factors Influencing Settlement in Australia." *Commonwealth Yearbook.* No. 11. Melbourne, 84–101.

1919   "The Physiographic Control of Australian Exploration." *Geographical Journal* 53:172–92.

"The Settlement of Tropical Australia." *Geographical Review* 8:84–115.

"Climatic Cycles and Evolution." *Geographical Review* 8:84–115.

1920   *Australian Meteorology: A Text-Book Including Sections on Aviation and Climatology.* Oxford: Clarendon Press.

"Agricultural Climatology of Australia." *Quarterly Journal of the Royal Meteorological Society* 46:331–55.

"Nature Versus the Australian." *Science and Industry* 2:459–72.

1921   "The Evolution and Distribution of Race, Culture and Language." *Geographical Review* 11:54–119.

1922   *British Antarctica (Terra Nova) Expedition 1910–13: The Physiography of McMurdo Sound and Granite Harbour Region.* London: Harrison.

"The Distribution of Future White Settlement: A World Survey Based on Physiographic Data." *Geographical Review* 12:375–402.

1924   "Geography and Australian National Problems." *Australasian Association for the Advancement of Science*, Report of 16th Meeting, Wellington, 433–87.

1925   With Dorothy Taylor. *The Geographical Laboratory*. Sydney: Sydney
            University Union.

1926   "The Frontiers of Settlement in Australia." *Geographical Review* 16:1–
            25.

1927   "The Topography of Australia." *Commonwealth Yearbook*. No. 20. Mel-
            bourne, 75–90.

            *Environment and Race: A Study of Evolution, Migration, Settlement and
            Status of the Races of Man*. London: Oxford University Press.

1928   "Glaciation in the South West Pacific." *Proceedings of the Pan-Pacific
            Science Congress, Tokyo* 2:1819–25.

            "Climatic Relations Between Antarctica and Australia." *Problems of Po-
            lar Research*. Edited by W.L.G. Jones. New York, 285–99.

            "The Status of the Australian States: A Study of Fundamental Geographical
            Controls." *Australian Geographer* 1:7–28.

1929   "Racial Migration Zones." *Human Biology* 2:34–62.

1930   *Antarctic Adventure and Research*. New York: Appleton.

            "Agricultural Regions of Australia." *Economic Geography* 6:109–34,
            213–42.

            "The Control of Settlement in Australia by Geographical Factors." *Pro-
            ceedings from the 6th Session of the Institute of International Relations*
            6:206–18. Berkeley.

1931   "The Nordic and Alpine Races and Their Kin: A Study of Ethnological
            Trends." *American Journal of Sociology* 37:67–81.

            Australia: A Geography Reader. Chicago: Rand McNally.

1932   "The Pioneer Belts of Australia." *Pioneer Settlement. American Geo-
            graphical Society Special Publication*. No. 14. New York, 360–91.

            "The Inner Arid Limits of Economic Settlement in Australia." *Scottish
            Geographical Magazine* 48:65–78.

1933   "The Australian Environment." *Cambridge History of the British Empire*
            7:3–23.

            "The Soils of Australia in Relation to Topography and Climate." *Geo-
            graphical Review* 23:108–13.

            Atlas of Environment and Race. Chicago: University of Chicago. (110
            maps and diagrams)

1935   "Geography: The Correlative Science." *Canadian Journal of Economic
            and Political Science* 1:535–50.

1936   *Environment and Nation: Geographical Factors in the Cultural and Po-
            litical History of Europe*. Toronto: University of Toronto Press; Chicago:
            University of Chicago Press.

1937   "Comparison of the American and Australian Deserts." *Economic Ge-
            ography* 13:260–68.

            "The Possibilities of Settlement in Australia." *Limits of Land Settlement*.

Edited by I. Bowman. New York, 195–227.

Environment, Race and Migration: Fundamentals of Human Distribution, with Special Sections on Racial Classification and Settlement in Canada and Australia. Toronto: University of Toronto Press; Chicago: University of Chicago Press.

1938   "Correlations and Culture: A Study in Technique." *British Association for the Advancement of Science. Report of Annual Meeting*, Cambridge, 103–38. Other versions published in *Nature* 142:737–41; *Scottish Geographical Magazine* 54:321–44; and *Pan-American Geologist* 70:241–62, 71:81–106.

1940   *Australia: A Study of Warm Environments and Their Effect on British Settlement.* London: Methuen; New York: Dutton.

1941   "The Climates of Canada." *Canadian Banker* 49:34–59.

1942   "British Columbia: A Study in Topographic Control." *Geographical Review* 32:372–402.

"Environment, Village and City: A Genetic Approach to Urban Geography, with some Reference to Possibilism." *Annuals Association of American Geographers* 32:1–67.

"The Role of Geography." *Education for Citizen Responsibilities*. Edited by F. L. Burdette. Princeton, 44:61.

1946   "Future Population in Canada: A Study in Technique." *Economic Geography* 22:67–74.

"Parallels in Soviet and Canadian Settlement." *International Journal* 1:144–58.

Our Evolving Civilization: An Introduction to Geopacifics. Toronto: University of Toronto Press.

"Newfoundland: A Study of Settlement with Maps and Illustrations." *Canadian Institute for International Affairs.* Toronto.

1947   *Canada: A Study of Cool Continental Environments and Their Effects on British and French Settlement.* London: Methuen.

1949   *Urban Geography: A Study of Sites, Evolution, Pattern and Classification in Villages, Towns and Cities.* London: Methuen.

1950   *Geography in the Twentieth Century.* London: Methuen.

"Northward Across Australia." *Proceedings of the Royal Canadian Institute* 15:32–33.

"Hobart to Darwin: An Australia Traverse." *Geographical Review* 40:548–74.

1951   "Fiji: A Study of Tropical Settlements." *Economic Geography* 27:148–62.

1952   "The Founding of the Society, 1927" (The Geographical Society of New South Wales, Silver Jubilee). *Australian Geographer* 6:3–4.

1953   With Dorothy J. Sievewright and Trevor Lloyd. *Southern Lands.* Toronto: Ginn.

1954	With Dorothy J. Sievewright and Trevor Lloyd. *Lands of Europe and Asia*. Toronto: Ginn.
1955	"Australia and Canada: A Comparison of Resources." A.N.Z.A.A.S. *Report of the 30th Meeting, Canberra 1954*, 277–315.
	"Australian Antarctica." *Proceedings of the Royal Australian Historical Society* 41:158–74.
1956	"Australia: Continental Comparisons." *Pacific Discovery* (California Academy of Sciences) (September–October):1–2.
1958	*Journeyman Taylor: The Education of a Scientist*. Edited by Alasdair Alphin MacGregor. London: Robert Hale.
1959	"Human Ecology in Australia." *Biography and Ecology in Australia*. Edited by A. Keast, R. L. Crocker, and C. S. Christian. Den Haag: Junk, 52–68.
1961	"Australia and Canada: A Study of Habitability as Determined by Environment." *Professional Geographer* 13:1–5.
1962	"How Geographers May Promote World Peace." *Geographical Outlook* (Ranchi, India) 3:1–4.
1963	"Geographers and World Peace: A Plea for Geopacifics." *Australian Geographical Studies* 1:3–17.
	"Probable Disintegration of Antarctica." *Geographical Journal* 129:190–91.

Chronology

1880	Born December 1 at Walthamstow, Essex, England.
1881	Lived in Serbia.
1884	Family returned to north of England.
1893	Family moved to Sydney, Australia.
1896	Attended King's School.
1899	Student at Sydney University. Began geological fieldwork in New South Wales.
1904	B.Sc. with honors in Physics and Geology.
1905	Bachelor of Engineering. Fieldwork extended to Victoria, South Australia, and Great Barrier Reef.
1906	Became Demonstrator in Geology, Sydney University.
1907	Gave first formal lecture in Geography at Sydney University. Awarded 1851 Science Research Scholarship to Cambridge University.
1909	Fieldwork in Alps, Riviera, and northern Europe.
1910	Representative of the Commonwealth Weather Service on Scott's expedition to Antarctica.
1913	Collated and edited material on Antarctic research as part of the Royal Geographical Society and the British Museum.

1916   D.Sc. from Sydney University. Elected advisor to Faculty of Science, Melbourne University.

1917   Thomson Gold Medal, Royal Geographical Society of Australasia (Queensland) for tropical research.

1921   Associate Professor of Geography at Sydney University.

1927   First President, Geographical Society of New South Wales.

1929   Professor of Geography at Chicago University.

1935   Foundation Professor of Geography, Toronto University. Advisor to Admiral Byrd's second expedition to Antarctica.

1940   President Association of American Geographers, first non-American to hold this office.

1942   Fellow of Royal Society of Canada.

1948   Advisor to the Interim Council of the Australian National University.

1950   Lecture tour of British universities.

1951   Retired and became Professor Emeritus of Toronto University. Honorary President of the new Canadian Association of Geographers.

1952   Returned to Sydney and became a council member of the Royal Society of New South Wales.

1954   Elected to Australian Academy of Science.

1959   First President, Institute of Australian Geographers.

1963   Died November 5 in Sydney.

References

James, Preston E., and Geoffrey J. Martin. 1981. *All Possible Worlds: A History of Geographical Ideas*. 2d ed. New York: Wiley.

Marshall, Ann. 1964. "Griffith Taylor." *The Geographical Review* 54:427–29.

Rose, John K. 1963. "Griffith Taylor." *Annals of the Association of American Geographers* 54:622–29.

Thales of Miletus

Thales was born circa 625 B.C. in the town of Miletus, in Ionia, and was later recognized by Aristotle as the founder of the Ionian philosophical school. Thales was probably among the first of the Greek philosophers to concern himself with questions about the earth and its relationship with other heavenly bodies, though some before him have undoubtedly been lost to us. What we know of Thales today is almost entirely derived from philosophers and those who chronicle the history of philosophy, not from direct knowledge of his work. *Aristotle, Seneca, Diodorus, and others preserved fragments of Thales's work for future generations.

Miletus was located on the eastern side of the Aegean Sea, near the mouth of the Meander River, and became a thriving commercial center, attracting merchants for trade. With these visitors came a wealth of knowledge about what was known in other areas, and Miletus became a center of intellectual ferment as well as commerce. Like so many other early Greek philosophers, Thales was an admirer of geometry and its applications. Additionally, he was trained in engineering, astronomy, and other forms of mathematics. His knowledge of astronomy was sufficient to allow him to predict an eclipse of the sun, which occurred in May of 585 B.C.

According to Kitto (1988:178), "The usual story of the absent-minded professor is told of Thales, that on a walk he was so intently looking up into the heavens that he tumbled into a well." Aristotle, however, is said to have tried to paint Thales in a more favorable light, not as a squanderer of time but as one capable of turning a profit if the need and opportunity arose (Kitto, 1988).

According to *Preston James and Geoffrey Martin (1981:17), "Thales was a practical businessman who at one time was able to corner the supply of olive oil. . . . He was also a genius, who is credited with a great variety of innovations and is often likened to Benjamin Franklin in the breadth of his contributions and the fertility of his imagination." His ability to ask questions, and to try to answer them with some combination of deduction and observation, as did so many of his successors, was important, even though he could be led astray by his own answers. For example, Thales deduced that the world was ultimately composed of water, a proposition that we would find no more than amusing today. It was, however, an explanation that could be subjected to testing, as opposed to theological explanations. Both the question, which many in his time would never have thought important at all, and the methods employed in search of an answer were significant. Unfettered by religious or mystic views, Thales sought to understand the world around him in "scientific" terms.

His philosophic thinking generated a movement that was built upon by a series of important successors. As Kitto (1988:178) so aptly phrased it, in speaking of the contributions of Thales, "It is as if the human mind for the first time took its toes off the bottom and began to swim, and swim with astonishing confidence." His immediate successor was Anaximander, and, in the view of James and Martin (1981:19), "Thales and Anaximander can be recognized as the originators of the mathematical study of geography."

Thales died ca. 547 B.C.

Selected Bibliography

His writings survive only in fragments, as quotations used by his successors (Kish:10).

Chronology

ca. 625 B.C.   Born in Greece.

                      Travelled as a merchant to Egypt, where he learned Egyptian mathematics and Chaldean astronomy.

585 B.C.   Predicted eclipse of the sun, which occurred on May 28.

ca. 547 B.C.   Died.

References

James, Preston E., and Geoffrey J. Martin. 1981. *All Possible Worlds: A History of Geographical Ideas*. 2d ed. New York: Wiley.

Kish, George. 1978. *A Source Book in Geography*. Cambridge, Mass.: Harvard University Press.

Kitto, H.F.D. 1988. *The Greeks*. London: Penguin Books.

Johann Heinrich
von Thünen

Johann Heinrich von Thünen was born in northwestern Germany on June 24, 1783. He attended secondary school in Jever, where he received additional instruction in advanced mathematics. In 1799 he left school to work on a farm, following his interest in agriculture.

Von Thünen's farm experience stimulated his interest in agriculture, and also in furthering his education, so in 1802 he decided to attend the agricultural college at Gross-Flottbeck. During his stay there, he began to carefully observe agricultural land-use patterns around Hamburg, concluding that Hamburg was indeed influencing those patterns directly. In 1803 he went to Celle, where he attended a seminar by Thaer, then on to the University of Göttingen, where he pursued a combination of interests, including economics, biology, philosophy, and languages.

In 1810 von Thünen purchased his own estate, which was located 23 miles southeast of Rostock. There he began farming, working constantly to improve soils and make other adjustments to improve productivity. At the same time, he remained interested in agricultural land-use patterns; so he collected data from his own farm and from other sources, and in his spare time began work on the problem of what determines agricultural land-use patterns.

The primary question posed by von Thünen was how farming systems would evolve relative to their distance from a central town or place. Essential to von Thünen's approach to the problem were the concepts of diminishing returns and economic rent. Over a period of years, von Thünen's work evolved into a book-length study of agricultural land-use patterns, published in 1826, *The Isolated State*, Part 1 (or *Der Isolierte Staat in Beziehung auf Landwirtschaft und Nationalökonomie*).

In *The Isolated State*, von Thünen developed a model of agricultural location in which the dominant variable affecting land-use patterns was the distance from a central market. His model operated within a restrictive set of assumptions, beginning with that of an isolated state within which one large central city represented the marketplace for agricultural commodities. That city was surrounded by a uniform (homogeneous) plain; the market was served by only one mode of transportation (cart and horse); and farmers sought to maximize their profits. Within this set of assumptions, he could focus on a single variable, transportation costs to the market, and ask what affect that alone would have on the differentiation of an agricultural landscape around the central city.

What von Thünen found was that a distinctive agricultural landscape would appear in his "ideal state," one set up by a series of rational responses by farmers to the constraint of variable costs associated with marketing their products. From this beginning set of assumptions, von Thünen moved on to relax some of them and see what would happen to land-use patterns. From his own experience, coupled with his theoretical interests, he introduced into the literature what is still considered to be a major model of agricultural location, a deductive model that provides an excellent start toward understanding why agricultural patterns develop the way that they do.

Interestingly, geographers were slow to recognize the importance of von Thünen's work, even thought nineteenth- and early twentieth-century geographers found agriculture of major interest. It was not until the 1960s that von Thünen's work attracted much attention in American geography, following the publication of a study by Peter Hall (1966). However, from that introduction until the present, von Thünen's work has remained an integral part of most discussions of agricultural location theory and agricultural land use, as is apparent by its inclusion in virtually all introductory economic geography texts. His work also served as a stimulus to research into agricultural patterns in both advanced and Third World countries.

Von Thünen continued to manage his farming enterprise. In 1830, however, he was awarded an honorary doctorate by the University of Rostock for his work on agricultural location theory. In 1848 he was elected as a representative to the German National Council, though he was never able to take his seat there. He died at his estate on September 22, 1850.

Selected Bibliography

1803   *Description of Agriculture in the Village of Gross-Flottbeck.*

1826   *The Isolated State.* Part 1.

1850   *The Isolated State.* Part 2. (Contains natural wage theory.)

Chronology

1783   Born June 24 in northwest Germany.

1796   Attended secondary school in Jever, and received supplementary instruction in calculus.

1799	Left the school in Jever to work on a farm. Interested in agriculture.
1802	Attended Agricultural College at Gross-Flottbeck in Holstein. Noticed the influence Hamburg and Altona had on surrounding areas.
1803	Attended Thaer's seminar in Celle. From Celle he went to the University of Göttingen, where he studied philosophy, biology, economics, and languages.
1810	Bought his own estate 23 miles southeast of Rostock; continuously tried to improve soils and production on this farm.
1819	First draft of *The Isolated State*.
1826	Publication of *The Isolated State*.
1830	Granted an honorary doctorate by the University of Rostock.
1848	Elected as a representative to the German National Assembly, but could not take his seat.
1850	Died September 22 at his estate.

Reference

Hall, Peter. 1966. *Von Thünen's Isolated State*. London: Pergamon.

Carl Troll

Carl Troll was born in the tiny Bavarian village of Gabersee, Germany, on December 24, 1899. His father was the medical director in a nerve clinic. While still a child, Troll was fortunate enough to go on holiday visits to relatives in Nuremberg and the Main Valley, where he was enthusiastic about rocks, plants, and the landscape. In his teen years, the Troll family moved to Munich, from where he made numerous weekend excursions to surrounding areas (Tilley, 1984).

Troll's university education began at Munich University in 1919, where he enthusiastically pursued courses in botany and geography. Between his university studies and his time in the field, Troll began to organize in his mind a view of landscapes that was primarily ecological. He focused his university studies on plant physiology and received his doctorate in 1921 at the young age of twenty-two. His interest in geography persisted, especially in what he termed "landscape ecology." Subsequent to his graduation, he qualified to teach a variety of courses in high school, travelled to Scandinavia, published his first work on glaciation, "Der diluviale Inn-Chiemseegletscher. Das geographische bild eines typischen Alpenvorlandgletschers" in 1924, and, in 1925, qualified as a lecturer in geography with a thesis entitled, "Einfluss der Ozeanität auf die Pflanzenwelt Mitteleuropas."

In the following year, he went to do fieldwork in South America, where he remained for three years studying geographical aspects of the Andes Mountains. He was able to take airplane rides over several areas, allowing him to collect air photos that he could later integrate with the collections of materials that he had accumulated on the ground.

In the autumn of 1929, Troll returned to Germany, where he took a position in Berlin as a professor of colonial geography, and in October of the following year, he married a fellow geographer, Elizabeth Kurschner. During the following decade, he published numerous papers based on his research in the Andes, covering topics from glaciology and botany to economic geography. A central theme for Troll during this decade was the relationship between vegetation and elevation in the tropical mountains of South America, as was apparent in such articles as "Die Landschaftsgurtel der tropischen Anden," published in 1932.

During the academic year 1933–34, Troll travelled to East Africa, looking at both the natural environment and its effects on colonial development. Then, in 1936, he was appointed Professor of Economic Geography at the Berlin University, and in the following year he had an opportunity to join the German Nanga Parbat Himalaya Expedition, where he produced a splendid vegetation map of the mountainous region. Following his return, Troll became Professor and Director of the Geography Department at Bonn University, where he remained until his retirement in 1965.

At Bonn Troll continued to produce articles on numerous topics, including such important works as "Luftbildplan und ökologische Bodenforschung," in 1939 and "Studien zur vergleichenden Geographie der Hochgebirge der Erde" in 1941. In 1946 Troll became Dean of the Faculty of Science at Bonn University, and continued his research along with his many other duties. The following year he founded the journal *Erdkunde*, a major geographical periodical, founded another publication, *Bonner Geographische Abhandlungen*, and published "Die Wissenschaftliche Geographie in Deutschland, 1933–1945," which was subsequently translated and published in the *Annals of the Association of American Geographers* in 1949. This work was a scholarly and thoughtful survey of the development of German geography during those years.

In 1948 Troll went to Zurich as a visiting professor at Zurich University. Two years later, he served as Chairman of the Commission for Research in Earth Sciences of the Mainz Academy of Science and Literature, and in the following year he was awarded the Vega Medal of the Royal Swedish Society of Anthropology and Geography, along with founding still another publication, *Arbeiten zur Rheinischen Landeskunde*.

During the 1950s, Troll continued tirelessly with his diverse research interests. In 1952 he was a visiting professor at the University of Wisconsin, did fieldwork in Mexico during part of 1953, published another major article, "Der Jahreszeitliche Ablauf des Naturgeschehens in den verschiedenen Klimagürteln der Erde," in 1955. In the last half of the decade he managed to serve as a visiting professor at the University of London for a year, re-found and co-edit another periodical, *Die Erde*, receive the Ritter Gold Medal of the Berlin Geographical Society and the Martin Behaim Gold Medal of the Franconian Geographical Society, and find himself elected as President of the International Geographical Union for 1960.

In that same year he became Rector of Bonn University. During 1962 he was a visiting professor at the University of Bergen, and in that same year received the Victoria Medal of the Royal Geographical Society of London. The following year he was awarded an honorary doctorate by Louvain University, and in 1964 he went to the University of Bucharest as a visiting professor. During that same year he received the *Albrecht Penck Medal from the German Quaternary Association.

In 1965 Troll retired from his geography position at Bonn University after forty years in academia and went as a visiting professor to the University of Ghent. In 1965 he also experienced his first heart problems but managed to continue doing research. He went on to a visiting professor post at the University of Liège in 1966, though he was starting to slow down. In the late 1960s, he organized several I.G.U. Commission Symposia, but in 1971 he had his second heart attack.

In 1975 Troll celebrated fifty years of university teaching, published his last article, "Vergleichende Geographie der Hochgebirge der Erde in landschafts-ökologischer Sicht," and attended the fortieth Conference of German Geographers, which met in Innsbruck that year. Troll died unexpectedly on July 21, 1975, in Bonn. Like *Alexander von Humboldt and Albrecht Penck, Troll had spent a lifetime in the field, making careful observations and incorporating them into explanations of natural processes.

Selected Bibliography

1924   "Der diluviale Inn-Chiemseegletscher. Das geographische bild eines typ-
            ischen Alpenvorlandgletschers." *Forschungen zur Deutschen Landes—
            und Volkskunde*. Vol. 23:121.

1925   "Die Landbauzonen Europas in ihrer Beziehung zur natürlichen Vegeta-
            tion." *Geographische Zeitung* 31:265–80.

1926   "Die jungglazialen Schotterfluren im Umkreis der Deutschen Alpen. Ihre
            Oberflächengestalt, ihre Vegetation ihr Landschaftscharakter." *Forschun-
            gen zur Deutschen Landes—und Volkskunde*. Vol. 24.

1929   "An expedition to the Central Andes, 1926–28." *Geographical Review*
            19:234–47.

1930   "Die wirtschaftsgeographische Struktur des tropischen Südamerika." *Geo-
            graphische Zeitung* 36:468–85.

1932   "Die tropischen Andenländer." *Handbuch der Geographische Wissen-
            schaft Südamerika*. Edited by F. Klute, 309–462.

1933   "Europäische Tropensiedlung, ihre Aussichten und ihre Grenzen." *Ko-
            loniale Rundschau* 25:32–36.

            "Die Kolonialgeographie als Zweig der allgemeinen Erdkunde." *Kolon-
            iale Rundschau* 25:121–29.

1935   "Gedanken und Bermerkungen zur ökologischen Pflanzen-geographie."
            Geographische Zeitung 41:380–88.

1936   "Termitensavannen." *Landerkundliche Forschung*. Festschrift für Norbert
            Krebs. Stuttgart, 275–312.

1939   "Gedanken zur Systematik der Anthropogeographie (zu H. Hassinger's:
            Die Geographie der Menschen)." *Zeitschrift für Gesellschaft für Erdkunde*.

Berlin, 210–15.

"Luftbildplan und ökologische Bodenforschung." *Zeitschrift für Gesellschaft für Erdkunde*. Berlin, 241–98. Reprinted in *Luftbildforschung und Landeskundliche Forschung, Erdkunde Wissen*. Wiesbaden. Vol. 12:1–69.

"Fortschritte der Luftbildforschung." *Zeitschrift für Gesellschaft für Erdkunde*. Berlin, 277–311.

1942   "Der Büsserschnee (Nieve de los Penitentes) in den Hochgebirgen der Erde." *Petermanns Geographische Mitteilungen*. (Erganz.) Vol. 210.

1943   "Die Stellung der Indianer—Hochkulturen im Landschaftsaufbau der tropischen Anden." *Zeitschrift für Gesellschaft für Erdkunde*. Berlin, 93–128.

"Thermische Klimatypen der Erde." *Petermanns Geographische Mitteilungen* 89:81–89.

1944   "Diluvialgeologie and Klima." *Geologische Rundschau* 34:305–25.

"Strukturboden, Solifluktion und Frostklimate der Erde." *Geologische Rundschau* 34:545–694. Translated as "Structure Solifluction and Frost Climates of the Earth." *USA SIPRE Trans*. No. 43. Wilmette, Ill. (1958).

1947   "Die Formen der Solifulktion und die periglaziale Bodenabtragung." *Erdkdunde* 1:162–75.

1948   "Der subnivale und periglaziale Zyklus der Denudation." *Erdkunde* 2:1–21.

1949   "Geographical Science in Germany During the Period 1933–45: A Critique and Justification." *Annals of the Association of American Geographers* 39:99–137.

1951   "Tatsachen und Gedanken zur Klimatypenlehre." *Geographische Studien Festschrift für Johann Solch*. Vienna, 184–202.

1952   "Halford J. Mackinder als Geograph und Geopolitiker." *Erdkunde* 6:177–78.

With B. Frenzel. "Die Vegetationszonen des nordlichen Eurasien während der letzten Eiszeit." *Eiszeit und Gegenwart* 2:154–67.

1953   "Ein Markstein in der Entwicklung der medizinische Geographie—Zum erscheinen von E. Rodenwaldt's Weltseuchenatlas." *Erdkunde* 7:60–64.

1954   "Über Alter und Bildung von Talmaandern." *Erdkunde* 8:286–302.

1956   "Das Wasser als Pflanzengeographischer Faktor." *Handbuch Pflanzenphysiologie*. 3:750–86. Edited by W. Rhuland. Berlin.

1958   "Climatic Seasons and Climatic Classification." *The Oriental Geographer* 2:141–65.

"Tropical Mountain Vegetation." *Proceedings of the 9th Pacific Scientific Congress* 20:37–46. Bangkok, 1956.

1959   "Die tropischen Grasländer (Savannen) unter dem Einfluss von Klima, Boden and Wasser." *Proceedings of the 18th International Geographical Congress* 1:302–07. Rio de Janeiro, 1956.

1960   "The Relationship Between the Climates, Ecology and Plant Geography of the Southern Cold Temperature Zone and of the Tropical High Mountains." *Proceedings of the Royal Society* 152:529–32. London.

1961   "Klima und Pflanzenkleid der Erde in dreidimensionaler Sicht." *Die Naturwissenschaften* 48:332.

1962   "Die Lokalwinde der Tropengebirge und ihre Einfluss auf Niederschlag und Vegetation." *Bonn Geographische Abhandlungen* 9:124–82.

1963   "Landscape Ecology and Land Development with Special Reference to the Tropics." *Journal of Tropical Geography* 17:1–11.

1964   "Karte der Jahreszeitenklimate der Erde." *Erdkunde* 18:5–28. Published also with text in English in H. E. Landsberg et al., *World Maps of Climatology*, Berlin-Gottingen-Heidelberg, 1963.

1965   "A Classification of Climates on an Ecological Basis (Explanation of a New Map of the Climates of the Earth)." *Consejo Superior de Investigaciones Cientificas Madrid.*

1966   "Herbert Lehmann." *Erdkunde* 20:1–5.

1966   "Herbert Lautensach's Lebenswerk." *Erdkunde* 20:241–52.

         "Plural Societies of Developing Countries: Aspects of Social Geography." *Proceedings, 20th International Geographical Congress*, London, 1964, 2–4.

1968   "Leo Waibel zum Gedächtnis." *Erdkunde* 22:63–65.

1971   "Landscape Ecology (Geoecology) and Biogeocoentology: A Terminological Study." *Geoforum* 8:43–46.

1973   "Julius Budel und die moderne Geomorphologie." *Erdkunde* 27:245–53.

         "High Mountain Belts between the Polar Caps and the Equator." *Artic and Alpine Research* 5/3(2):19–27.

         "The Upper Timberlines in Different Climatic Zones." *Arctic and Alpine Research* 5/3(2):3–18.

Chronology

1899   Born December 24 at Gabersee, Bavaria, Germany.

1919   Graduated from Munich University.

1921   Ph.D. from Munich University.

1922   Assistant in Geography Department of Munich University.

1924   Fieldwork in Scandinavia.

1925   Lecturer in Geography, Munich University.

1926   Began fieldwork in Bolivian, Peruvian, and Chilean Andes.

1928   Silver Medal, Berlin Geographical Society.

1930   Appointed Associate Professor of Overseas and Colonial Geography.

1934   Fieldwork in eastern Africa.

1936	Appointed Professor of Economic Geography, Berlin University.
1937	Scientist on the German Nanga Parbat Himalaya Expedition.
1938	Professor and Director of the Geography Department, Bonn University.
1946	Dean, Faculty of Science, Bonn University.
1947	Founding editor of *Erkunde* and *Bonner Geographische Abhandlungen*.
1950	Chairman of the Commission for Research in Earth Sciences of the Mainz Academy of Science and Literature.
1951	Founding editor of *Colloquium Geographicum*.
1952	Founding editor of *Arbeiten zur Rheinischen Landeskunde*. Visiting Professor, University of Wisconsin at Madison.
1956	Visiting Professor at University of Brazil.
1958	Visiting Professor at University of London.
1959	Awarded Ritter Gold Medal of the Berlin Geographical Society and the Martin Behaim Gold Medal of the Franconian Geographical Society.
1960	Elected President of International Geographical Union (I.G.U.) in Stockholm. Appointed Rector, Bonn University.
1962	Awarded Victoria Medal of the Royal Geographical Society, London. Visiting Professor at University of Bergen.
1963	Awarded honorary D.Sc., Louvain University.
1964	Visiting Professor, University of Bucharest. Appointed member of U.N.E.S.C.O. Advisory Committee for Natural Resource Research. Awarded Albrecht Penck Medal of the German Quaternary Association.
1965	Retired from Chair of Bonn University and made Emeritus Professor. Honorary Ph.D. from University of Vienna. Visiting Professor, University of Ghent. First heart attack.
1968	Chairman of I.G.U. Commission on High-Altitude Geoecology established at its New Delhi Congress.
1971	Second severe heart attack.
1972	Organized and attended I.G.U. Commission on High-Altitude Geoecology Symposium in Calgary, relinquished its chairmanship.
1974	Organized I.G.U. Commission Symposium in Mainz.
1975	Celebrated fifty years as a university lecturer, January 31. Attended 40th Conference of German Geographers in Innsbruck. Died July 21 in Bonn.

Reference

Tilley, Philip D. 1984. "Carl Troll." *Geographers Biobibliographical Studies* 8:111–24.

Yi Fu Tuan

Many geographers today believe Yi Fu Tuan is one of the foremost spokespersons for the humanistic approach to geography. He was born on December 5, 1930, in Tientsin, China, around the time of the Japanese invasion. During his first decade of life, his family moved a number of times to escape the Japanese. In 1940 he left the country and went first to Australia, then in 1946 on to the Philippines; finally he ended up in London when his father was transferred to the Chinese Embassy in Britain.

Tuan was sixteen years of age when he arrived in Britain, and because he was too young to enter the university, he enrolled in a preparatory school for university entrance examinations. In 1947 he entered University College, London as an external student and the following year transferred from London to Oxford University. He was tempted to major in philosophy at Oxford but felt it dealt in high abstractions, and he did not think he had the temperament or talent to work in that area. His travel experiences as a child, along with his interest in questions concerning human beings in nature, led him to geography and earth science, a more down-to-earth endeavor.

Tuan liked Oxford immensely. It was exciting, and for the first time he felt that learning could be enjoyed; however, except for the subfield of geomorphology, Tuan found most of the geography program at Oxford boring. He completed his education at Oxford in 1951 and was awarded both a bachelor's and a master's degree.

Tuan was familiar with the work of John Kesseli and *Carl Sauer at Berkeley and decided to continue his graduate education there. He arrived at Berkeley in 1951 at the age of twenty to begin a Ph.D. program. He could follow his interest in geomorphology with Kesseli and his interest in man and nature with Sauer. When he went on his first field trip at Berkeley to California's Mohave Desert, he was "dumbfounded." He could actually see in the real world the landforms that had been described in textbooks but that had remained something hidden under the vegetation in England. He fell in love with the desert and decided that his dissertation would deal with some aspect of desert landforms. He taught for two years at Indiana University while working on his dissertation, which he finished in 1957. Upon graduation from Berkeley in 1957 he accepted a post-doctoral fellowship in statistics at the University of Chicago in 1958.

The year at Chicago was an important turning point in Tuan's career. He realized that the types of questions he was asking about landforms were basically historical and the statistical or modeling techniques he had learned were not appropriate. He also realized that he was inadequately trained in math and statistics. In reflecting on his experiences at Chicago, Tuan commented (Browning, 1982:120):

It has been of great benefit to me in a negative sense. If I had not had that year of total exposure to statistics, I would always have the question in my mind, "Shouldn't I do something in that field?" Since I've had this experience, it doesn't bother me and I could wholeheartedly swing to the other extreme. This other extreme, the interest in the broad questions of man and nature, has always been there from undergraduate days.

In 1959 Tuan accepted a position at the University of New Mexico in Albuquerque. His publications in the late 1950s and early 1960s primarily had dealt with his work in geomorphology, but he liked the University of New Mexico, and his research began to take on a more humanistic flavor. He published several articles in *Landscape* that dealt with humanistic interpretations of landscape features.

In 1965 Tuan accepted a position at the University of Toronto that was especially appealing since he had the opportunity to teach part time in the Department of Landscape Architecture. He stayed at Toronto for two years and then went on to the University of Minnesota, where he rose through the academic ranks to Professor of Geography and East Asian Studies. In his twenty years at Minnesota, Tuan wrote many scholarly articles and books. His most influential books at the time were *Topophilia: A Study of Environmental Perception, Attitudes, and Values* and *Space and Place: The Perspectives of Experience*. These books illustrate what Tuan calls "systematic humanistic geography."

In 1983 Tuan left Minnesota to take a position at the University of Wisconsin-Madison, where he is currently John Kirtland Wright Professor and Vilas Research Professor of Geography. According to Tuan (Personal correspondence, November 16, 1990), "What I am about is best represented, I think, by my last four books: *Segmented Worlds and Self* (1982); *Dominance and Affection* (1984); *The Good Life*; and *Morality and Imagination* (1989)."

Tuan's colleagues have recognized his contributions, and he has received the Award for Meritorious Contribution to Geography from the Association of American Geographers (1973) and the Cullum Geographical Medal from the American Geographical Society (1987). In 1985 he was awarded the Doctor of Environmental Studies, *honoris causa*, from the University of Waterloo, Canada.

Selected Bibliography

1954   "Types of Pediment in Arizona." *Yearbook of Pacific Coast Geographers* 16:17–24.

1957   "Use of Simile and Metaphor in Geographical Description." *Professional Geographer* 9:8–11.

1959   *Pediments in Southeastern Arizona.* University of California Publications in Geography. Vol. 13.

1962   "Structure, Climate, and Basin Land Forms in Arizona and New Mexico." *Annals of the Association of American Geographers* 52:51–68.

1963   "Architecture and Human Nature." *Landscape* 13:16–19.

1968   "Lewis Mumford and the Quality of Life." *Geographical Review* 58:570–73.

            The Hydrological Cycle and the Wisdom of God. University of Toronto Department of Geography Research Publications No. 1.

1970   *China.* London: Longman.

1971   *Man and Nature.* Resource Paper No. 10, Commission on College Geography, Association of American Geographers, Washington, D.C.

1972   "Environmental Psychology: A Review." *Geographical Review* 62:245–56.

1974   *Topophilia: A Study of Environmental Perception, Attitudes, and Values.* Englewood Cliffs, N.J.: Prentice-Hall.

1975   "Place: An Experiential Perspective." *Geographical Review* 65:151–65.

1977   *Space and Place: The Perspectives of Experience.* Minneapolis: University of Minnesota Press.

1978   "The City: Its Distance from Nature." *Geographical Review* 68:1–12.

1980   *Landscape of Fear.* New York: Pantheon.

1982   *Segmented Worlds and Self: Group Life and Individual Consciousness.* Minneapolis: University of Minnesota Press.

1983   "Moral Ambiguity in Architecture." *Landscape* 27:11–17.

1984   "Continuity and Discontinuity." *Geographical Review* 74:245–56.

            Dominance and Affection: The Making of Pets. New Haven: Yale University Press.

1985   "The Landscapes of Sherlock Holmes." *Journal of Geography* 84:56–60.

1986   *The Good Life.* Madison: University of Wisconsin Press.

            "Strangers and Strangeness." *Geographical Review* 76:10–19.

1989   *Morality and Imagination: Paradoxes of Progress.* Madison: University of Wisconsin Press.

            "Cultural Pluralism and Technology." *Geographical Review* 79:269–79.

1990   "Realism and Fantasy in Art, History, and Geography." *Annals of the Association of American Geographers* 80:435–46.

Chronology

1930	Born on December 5 in Tientsin, China.
1951	Graduated from the University of Oxford with a B.A. and an M.A.; went to the University of California at Berkeley for work on a Ph.D.
1956	Took a position at Indiana University.
1957	Awarded a Ph.D. from the University of California at Berkeley.
1958	Spent a year as a post-doctoral student in statistics at the University of Chicago.
1959	Accepted a position in the Geography Department at the University of New Mexico.
1965	Went to the University of Toronto.
1967	Took a position at the University of Minnesota.
1970	Published *China*.
1974	Published *Topophilia*.
1977	Published *Space and Place*.
1982	Published *Segmented Worlds and Self*.
1983	Went to the University of Wisconsin at Madison as Professor of Geography.
1984	Published *Dominance and Affection*.
1986	Published *The Good Life*.
1987	Awarded the Cullum Geographical Medal from the American Geographical Society.
1989	Published *Morality and Imagination*.

Reference

Browning, Clyde E. 1982. *Conversations with Geographers: Career Pathways and Research Styles*. Studies in Geography No. 16, Chapel Hill: University of North Carolina, Department of Geography.

Edward Louis Ullman

Edward Louis Ullman was born in 1912. As a youngster he enjoyed statistics about cities and maps and was encouraged by his parents to broaden his knowledge. His father, a classics scholar, took a position in Iowa City when Edward was seven. Later the family lived in Rome for a year, then in Chicago.

Among the characteristics of places that Ullman found particularly interesting were transportation systems and patterns. While a student at the University of Chicago, he worked for a local travel agency, where he learned about various forms of transportation, schedules, and numerous other details. After receiving his B.A. from the University of Chicago in 1934, he went to Harvard for an M.A., which he received in 1935. From Harvard he returned to the University of Chicago for his Ph.D., which he received in 1942.

During his student years, Ullman also gained some teaching experience at Washington State and Indiana University. In both places he was an instructor of economic geography. In 1946 he took a position at Harvard as an Assistant Professor in the Regional Planning Department, where he stayed until 1951, working his way up to the Associate Professor rank. In 1951 he moved to the University of Washington, where he became a full Professor in the Department of Geography, a position that he would hold for the rest of his life.

In some respects Ullman was like *J. Russell Smith, committed to applying geography to solve real problems. During World War II, Ullman worked as Chief of the Transport Section, Research and Analysis Branch, of the Office of Strategic Studies, a position that allowed him to expand and utilize his knowledge of transportation systems.

By the end of the 1930s, Ullman's major research foci had been defined: cities, transportation systems, and regional development. His first major article, "A Theory of Location for Cities," was published in 1941, and in 1943 he published *Mobile: Industrial Seaport and Trade Center*. Two years later he coauthored another influential article, "The Nature of Cities," with *Chauncy

Harris, whom he had met in his undergraduate days at the University of Chicago. Two further articles, "The Railroad Pattern of the United States," published in 1949, and "Rivers as Regional Bonds: The Columbia-Snake Example," demonstrated the breadth and depth of Ullman's thinking. His urban interests were pursued again in "Urban Geography," written with Harold Mayer and published in 1954 in *American Geography: Inventory and Prospect*.

In 1956 Ullman published another widely acclaimed article, "The Role of Transportation and the Bases for Interaction," and in that same year served as a transportation consultant to the Stanford Research Institute's survey of transportation in the Philippines, out of which came a coauthored publication, *An Economic Analysis of Philippine Domestic Transportation*. In the following years, he served as a consultant on regional development in Sardinia and on a Department of Commerce study on San Francisco. During that time, Ullman published a pioneering study of commodity flows, *American Commodity Flow: A Geographical Interpretation of Rail and Water Traffic Based on Principles of Spatial Interchange*. He received the Citation for Meritorious Contribution to the Field of Geography from the Association of American Geographers in 1958. In 1959 he became Director of the Meramec Basic Research Project in St. Louis, a position that he held until 1961.

During the 1960s, Ullman continued to work enthusiastically on a number of projects, including work with Michael Dacey on the minimum requirements approach to measuring the urban economic base, geography and underdevelopment, and geographic theory and prediction. In 1969 his last book, *The Economic Base of American Cities*, was published. In the 1970s one of his main interests became the trade-offs that existed between time and space, an idea developed most fully in his last major article, "Space and/or Time: Opportunity for Substitution and Prediction," published in 1974.

Edward Ullman died in 1976. In writing about Ullman's contributions in the following year, Harris (1977:599) said, "Finally it may be noted that Ullman was interested in developing concepts and theories in geography. . . . He felt that the use of the comparative method, coupled with theory, quantitative analysis, and specialized knowledge of some systematic topics provided the best basis for the discipline of geography."

Selected Bibliography

1936   "The Historical Geography of the Eastern Boundary of Rhode Island."
            Research Studies of the State College of Washington 4(2):67–87. Pullman.

1938   "Political Geography in the Pacific Northwest." *Scottish Geographical Magazine* 54:236–39.

1939   "The Eastern Rhode Island–Massachusetts Boundary Zone." *Geographical Review* 29:291–302.

1941   "A Theory of Location for Cities." *American Journal of Sociology* 46:853–64.

1943   *Mobile: Industrial Seaport and Trade Center*. Chicago: Department of
            Geography, University of Chicago, 167pp.

1945   With Chauncy D. Harris. "The Nature of Cities." *Annals of the American
            Academy of Political and Social Science* 242:7–17.

1949   "The Railroad Pattern of the United States." *Geographical Review*
            39:242–56.

            "Mapping the World's Ocean Trade: A Research Proposal." *Professional
            Geographer* 1(2):19–22.

            Maps of Metropolitan Boston. Boston: The Boston Globe.

1951   "Rivers as Regional Bonds: The Columbia-Snake Example." *Geograph-
            ical Review* 41:210–25.

            *The Railroads of the United States Classified According to Capacity and
            Importance*. Maps. New York: Simmons-Boardman.

1953   "Are Mountains Enough?" *Professional Geographer* 5(4):5–8.

            "Human Geography and Area Research." *Annals of the Association of
            American Geographers* 43:54–66.

1954   With Harold M. Mayer. "Urban Geography." Chapter 6 in *American
            Geography, Inventory and Prospect*. Edited by Preston E. James and
            Clarence F. Jones. Syracuse, N.Y.: Syracuse University Press for the
            Association of American Geographers, 142–66.

            With H. M. Mayer. "Transportation Geography." Chapter 13 in *American
            Geography*, 310–32.

            "Amenities as a Factor in Regional Growth." *Geographical Review*
            44:119–32.

1954   "Geography as Spatial Interaction." *Interregional Linkages*. Proceedings
            of the Western Committee on Regional Economic Analysis, Social Science
            Research Council, Berkeley, California, 1–12.

1955   "Die wirtschaftliche Verflechtung verschiedener Regionen der U.S.A. be-
            trachtet am Güteraustausch Connecticuts, Iowas and Washingtons mit den
            anderen Staaten." *Zeitschrift der Gesellschaft für Erdkunde zu Berlin*
            7(2):129–64.

1956   "The Role of Transportation and the Bases for Interaction." *Man's Role
            in Changing the Face of the Earth*. Edited by William L. Thomas, Jr.
            Chicago: University of Chicago Press, 862–80.

1957   With R. O. Shreve, H. E. Robison, R. K. Arnold, J. W. Landregan, and
            J. A. McCunniff. *An Economic Analysis of Philippine Domestic Trans-
            portation*. 7 vols. Menlo Park, Calif.: Stanford Research Institute, 1129pp.

            *American Commodity Flow: A Geographical Interpretation of Rail and
            Water Traffic Based on Principles of Spatial Interchange*. Seattle: Uni-
            versity of Washington Press, 215pp. Reprinted in 1959, 1967.

1958   "Regional Development and the Geography of Concentration." *Papers
            and Proceedings of the Regional Science Association* 4:179–98.

1959   "Sources of Support for the San Francisco Bay Area Economic Base."

Future Development of the San Francisco Bay Area, 1960–2020. U.S. Department of Commerce, Office of Area Development. Washington, D.C.: U.S. Government Printing Office, 34–40.

1960   "Trade Centers and Tributary Areas of the Philippines." *Geographical Review* 50:203–18.

"Geographical Theory and Underdeveloped Areas." *Essays on Geography and Economic Development.* Edited by Norton Ginsburg. Chicago: University of Chicago, Department of Geography Research Paper No. 62, 26–32.

With Michael F. Dacey. "The Minimum Requirements Approach to the Urban Economic Base." *Papers and Proceedings* 6:175–94. Regional Science Association.

1961   With Ronald R. Boyce and Donald J. Volk. *The Meramec Basin: Water and Economic Development.* 3 vols. St. Louis, Mo.: Meramec Basin Research Project, Washington University.

1962   With Donald J. Volk. "An Operational Model for Predicting Reservoir Attendance and Benefits: Implications of a Location Approach to Water Recreation." *Papers of the Michigan Academy of Sciences, Arts and Letters* 47:473–84.

"Notes on Theory and Practice of Economic Regionalization in the United States." *Documentacja Geograficzna. Polska Akademia Nauk. Instytut Geografii.* 1:90–97.

"The Nature of Cities Reconsidered." *Papers and Proceedings* 9:7–23. Regional Science Association, Presidential Address.

1967   "Geographical Prediction and Theory: The Measurement of Recreation Benefits in the Meramec Basin." *Problems and Trends in American Geography.* Edited by B. Cohen. New York: Basic Books, 124–45.

1968   "Minimum Requirements after a Decade: A Critique and Appraisal." *Economic Geography* 44:364–69.

"The Primate City and Urbanization in Southeast Asia: A Preliminary Speculation." *Papers on Problems of Development in Southeast Asia.* No. 31. New York: The Asia Society.

1969   With Michael F. Dacey and Harold Brodsky. *The Economic Base of American Cities: Profiles for the 101 Metropolitan Areas over 250,000 Population Based on Minimum Requirements for 1960.* Seattle: University of Washington Press.

1970   "The Urban Problem and the University." *University of Washington Report* 1(2) (April 27):6–8.

1971   "The Pacific Northwest Community: Austerity, Amenity, and Higher Education." *University of Washington Business Review* 30(3):14–24.

1974   "The City and Environmental Quality, Especially Air Pollution Sources and Costs." *Der Mensch und die Bioshpäre.* Proceedings of U.N.E.S.C.O. Conference. No. 20 on Man and the Biosphere (1971). Pullach bei München: Verlag Dokumentation, 10–27.

"Space and/or Time: Opportunity for Substitution and Prediction." *Transactions of the Institute of British Geographers* 63:125–39.

1975   "Intercity Ground Passenger Transportation." Panel Report. *Symposium on Transportation Issues, September 17, 18, 19, 1975, The Mitre Corporation.* McLean, Virginia, 158–66.

Chronology

1912   Born.

1933   Attended University of Chicago.

1934   Received his B.A. from University of Chicago.

1935   M.A. from Harvard University.

1942   Earned Ph.D. from University of Chicago.

1943   Chief of the Transport Section, Research and Analysis Branch of the Office of Strategic Services.

1946   Moved to Harvard, where he became Associate Professor of Regional Planning (until 1951).

1951   Professor of Geography at the University of Washington (until 1976).

1954   President of American Association of University Professors.

1959   Director of the Meramec Basin Research Project, St. Louis.

1965   President of the Washington Center for Metropolitan Studies, Washington, D.C.

1974   Member of Board of Directors of Amtrak.

1976   Died.

Reference

Harris, Chauncy D. 1977. "Edward Louis Ullman, 1912–1976." *Annals of the Association of American Geographers* 67:595–600.

Nikolai Ivanovich Vavilov

Nikolai Vavilov was one of the most influential scientists in Soviet and international science in the twentieth century. He had a broad array of interests including botany, agronomy, genetics, and geography. He travelled widely between World War I and World War II and had a respected international reputation. The son of a Moscow merchant of peasant background, he was born on November 25, 1887, in Moscow. He was one of four children in the Vavilov household, all of whom turned to science for a career. Two of the Vavilov children, Nikolai and his brother Sergei, eventually became members of the Academy of Sciences of the U.S.S.R.

Vavilov graduated from the Moscow Agricultural Institute in 1911 and the following year went on a two-year trip to visit the principal biological laboratories in Western Europe. He completed his postgraduate thesis in Great Britain and while there developed his lifelong interest in global research. He became a professor at Sartov University in 1917 and it was here that he developed his law of homologous series—that related species develop similar variations (Harris, 1991:118).

In 1921 he left Sartov University to take a position as head of the Branch of Applied Botany in Petrograd. During this year he also made an extensive trip to the United States to study agricultural research that was being conducted by the Bureau of Plant Industry of the United States Department of Agriculture.

"Three activities of Vavilov are of particular geographic interest," according to *Chauncy D. Harris (1991:118), "his geographical explorations, his leadership of the Branch of Applied Botany and its successors, and his presidency of the Geographical Society."

Vavilov's travels were extensive, and during a period when few Soviet citizens travelled, he managed to visit five continents and fifty-two countries. These trips were important scientific excursions and enabled him to gather and analyze a great deal of data. "He spent half a year in Afghanistan in 1924, worked in the

Mediterranean, North Africa, and the Near East in 1926–27, visited East Asia in 1929 and made repeated journeys to the Americas between 1921 and 1933, with particularly detailed observations in Mexico, Guatemala and Honduras in 1930, and in South America in 1932–33'' (Harris, 1991:118).

Vavilov's concern for agricultural geography was manifested in the early agricultural map of the Soviet Union he developed, along with an 84-page text to explain the distributions. His greatest geographical contribution, however, was his development of the concept of centers of origin of cultivated plants. His ideas and publications became widely known to western geographers, and reviews and comments of his work appeared in *The Geographical Review* in the United States and *The Geographical Journal* in Great Britain. According to Harris (1991:119), ''Vavilov's wide-ranging intellectual curiosity, his acute eye for the landscape and for geographical patterns, his passion for exact recording of field observations, and his seminal search for the wider implications, generalizations, regularities and even laws—all these are reminiscent of other great geographers.''

Under the leadership of Vavilov, the Branch of Applied Botany and its successors organized several hundred expeditions to study cultivated plant resources and agriculture. He established one of the world's largest seed banks at the institute, which in 1940 included more than 250,000 seed specimens. A geographical network of experiment stations was set up by Vavilov, for which he received the gold medal of the International Congress on Agriculture in Rome in 1927.

Shortly after his move to Petrograd in 1921, Vavilov had joined the Geographical Society of the U.S.S.R. Four years later he had received the Przhevalsky gold medal of the Society for his contributions to the geographical knowledge of Afghanistan. From 1931 to 1940 he served as President of the Geographical Society and was a strong and imaginative leader. During his tenure as president, membership in the society more than doubled.

During the 1930s, Vavilov increasingly feel out of favor with the Central Committee of the Communist Party of the Soviet Union. He was banned from foreign travel in 1934, and when he challenged the guru of Soviet genetics, T. D. Lysenko, he was arrested and sentenced to death in a secret trial in 1941. The death sentence was later commuted to twenty years imprisonment, but Vavilov died from starvation in Saratov prison on January 26, 1943, and was buried in an unmarked grave. Recently, a senior Soviet geographer and botanist wrote (Rodin, 1988:664–65): ''We found out about his subsequent fate only much later. An unforgivable crime was committed. There has hardly been a more tragic fate since Galileo; the man who sought to give bread to the people died of starvation. . . . He was a hero who gave his life for his scientific beliefs.''

Selected Bibliography

1914   ''Immunity to Fungous Diseases as Physiological Test in Genetics and
                     Systematics, Exemplified by Cereals.'' *Journal of Genetics* 4:49–65.

1922	"The Law of Homologous Series in Variation." *Journal of Genetics* 12:47–89.
	Field Crops of South-Eastern European Russia. Petrograd.
1926	*Studies on the Origin of Cultivated Plants*. Leningrad.
1929	"The Origin of Cultivated Plants." *Proceedings of the International Congress on Plant Science* 1:167–69.
1930	"Science and Technique Under Conditions of a Socialist Reconstruction of Agriculture." *Proceedings of the Second International Conference of Agricultural Economics*, Menasha, Wis.: George Banta, 336–42.
1931	"The Problem of the Origin of the World's Agriculture in Light of the Latest Investigations." *Science at the Crossroads*. London: Kniga, 95–106.
	"The Linnean Species as a System." *Fifth International Botanical Congress*. Cambridge: Cambridge University Press.
1932	"The World Centres of the Origin of Agriculture and the Soil Map of the World." *Proceedings and Papers of the Second International Congress of Soil Science* 4:81–85.
1951	*Selected Writings of N. I. Vavilov*. New York: Ronald.
1960	*World Resources of Cereals, Leguminous Seed Crops and Flax, and Their Utilization in Plant Breeding: Agroecological Survey of the Main Field Crops*. Washington, D.C.: National Science Foundation and the United States Department of Agriculture.

Chronology

1887	Born in Moscow, November 25.
1906	Graduated from Moscow Commercial School.
1911	Graduated from the Moscow Agricultural Institute.
1917	Took position as Professor at Sartov University.
1921	Became Head of the Branch of Applied Botany in Petrograd and made extensive trip to the United States to study agricultural research.
1922	Publication of *Field Crops of South-Eastern European Russia*.
1924	Went on research trip to Afghanistan.
1926	Awarded the Lenin Prize and published *Studies on the Origin of Cultivated Plants*.
1927	Awarded the gold medal by 13th International Congress on Agriculture.
1929	Became President of the Lenin All-Union Academy of Agricultural Sciences.
1930	Research trip to Mexico and Central America.
1931	Became President of the Russian Geographical Society.
1939	Elected Honorary President of the 7th International Congress of Genetics.

1941	Sentenced to death by a Military Collegium of the Supreme Court of the U.S.S.R. in a closed session.
1942	Death sentence commuted to detention in corrective labor camp.
1943	Died of starvation in prison in Saratov, January 26.
1955	Posthumously rehabilitated.

References

Harris, Chauncy D. 1991. "N. I. Vavilov." *Geographers Biobibliographical Studies* 13:117–33.

Rodin, L. 1988. "N. I. Vavilov, Geographer and Explorer." *Soviet Geography* 29:658–65.

Paul Vidal de la Blache

Paul Vidal de la Blache, born Paul Marie Joseph Vidal-Lablache, was born in the small French village of Pézenas in southern France on January 22, 1845. His father taught language and literature in the French lycée system, and so moved frequently among locations. At the same time, he encouraged Paul's schooling and interests.

In 1858, after excelling in his early schooling, Vidal was drawn to Paris, where he entered the Lycée Charlemagne to prepare himself in the classics. Five years later, he entered the École Normale Supérieure, and in 1866 he was at the top of the list for the *agrégation* in history and geography. His preparation, however, was primarily in history and secondarily in historical geography.

Following that, Vidal taught at the lycée at Carcassonne for three months, then, in January 1867, was offered an appointment in the École Française d'Athènes, which he accepted. His focus was on archaeology and epigraphy, and his first publication, *Hérode Atticus: Étude critique sur sa vie*, his doctoral thesis for the University of Paris, published in 1872, came out of that work. At the same time, living in Athens gave Vidal an opportunity to travel widely throughout the Mediterranean region, including Greece, Italy, and Asia Minor. During his stay with the school he also was introduced to the geographic works of *Alexander von Humboldt and *Carl Ritter, two of the leading voices in German geography, volumes of both *Kosmos* and *Erdkunde* had appeared by that time.

Vidal returned to France in January 1870 and married Laure Marie Elisabeth Mondot in the spring of that same year. The French loss of the France-Prussian war in the following year left an indelible impression on Vidal, and job scarcity weighed upon him as well. Finally he found a job in the Lycée d'Angers for the 1871–72 school year, and there defended his doctoral thesis at the Sorbonne. Following receipt of his doctorate, he was offered a position as *chargé de cours* in history and geography beginning in the fall of 1872 at the University of Nancy (Baker, 1988).

At the beginning of 1873, Vidal began his first lectures on geography, along with the development of a curriculum in geography, despite his limited knowledge of the subject. Until then, geography had been badly neglected in France, and a movement was begun to improve its teaching and status in the schools and universities. In order to succeed, Vidal established connections with several prominent German geographers, including *Ferdinand von Richthofen and *Friedrich Ratzel, and travelled frequently to Germany. In 1873, Vidal also published *La Péninsule Européenne: L'Océan et la Méditerranée*.

In 1875 he received the title of professor of geography at the University of Nancy. Both his teaching and his research interests were focused on geography by this time. The latter was being reflected in articles such as "L'Europe méridionale et le monde méditerranéen," which was published in 1875, and "Remarques sur la population de l'Inde anglaise, avec une carte de la densité de la population," published in 1877.

In November 1877, Vidal accepted a new position in geography at the École Normale Supérieure, his alma mater in Paris. In 1881 he acquired additional duties there as *sous-directeur* in the Section of Lettres. In 1883 he took on additional duties with a supplementary appointment as professor of geography at the École Normale Supérieure d'Institutrices de Fontenay-aux-Roses. His stay at the school was a lengthy one, and here he began to train his first serious students and followers. During the 1880s, his research flourished. *La terre. Géographie physique et économique: Histoire sommaire de découvertes* was published in 1883, and in 1889 *États et nations de l'Europe: Autour de la France* appeared, with several other publications in between.

Into the 1890s, Vidal continued to be a productive scholar and teacher. In 1891 the *Annales de Géographie* began publication, co-founded by Vidal and M. Dubois, a colonial geographer, and Vidal's excellent *Histoire et Géographie: Atlas général* appeared in 1894. In December 1898, he was nominated to the chair of geography at the University of Paris (Sorbonne), which was to be his final academic appointment. By this time in his career, Vidal had rejected environmental determinism and had formulated the concept of "possibilism." He argued heavily in favor of the importance of studying small regions, though he was concerned with how regions should be defined. He also argued that both the physical environment and people needed to be studied together. As the twentieth century began, Vidal continued his research. In 1903 the *Tableau de la géographie de la France*, recognized even now as a classic in geographical studies, was published; in 1904 he attended the International Geographical Congress in Washington, D.C.; and in 1906 he was elected to be a member of the Institut de France, which is in the Académie des Sciences Morales et Politique.

Vidal retired from the Sorbonne in 1909. Subsequent years brought him several major professional recognitions, including the Commandeur de la Légion d'Honneur in 1912, an honorary professorship at the Sorbonne in 1914, and the Charles Daly gold medal from the American Geographical Society in 1915. *La France de l'Est* was published in 1917. In January of 1918 Vidal became president of the Académie de Sciences Morales et Politiques, but it was a term that he would not be able to fulfill because he died in southern France on April 5 of that year, stricken by a heart attack. His last major work, *Principes de géographie humaine*, was published posthumously in 1922 thanks to a considerable amount of work by his son-in-law, Emmanuel de Martonne.

According to *Preston James and Geoffrey Martin (1981:193), "The French school of geography under the leadership of Vidal achieved a notable balance between physical and human components. The French geographers of that period were not bothered by an apparent dichotomy between physical geography and human geography, the way the Germans were." Vidal's work in geography was carried on by such able students as Jean Brunhes and Emmanuel de Martonne. Even today, French geographers speak of *la tradition vidalienne*, so important was Vidal to the development of geography in France.

Selected Bibliography

1872   *Hérode Atticus: Étude critique sur sa vie*. Paris: Ernest Thorin.

            Commentatio de Titulis Funebribus Graecis in Asia Minore. Paris: Ernest Thorin.

1873   *La Péninsule Européenne: L'Océan et la Méditerranée*. Paris: Berger-Levrault.

            "La côte allemande de la mer du Nord." *Rev. Polit. Litt.* 3(10):219–22. 2d series.

1874   "Le relief du sol de l'Europe centrale et le massif des Alpes." *Rev. Polit. Litt.* 3(28):647–52.

1875   "L'Europe méridionale et le monde méditerranéen." *Rev. Polit. Litt.* 4(32):750–54.

            "Les empires anglais et russe en Asie." *Rev. Polit. Litt.* 5(25):582–87.

1877   "Remarques sur la population de l'Inde anglaise, avec une carte de la densité de la population." *Bull. Soc. Géogr.* 13:5–34. Paris. 6th series.

            "Les voies de communication de l'Inde." *Rev. Sci.* 6(41):957–72. 2d series.

1880   *Marco Polo: Son temps et ses voyages*. Paris: Hachette.

1883   *La terre. Géographie physique et économique: Histoire sommaire des découvertes*. Paris: C. Delagrave.

1885   "De quelques réformes dans la terminologie géographique de la France." *Revue Géographie* 17:169–73.

            Collection de cartes murales accompagnées de notices. Paris: A. Colin.

1886   "Des rapports entre les populations et le climat sur les bords européens de la Méditerranée." *Revue Géographie* 19:401–19.

1888   "Des divisions fondamentales du sol français." *Bull. Lit.* 2(1):1–7.

1889   *États et nations de l'Europe: Autour de la France*. Paris: C. Delagrave.

1891   With P. Camena d'Almeida. *Cours de géographie à l'usage de l'enseignement secondaire: programmes de 1890.* 4 vols. Paris: A. Colin.

1894   *Histoire et Géographie: Atlas général.* Paris: A. Colin.

1896   "Le principe de la géographie général." *Annales de Géographie* 5(20):129–42.

          "Les voies de commerce dans la *Géographie* de Ptolémée." *C.R. Acad. Inscr. et Belles-Lettres* 24:420–22, 456–83. 3d series.

1898   "La géographie politique à propos des écrits de M. Frédéric Ratzel." *Annales de Géographie* 7(32):97–111.

1899   "Leçon d'ouverture de cours géographie à la Sorbonne." *Annales de Géographie* 8(38):97–109.

          "De l'habitation sur les plateaux limoneux du nord de la France." *Communication to Seventh International Geographical Congress Berlin.* Berlin: W. H. Kuhl, 498–501.

1902   *La rivière Vincent Pinzon: Étude sur la cartographie de la Guyane.* Paris: Université de Paris, Bibliothèque de la Faculté des Lettres.

1903   *Tableau de la géographie de la France.* Paris: Hachette. Translated into English by H. C. Brentnall, the first part was published as *The Personality of France.* 1928. London: Christophers.

          "La géographie humaine: Ses rapports avec la géographie de la vie." *Revue de Synthèse Historique* 7(20):219–40.

          "De la signification populaire des noms de pays." *Congresso Internazionale di Scienze Storich* 10:11–17. Rome, 1904.

1904   "Rapports de la sociologie avec la géographie." *Revue Internationale de Sociologie* 12(5):309–13.

          "Application des lignes d'équidistance à l'étude anthropogéographique de la Méditerranée." *Communication to Rep. 8th Int. Geogr. Congr.* (1905). Washington, D.C. 676–77.

1905   "La conception actuelle de l'enseignement de la géographie." *Annales de Géographie* 14(75):193–207.

          "A travers l'Amérique du Nord." *Rev. Paris.* 12(5):513–32.

1906   "Le peuple de l'Inde d'après la série des recensements." *Annales de Géographie* 15(82):353–75; 15(84):419–42.

1908   "De l'interpretation géographique des paysages." Communication to the Geneva Congress of 1908. *9th Congress International Geographical Society* 3:59–64. Genève, 1911.

1909   "Régions naturelles et noms de pays." *J. Savants*, 389–401, 454–62.

1910   "Régions françaises." *Rev. Paris* 17(6):821–49.

1911   "Sur la relativité des division régionales." *Athena* 11:1–8.

          "Les genres de vie dans la géographie humaine." *Annales de Géographie* 20(111):193–212; 20(112):289–304.

1912	"Sur le sens et l'objet de la géographie humaine." *Rev. Polit. Litt.* 50(17):513–15.
1913	"Des caractères distinctifs de la géographie." *Annales de Géographie* 22(124):289–99.
1914	"Sur l'esprit géographique." *Rev. Polit. Litt.* 52(18):556–60.
1915	"La formation de la France de l'Est." *Rev. Paris* 22(6):449–76, 741–59.
1916	"Évolution de la population en Alsace-Lorraine et dans les départements limitrophes." *Annales de Géographie* 25(34):97–115; 25(135):161–80.
1917	"La rénovation de la vie régionale." *Foi et vie: Les questions du temps présent.* 9:103–10. Paris: Cahier B.
	La France de l'Est (Lorraine, Alsace). Paris: A. Colin.
	"La frontière de la Sarre d'après les traités de 1814 et 1815." *Travaus du Comité d'Etudes.* Paris, 79–101.
	"La répartition des hommes sur le globe." *Annales de Géographie* 26(140):81–93; 26(142):241–54.
	"Les grande agglomérations humaines: Afrique et Asie." *Annales de Géographie* 26(144):401–22.
1918	"Les grande agglomérations humaines: Europe—remarques générales." *Annales de Géographie* 27(146):92–101.
	"Les granges agglomérations humaines: Regions Meditérranéennes." *Annales de Géographie* 27(147):174–87.
1922	*Principes de géographie humaine.* Published posthumously from the manuscripts of Vidal de la Blache by Emmanuel de Martonne. Paris: A. Colin.
1926	*Principles of Human Geography.* Translated by Millicent Todd Bingham. New York: Holt.

Chronology

1845	Born January 22 at Pézenas, France.
1858	After early schooling in southern France, sent to Lycée Charlemagne, Paris, for a classical education.
1863	Entered the École Normale Supérieure.
1867	Nominated as a member of the École Française d'Athènes. Travelled in Italy, Greece, and Asia Minor.
1870	Returned to France.
1872	Defended his thesis for the doctorate in letters at the Sorbonne in January. In October, appointed "chargé de cours" in history and geography in the Faculty of Letters of the University of Nancy.
1875	Professor of Geography at Nancy.
1883	Supplementary appointment as Professor of Geography at the École Normale Supérieure d'Institutrices de Fontenay-aux-Roses.

1898	Nomination in December to Chair of Geography in the Faculty of Letters at the Sorbonne.
1904	Attended the International Geographical Congress in Washington.
1906	Elected member of the Institut de France, in the Académie des Sciences Morales et Politique.
1908	Assigned to the École Libre des Sciences Politiques (until 1917).
1909	Retired from the chair of geography at the Sorbonne.
1912	Commandeur de la Légion d'Honneur.
1914	Honorary professorship of the Sorbonne.
1915	Awarded Charles Daly Gold Medal of the American Geographical Society.
1918	In January became President of the Académie de Sciences Morales et Politiques. Died suddenly, April 5 at Tamaris-sur-Mer.

References

Baker, S.J.K. 1988. "Paul Vidal de la Blache." *Geographers Biobibliographical Studies* 12:189–201.

James, Preston E., and Geoffrey J. Martin. 1981. *All Possible Worlds: A History of Geographical Ideas*. 2d ed. New York: Wiley.

Gilbert F. White

Gilbert F. White was one of the pioneering geographers to study natural resources and hazards, and the human environment. In his more than fifty years of professional work, he has been a civil servant, college administrator, scientist, and educator. He was born in Chicago on November 26, 1911, the son of a railroad man. His father decided to settle near Chicago so his young children would eventually be able to attend the new university being formed there. White worked summers on his father's ranch in Wyoming, only to see the ranch lost in the 1930s during the Depression.

White received his S.B. from the University of Chicago and in 1934 took a position as geographer with the Mississippi Valley Committee, part of the National Resources Planning Board. White was recommended for the position by his mentor at the University of Chicago, Harlan H. Barrows, who emphasized the interaction between people and the natural habitat. As Barrows said in his 1923 presidential address to the Association of American Geographers (Barrows, 1923:3): "Geography will aim to make clear the relationships existing between natural environments, and the distribution and activities of man." Beyond this legacy, Barrows emphasized the role of geography in public service. These ideas rubbed off on Gilbert White, and his first job as a geographer was as a public servant.

While White worked for the National Resources Planning Board, he also completed his doctoral work and was awarded a Ph.D. from the University of Chicago. His doctoral dissertation, *Human Adjustment to Floods*, according to Kates and Burton (Vol. 1, 1986:10),

may well have been the most influential dissertation in U.S. geography. . . . It quickly found its way into the hands of scholars, scientists, planners, and administrators. . . . This work still serves as a remarkable blueprint for the enormous changes in the attitudes and policies of floodplain adjustment that were to take place over the next forty years.

During the late 1930s and early 1940s, White published a series of papers dealing with economic issues in floodplain development, the need for land management and regulation, and methods of forecasting effects. White left the National Resources Planning Board in 1940 to take a position as a staff member of the Bureau of the Budget in the Executive Office of the President of the United States. This work in public service convinced White of the problems in contemporary approaches to water management, and according to Burton and Kates (Vol. 2, 1986:117), "Ever since, through the scholarly literature and advice to governments and international agencies, White has helped pioneer major innovations in water resources policies."

After having joined the Society of Friends (Quakers) in 1940, White spent the war years in France as a conscientious objector in relief work; he later worked with the American Friends Service Committee in Philadelphia on relief for China and India during 1944–45.

In 1946 White accepted the presidency of Haverford College, a small Quaker institution in Pennsylvania. When he started, Haverford had eighty students and was in considerable turmoil; when he left, after almost ten years, it had 450 students, was financially stable, and had a new curriculum.

White left Haverford in 1956 to become chairman of the Department of Geography at the University of Chicago. He emphasized the importance of a student-centered program and encouraged students to conduct research on areas with public consequence. While White was at Chicago he was elected president of the Association of American Geographers, and one of his important projects was the development of the High School Geography Project, a program whose objective was to develop a new geography curriculum.

In 1970 White left the University of Chicago to become Professor of Geography and Director of the Institute of Behavioral Science at the University of Colorado at Boulder. Several years later, he became Director of the Natural Hazards Research Applications and Information Center at Boulder.

White has received numerous awards for his work including the Distinguished Service Award, Association of American Geographers (1955, 1974); the Quantrell Award for Excellence in Undergraduate Teaching (1967); the Daly Medal from the American Geographical Society (1971); the Eben Award from the American Water Resources Association (1972); the Thomas Jefferson Award from the University of Colorado (1973); the Environmental Award from the National Academy of Science (1980); Master Teacher Award from the National Council for Geographic Education (1985); the United Nations Sasakawa International Environment Prize (1985); National Wildlife Federation Conservation Award (1986); the Anderson Medal from the Association of American Geographers (1986); the Tyler Prize for Environmental Achievement (1987); the Distinguished Contribution Award from the International Society of Risk Assessment (1987); and the Laureat d'Honneur from the International Geographical Union (1988).

Selected Bibliography

1935   "Shortage of Public Water Supplies in the United States During 1934."
         Journal of the American Water Works Association 27:841–54.

1936   "The Limit of Economic Justification for Flood Protection." *The Journal
         of Land and Public Utility Economics* 12:133–48.

1942   *Human Adjustment to Floods.* Chicago: University of Chicago Department
         of Geography, Research Paper No. 29.

1949   "Toward an Appraisal of World Resources." *Geographical Review*
         39:625–39.

1950   "National Executive Organization for Water Resources." *American Po-
         litical Science Review* 44:593–610.

1956   Editor of *The Future of Arid Lands.* Washington, D.C.: American As-
         sociation for the Advancement of Science.

1960   *Science and the Future of Arid Lands.* Paris: United Nations Educational,
         Scientific and Cultural Organization (U.N.E.S.C.O.).

1962   With E. de Vries, H. B. Dunkerley, and J. V. Krutilla. *Economic and
         Social Aspects of Lower Mekong Development: A Report to the Committee
         for Coordination of Investigations of the Lower Mekong Basin.*

         *Social and Economic Aspects of Natural Resources: A Report to the Com-
         mittee on Natural Resources.* Washington, D.C.: National Academy of
         Sciences, Publication 1000–G.

1964   *Choice of Adjustment to Floods.* Chicago: University of Chicago, De-
         partment of Geography, Research Paper No. 93.

1969   *Strategies of American Water Management.* Ann Arbor: University of
         Michigan Press.

1972   "Collaboration in Natural Hazards Research." *Geographical Review*
         62:280–81.

         With D. J. Bradley and Anne White. *Drawers of Water: Domestic Water
         Use in East Africa.* Chicago: University of Chicago Press.

1973   *Man-Made Lakes: Their Problems and Environmental Effects.* Washing-
         ton, D.C.: American Geophysical Union.

1974   Editor of *Natural Hazards: Local, National and Global.* New York: Oxford
         University Press.

         "Edward A. Ackerman, 1911–1973." *Annals of the Association of Amer-
         ican Geographers* 64:297–309.

1975   With J. Eugene Haas. *Assessment of Research on Natural Hazards.* Cam-
         bridge, Mass.: MIT Press.

1978   With Ian Burton and Robert W. Kates. *The Environment as Hazard.* New
         York: Oxford University Press.

1982   With M. W. Holdgate and M. Kassas. "World Environmental Trends
         Between 1972 and 1982." *Environmental Conservation* 9:11–29.

1984	With J. London. *The Environmental Effects of Nuclear War*. Boulder: Westview.
1986	With Anne U. White. "Potable Water for All: The Egyptian Experience with Rural Water Supply." *Water International* 11:54–63.
1988	"Glasnost and Ecology: Three Reports from the Soviet Union." *Environment* 30:4–5.

Chronology

1911	Born November 26 in Chicago.
1934	Graduated with an S.B. from the University of Chicago and took position as geographer with the Mississippi Valley Committee, National Resources Planning Board.
1940	Spent war years in France with the Society of Friends.
1942	Awarded Ph.D. from the University of Chicago and published *Human Adjustment to Floods*.
1946	Appointed President of Haverford College.
1956	Appointed Chairman of the Department of Geography at the University of Chicago and published *The Future of Arid Lands*.
1961	Elected President of the Association of American Geographers and named consultant to the Lower Mekong Coordinating Committee.
1967	Awarded the Quantrell Award for Excellence in Undergraduate Teaching.
1969	Published *Strategies of American Water Management*.
1970	Appointed Professor of Geography and Director of the Institute of Behavioral Science at the University of Colorado at Boulder.
1971	Awarded the Daly Medal of the American Geographical Society.
1974	Published *Natural Hazards: Local, National and Global*.
1980	Received the Environmental Award from the National Academy of Sciences.
1985	Received the Master Teacher Award from the National Council for Geographic Education and the United Nations Sasakawa International Environment Prize.
1986	Publication of *Geography, Resources, and Environment: Selected Writings of Gilbert F. White*.
1988	Received the Laureat d'Honneur from the International Geographical Union.
1989	Received the Bonfils-Stanton Foundation Award.

References

Barrows, H. H. 1923. "Geography as Human Ecology." *Annals of the Association of American Geographers* 13:1–14.

Kates, Robert W., and Ian Burton. 1986. *Geography, Resources, and Environment: Themes From the Work of Gilbert F. White*. Vol. 1 and 2. Chicago: University of Chicago Press.

Sidney William Wooldridge

Sidney William Wooldridge, one of the most important figures in twentieth-century British geography, was born in Hornsey, in North London, on November 16, 1900. While Sidney was still quite young, the Wooldridge family moved to Surrey for a period, where he began his schooling, then back to another section of North London, Winchmore Hill, where he continued.

Wooldridge developed an early interest in natural landscapes and in being in the field. In 1918 he went to King's College in London, where he began working toward a degree in geology. At the time *Laurence Dudley Stamp had just completed a degree in geology and was working toward a geography degree. Wooldridge received a first-class honors degree in geology in 1921, the same year in which appeared his first publication, "Evidence of Folding in the Tertiary and Cretaceous Rocks near South Mimms and Ridge Hill."

For his degree work, Wooldridge specialized in petrology, though before long geomorphology became his favorite subject. While working as a Demonstrator at King's College, he went on to finish his M.Sc. and D.Sc. degrees, the latter in 1927. In 1923 he had become the founding member of the Weald Research Committee for the Geologists' Association, and in 1925 he had been advanced to a position as Assistant Lecturer in the Department of Geology and Geography at King's College. With the receipt of his doctorate in 1927, Wooldridge was appointed Lecturer in the Department of Geology and Geography, which was then combined with the Geography Department at the London School of Economics, forming the Joint School of Geography. The Joint School became a major geography program in the following decade.

Wooldridge's role was first as a geologist, then gradually increasingly more as a physical geographer. His enthusiasm for fieldwork, coupled with his own field research in the landscapes of southeast England, especially the Weald, made him an invaluable member of the Joint School. Along with his teaching, he published numerous articles during the 1920s, virtually all dealing with the geomorphology of local landscapes. In 1928 he received the Geological Society award from the Daniel Pidgeon Fund, and in 1932 shared, with F. Gossling, the Foulerton Prize from the Geologist's Association. In 1933 he became one of the founding members of the Institute of British Geographers.

In 1934 he married another geographer, Edith Mary Stephens, who later taught geography at Enfield County School. Wooldridge's extensive fieldwork and publications helped him in the writing, with R. S. Morgan, of a successful text, *The Physical Basis of Geography: An Outline of Geomorphology*, which was published in 1937. Though he continued to work primarily in the realm of geomorphology, his geographic horizons broadened somewhat during the 1930s, as is apparent in such publications as "The Loam Terrains of South-East England and their Relation to its Early History" and "Some Aspects of the Saxon Settlement in South-East England and their Relation to Its Early History," articles that he coauthored with D. L. Linton in 1933 and 1935, respectively.

Chance played the final role in converting Wooldridge from geologist to geographer, when the Joint School was split up during World War II and moved to two separate locations, with King's College going to Bristol and the London School to Cambridge. Wooldridge was the sole geographer in King's College's Bristol geography program. In 1942 he was awarded a Readership in Geography, official recognition of his conversion. The war impacted seriously on Wooldridge's research program as well, with much of his spare time devoted to work for the Admiralty Naval Intelligence Department rather than fieldwork.

In 1944 Wooldridge accepted a Chair of Geography at Birkbeck College in the University of London, though he was less than eager to leave King's College. He was appointed a member of the Government Advisory Committee on Sand and Gravel in 1946, and in the following year returned to King's College as Professor of Geography in the newly created Department of Geography. He served as president of the Institute of British Geographers in 1949 and 1950, and in 1950 was also president of the geography section of the British Association for the Advancement of Science, which met that year in Birmingham.

In 1952 Wooldridge was Chair of the Field Studies Council, and two years later he served as president of the Geographical Association and was also appointed Commander of the Order of the British Empire. Unfortunately, in 1954 he experienced his first serious health problem, a cerebral thrombosis, from which he did manage to recover reasonably well, though his recovery required many months. In 1956 he was elected a Fellow of King's College, London, and in the following year was awarded the Victoria Medal of the Royal Geographical Society, to which he was elected a Fellow in 1959. In 1962 he became president of the King's College London Association and was elected an honorary member of the Geologist's Association.

Wooldridge died on April 25, 1963, in Halliday Hall at King's College. Though his influence on British geography had been considerable, he left behind a mixed legacy. In recently reviewing some of Wooldridge's work, however, Perry (1990:230) wrote that "to Wooldridge, the unity of geography was not a matter of convenience and momentum but of intellectual integrity and interdependence. It may well be that financial stringency rather than intellectual concern will force geographers to recover the generalist tradition, and perhaps with it regional geography.''

Selected Bibliography

1921   ''Evidence of Folding in the Tertiary and Cretaceous Rocks near South Mimms and Ridge Hill.'' *Proceedings of the Geologists Association* 32:227–31.

1923   With A. K. Wells. ''The Mechanism of Sedimentation Cycles.'' *Geological Magazine* 60:545–50.

            With A. K. Wells. ''Notes on the Geology of Epping Forest.'' *Proceedings of the Geologists Association* 34:244–52.

            ''The Geology of the Rayleigh Hills.'' *Proceedings of the Geologists Association* 34:314–22.

            With L. D. Stamp. ''The Igneous and Associated Rocks of Llanwrtyd (Brecon).'' *Quarterly Journal of the Geological Society* 79:16–46.

            With H. W. Cornes. ''A System of Basic Intrusions at the Northern End of the Island of Sark.'' *Geological Magazine* 60:500–05.

1924   ''The Bagshot Beds of Essex.'' *Proceedings of the Geologists Association* 35:359–83.

1925   With analyses by G. M. Stockley. ''The Petrology of Sark.'' *Geological Magazine* 62:241–52.

            With A. J. Bull. ''The Geomorphology of the Mole Gap.'' *Proceedings of the Geologists Association* 36:1–10.

            With D.M.C. Gill. ''The Reading Beads of Land End, Bucks and their Bearing on some Unsolved Problems of London Geology.'' *Proceedings of the Geologists Association* 36:146–73.

            With H. Dewey et al. ''The Geology of the Canterbury District.'' Sections 1, 3, 4. *Proceedings of the Geologists Association* 36:257–84.

            ''On a Section at Rayleigh, Essex, Showing a Transition from London Clay to Bagshot Sand.'' *Essex Nat.* 21:112–18.

1926   ''The Geology of Essex.'' *Essex: An Outline Scientific Survey, Southeast, Union Sci. Soc. Congr. Handbk.*, 7–27.

            With F. Gossling. ''On Outliers of Lenham Beds at Sanderstead, Surrey.'' *Proceedings of the Geologists Association* 37:92–101.

            ''The Structural Evolution of the London Basin.'' *Proceedings of the Geologists Association* 37:162–96.

            ''The Progress of London Geology.'' *Science Progress* 20:517–23.

1927   ''The Pliocene Period in Western Essex and the Pre-Glacial Topography of the District.'' *Essex Nat.* 21:247–68.

"The Pliocene History of the London Basin." *Proceedings of the Geologists Association* 38:49–132.

1928   "The 200-Foot Platform in the London Basin." *Proceedings of the Geologists Association* 39:1–26.

With B. R. Saner. "River Development in Essex." *Essex Nat.* 22:244–50.

With A. J. Bull. "Report of the Weald Research Committee." *Proceedings of the Geologists Association* 39:223–37.

1929   "The Alleged Pliocene of Buckinghamshire and Hertfordshire." A discussion, with R. L. Sherlock et al. *Proceedings of the Geologists Association* 40:363–69.

1931   With D. J. Smeetham. "The Glacial Drifts of Essex and Hertfordshire and Their Bearing upon the Agricultural and Historical Geography of the Region." *Geographical Journal* 78:243–69.

With A. K. Wells. "The Rock Groups of Jersey, with Special Reference to Instrusive Phenomena." *Proceedings of the Geologists Association* 42:178–215.

1932   "The Cycle of Erosion and the Representation of Relief." *Scottish Geographical Magazine* 48:30–36.

"The Physiographic Evolution of the Longon Basin." *Geography* 17:99–116.

With F. J. Richards. "Climatic Changes in South-East India during Early Palaeolithic Times." *Geological Magazine* 69:193–205.

1933   "The Loam Terrains of South-East England and Their Relation to Its Early History." *Antiquity* 7:297–310.

1934   "The River Mole: Its Physiography and Superficial Deposits." *Proceedings of the Geologists Association* 45:35–69.

1935   With D. L. Linton. "Some Aspects of the Saxon Settlement in South-East England and their Relation to Its Early History." *Geography* 20:161–75.

"The Eocene and Pliocene Deposits of Lane End, Buckinghamshire." *Quarterly Journal of the Geological Society* 91:193–317.

1936   With J. F. Kirkaldy. "River Profiles and Denudation Chronology in Southern England." *Geological Magazine* 73:1–16.

1936   "The Soils of Britain and their Classification." *Geography* 21:112–17.

"The Anglo-Saxon Settlement." *An Historical Geography of England before A.D. 1800.* Edited by H. C. Darby. Cambridge, 88–132.

1937   With R. S. Morgan. *The Physical Basis of Geography: An Outline of Geomorphology.* London.

1938   With J. F. Kirkaldy. "Notes of the Geology of the Country around Haslemere and Midhurst." *Proceedings of the Geologists Association* 49:135–47.

With D. L. Linton. "Some Episodes in the Structural Evolution of South-East England, Considered in Relation to the Concealed Boundary of Meso-

Europe." *Journal of Geomorphology* 1:40–54.

"Town and Rural Planning: The Physical Factors in the Problem." *Geography* 23:90–93.

"The Glaciation of the London Basin and the Evolution of the Lower Thames Drainage System." *Quarterly Journal of the Geological Society* 94:627–67.

1939   With D. L. Linton. "Structure, Surface and Drainage in South-East England." *Trans. Pap. Institute of British Geographers*, no. 10. This monograph was republished by George Philip and Son in 1955.

1945   "The Land of Britain: The Report of the Land Utilisation Survey of Britain." Vol. 4: *North England*. Part 51: "Yorkshire, North Riding." Edited by L. D. Stamp, 351–417.

            The Geographer as Scientist. Inaugural lecture at Birkbeck College, University of London.

1946   "Some Geographical Aspects of the Greater London Regional Plan." *Trans. Pap. Institute of British Geographers*. No. 11:1–20.

1947   "Geographical Science in Education." *Geographical Journal* 109:26–37.

1948   *The Role and Relations of Geomorphology*. Inaugural lecture at King's College, University of London.

            With A. A. Miller and W.G.V. Balchin. *Guide to Excursion A.11, London to Wales, 18th Int. Geol. Congr. London*.

1949   "Geomorphology and Soil Science." *Journal of Soil Science* 1:31–34.

1949   "The Weald and the Field Sciences." *Advancement of Science* 6:3–11.

            "On Taking the "GE" out of Geography." *Geography* 34:9–18.

1950   With S. H. Beaver. "The Working of Sand and Gravel in Britain: A Problem in Land Use." *Geographical Journal* 115:42–57.

            "Some Features in the Structure and Geomorphology of the Country around Fernhurst, Sussex." *Proceedings of the Geologists Association* 61:165–90.

            "Reflections on Regional Geography in Teaching and Research." *Trans. Pap. Institute of British Geographers*. No. 16:1–11.

1951   "The Upland Plains of Britain—Their Origin and Geographical Significance." *Advancement of Science* 7:124–49.

            "The Progress of Geomorphology." *Geography in the Twentieth Century*. Edited by G. Taylor, 165–77.

            With W. G. East. *The Spirit and Purpose of Geography*. London.

1952   "The Conservation of Natural Resources." *Journal of the Town Planning Institute* 38:134–40.

            "The Changing Physical Landscape of Britain." *Geographical Journal* 118:297–308.

1953   With F. Goldring. *The Weald*. London.

Sidney William Wooldridge 347

"Some Marginal Drainage Features of the Chalky Boulder Clay Ice-Sheet in Hertfordshire." *Proceedings of the Geologists Association* 64:208–31.

1954   "The Physique of the South-West." *Geography* 39:231–42.

1955   With H.C.K. Henderson. "Some Aspects of the Physiography of the Eastern Part of the London Basin." *Trans. Pap. Institute of British Geographers.* No. 21:19–31.

"The Status of Geography and the Role of Field Work." Presidential address to the Geographical Association. *Geography* 40:73–83.

"The Study of Geomorphology." *Geographical Journal* 121:89–90. (Review article on W. M. Davis, *Geographical Essays*, 2d ed.).

1956   *The Geographer as Scientist.* (A collection of selected, previously published articles from 1931 on.)

1956   "On Understanding a Piece of Country." *Annual Report, Field Studies Council, 1955–56*, 27–33.

1959   *An Outline of Geomorphology: The Physical Basis of Geomorphology.* 2d ed. of 1937 work.

Chronology

1900   Born November 16 in Hornsey (North London).

1918   Entered King's College, University of London.

1921   First-class honors, B.Sc. degree in Geology.

1922   Appointed Demonstrator in Geology at King's College.

1923   Master of Science in Geology. Founder member of Weald Research Committee for the Geologists' Association.

1925   Assistant Lecturer in Geology and Geography at King's College.

1927   D.Sc. degree in Geology. Promoted to Lecturer in Geology and Geography at King's College, University of London.

1933   Founder member of the Institute of British Geographers.

1936   Geological Society grant from Lyell Fund.

1939   Outbreak of World War II, temporary evacuation of King's College to Bristol.

1942   Promoted to Reader in Geography in the Department of Geology and Geography at King's College.

1944   Professor of Geography at Birkbeck College, University of London.

1946   Appointed a member of the Government Advisory Committee on Sand and Gravel.

1947   Professor of Geography in the newly created Department of Geography at King's College.

1949   President of the Institute of British Geographers.

1950   President of the Geography Section of the British Association for the Advancement of Science.

1952	Chairman of the Field Studies Council.
1954	President of the Geographical Association. Appointed Commander of the Order of the British Empire.
1956	Elected a Fellow of King's College, London.
1957	Awarded Victoria Medal of the Royal Geographical Society.
1959	Elected a Fellow of the Royal Society.
1962	President of King's College London Association. Elected Honorary Member of the Geologists Association.
1963	Died suddenly at Halliday Hall, King's College on April 25.

Reference

Perry, Peter J. "S. W. Wooldridge: The Geographer as Humanist." *Transactions of the Institute of British Geographers* 15:227–31.

Appendices

Appendix 1: Alphabetical List

Amundsen, Roald (1872–1928)
Aristotle (384 B.C.–322 B.C.)
Atwood, Wallace Walter (1872–1949)
Baulig, Henri (1877–1962)
Berry, Brian J. L. (1934–   )
Borchert, John R. (1918–   )
Bowman, Isaiah (1878–1950)
Brigham, Albert Perry (1855–1932)
Büsching, Anton Friedrich (1724–1793)
Christaller, Walter (1893–1969)
Cook, Captain James (1728–1779)
Copernicus, Nicolaus (1473–1543)
Cotton, Charles Andrew (1885–1970)
Cressey, George Babcock (1896–1963)
Crist, Raymond E. (1904–   )
Darwin, Charles (1809–1882)
Davis, William Morris (1850–1934)
De Geer, Sten (1886–1933)
Dokuchaev, Vasily Vasilyevich (1846–1903)
Eratosthenes (ca. 275 B.C.–195 B.C.)
Geikie, James (1839–1915)
Gilbert, Grove Karl (1843–1918)
Goode, John Paul (1862–1932)
Gottmann, Jean (1915–   )
Guyot, Arnold Henry (1807–1884)
Haggett, Peter (1933–   )
Harris, Chauncy D. (1914–   )
Harvey, David W. (1935–   )
Haushofer, Karl (1869–1946)
Herodotus (ca. 484 B.C.–424 B.C.)
Hettner, Alfred (1859–1941)
Humboldt, Alexander von (1769–1859)
Huntington, Ellsworth (1876–1947)
James, Preston Everett (1899–1986)
Jefferson, Mark (1863–1949)

Kant, Immanuel (1724–1804)
Köppen, Wladimir (1846–1940)
Kropotkin, Pyotr (1842–1922)
Mackinder, Halford John (1861–1947)
Marsh, George Perkins (1801–1882)
Maury, Matthew Fontaine (1806–1873)
Meinig, Donald W. (1924–   )
Mill, Hugh Robert (1861–1950)
Muir, John (1838–1914)
Mumford, Lewis (1895–   )
Münster, Sebastian (1488–1552)
Nansen, Fridtjof (1861–1930)
Parsons, James J. (1915–   )
Penck, Albrecht (1858–1945)
Powell, John Wesley (1834–1902)
Ptolemy (ca. A.D. 100–A.D. 170)
Ratzel, Friedrich (1844–1904)
Ravenstein, Ernst Georg (1834–1913)
Reclus, Élisée (1830–1905)
Richthofen, Ferdinand Freiherr von (1833–1905)
Ritter, Carl (1779–1859)
Robinson, Arthur H. (1915–   )
Russell, Richard Joel (1895–1971)
Salisbury, Rollin D. (1858–1922)
Sauer, Carl Ortwin (1889–1975)
Scoresby, William (1789–1857)
Semple, Ellen Churchill (1863–1932)
Shackleton, Ernest (1874–1922)
Smith, Joseph Russell (1874–1966)
Somerville, Mary (1780–1872)
Stamp, Laurence Dudley (1898–1966)
Smith, Joseph Russell (1874–1966)
Strabo (ca. 64 B.C.–A.D. 20)
Taylor, Thomas Griffith (1880–1963)

Thales of Miletus (ca. 625 B.C.–
  547 B.C.)
Thünen, Johann Heinrich von (1783–
  1850)
Troll, Carl (1899–1975)
Tuan, Yi Fu (1930–   )

Ullman, Edward Louis (1912–1976)
Vavilov, Nikolai Ivanovich (1887–1943)
Vidal de la Blache, Paul (1845–1918)
White, Gilbert F. (1911–   )
Wooldridge, Sidney William (1900–
  1963)

Appendix 2: Chronological List

Thales of Miletus (ca. 625 B.C.–547 B.C.)

Herodotus (ca. 484 B.C.–424 B.C.)

Aristotle (384 B.C.–322 B.C.)

Eratosthenes (ca. 275 B.C.–195 B.C.)

Strabo (ca. 64 B.C.–A.D. 20)

Ptolemy (ca. A.D. 100–A.D. 170)

Copernicus, Nicolaus (1473–1543)

Münster, Sebastian (1488–1552)

Büsching, Anton Friedrich (1724–1793)

Kant, Immanuel (1724–1804)

Cook, Captain James (1728–1779)

Humboldt, Alexander von (1769–1859)

Ritter, Carl (1779–1859)

Somerville, Mary (1780–1872)

Thünen, Johann Heinrich von (1783–1850)

Scoresby, William (1789–1857)

Marsh, George Perkins (1801–1882)

Maury, Matthew Fontaine (1806–1873)

Guyot, Arnold Henry (1807–1884)

Darwin, Charles (1809–1882)

Reclus, Élisée (1830–1905)

Richthofen, Ferdinand Freiherr von (1833–1905)

Powell, John Wesley (1834–1902)

Ravenstein, Ernst Georg (1834–1913)

Muir, John (1838–1914)

Geikie, James (1839–1915)

Kropotkin, Pyotr (1842–1922)

Gilbert, Grove Karl (1843–1918)

Ratzel, Friedrich (1844–1904)

Vidal de la Blache, Paul (1845–1918)

Dokuchaev, Vasily Vasilyovich (1846–1903)

Köppen, Wladimir (1846–1940)

Davis, William Morris (1850–1934)

Brigham, Albert Perry (1855–1932)

Penck, Albrecht (1858–1945)

Salisbury, Rollin D. (1858–1922)

Hettner, Alfred (1859–1941)

Mackinder, Halford John (1861–1947)

Mill, Hugh Robert (1861–1950)

Nansen, Fridtjof (1861–1930)

Goode, John Paul (1862–1932)

Jefferson, Mark (1863–1949)

Semple, Ellen Churchill (1863–1932)

Haushofer, Karl (1869–1946)

Amundsen, Roald (1872–1928)

Atwood, Wallace Walter (1872–1949)

Shackelton, Ernest (1874–1922)

Smith, Joseph Russell (1874–1966)

Huntington, Ellsworth (1876–1947)

Baulig, Henri (1877–1962)

Bowman, Isaiah (1878–1950)

Taylor, Thomas Griffith (1880–1963)

Cotton, Charles Andrew (1885–1970)

De Geer, Sten (1886–1933)

Vavilov, Nikolai Ivanovich (1887–1943)

Sauer, Carl Ortwin (1889–1975)

Christaller, Walter (1893–1969)

Mumford, Lewis (1895–   )

Russell, Richard Joel (1895–1971)

Cressey, George Babcock (1896–
1963)

Stamp, Laurence Dudley (1898–1966)

James, Preston Everett (1899–1986)

Troll, Carl (1899–1975)

Wooldridge, Sidney William (1900–
1963)

Crist, Raymond E. (1904–   )

White, Gilbert F. (1911–   )

Ullman, Edward Louis (1912–1976)

Harris, Chauncy D. (1914–   )

Gottmann, Jean (1915–   )

Parsons, James J. (1915–   )

Robinson, Arthur H. (1915–   )

Borchert, John R. (1918–   )

Meinig, Donald W. (1924–   )

Tuan, Yi Fu (1930–   )

Haggett, Peter (1933–   )

Berry, Brian J. L. (1934–   )

Harvey, David W. (1935–   )

Appendix 3: Country of Birth

China

Tuan, Yi Fu (1930–   )

Egypt

Ptolemy (ca. A.D. 100–A.D. 170)

France

Baulig, Henri (1877–1962)
Gottmann, Jean (1915–   )
Reclus, Élisée (1830–1905)
Vidal de la Blache, Paul (1845–1918)

Germany

Büsching, Anton Friedrich (1724–1793)
Christaller, Walter (1893–1969)
Haushofer, Karl (1869–1946)
Hettner, Alfred (1859–1941)
Humboldt, Alexander von (1769–1859)
Kant, Immanuel (1724–1804)
Köppen, Wladimir (1846–1940)
Münster, Sebastian (1488–1552)
Penck, Albrecht (1858–1945)
Ratzel, Friedrich (1844–1904)
Ravenstein, Ernst Georg (1834–1913)
Richthofen, Ferdinand Freiherr von
   (1833–1905)
Ritter, Carl (1779–1859)
Thünen, Johann Heinrich von (1783–
1850)
Troll, Carl (1899–1975)

Greece

Aristotle (384 B.C.–322 B.C.)
Eratosthenes (ca. 275 B.C.–195 B.C.)
Herodotus (ca. 484 B.C.–424 B.C.)
Thales of Miletus (ca. 625 B.C.–547 B.C.)

New Zealand

Cotton, Charles Andrew (1885–1970)

Norway

Amundsen, Roald (1872–1928)
Nansen, Fridtjof (1861–1930)

Poland

Copernicus, Nicolaus (1473–1543)

Russia

Dokuchaev, Vasily Vasilyovich (1846–
   1903)
Kropotkin, Pyotr (1842–1922)
Vavilov, Nikolai Ivanovich (1887–1943)

Sweden

De Geer, Sten (1886–1933)

Switzerland

Guyot, Arnold Henry (1807–1884)

Turkey

Strabo (ca. 64 B.C.–A.D. 20)

United Kingdom

Berry, Brian J. L. (1934–   )
Cook, Captain James (1728–1779)
Darwin, Charles (1809–1882)
Geikie, James (1839–1915)
Haggett, Peter (1933–   )
Harvey, David W. (1935–   )
Mackinder, Halford John (1861–1947)
Mill, Hugh Robert (1861–1950)
Muir, John (1838–1914)
Scoresby, William (1789–1857)
Shackelton, Ernest (1874–1922)
Somerville, Mary (1780–1872)
Stamp, Laurence Dudley (1898–1966)
Taylor, Thomas Griffith (1880–1963)
Wooldridge, Sidney William (1900–1963)

United States

Atwood, Wallace Walter (1872–1949)
Borchert, John R. (1918–   )

Bowman, Isaiah (1878–1950)
Brigham, Albert Perry (1855–1932)
Cressey, George Babcock (1896–1963)
Crist, Raymond E. (1904–   )
Davis, William Morris (1850–1934)
Gilbert, Grove Karl (1843–1918)
Goode, John Paul (1862–1932)
Harris, Chauncy D. (1914–   )
Huntington, Ellsworth (1876–1947)
James, Preston Everett (1899–1986)
Jefferson, Mark (1863–1949)
Marsh, George Perkins (1801–1882)
Maury, Matthew Fontaine (1806–1873)
Meinig, Donald W. (1924–   )
Mumford, Lewis (1895–   )
Parsons, James J. (1915–   )
Powell, John Wesley (1834–1902)
Robinson, Arthur H. (1915–   )
Russell, Richard Joel (1895–1971)
Salisbury, Rollin D. (1858–1922)
Sauer, Carl Ortwin (1889–1975)
Semple, Ellen Churchill (1863–1932)
Smith, Joseph Russell (1874–1966)
Ullman Edward Louis (1912–1976)
White, Gilbert F. (1911–   )

Index